FOUND PHOTOS *of* YELLOWSTONE

YELLOWSTONE'S HISTORY IN TOURIST AND EMPLOYEE PHOTOS

1880 TO 1940

PHOTOGRAPHS FROM MICHAEL H. FRANCIS COLLECTIONS
TEXT BY AMY GRISAK
CAPTIONS BY AMY GRISAK AND LEE WHITTLESEY
FOREWORD BY LEE WHITTLESEY

RIVERBEND PUBLISHING

Found Photos of Yellowstone

Published by Riverbend Publishing, Helena, Montana

ISBN: 978-1-60639-131-0

Printed in the USA

1 2 3 4 5 6 7 8 VP 26 25 24 23 22 21

Cover and text design by Sarah Cauble, sarahcauble.com

Riverbend Publishing
P.O. Box 5833
Helena, MT 59604
1-406-449-0200
riverbendpublishing.com

ACKNOWLEDGEMENTS

It is hard to believe I started collecting Yellowstone National Park photos in 1974. So many people have helped me through the years, too many to mention them all, but I would like to recognize the help of several who have made this book possible.

I am especially indebted to the former park historian Lee Whittlesey. He has spent hundreds of hours with me looking over photos and helping to make historical identification for over 10,000 photos. He also volunteered to help with captions for this book. This book was made much better because of his expertise.

Two Yellowstone collectors have been especially helpful in allowing me access to their extensive collections Bob Reynolds and Jay C. Lyndes. Some of the fun and informative photos in the book have been graciously donated for use by these two individuals. Thanks for your help and friendship.

My family has always been supportive of my projects, especially my wife Victoria and my mother Derline. My mother-in-law Gayle Laeder donated family albums of her relatives' visit to the park. My sister Karelle for years has found fun Yellowstone National Park items, including old images, to add to my collection.

Others who have shared expertise or donated photos are friends Betsy Watry, Ruth and Leslie Quinn, M.A. Bellingham, Rocco Paperiello, John Alley, Rick and Karen Hoeninghausen, and Jessica Moody.

I cannot imagine what direction this book would have taken without author Amy Grisak. She has spent countless hours in the past two years researching the images I keep sending to her and coming up with fun exciting interpretive history for each. Thank you for your patience and persistence!

Last on my list, but of great importance, is the publisher of Riverbend Publishing, Chris Cauble. After he looked at some of my collection, he had the vision to see the importance of using never-before-seen photography to help tell the history of Yellowstone National Park. He was always available to help with photo selections and caption questions. Thank you, Chris, for making this idea a reality.

Michael Francis

CONTENTS

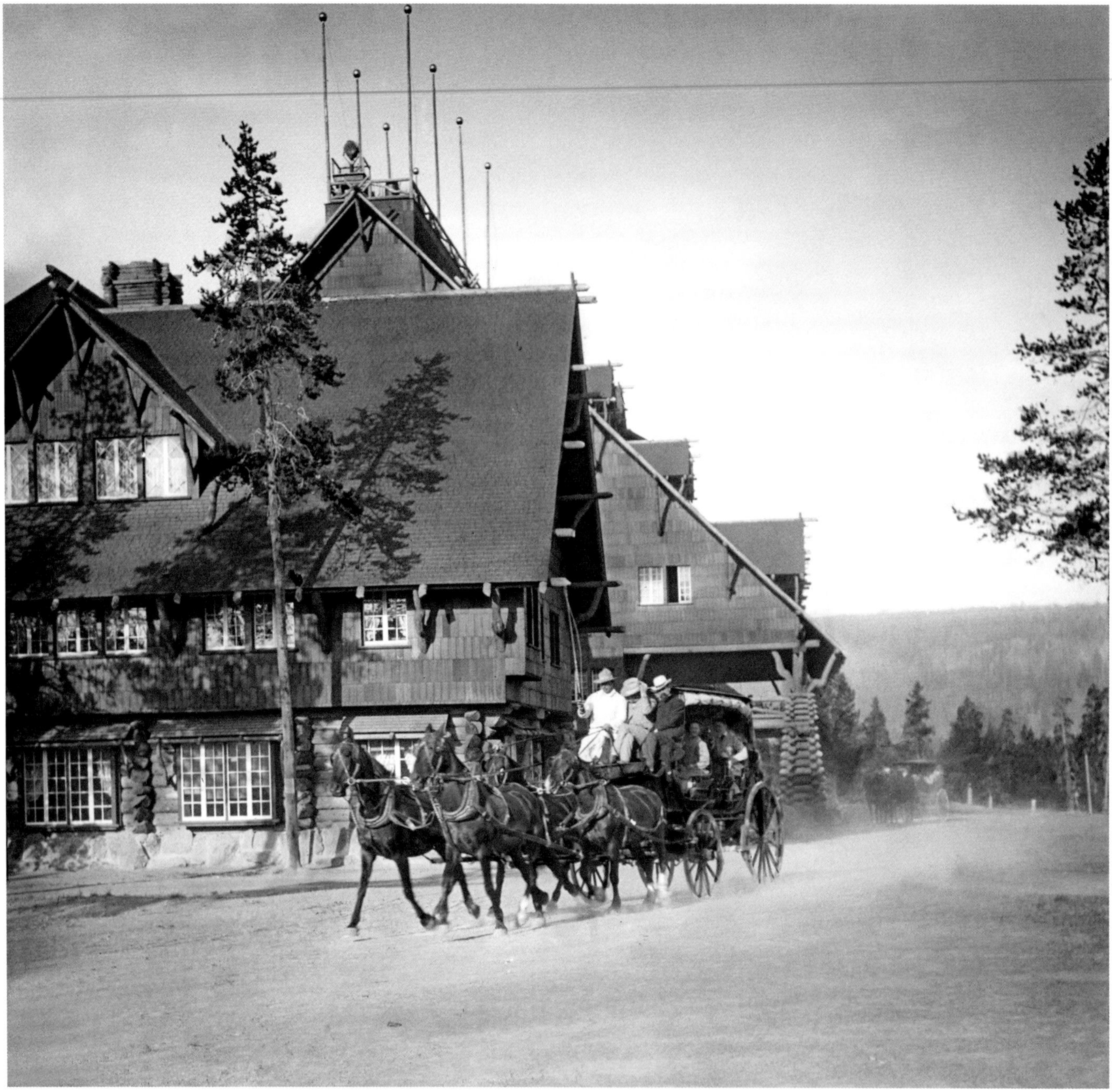

A four-horse stagecoach with the driver and park visitors wearing dusters departs the Old Faithful Inn in 1906, two years after the inn opened. These smaller coaches typically carried ten passengers on the Grand Loop tour. Notice there is one spotlight on the roof of the inn, which was used to illuminate Old Faithful Geyser's eruptions at night. The eight flagpoles on the roof flew the United States flag, along with flags representing Montana, Wyoming, and Idaho.

FOREWORD

Yellowstone National Park is a location of many wonders and a history that photographs have documented since 1871. The place that the nation's journalists called "Wonderland" even before the U.S. Congress declared it the world's first national park in 1872 has been fertile fodder for photographers for nearly one hundred fifty years.

Michael Francis's book *Found Photos of Yellowstone* (volume one) will show you a whole lot of these historical photos that you have likely never seen, even if you are a Yellowstone expert. Many of us had no idea that they existed, and most of these pictures have probably never been seen by anyone except the people who originally took or owned them and Michael Francis himself.

That of course is the story of photographs everywhere, but where the famous place of Yellowstone is concerned, Francis owns one of the nation's largest personal collections at more than 11,000 images. In this volume, he has also been allowed to select and add to them numerous images from another of the country's largest YNP compilations, that of the Jay Lyndes Family Collection. Jay has graciously allowed Francis to take pictures of his items in order for Michael to assist Lyndes with the cataloging of that collection.

I have a personal connection to this book, because Michael Francis is an old Yellowstone friend of mine whom I have known as a fellow park employee since 1981, a period of nearly forty years. We kept in touch through many intervening years while I became Yellowstone National Park's Historian and he produced thirty-five books as a photographer and YNP collector, including the well-known *Yellowstone Postcard Checklist* (J. Michael Bodell and Kathie Burke, 1995, 2006). Mike Francis worked in Yellowstone from 1974 through 1989, but he never really left the great park, because of owning his own touring business there, as well as the continuing sales to park concessioners of his postcards, posters, calendars, books, and other YNP products.

Mike and I have spent hundreds of hours looking at these photographs together and exchanging information about them. While we were working together, he would often tell me the story about how he obtained a given photograph, I would tell him what the photo was about with some of its background story, and then he would ask probing questions that usually resulted in more and better information for both of us. Our discussions usually revealed a richer tapestry between the photograph's literal depictions and its deeper meanings.

Speaking of literal depictions, I learned in the first ten years of the twenty-first century that advancing technology had suddenly allowed old photographs to be electronically scanned at a higher resolution and then enlarged, so that we could see the previously hidden parts of a given photograph. This technology opened a new "window on the past" that revealed a more-detailed world for professional historians like me. We could now clearly see faces and identify them, where before, the photos had been too small. We could see details on and around buildings; and we could see dogs, children, and other people who had not been obvious before. Thus, we were suddenly able to make better sense of hundreds of historical photographs and to more thoroughly understand how they fit into landscapes and the history of entire regions.

As I pointed some of these details out to Michael Francis, he caught the "spirit" of it and began pointing out other details in other photos to me. It was one more way that our exchanges became fruitful and even more important.

For example, when Francis showed me a photo of a park cabin that was labeled "Mud Geyser Soldier Station," I did a doubletake. After looking at it closely and comparing it to one other known photo that bore a similar caption, I suddenly realized that the other photo was not of "Mud Geyser Soldier Station" and that what Michael possessed was most likely the only known true photograph of the U.S. Army's patrol station at that location—south of present Mud Geyser, built in 1895, and long ago moved, demolished, and omitted from the park's list of existing structures. You will probably love this photo on page 146 of a single soldier with his dog and two cats at a lonely soldiers' station and likely taken in 1895 or 1896.

Other photos here will probably entertain you thoroughly, such as the photo on page 6, which captures the spirit of the time by showing a wonderful, four-horse stagecoach taking off at a brisk trot from a newly built Old Faithful Inn, catapulting its occupants into a day's worth of Yellowstone adventure. Or the photo on page 31, which will transport you to around 1890. It startled Mike and me when we realized that it depicted a hotel-building we did not recognize. A bit of research revealed that it was the second hotel of four total at Norris Geyser Basin—a stagecoach-era hotel that lasted only a few years before it burned to the ground, such that virtually no photos were heretofore known of it.

I am looking forward to subsequent volumes in this series. Meanwhile, you can begin perusing the photos in this first volume, and reading the captions. Whether you are a longtime Yellowstone afficionado, a relatively new fan of the Grand Old Park, or a complete novice to Wonderland who merely loves historical photos, you will have a great time gazing at these images.

I envy you the novelty of the experience.

Lee H. Whittlesey
Yellowstone National Park Historian (retired)

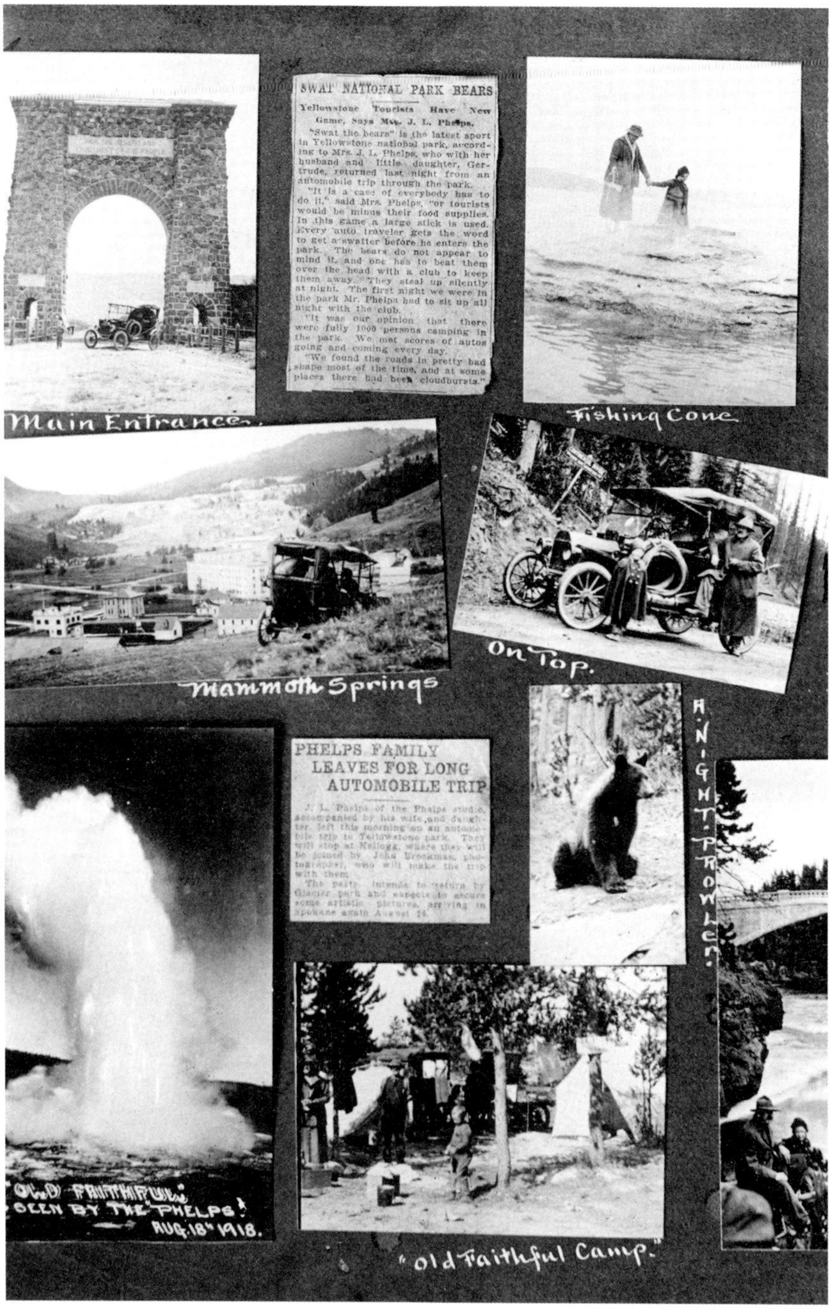

A page from the Phelps family's scrapbook of their visit to Yellowstone in August 1918 shows several park highlights, including the Roosevelt Arch at the north entrance in Gardiner framing their family automobile, a grand view of Mammoth Hot Springs and the Mammoth Hot Springs Hotel, and the mother and daughter peering into Fishing Cone on Yellowstone Lake. In addition, there are clippings from their hometown newspaper in Spokane, Washington. One snippet describes the apparently common practice of "swatting" campground bears with sticks to keep them from food supplies.

INTRODUCTION

It all started with a postcard. Shortly after graduating from Great Falls High School in Great Falls, Montana, in 1971, Michael Francis and his younger brother embarked on a grand adventure to Yellowstone National Park. Even though they slept in a park campground right next to the restrooms, he was hooked. The first postcard he purchased during this road trip turned into a lifetime of collecting Yellowstone memorabilia. *Found Photos of Yellowstone* showcases the best images from over fifty years of finding these jewels.

Mike acquired many of the early pieces perusing estate sales, but his first breakthrough was in 1974 when one of the Hamilton stores sold Haynes postcards for a penny-a-piece. Mike splurged and bought a dollar's worth. But his collection truly blossomed upon the dawn of eBay. Now the contents of family scrapbooks or photos tucked away in attics were at his fingertips. The resulting assemblage, which is carefully catalogued and documented, is what retired park historian Lee Whittlesey believes is the largest collection of Yellowstone photos in private hands.

Deeply enamored with Yellowstone, Mike began working in the park in 1974, launching a fifteen-year career immersed in the inner workings of the hotels and lodges. Also during this time, he picked up his first camera, launching his highly successful photography career. Although he spent decades guiding other photographers on tours throughout the world, Yellowstone is still his favorite place on earth, and he returns regularly visiting familiar places and friends. Mike takes particular delight in looking for the locations of former structures or natural features displayed in historic photos, and with his decades' long friendship with Lee Whittlesey, he appreciates being able to confirm the exact locations.

With the sheer volume of this fifty-plus year collection, there are images that surprise even the most well-versed Yellowstone historians. It demonstrates how much Yellowstone has changed, while remaining remarkably the same on many fronts: Everyone travels the same park loop, and typically stops at the most popular attractions, all the while experiencing a similar visceral reaction as those who witnessed them over a century ago.

One obvious difference is the evolution of clothing styles. Today our casual society sports sandals and shorts, whereas at the turn of the century Yellowstone visitors were far more formal. In these images, women explore rough terrain in full length skirts or dresses, long-sleeved blouses, and always the fashionable hat. Men strolled along the rudimentary boardwalks, or climbed upon the thermal features, in suit and ties, and as with the ladies, often donned the popular style cap of the time. Throughout the decades exhibited in this compilation, the change to less restrictive—and one might say scandalous, at least for the time—garb in the form of just below the knee-length skirts or knickers for the ladies, and more comfortable options for the gentlemen.

The greatest change between then and now is probably the way that we interact with the wonders of Yellowstone. In many of these images we see visitors standing precariously near, or even on, fragile and potentially dangerous thermal features. As we know, the U.S. Army was rallied in 1886 with one of its primary goals to protect these natural features from the public and those wishing to exploit its resources. We often think of damage, such as graffiti, as being a modern phenomenon, but there are instances during the military involvement when people were discovered, and in some instances, marched back to the location to clean it. Theoretically, we now comprehend the severity of seemingly innocent damage, which is often permanent, particularly with the park's visitation exceeding four million people every year. Even though we see people in these photos standing right next to a geyser or one of the other wonders of the park, we cannot follow suit.

This also holds true when it comes to wildlife. For many decades the allure of seeing a bear begging along the side of the road was an enormous attraction. In photos from this period, we see the cute, and often comical, black bears taking food directly from people, enjoying a sip of soda, or boldly climbing into the window of an automobile. What we do not see are the injuries caused when a guest runs out of a favorite treat and the bear demands more, or the expensive damage done because when you have a bear in the car, you have a mess on your hands. Fortunately, we now understand the ramifications of food habituated wildlife, whether it is a grizzly or a ground squirrel, and we feeding wildlife is prohibited for good reason.

One of the greatest lessons learned from this collection is to never take even the simplest moments for granted. We delight in discovering photos of these former structures, watching employees thoroughly enjoy themselves even in the most mundane tasks, as well as intimate moments such as the interior of the hotel room or the kitchen staff taking a break between meal preparations. Examining these photos, we experience the park through other peoples' eyes, but we can make our own memories. Mike reminds us all to take pictures of the buildings and the interior shots of the places we love because one day there might be another opportunity to share our perspective to generations long into the future.

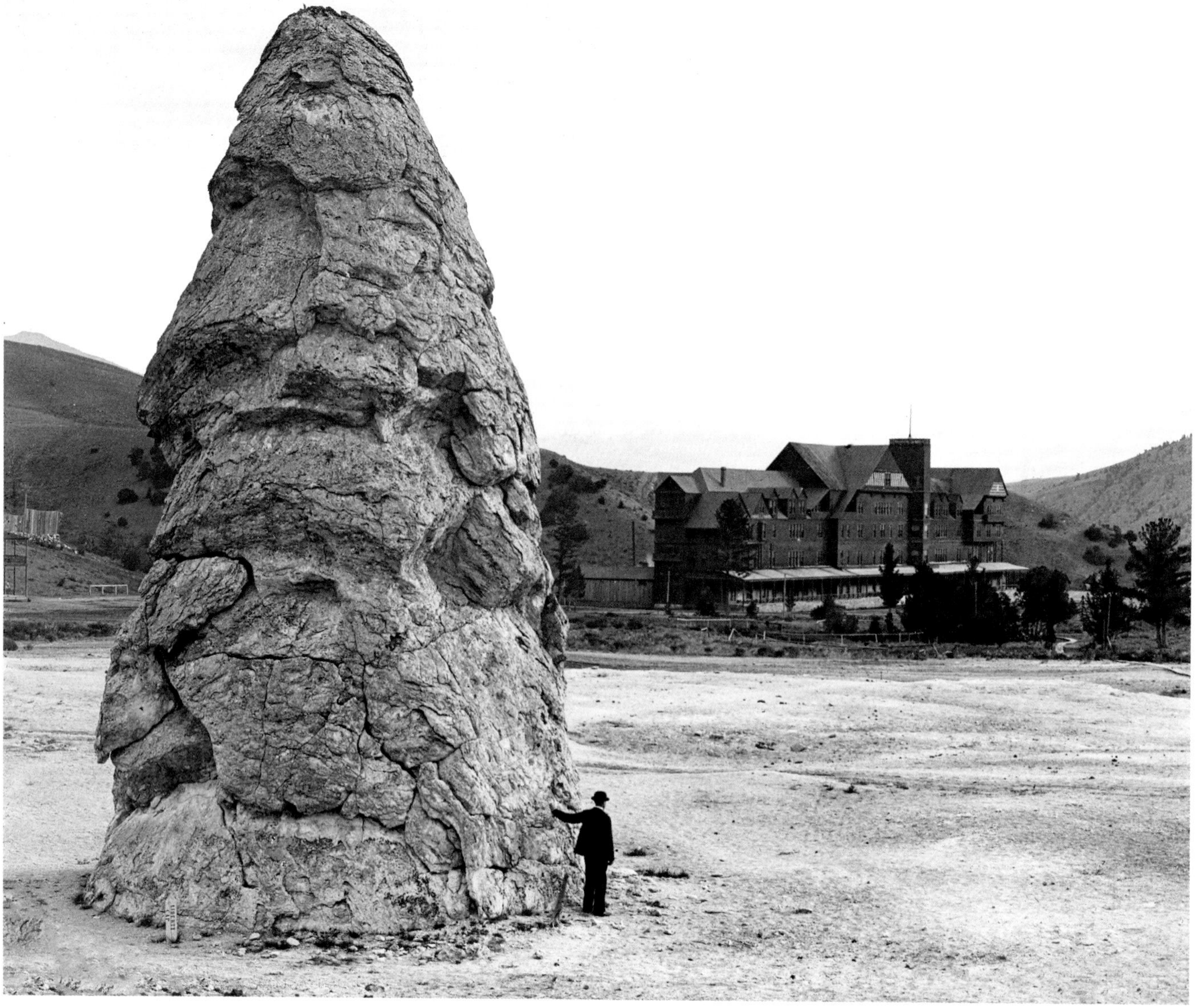

The 37-foot-tall Liberty Cap is a thermal feature as recognizable as the distinct white terraces at Mammoth Hot Springs. Here a park visitor standing next to it offers a sense of scale in this circa-1900 photo. The four-story Mammoth Hot Springs Hotel is in the background. Tall, long, and narrow, it was considered gangly and somewhat out-of-place until it was drastically renovated in 1913, reducing the height and adding the North Wing. During reconstruction in 1936, the North Wing was the only section of the older hotel incorporated into the new design.

CHAPTER 1

From Rustic to Refined

Early visitors of this practically mythical area were a hardy, resourceful bunch. Beginning in 1871, the year prior to the official designation as a national park, Yellowstone's only permanent lodging was the primitive McCartney Hotel in Mammoth Hot Springs, a single-story log cabin that provided a roof over one's head, yet little else. More often, visitors hauled their massive tents and gear, relying on their own resources to make or break their adventure.

From these humble beginnings, the history of hotel development in the park is a succession of construction, renovations, and in many cases, demolition. As more visitors ventured to see the unrivaled beauty and other-worldly features with their own eyes, there was a call for more comfortable accommodations, particularly with the goal of some entrepreneurs to entice wealthy Easterners to "See America First." What often began as a humble structure, sometimes cobbled together with embarrassing flaws, was often transformed over the years to hotels that rivaled their European counterparts marrying luxury with Yellowstone's natural wonders.

These photos give us a glimpse of what early visitors witnessed as the park's hotels evolved from rustic accommodations into places worthy of their world-class location and status. It's fascinating to view the construction of some of the buildings, as well as gain an appreciation of how much some of them have changed—or remained in the same form we cherish to this day. Regardless of the evolution of the hotels themselves, it is this sense of place that draws each of us to revel in the lives of these beloved structures.

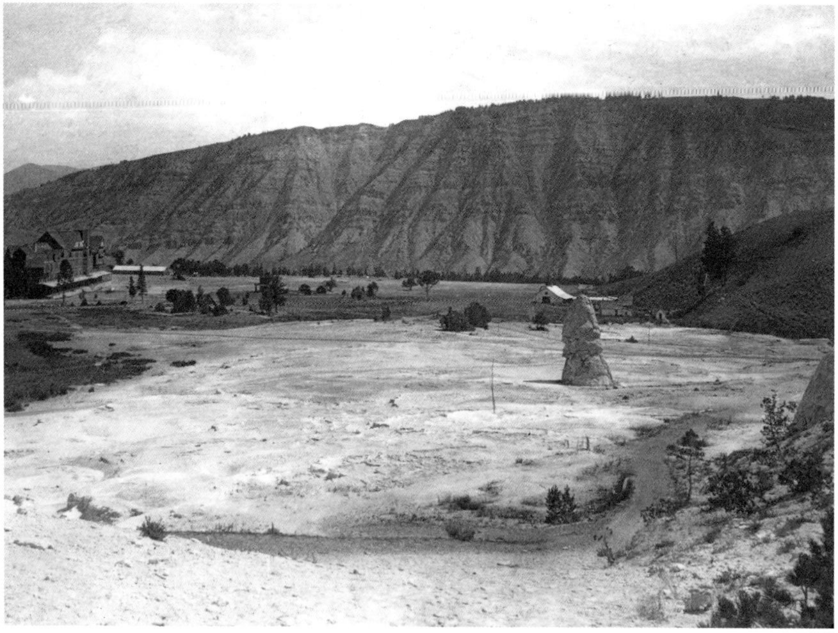

This overview of the Mammoth Hot Springs area shows a rare view of the stagecoach road in 1885 or 1886, which is visible in the lower right of the photo, between Liberty Cap and Devil's Thumb. When visitors left Mammoth Hot Springs Hotel, located to the distant left in this photo, they traveled past Liberty Cap to the base of the Mammoth terraces. Because it was difficult for the horses to haul fully loaded coaches up the steep slope that skirted the terraces, passengers disembarked at the bottom and walked up the terraces, exploring their wonders along the way, before meeting the coach at the top. The building behind and to the left of Liberty Cap was a large stable built by James A. Clark. Clark owned a company that transported tourists via stagecoach from 1884 to 1887 when he transferred his transportation lease to another party. The building that is difficult to see behind and to the right of Liberty Cap was originally James Clark's residence, which he sold to stage coacher George Wakefield in 1888.

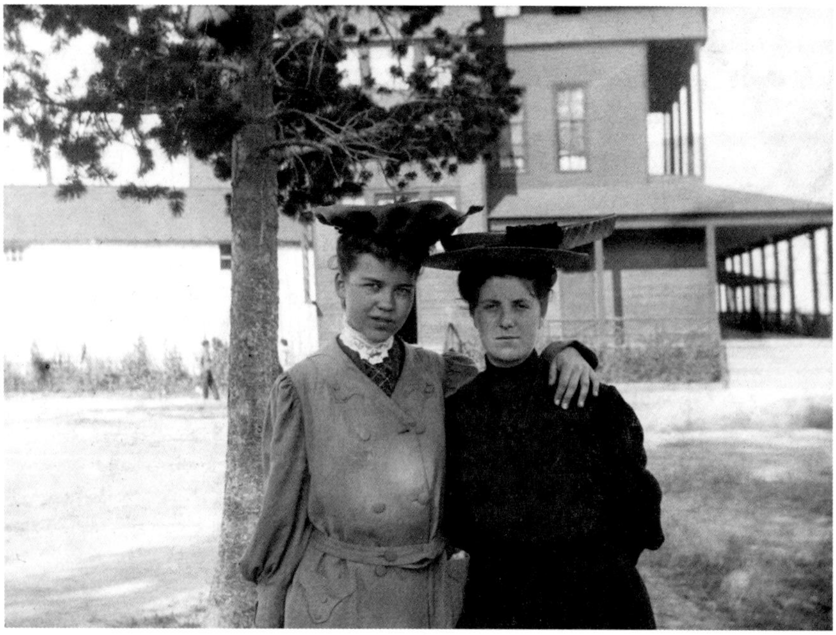

Annie and Mabelle Wagner, who were possibly sisters, pose at the west end of the Mammoth Hot Springs Hotel in 1905. This view of the side of the hotel demonstrates how the 414-foot-long building was narrow, reaching only 56-feet wide. Numerous documents indicate that guests could feel the building sway in high winds.

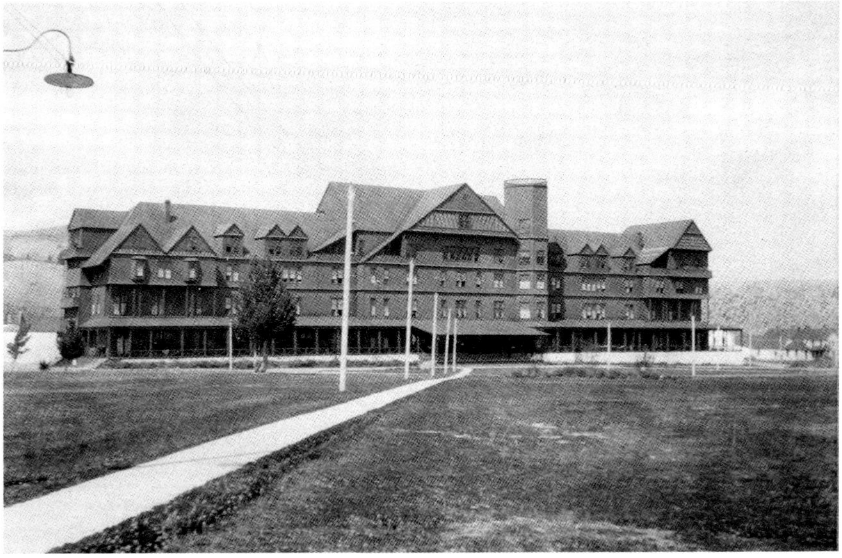

This image of the 151-room Mammoth Hot Springs Hotel in 1910 shows its original design, including the steeply pitched red roof and terra-cotta-and-green exterior. The wooden veranda stretched the entire 414-feet length of the grand structure. Significant renovations took place in 1913, including reducing the angle of the roof and increasing the occupancy up to 600 guests. The Yellowstone National Park Improvement Company strove for elegance in its new hotels, including wiring at least a portion of its lodging for indoor and outdoor lighting as early as 1883. (Note the outdoor light at upper left.) These new features were powered by a Weston Dynamo, an electrical generator that produced direct current, of the U.S. Electric Lighting Company. Park officials encouraged the complete electrification of all the buildings by 1887 to eliminate the risk of fire from kerosene lanterns.

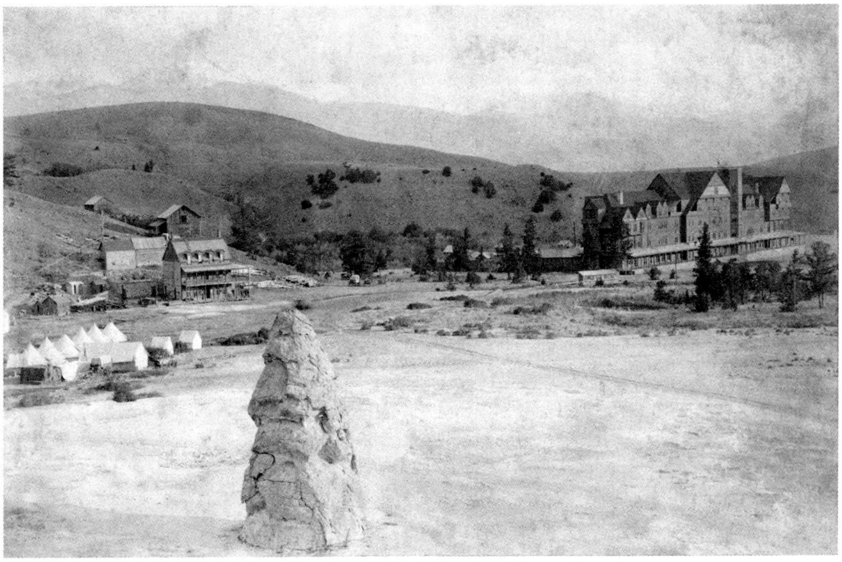

This photo is an overview of the Mammoth area in 1886, the year the U.S. Army arrived in the park. In the foreground is the Liberty Cap geological feature, and, from left to right, the tents of the first U.S. Army encampment, the Cottage Hotel and other buildings of "Henderson Town" (beyond the tents), the 1884 bathhouse for hotel guests (the small, flat-roofed rectangular building in front of and to the left of the hotel), and the Mammoth Hot Springs Hotel. The buildings around the Cottage Hotel were dubbed "Henderson Town" after the George L. Henderson family, who catered to guests within Yellowstone for more than three decades.

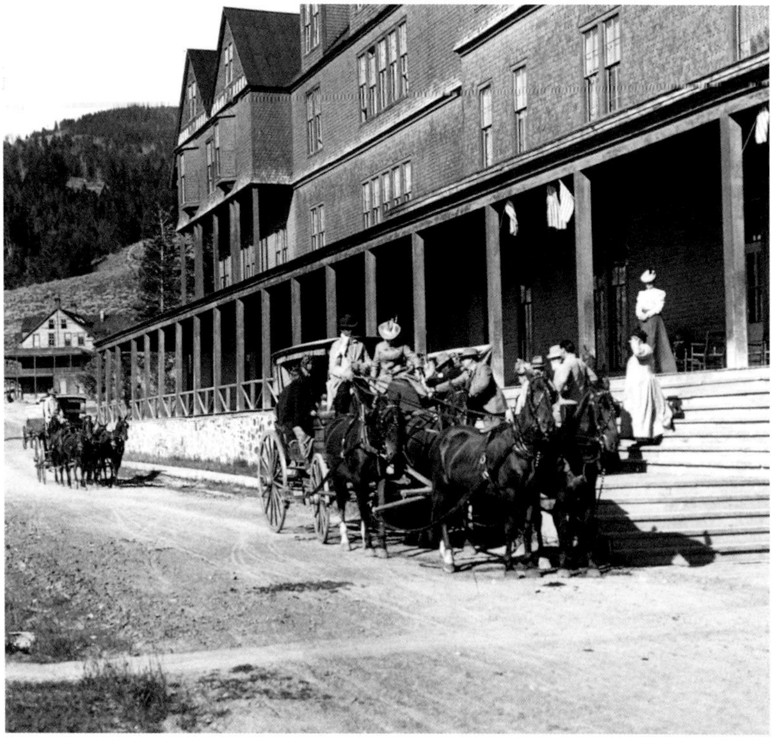

After arriving in Cinnabar on the Northern Pacific Railroad from 1883-1902, or in Gardiner on the Northern Pacific Railway from 1903-1916, many train passengers climbed aboard horse-drawn coaches to travel the final miles to the Mammoth Hot Springs Hotel, commencing their park adventure. The Cottage Hotel, visible in the left background of the photo, was a lower-cost option for some travelers. It was constructed in 1885 and operated by George L. Henderson, one of the park's earliest interpreters who often guided parties in the park and drove stagecoaches for his own fleet.

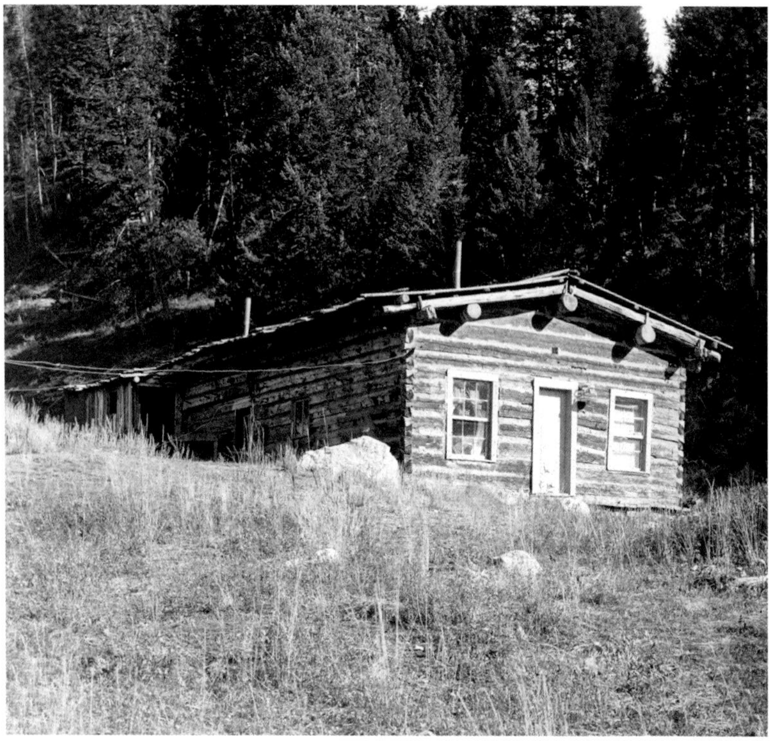

While not considered plush accommodations, the hewn-log McCartney Hotel was the first commercial lodging within Yellowstone. It was constructed in 1871 by James McCartney and Harry Horr at the mouth of Clematis Gulch, near the current trail to the Beaver Ponds in Mammoth Hot Springs. Throughout the 1870s, McCartney and Horr built many other structures, including one that they rented to George L. Henderson and his family for the Mammoth Hot Springs post office and their private dwelling. In 1902, Sam Toy (Toi) took over the original hotel building, using it as a laundry facility until it burned in December 1912.

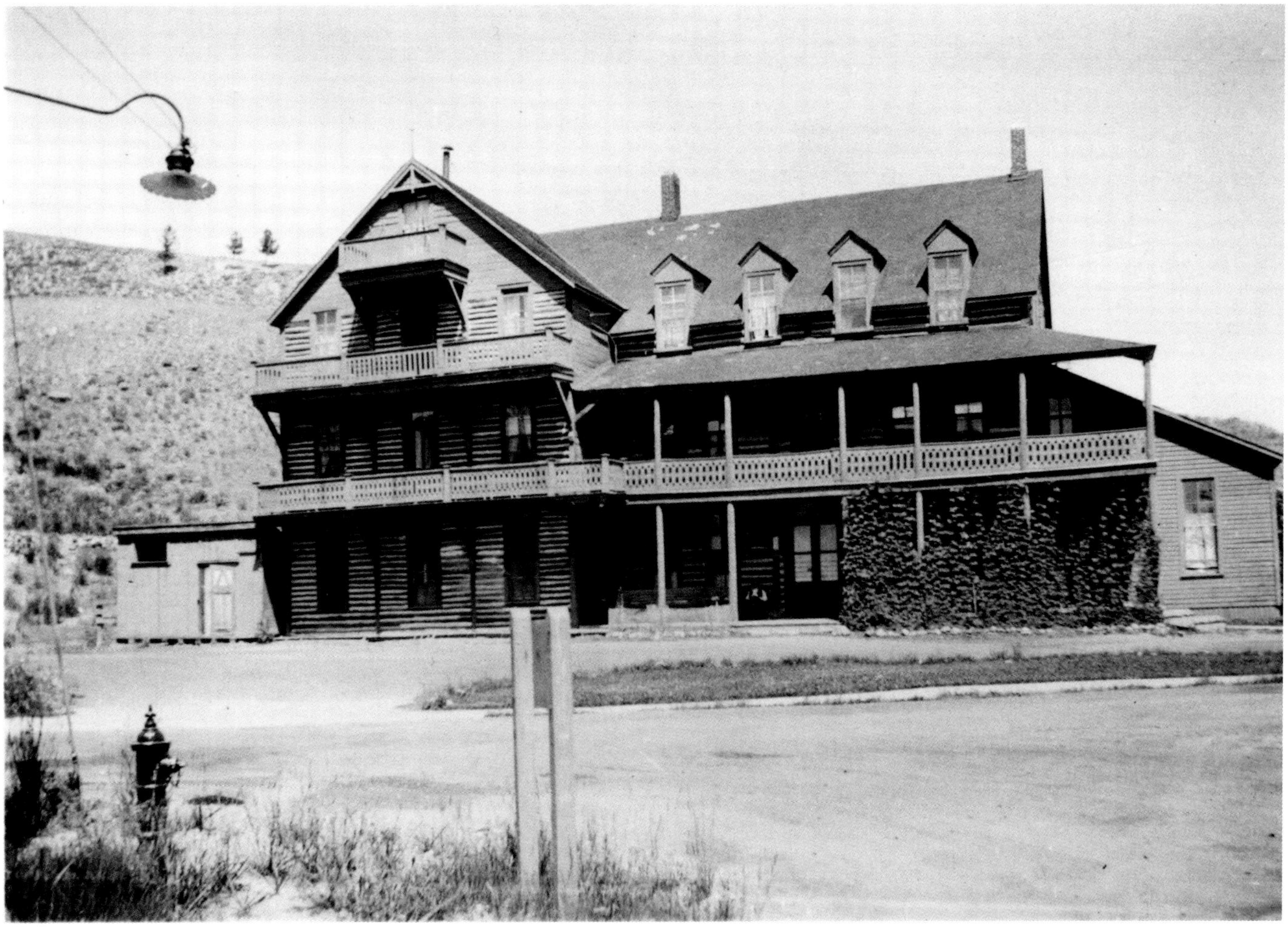

Built in 1885 by George L. Henderson and his family, the three-story, no-frills Cottage Hotel offered comfortable visitor accommodations for $2.50 per day versus the $4 daily charge of the National Hotel, which was called the Mammoth Hot Springs Hotel by 1883. Originally housing guests throughout the year—its grand opening was Christmas Day, 1885—the Cottage Hotel was the centerpiece of "Henderson Town," where George L. Henderson and his five children were active figures in the early days of the park. In 1889, the Hendersons sold the hotel to the Yellowstone Park Association. The company retained Henderson as a spokesperson and consummate park interpreter for its guests.

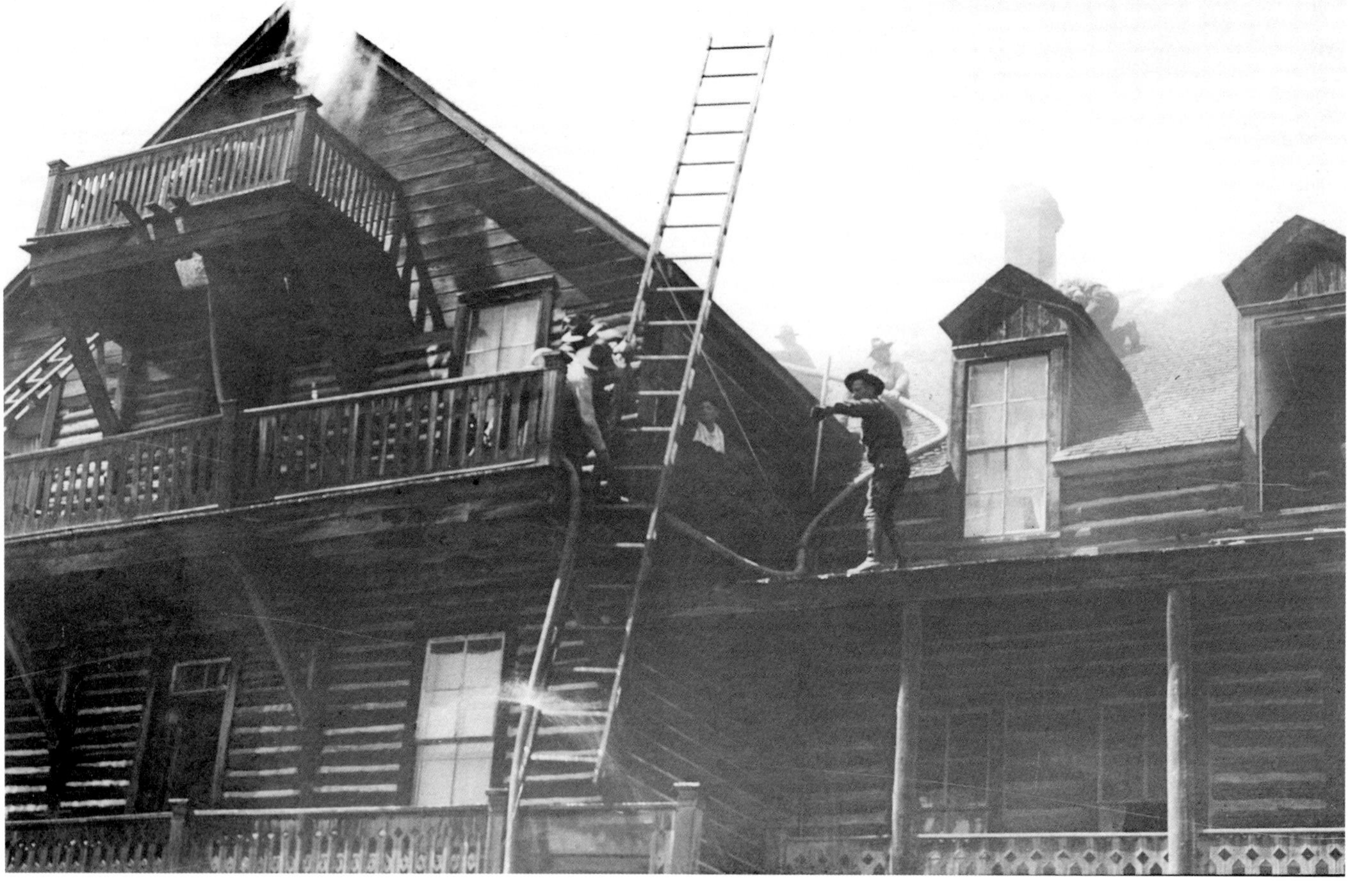

The Cottage Hotel was being used as an employee dormitory when it caught fire in 1910. Soldiers from nearby Fort Yellowstone formed a fire brigade (shown here), rescuing residents and belongings while dousing the flames. Even their waking of Ms. "Tweet-tweet," a partially dressed female employee slumbering in one of the upstairs bedrooms after her night shift at the Mammoth Hot Springs Hotel, did not deter the troops from their mission. They gave her a blanket and continued saving the structure and its contents. Standing idle for a decade after the fire, the Cottage Hotel was remodeled in 1921 and continued its life as an employee dormitory until the National Park Service demolished the historic building in 1964, two years prior to the National Historic Preservation Act, which would have saved this cultural representation of early visitation in Yellowstone.

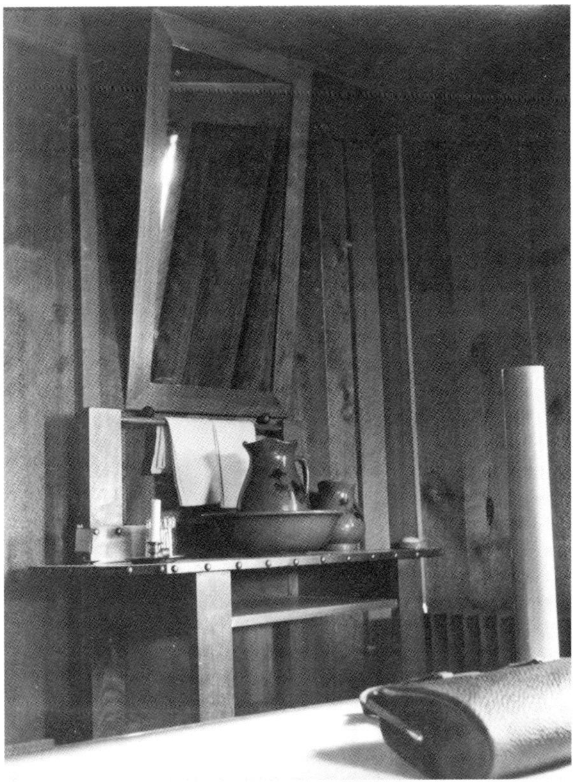

Without a flash built into the camera, indoor photography was exceptionally difficult in the early 1900s, yet this photo taken on July 22, 1909, gives us a rare glimpse inside a room in Old Faithful Inn. A simple basin and pitcher sit upon the washstand, with a clean set of folded towels hanging behind them. To the left, a drinking glass is turned upside-town, ready for use, and a partially burnt candle with a box of matches behind it are within easy reach when the sun sets. A large mirror tilts from the wall. Manufactured by Charles Limbert of Grand Rapids, Michigan, the wooden washstand was one of the many pieces, including table lamps, fashioned in the Mission style, some of which are used in the rooms of the Old House to this day. Apparently, the guest who took this photo placed a leather club-bag on the four-post bed.

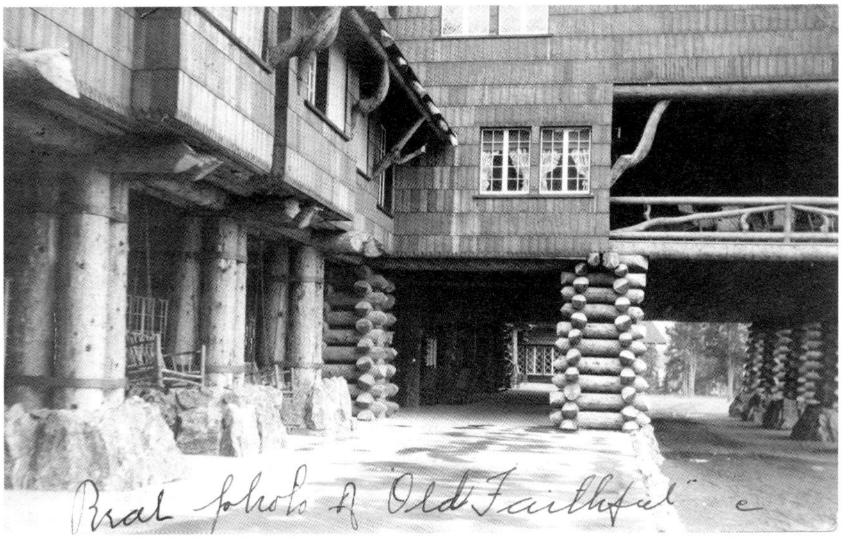

The visually interesting porch in this 1909 image of the Old Faithful Inn is evidence of architect Robert Reamer's goal to create rustic charm for refined guests. Crews harvested timber from nearby areas in the park, specifically setting aside oddly shaped pieces for railings and other visible features. The Old Hickory Furniture Company created the hickory and wicker furniture specifically for Old Faithful Inn, while the Mission-style pieces, which were popular in the early 1900s, were commissioned to Charles Limbert for their construction. Known for its clean, structural—very unpretentious—lines, the Mission design departed from ornate Victorian furniture. Some of the original chairs and writing desks are still used today.

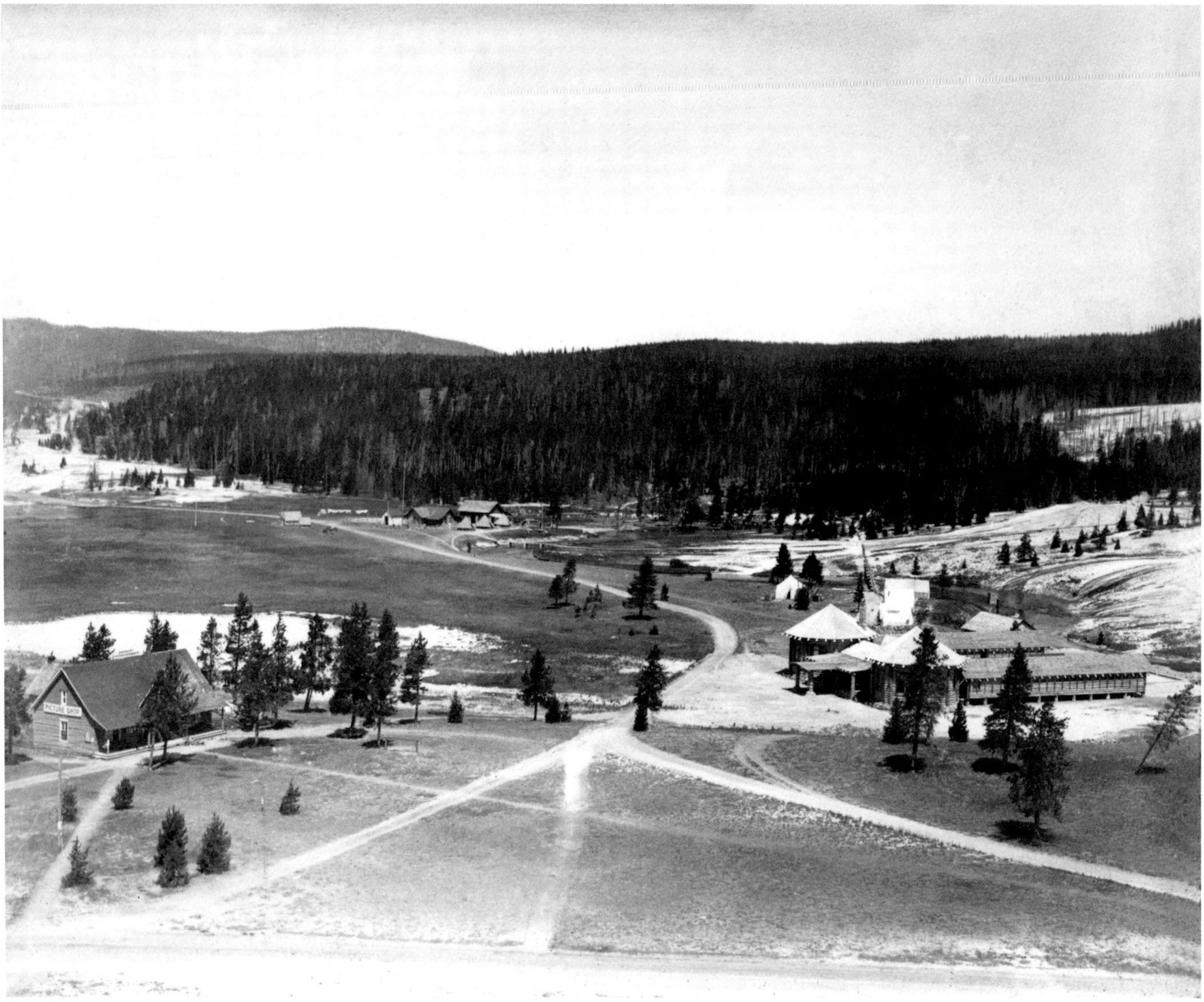

This photo provides a view from the top of Old Faithful Inn in the Upper Geyer Basin, prior to 1934. The overview shows buildings and roads that no longer exist today. On the right of the image, the second bathhouse, which was built in the basin by Henry P. Brothers in 1927, was an open-air pool supplied with water from Solitary Geyser. When Charles Hamilton purchased the swimming pool from Henry Brothers in 1933, he renovated it and then built a much larger log structure the following year, but did not relocate the pool as the National Park Service had requested. After years of battles with the National Park Service because the pool tapped into a thermal feature and obstructed views of Old Faithful Geyser from the Grand Loop Road, it was closed in 1950 and demolished in 1951. The Haynes Photo Shop (near left) was built in 1897, and was eventually moved to near the first Snow Lodge in 1974. The U.S. Army's soldier station is at the rear of the area photo.

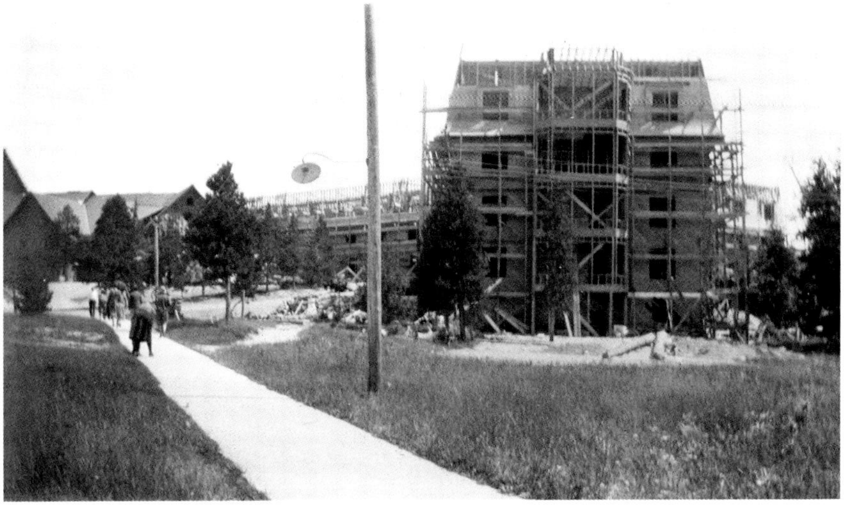

Guests stroll along a sidewalk during the construction of the West Wing, an addition to Old Faithful Inn, in 1926. Because visitation significantly increased within two decades of the inn's initial opening in 1904, the Y-shaped, four-story wing was a much-needed expansion, adding 150 guest rooms and 95 baths, bringing the inn's total to 340 rooms. During this renovation, builders added the extended carriage entrance to the front of the inn and expanded the lobby by 30 feet.

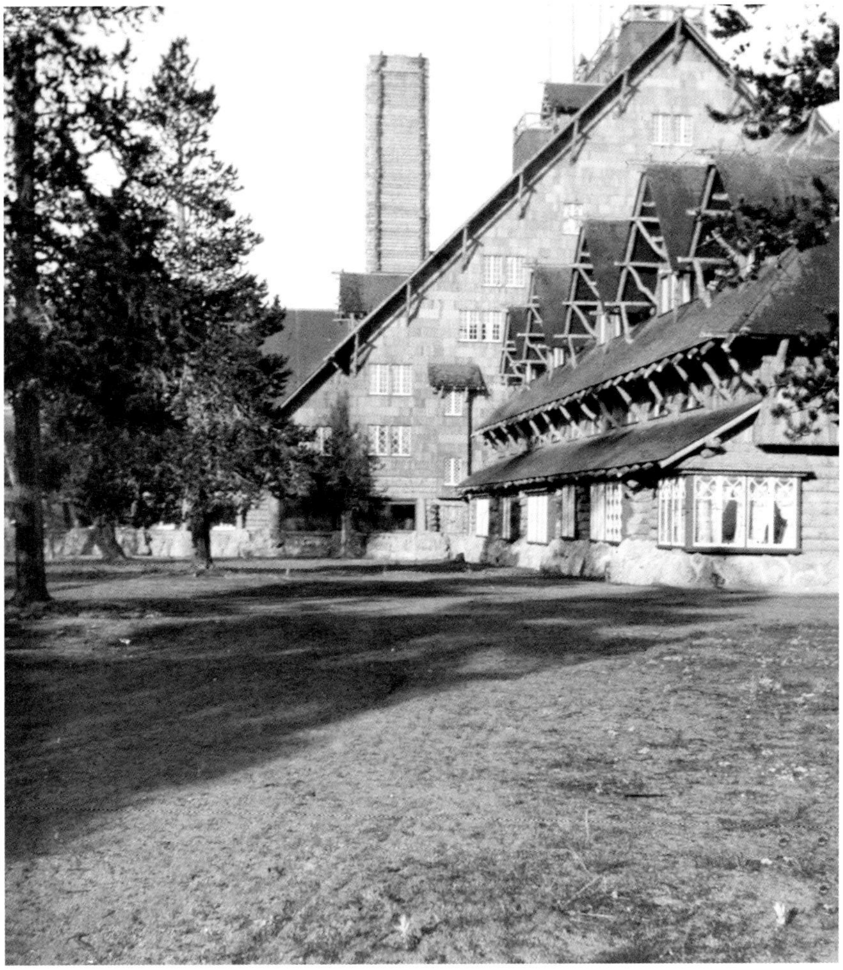

This photo, taken prior to 1913, is an eastern aspect of Old Faithful Inn showing the "Old House" before the addition of the East Wing in 1913-1914, which added 100 rooms. Architect Robert Reamer was integral in the popularity of this now classic "parkitecture" style: incorporating natural materials and organic design into structures situated in inherently wild areas. Built using rustic-looking logs and volcanic stone with steep-sloping roof lines—plus equally angled dormers—it gave the feeling that this massive building grew organically from the dynamic landscape. *Photo by Edward M. Rice.*

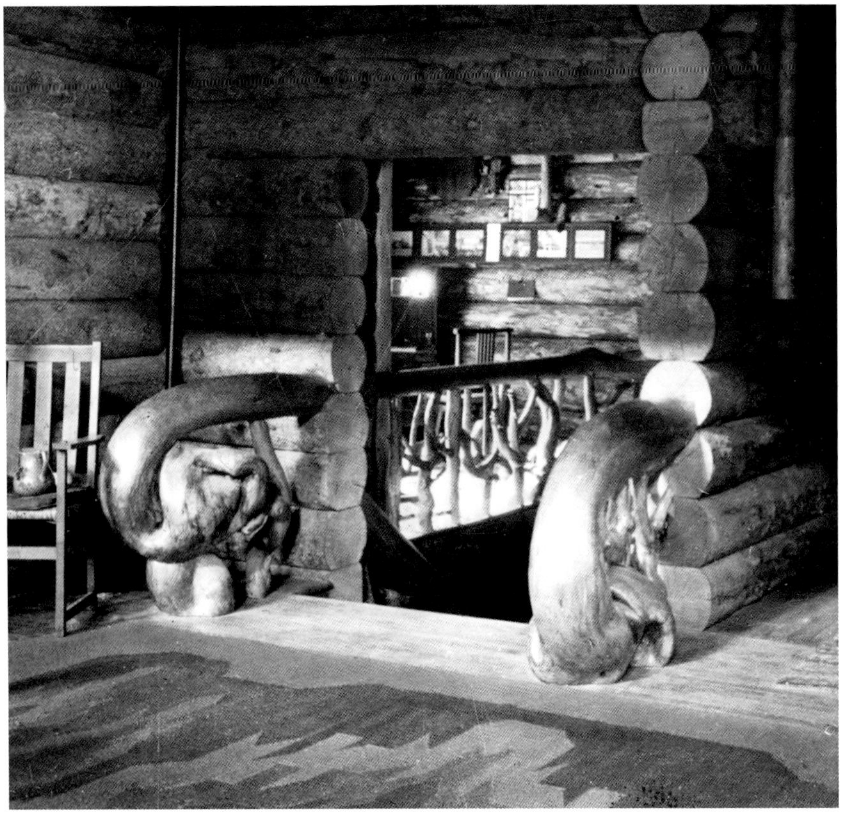

Architect Robert Reamer directed workers to use the twisted and gnarled "freaks of the forest" to accentuate the railings and decorative features within Old Faithful Inn, such as these steps that led down to the wine cellar. The Mission-style chair sitting to the left of the stairway is typical of much of the furniture commissioned for the inn from Charles Limbert of Michigan. Adelaide Child, the wife of Yellowstone Park Association president Harry Child, acquired much of the furniture and accessories during the construction of the "Old House" in 1904. *Photo by E. B. Thompson.*

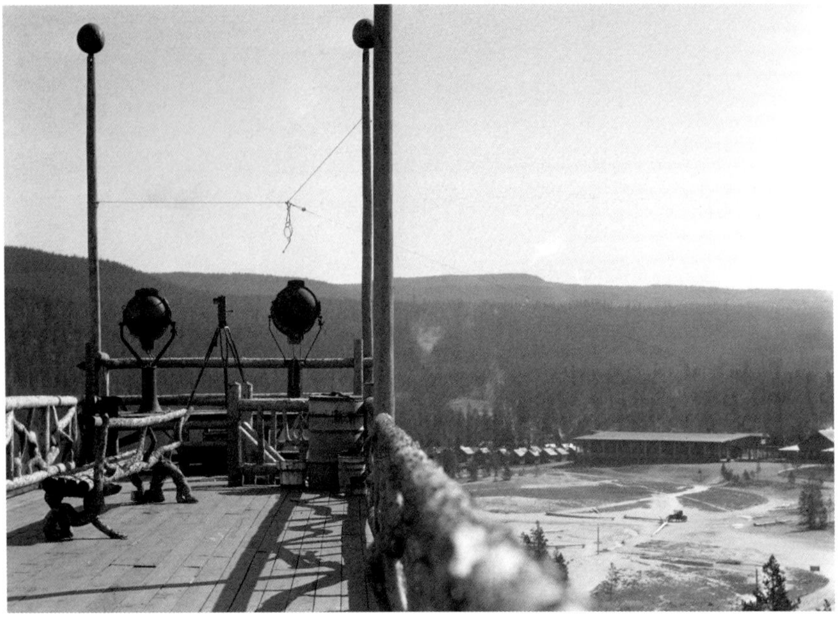

This is a circa-1920s view of the roof top of Old Faithful Inn with the Old Faithful Camp (today's Old Faithful Lodge) in the background. The sturdy-looking bench built from gnarled lodgepole pines gave people a prime seat to view the entire area, including night scenes. The dual spotlights at the far end were used to illuminate Old Faithful Geyser at night—and sometimes highlighted "rotten loggers," amorous couples attempting to find a little seclusion in the dark. In the early years there was a single spotlight. Nobody knows exactly when the dual lights were installed.

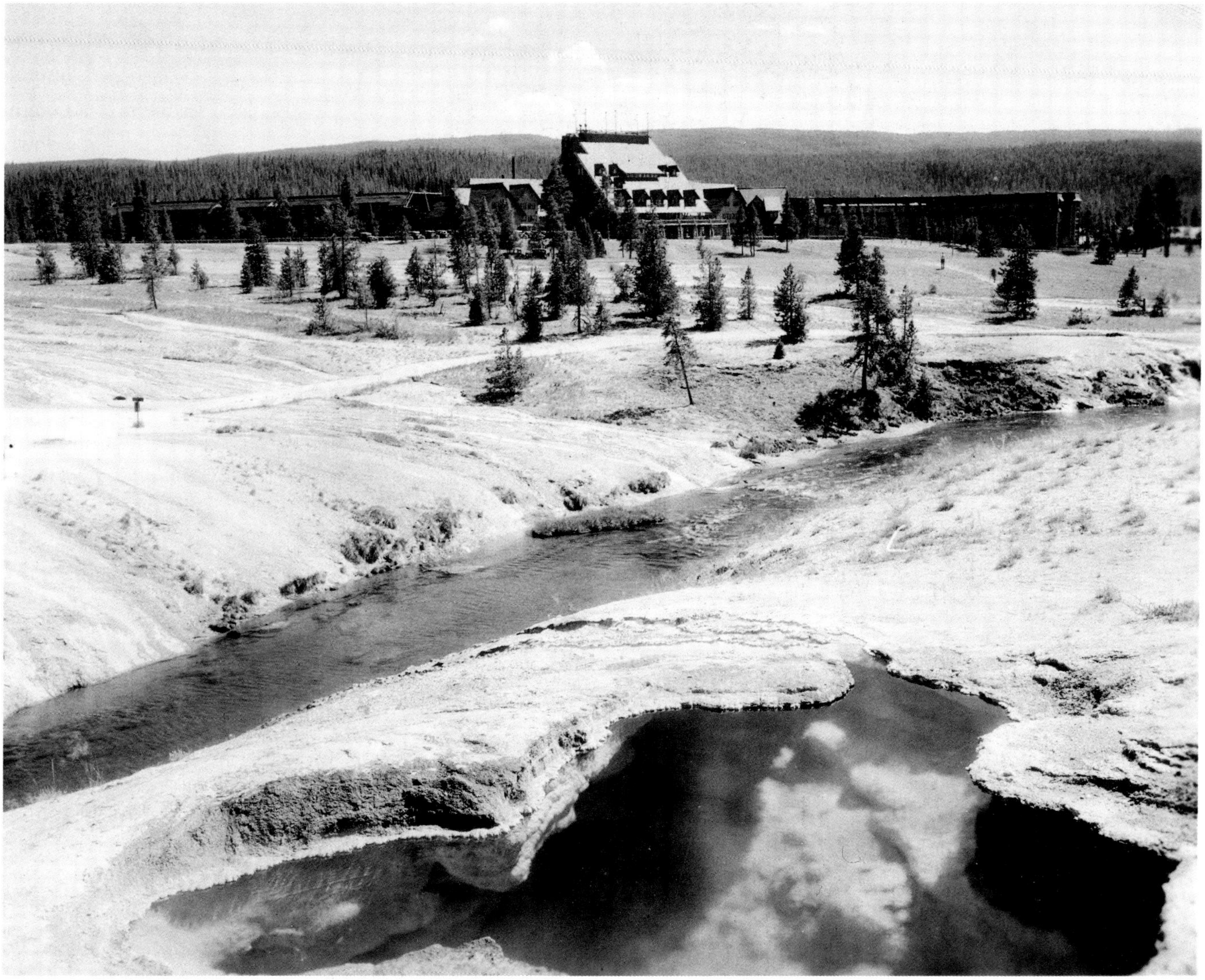

The foreground of this image provides a glimpse into the depths of Cascade Geyser, which is part of the Geyser Hill Group of hot springs along the north bank of the Firehole River. This geyser was active in the early days of the park with eruptions as high as 40 feet, and was one of the many thermal attractions that made the Upper Geyser Basin so popular. In recent times, this feature has been mostly inactive. Situated in the background of this 1929 photo, the expansive Old Faithful Inn stretched 836 feet across the landscape, including the spacious West Wing addition built the prior year.

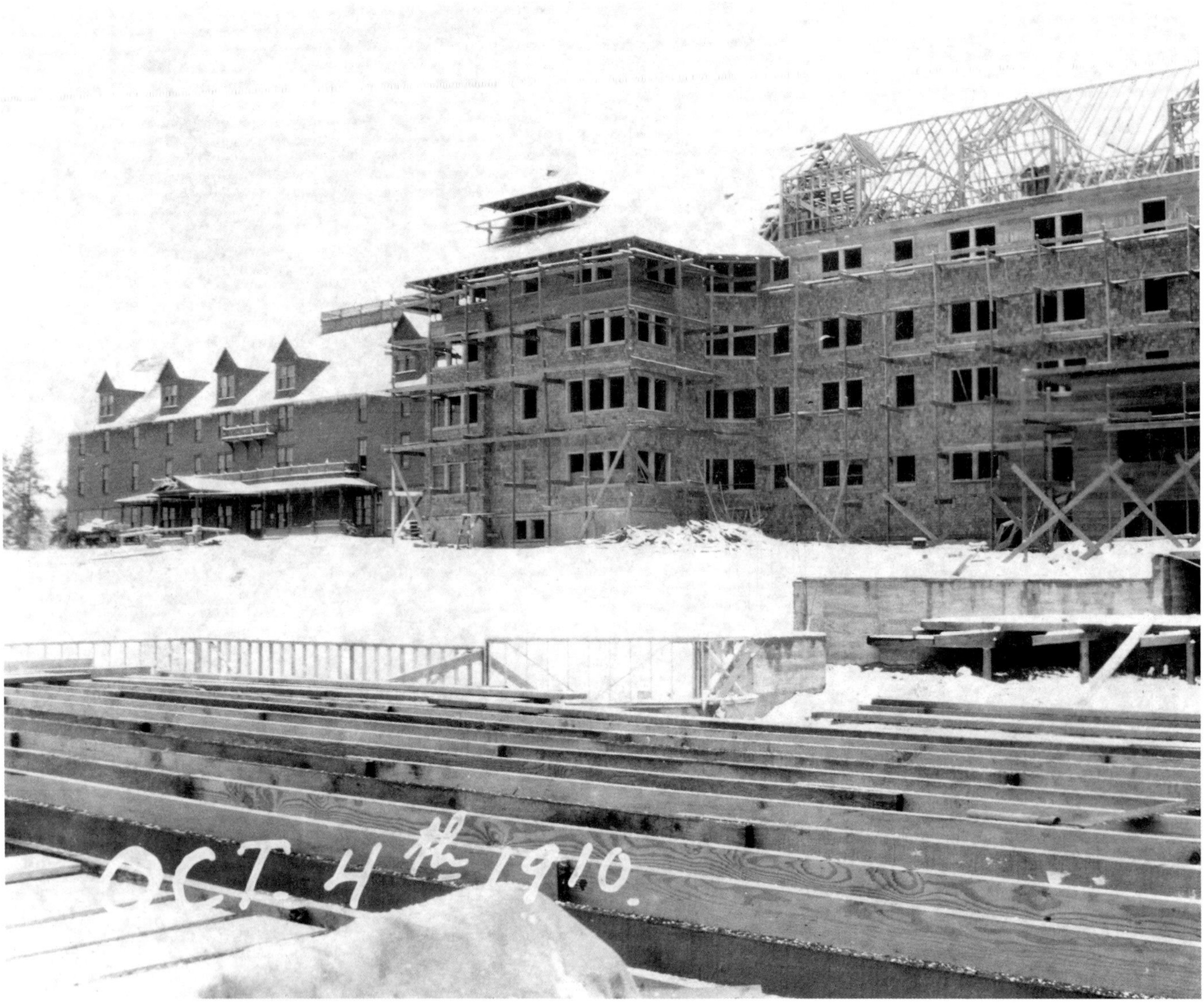

The snow-covered construction site in this photo dated October 4, 1910, shows the progress incorporating the second version of the Canyon Hotel into the new and what was ultimately the largest structure built within Yellowstone. The completed building measured a mile in circumference, all the while maintaining an affinity with its natural surroundings. With 375 rooms, 75 of which held private baths, the new Canyon Hotel was the pinnacle of refinement at that time. In addition to electricity and comfortable accommodations, the hotel boasted a splendid lounge, bowling alley, and billiard rooms—all intended to encourage a lively social scene. Condemned for demolition in 1958 due to a long-failing foundation, the beloved hotel burned to the ground on August 8, 1960, from an undetermined cause. Many believed it was a fitting end, as the Wyoming State Tribune stated, "The Great Lady Chose a Sudden Death."

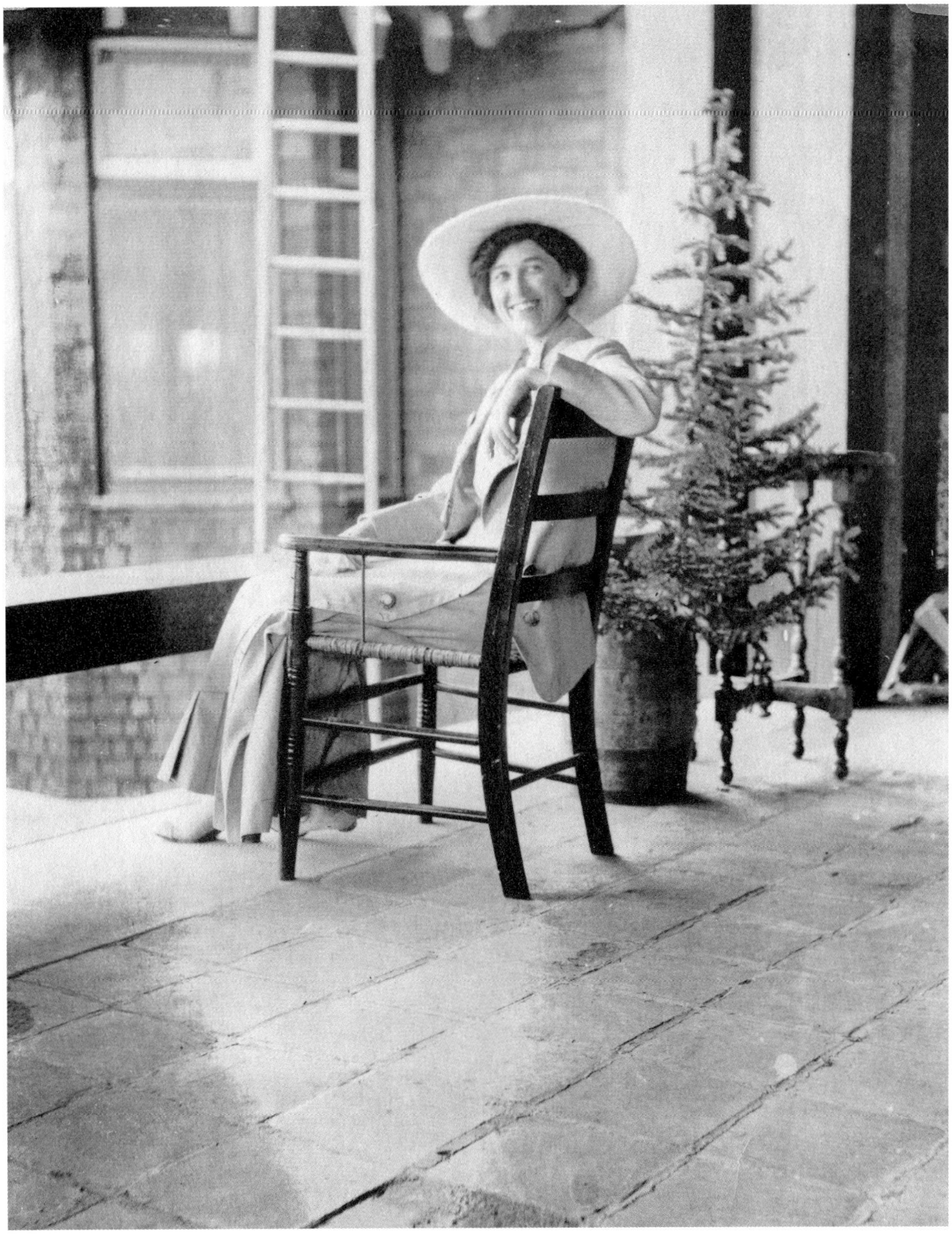

A smiling visitor wears a fashionable wide-brimmed hat as she poses for her photo on the tile porch at the third Canyon Hotel, circa 1911. Note the well-made chair and the decorative potted evergreen behind her. Completed that year, the Canyon Hotel brought to the park the elegance of the finest European accommodations, including 1,500 pieces of custom-made furniture, many of which were created by the McHugh Willow Furniture Company of New York.

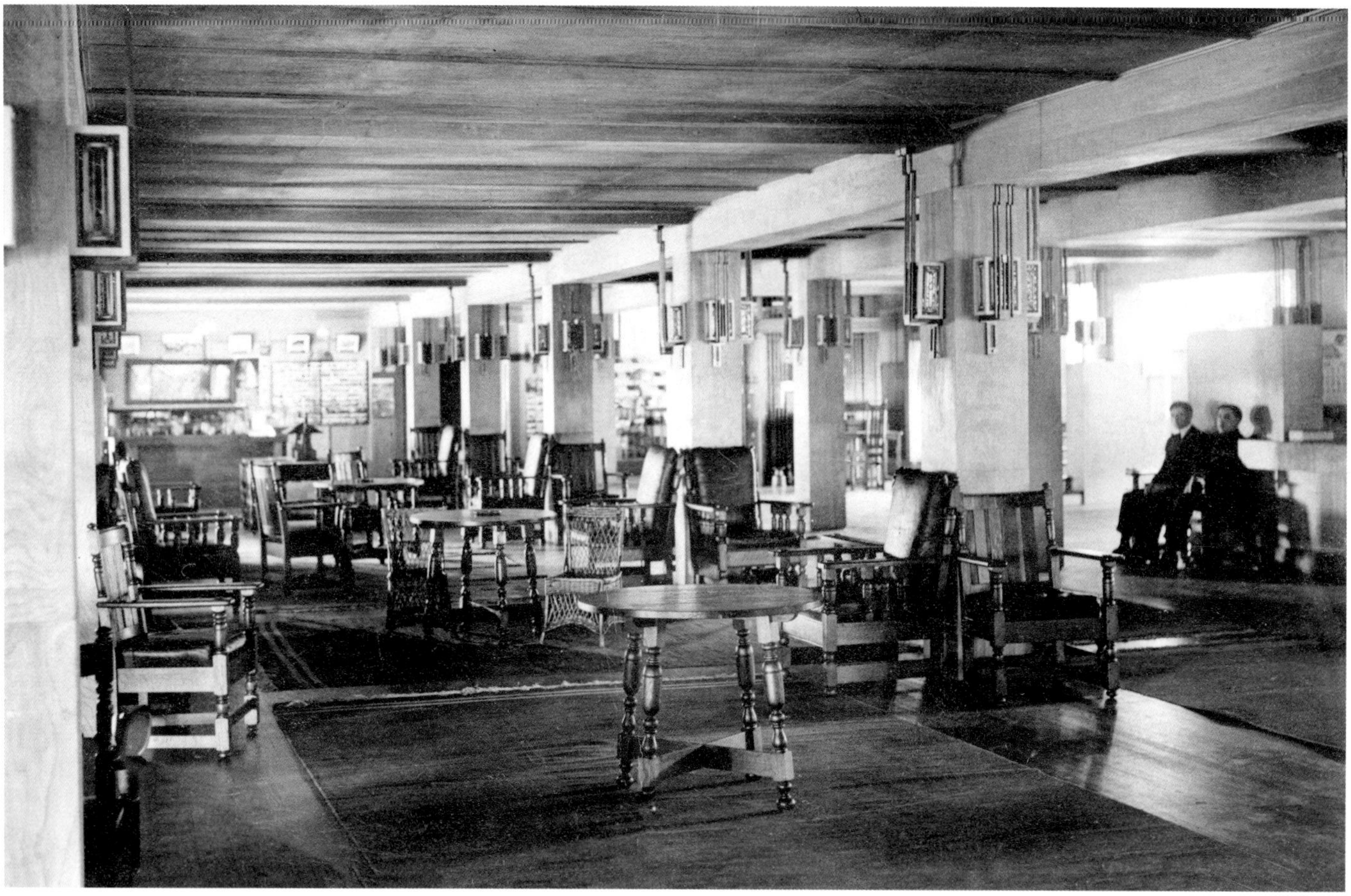

This is a view of the grand lobby inside the third rendition of the Canyon Hotel; the lobby was 65-feet wide and 118-feet long. The registration desk welcomed visitors through the main doors, and electric elevators transported guests and luggage to the upper floors. Note the wall-mounted light fixtures, some of which were salvaged and installed in Frank Lloyd Wright's Blair Residence in Cody, Wyoming, before the Canyon Hotel burned in 1960. This is particularly fitting because Frank Lloyd Wright's influence, including the Prairie Style of the Canyon Hotel, is evident in much of Robert Reamer's work. Reamer's goal of melding the structure, particularly as massive as it was, into the landscape was visionary. In his pamphlet on the Canyon Hotel, *A Miracle in Hotel Building*, John H. Rafferty quoted Reamer as saying, "I built it in keeping with the place where it stands. Nobody could improve upon that. To be at discord with the landscape, would be almost a crime. To try to improve upon it, would be an impertinence." The Haynes Photo Shop was located towards the far end of the lobby, and in the 1928 *Haynes Guide*, Frank J. Haynes commented on what a pleasure it was to spend the day at the grand hotel.

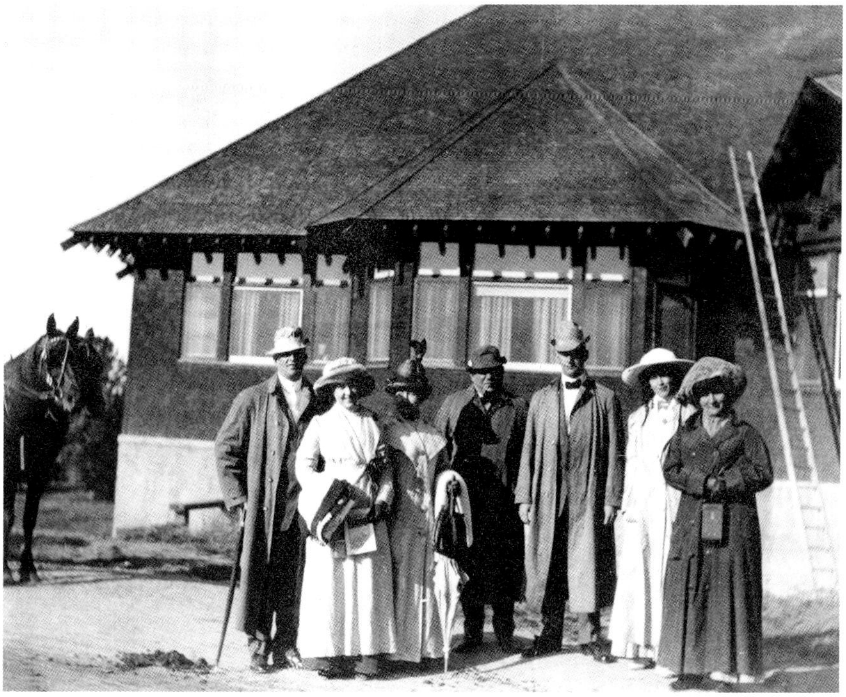

This is a group photo of guests waiting outside the third Canyon Hotel, circa 1911. These tourists either just arrived or are preparing to leave via a horse-drawn coach because they are dressed in long dusters, a necessity to avoid being coated in dirt. Bandanas and scarves were also used to keep the grit out of mouths and lungs. While seeing Yellowstone from a stagecoach was the primary mode of travel until August 1915, it was difficult to view the landscape because of the dust raised by the stagecoaches, unless your coach led the line or kept its distance from the others. Notice the woman on the left holds a pamphlet or travel guide, and the lady standing behind her has two feathers decorating her hat. The woman on the far right carries a folding camera. Such cameras were made by several companies, including Kodak and Seneca. The small and rugged designs were popular with travelers.

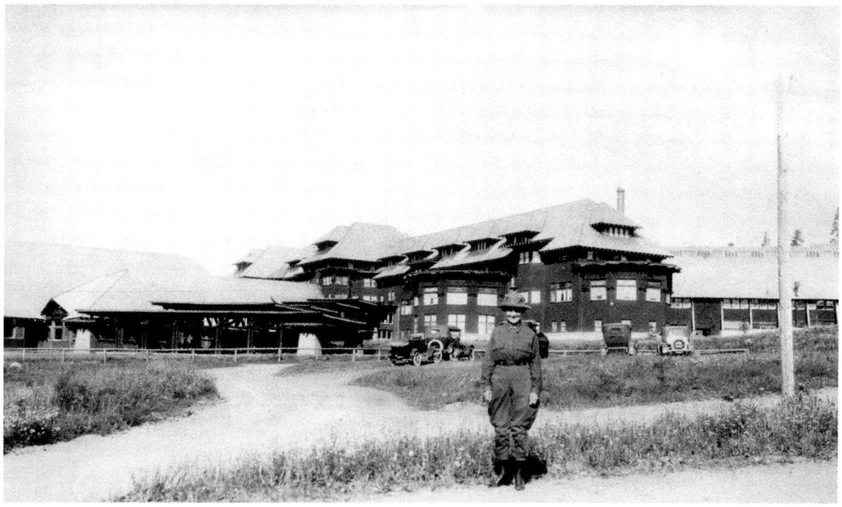

A woman dressed for her "Wonderland" adventure wears knicker-style sports pants and a practical bucket hat as she poses in front of the third Canyon Hotel in July 1921, nearly a decade after its opening in August 1911. Architect Robert Reamer designed the sprawling structure to bring the outdoor ambience indoors without compromising comfort and refinement. Stretching 750-feet long, the hotel had enormous windows that highlighted the panoramic views that Thomas Moran, the famous artist who brought Yellowstone's astounding landscape to the attention of the public and Congress, painted during his park visits in 1871 and 1872.

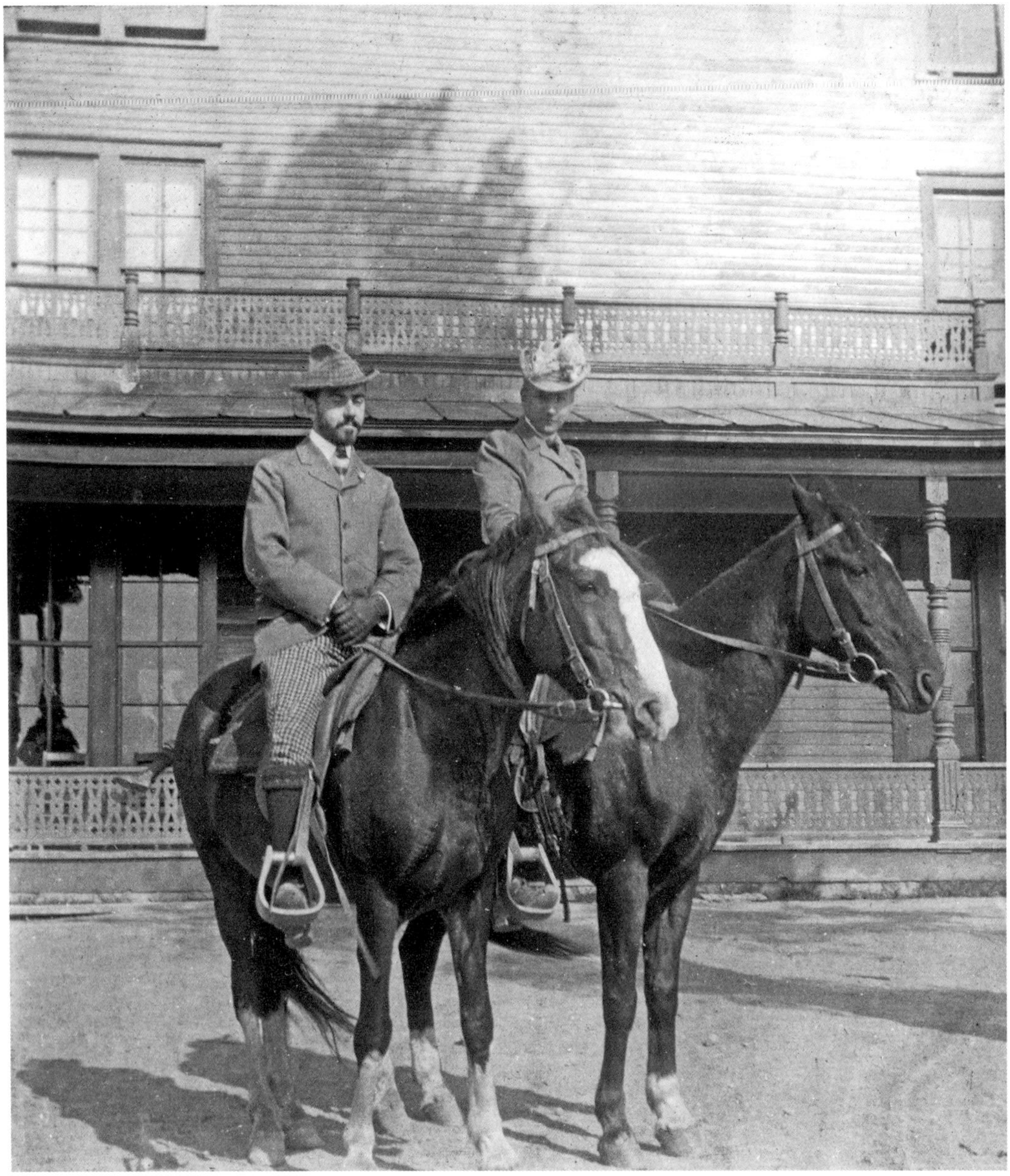

Wearing a sportsman's outfit typical of the early 1900s--including canvas gaiters, a wool Homburg hat, and leather gloves--this gentleman and his female counterpart pose on horseback in front of the second Canyon Hotel. The equally fashionable lady wears an upswept hairstyle along with a feather-decorated hat angled over her face. At the turn of the twentieth century, millions of birds, from hummingbirds to eagles, were killed to satisfy the nearly insatiable demand to adorn women's hats and accessories. Spearheaded by John James Audubon and other conservationists, the 1918 Migratory Bird Treaty Act finally ended this practice.

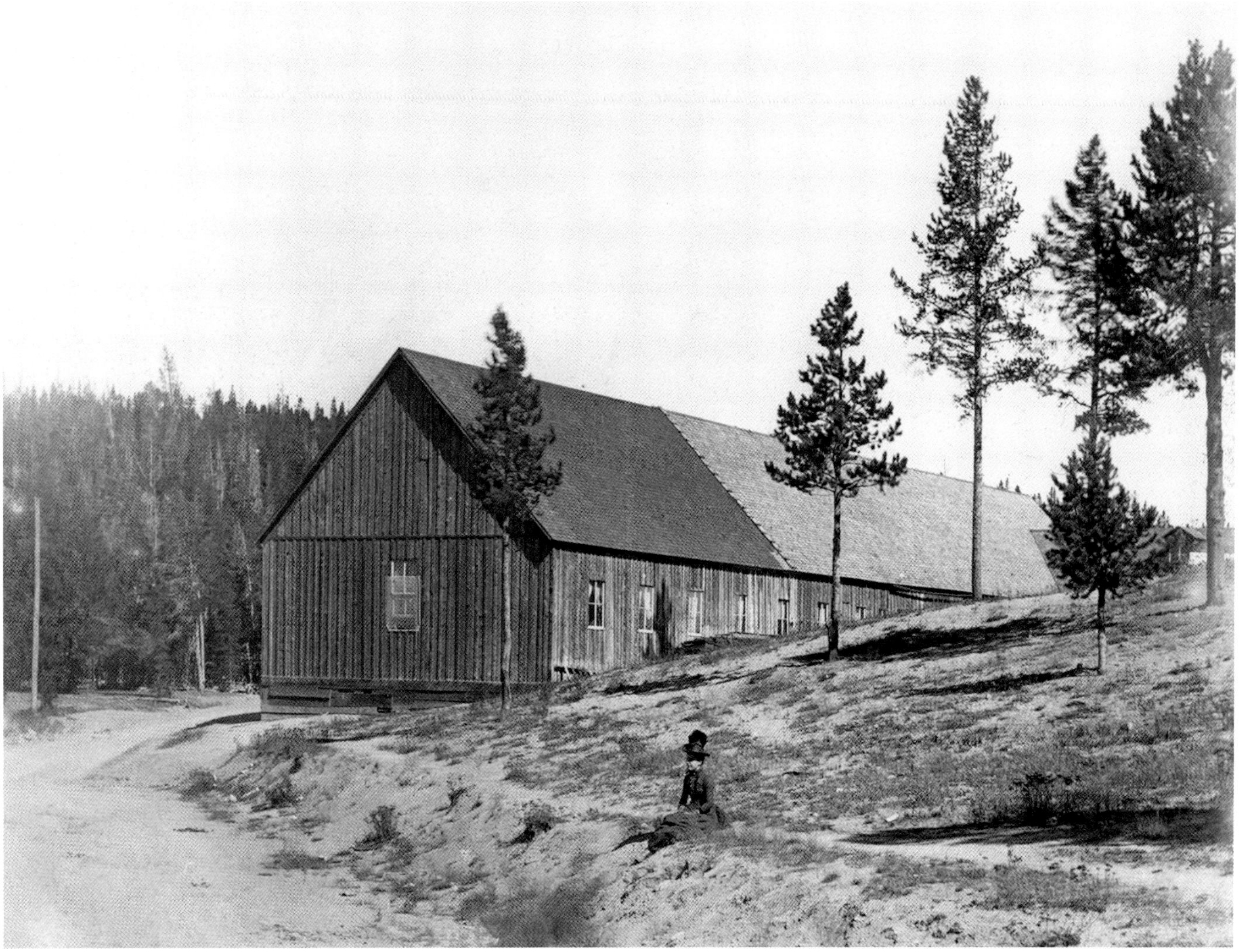

This photo shows the second Norris Hotel, located near the Norris Geyser Basin, sometime between 1887 and 1892. A young female visitor sits on the bank above the road, along what appears to be a walking path. She wears a dark, full-length dress with a high collar, dark gloves, and a dark-colored hat possibly adorned with feathers, a common fashion accessory of this era. The Yellowstone Park Association (YPA) built the first Norris Hotel in the fall of 1886 on a hill south of and across from the Gibbon River and the Soldier Station. The YPA opened it in June 1887, but it burned down after only a month of welcoming guests. Toward the end of the same year, the YPA cobbled together a rudimentary, rectangular, part-tent building that offered 20 rooms for guests, along with a common hall where most visitors only ate lunch. This second Norris Hotel, located just east of the first building and at the bottom of the same hill, burned in 1892. Tents and various primitive structures on essentially the same site served as the third hotel until 1901. In that year, the YPA built the final Norris Hotel on the north edge of Porcelain Terrace, providing 25 rooms for guests. Automobiles changed the nature of visitation after 1915, leading to the closure of the fourth Norris Hotel at the end of the 1916 season. Workmen demolished the building in 1927.

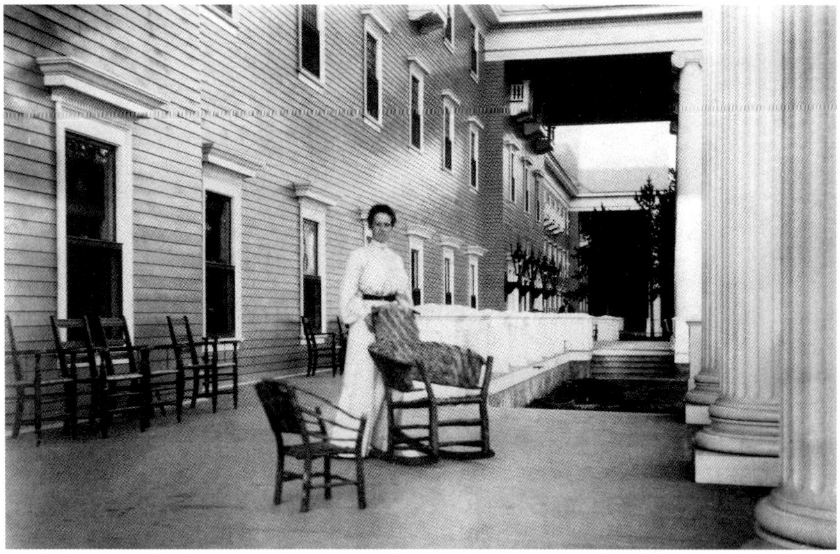

A guest poses near one of the hickory chairs on Lake Hotel's wooden veranda. She wears the full-length, flowing dress with a high neckline that was typical of the fashion at the turn of the twentieth century. This dramatic outdoor space, where visitors socialized as they soaked in the wonders of Yellowstone Lake and the surrounding areas, stretched the entire 720-feet length of the hotel. Unfortunately, the beloved wooden veranda was replaced with concrete during the renovations from 1918-1919. Although the veranda is gone, a handful of these original hickory chairs are still in use.

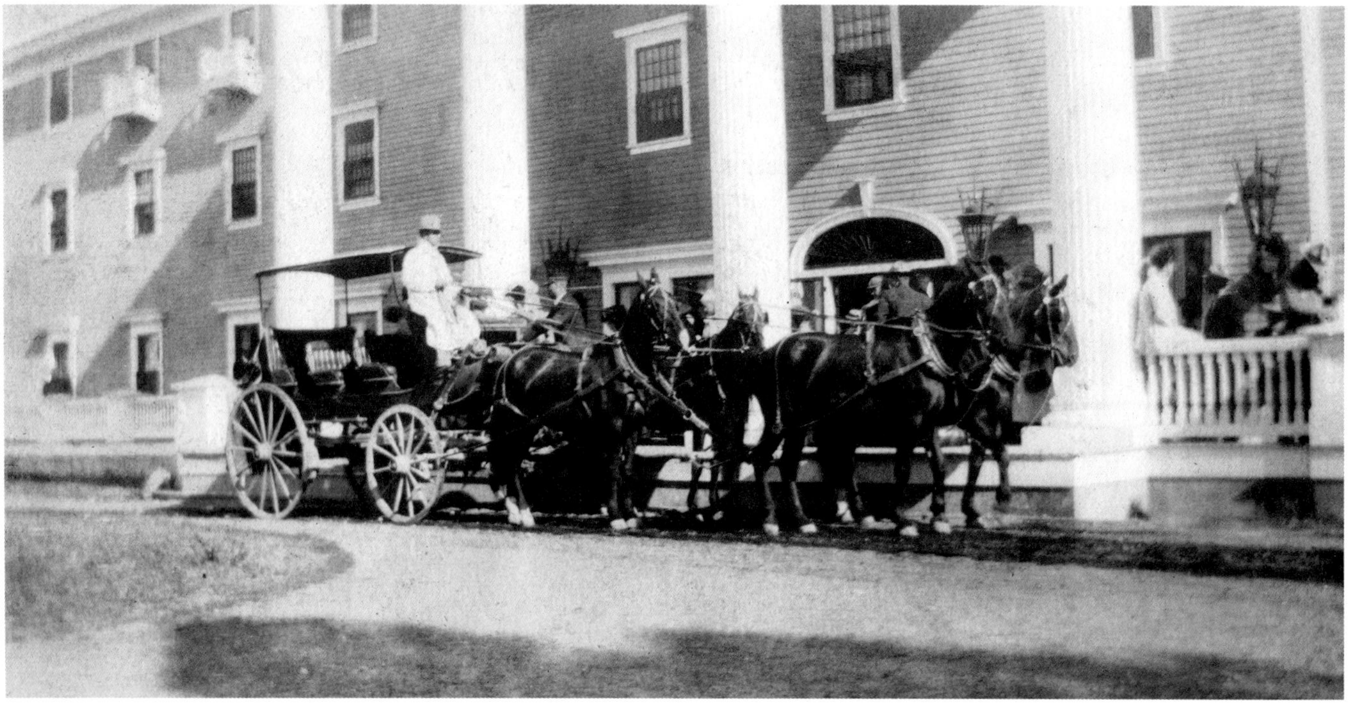

This photo, most likely taken prior to 1916, shows a four-horse open coach pulled up to the entrance of Lake Hotel. The driver wears a duster to mitigate the dust from the primitive road system. The guests on the veranda might have just disembarked, or are preparing to leave, as they are dressed for travel. After the hotel's renovations in 1903-1904, staying at this welcoming and elegant hotel was a highlight for many park guests, including President Calvin Coolidge in 1927.

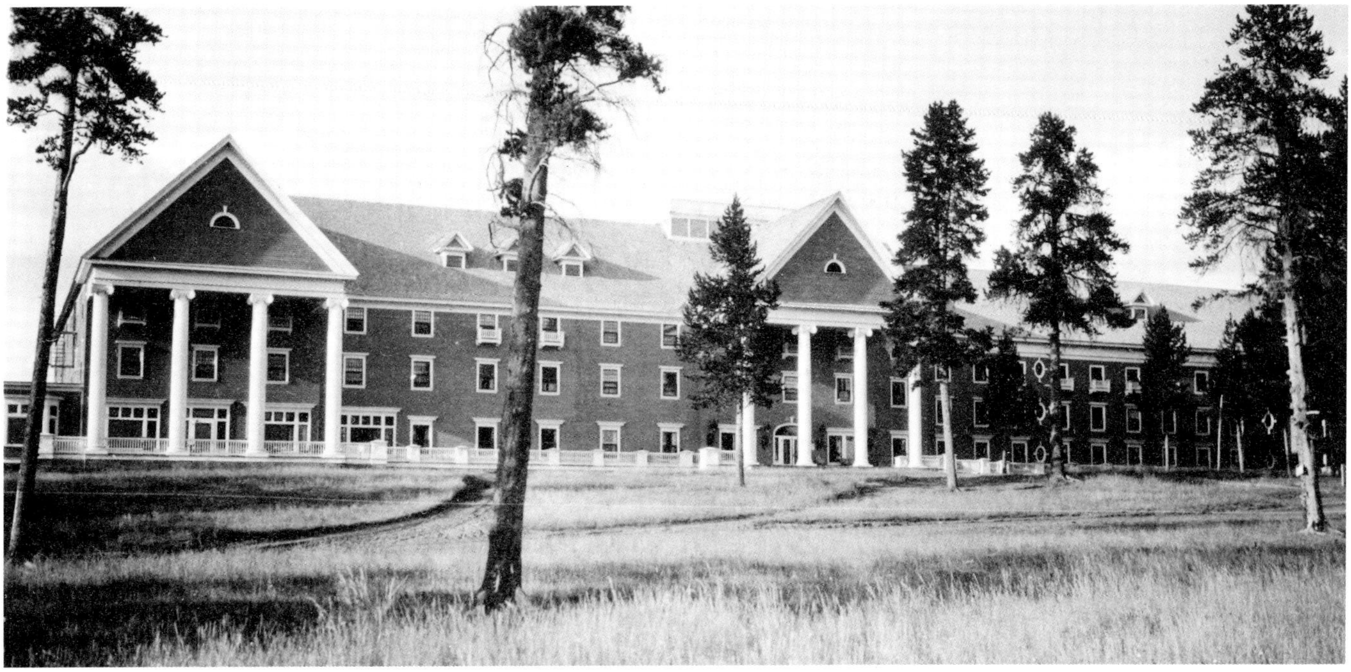

This is the view that welcomed guests as they approached Lake Hotel in August 1916. In 1903-1904, architect Robert Reamer completely revamped the simple structure of the hotel, creating a neoclassical appearance that earned the hotel the moniker "The Colonial" due to its distinguished new appearance. A dozen 50-foot-tall columns supported porticos on either end of the hotel, as well as in the center. A half-dozen dormers, three on each side of the central portico, mimicked the rooflines. Large windows, and the locally sourced, pine clapboard siding painted soft yellow with white trim, created an elegant atmosphere. In this photo, notice the widow's walk on the roof, which was part of the original design. Guests sometimes ventured to this observation deck to enjoy exceptional views; the feature was removed around 1919.

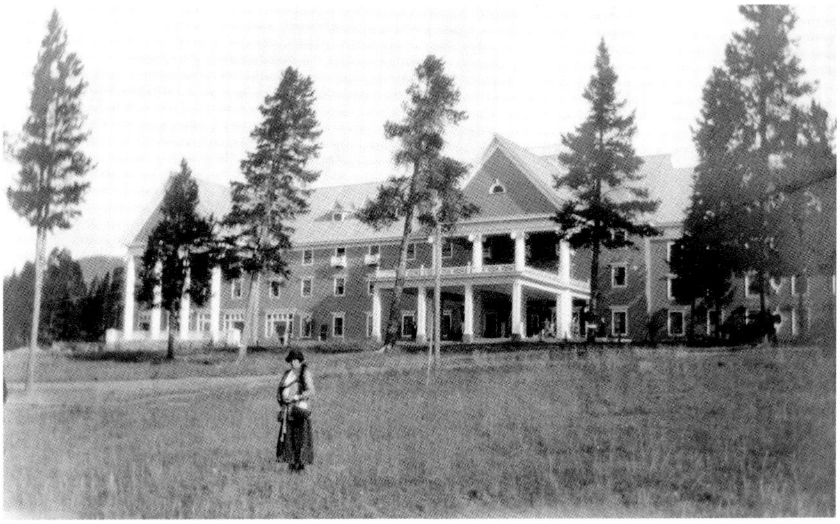

This park visitor stands in the spacious front meadow of the Lake Hotel, often called "The Colonial" during the time of this circa-1915 photo. The woman's long skirt ends just above the ankles and is indicative of what was called a "fuller skirt." It also appears that she is carrying a purse or basket on her left arm. The porte-cochere, the large, covered area in the center of the hotel, allowed guests to step out of their automobiles in protected comfort. It was added in 1918-1919 when the hotel was closed during World War I.

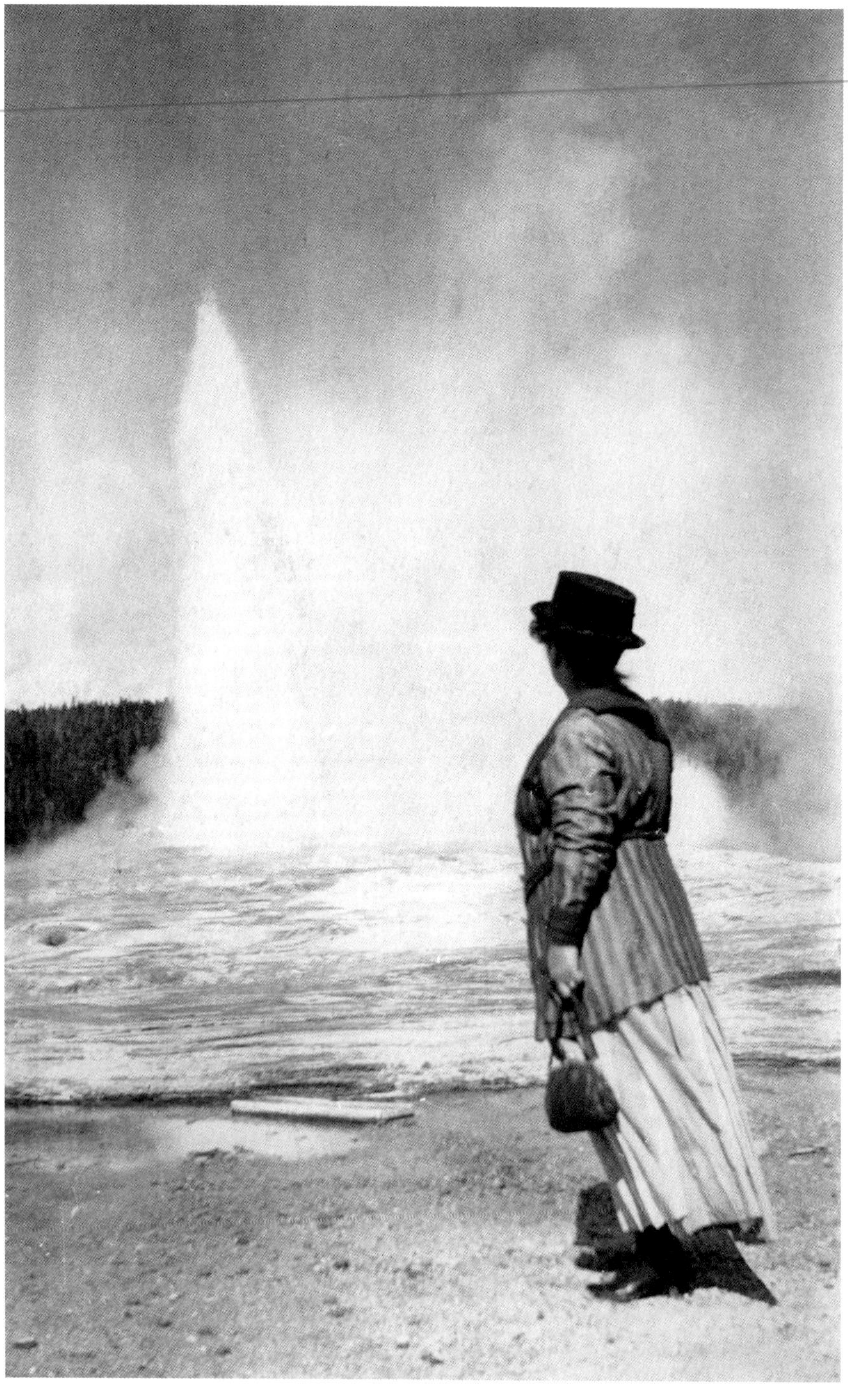

Named during the 1870 Washburn Expedition, Old Faithful delighted these explorers with its predictable nature and impressive display. Here a woman holding a handbag and wearing a fashionable dark-hued hat watches Old Faithful, either when it was building up to an eruption or quieting after one, circa-1910.

CHAPTER 2

The Wonders of Wonderland

Regaled by stories of abundant wildlife, geysers, and petrified forests, initial descriptions of Yellowstone came off as wildly exaggerated tales. The reality was far more splendid. After the Washburn-Langford-Doane Expedition of 1870 and the Hayden Expedition the following year, solid evidence—including the scenery recorded by the brilliant artwork of Thomas Moran—inspired the public to visit this treasure the nation wisely chose to preserve.

This "Wonderland," as it was called, did not disappoint. Geysers erupted high over visitor's heads while mud pots bubbled at their feet, offering experiences never seen before by most people. During these first decades, most tourists traveled with guides who shared what they knew--or made up stories when they didn't—about the wondrous beauty and astounding thermal features.

It was a challenge for early park officials to protect the thermal features, as well as the welfare of the visitors. For example, there were very few boardwalks to keep people from falling through the sometimes-shallow crust of thermal areas. Some of the early photographs show visitors stepping to the very edge of geysers or hot springs, or sitting upon thermal features, without regard for their own safety or the fragility of what brought them to Yellowstone in the first place. Of course, this type of intimate experience with Old Faithful Geyser, or any of the others, is no longer permitted because the consequences are understood.

Yellowstone is like no other place on earth. Its otherworldly allure attracted visitors seeking to have adventures and take stories home, and it did not disappoint. They saw many of the park's features up close, which makes it interesting to view these images from their unique perspective.

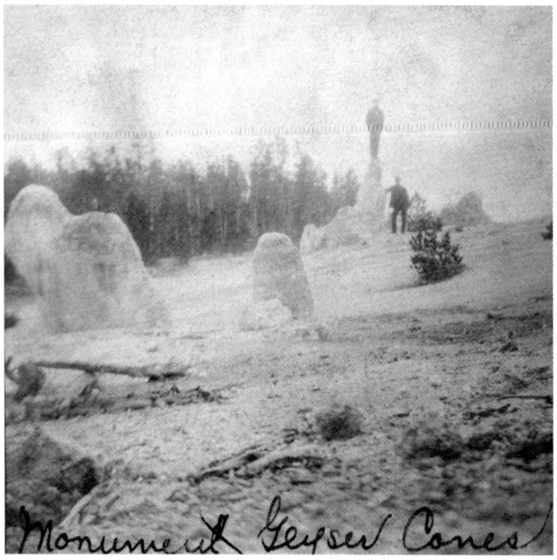

This circa-1900 image shows visitors posing among the ghostly thermal features of Monument Geyser Basin. One of the men is standing on a siliceous sinter cone, an act which is illegal today because of the potential for damage to the structure. These mostly dormant geysers, along with a few steaming vents and the larger Monument Geyser, are unlike any others in the park because they may have originated under water. Found high above Gibbon Meadows, these thermal features lie at the end of a steep but short trail that gains more than 600 feet.

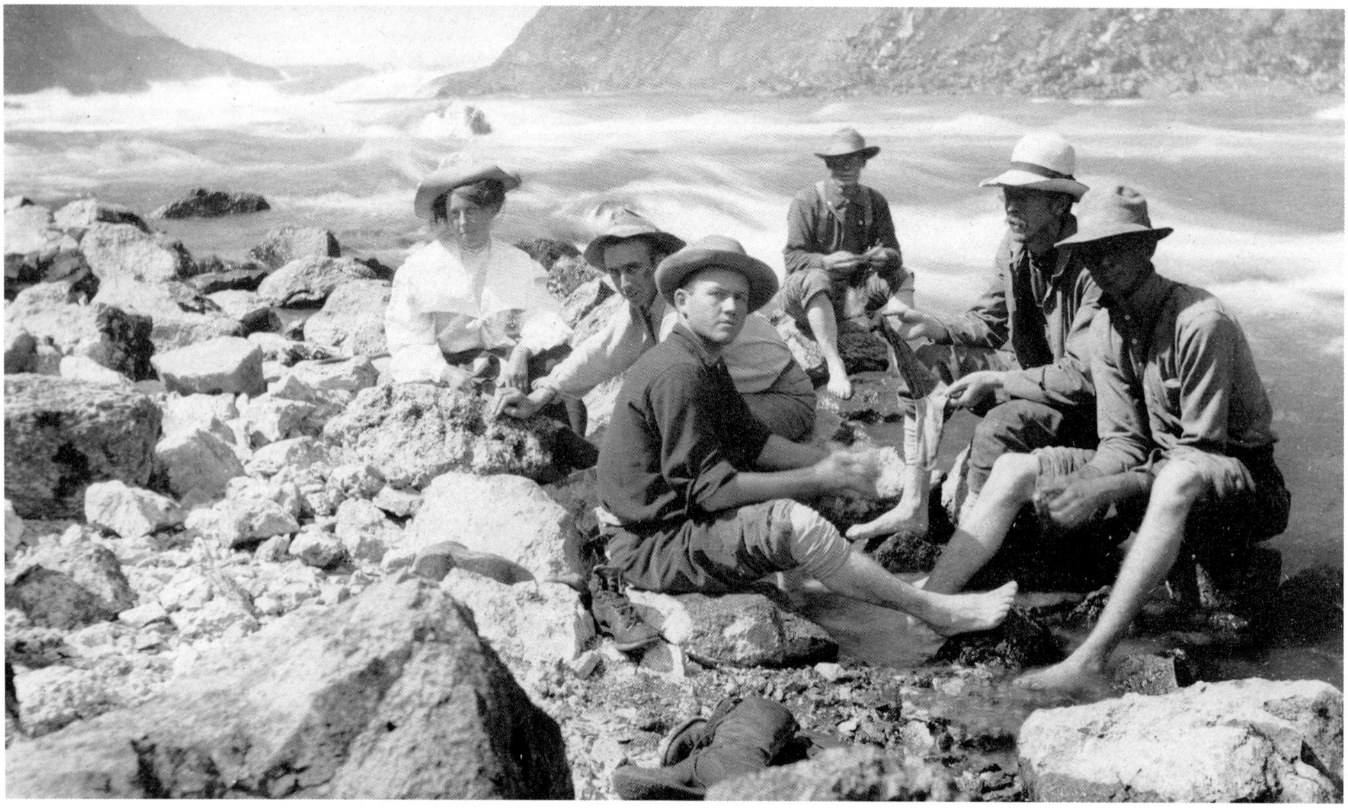

A group of park visitors rests after an arduous descent to the bottom of the Grand Canyon of the Yellowstone, just below the Lower Falls, in this circa-1910 photo. To reach this spot they carefully made their way 300 feet down the rugged, steep, and rickety Uncle Tom's Trail. A few minutes cooling their bare feet in the water were well-deserved, even if the display breached societal norms of mixed company of the day.

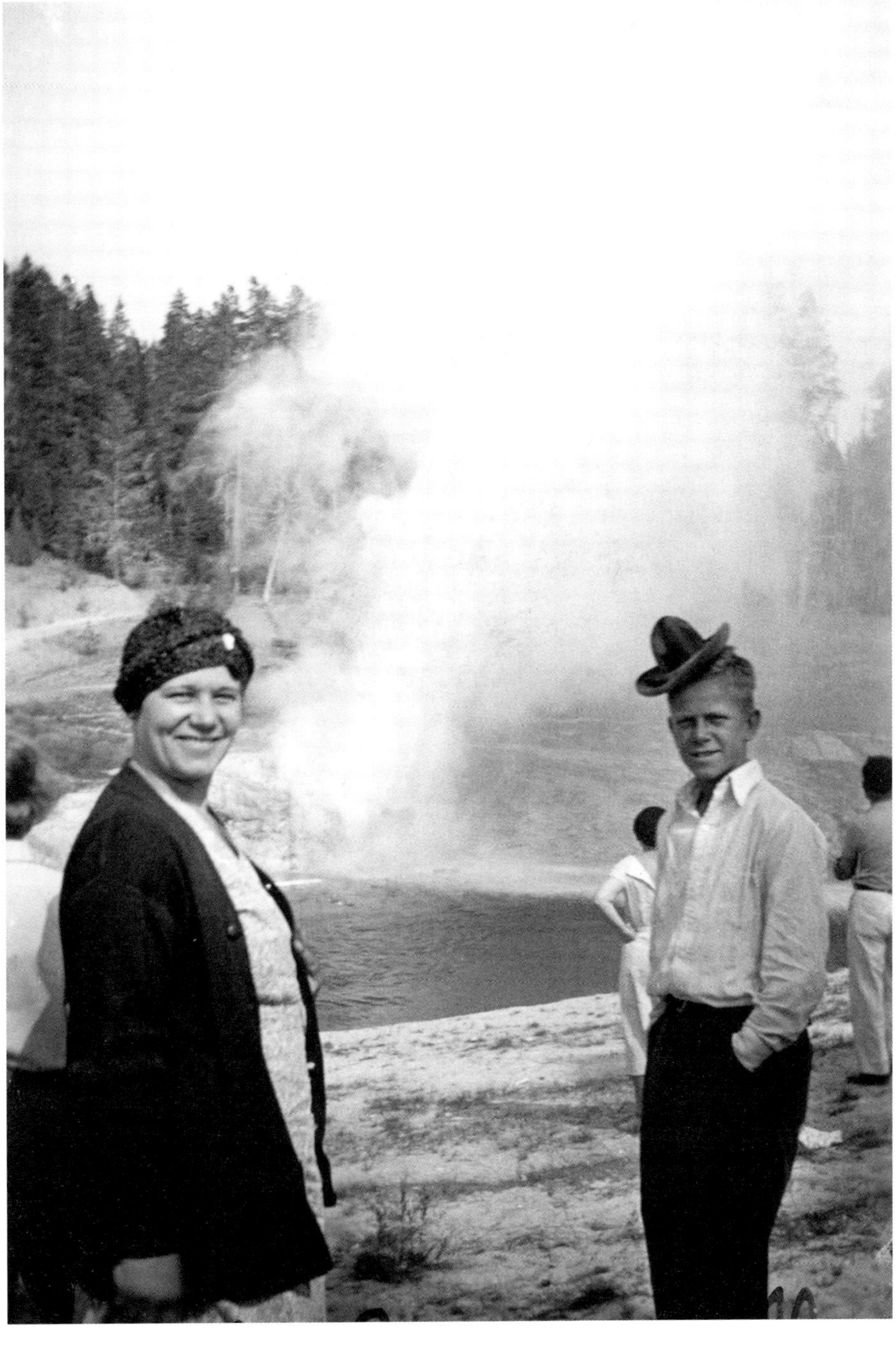

Visitors, including a young man wearing a miniature cowboy hat, watch Riverside Geyser erupting on the Firehole River in August 1934. The geyser's column of water often arched over the river, creating a rainbow in its spray. It continues to be a crowd favorite.

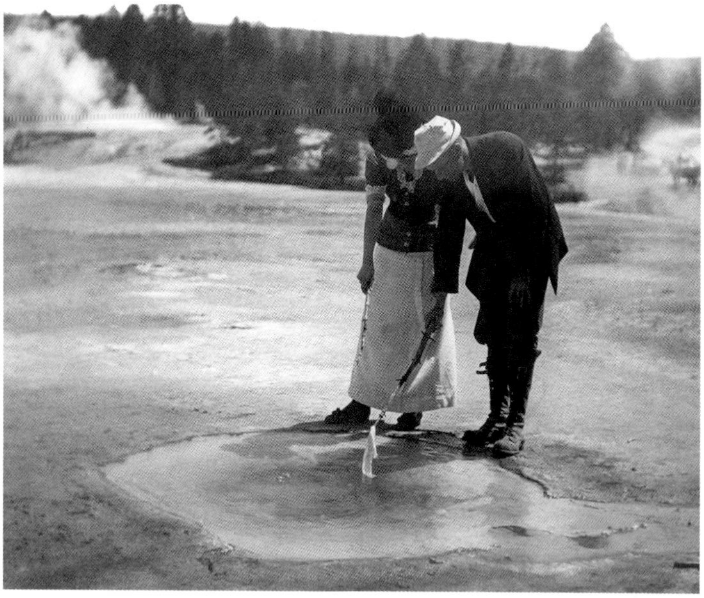

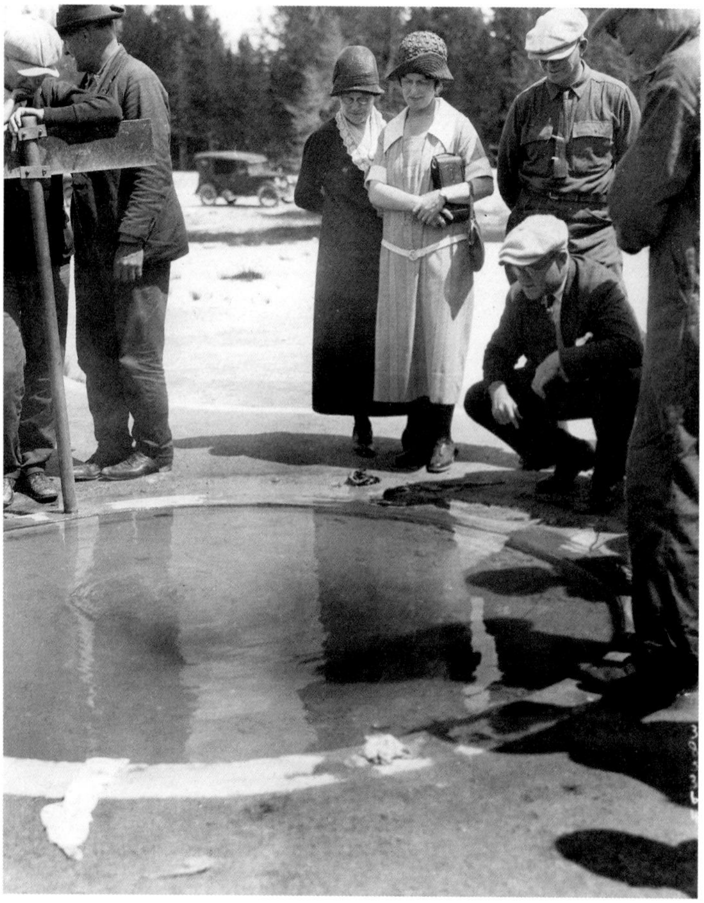

In its heyday, Handkerchief Pool, a thermal spring in Black Sand Basin west of Old Faithful village, was as popular as Old Faithful Geyser because of its interactive display. When visitors placed a handkerchief or small piece of cloth in the pool, they watched it float for a moment before it was sucked into the water, disappearing into the depth of the spring. Usually within a few minutes, the cloth miraculously reappeared, completely clean. The earlier photo (top), shows a couple with a handkerchief or cloth at the spring. A horse is visible in the far-right background, so there is a good chance the visitors are part of a day tour on horseback. The photo was most likely taken prior to 1918, before there was a concrete ring and solid walking path leading to Handkerchief Pool. In the photo, taken by C. E. Griesman, the woman wears a walking skirt, a practical garment common in the early 1900s. The group of visitors with the automobile in the background (bottom) surely did not realize they were some of the last to enjoy the handkerchief trick when this photo was taken on July 11, 1925. The iconic thermal spring ceased to function in 1926 after a visitor shoved a log into the vent. When the thermal feature was cleaned three years later, pieces of cloth, coins, hairpins, and a horseshoe, among other debris, were removed, yet the plumbing system was never the same. Note the concrete ring around the pool and the metal signpost; both were later removed.

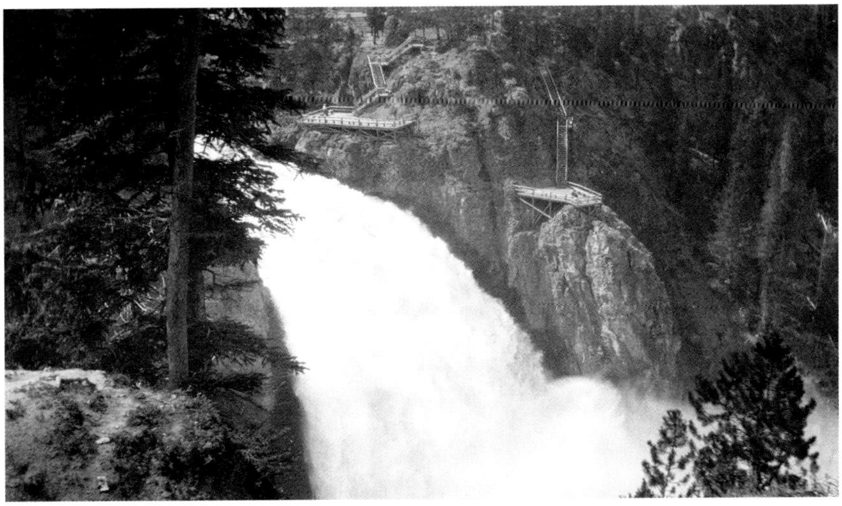

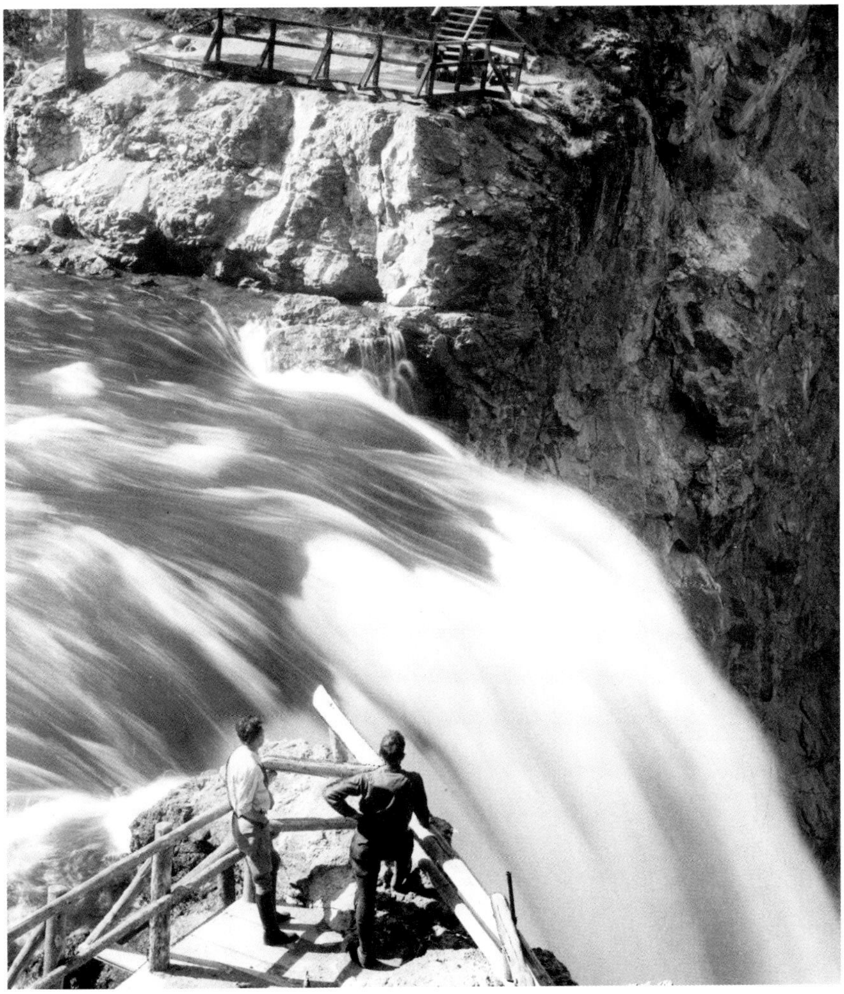

The splendor of the Grand Canyon of the Yellowstone was one of the features painted by artist Thomas Moran, who helped convince the U.S. Congress to protect this natural wonder—and many other features in this region that is larger than Delaware and Rhode Island—as our first national park. Since the earliest days of the park, the Upper and Lower Falls of the Yellowstone River drew visitors who wished to be as close as possible to their magnificence. In this circa-1920s photo (top), two of the viewing platforms on the north side of the Upper Falls are visible. The wooden decks placed guests on the brink of the falls, allowing them to experience the power of the water. These decks were originally created around 1906 to give visitors exceptional views and provide seating so people could rest before climbing the stairs back to the canyon rim. This area is now located along the North Rim Trail. The lower viewing platform was damaged after 1934 and permanently removed. The second photo (bottom) shows two men standing on the Sunset Point platform, mostly likely in the 1930s, looking at the Lower Falls. While this viewing area was eliminated around the time of World War II, the platform visible on the other side of the river was located where the current viewing deck is today.

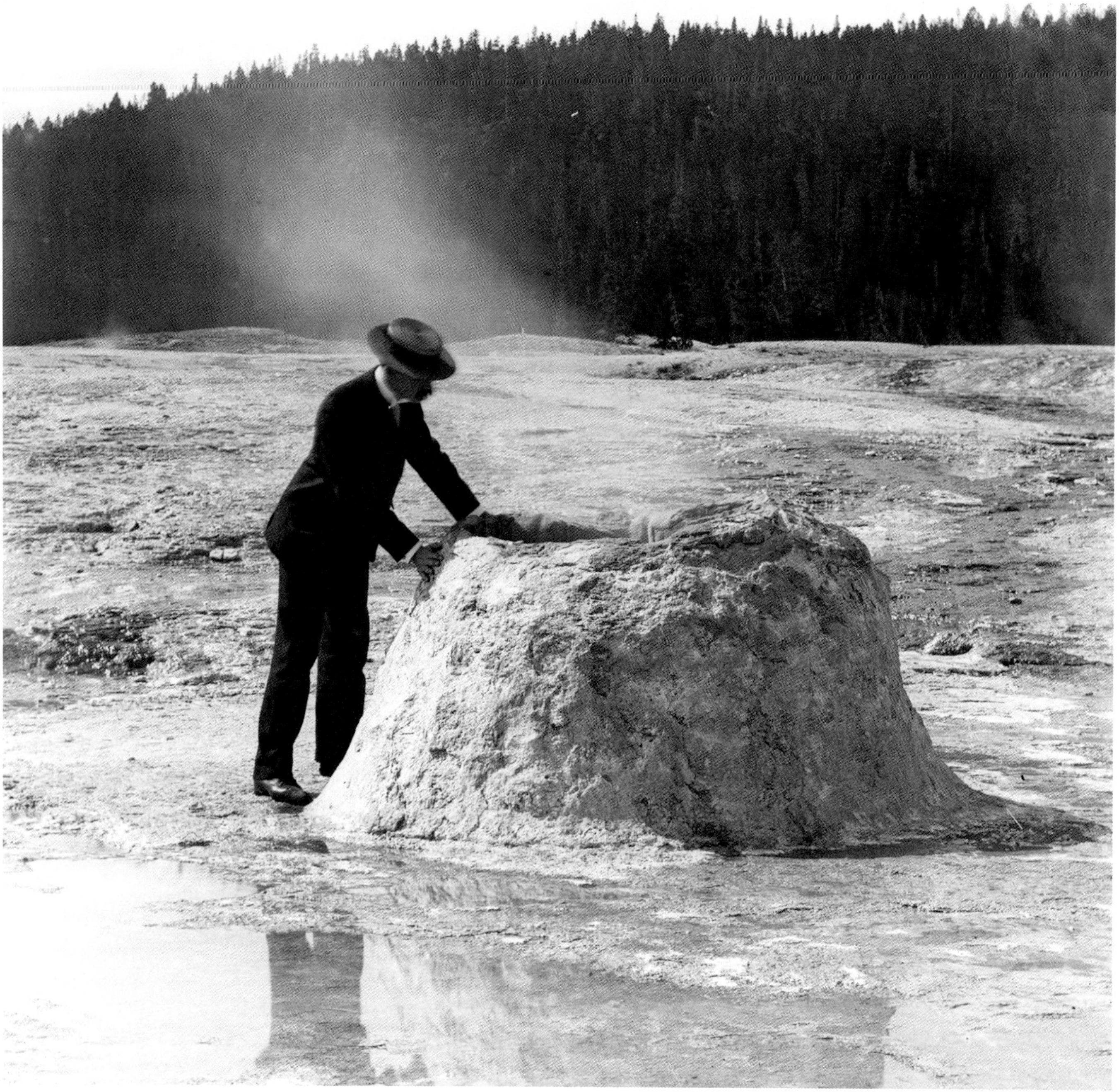

A well-dressed gentleman sporting a straw boater hat peers into the vent of Beehive Geyser, near Old Faithful Geyser on Geyser Hill, in this circa-1910 photo. This stubby cone has always been a favorite of tourists because it erupts so high, spewing water 150 to 200 feet in the air. These days a boardwalk brings visitors close to the geyser but not where this gentleman walked; to prevent damage to the thermal feature and to keep people safe, visitors must stay on the boardwalk.

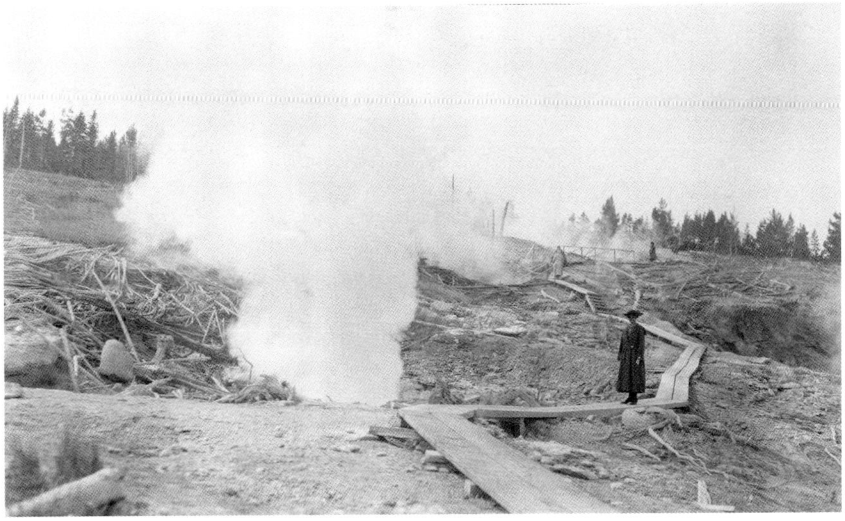

This photo, likely taken between 1910 and 1916, shows a woman visiting Ledge Geyser in Norris Geyser Basin. She walks on a rudimentary boardwalk made of planks. Building walkways within thermal areas has always been challenging due to the evolving nature of the thermal features and the soil. Because of this, paths often had to be rerouted as new thermal features formed or existing features changed their activity. Ledge Geyser, the second largest geyser in the Norris Geyser Basin (Steamboat Geyser is the largest), erupts at an angle, spraying water and steam 220 feet from the crater, and has long been a favorite.

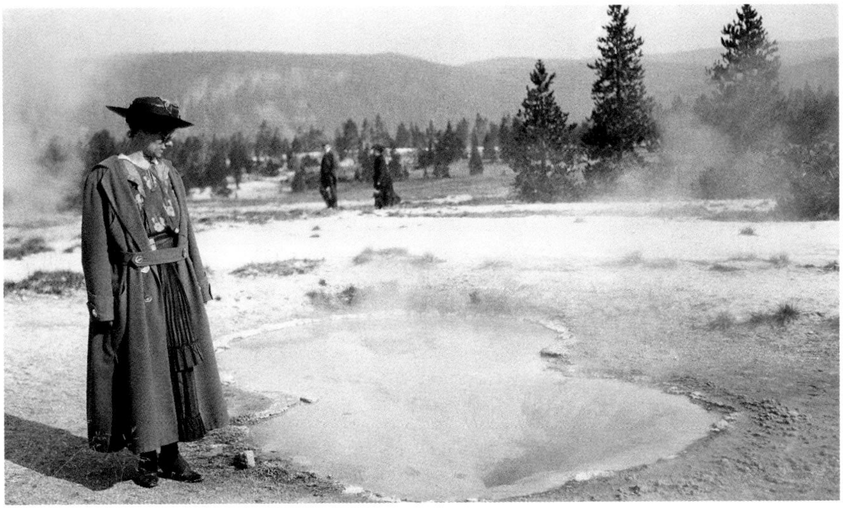

In this photo, a woman gazes into the pale blue and orange colorations of Belgian Pool in the Upper Geyser Basin. Because she is wearing a skirt with higher hemlines, and no corset, this photo was most likely taken around 1915, when fashion throughout the world was impacted by World War I and shifted towards more practical designs. There was no recorded name for the thermal spring when this photo was taken; it was later called Belgian Pool because of the death of a Belgian journalist. On July 3, 1929, the journalist was running to witness an eruption of Castle Geyser when he accidentally fell into this spring. More than half of his body was burned; he died two days later at Mammoth Hot Springs.

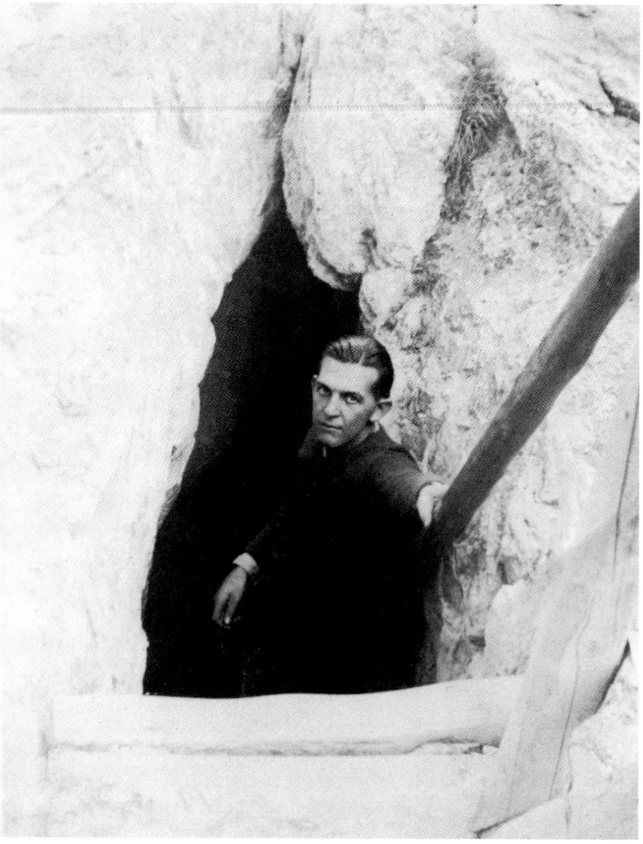

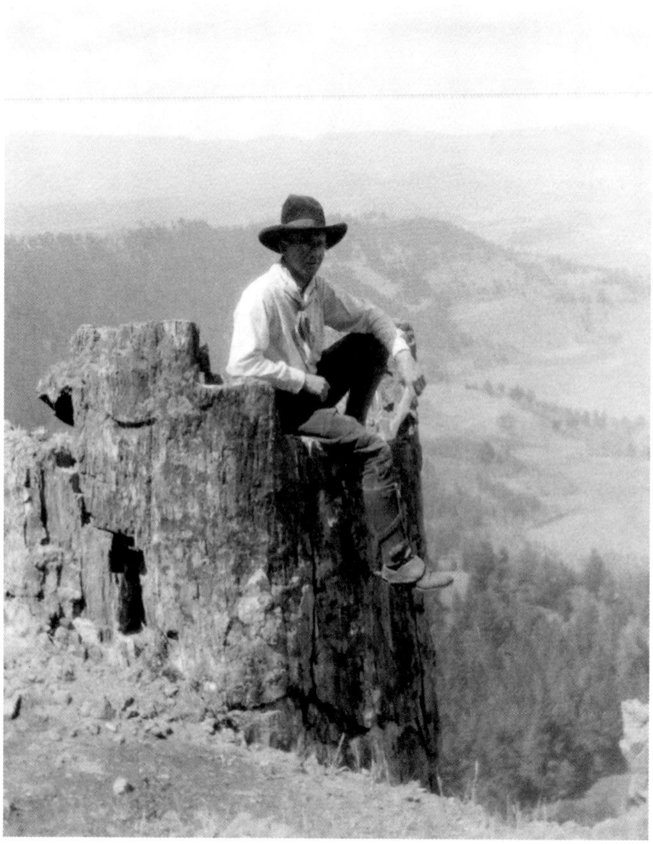

In 1884, George L. Henderson, the original builder and owner of the Cottage Hotel and a longtime park interpretative guide, installed a ladder through this narrow opening to allow visitors on his walking tours to descend into the otherworldly realm of Devil's Kitchen, the cave of an extinct hot spring situated east of Bath Lake at Mammoth Hot Springs. Beginning in the early 1870s, this area beckoned explorers to experience what an underworld might feel like. Visitors descending into the warm, sulfurous, dark cavern reportedly experienced a "queer sensation," most likely caused by breathing poisonous gases accumulating within the confined space. Animal bones sometimes littered the cavern floor, either from animals that succumbed to the poisonous gases or were unable to escape the cavern. This photo taken in September 1931 shows a gentleman descending into the crevice. The ladder was removed in 1939, and visitors were prohibited from exploring the feature due to valid safety concerns.

In this circa-1920s photo, a cowboy sits on a petrified tree on Specimen Ridge. Many visitors rode horses during day rides, so it is difficult to know if this person was a wrangler or a guest. Petrified trees formed when ancient trees were buried quickly in silica-rich sediments from volcanic events; silica and other minerals dissolved in the groundwater seeped into the plant material and replaced some of it, forming a hard fossil. Scientists believe the fossilized remnants on Specimen Ridge date back 50 million years to a period when sequoias and various species of deciduous trees grew in the area. While geologists initially thought this area was a fossilized forest, more recent research indicates the trees might have been uprooted and thrust downhill in a mud flow after a major volcanic event. Today, visitors can still hike to Specimen Ridge—and see this tree—although the trek is along an unmaintained trail.

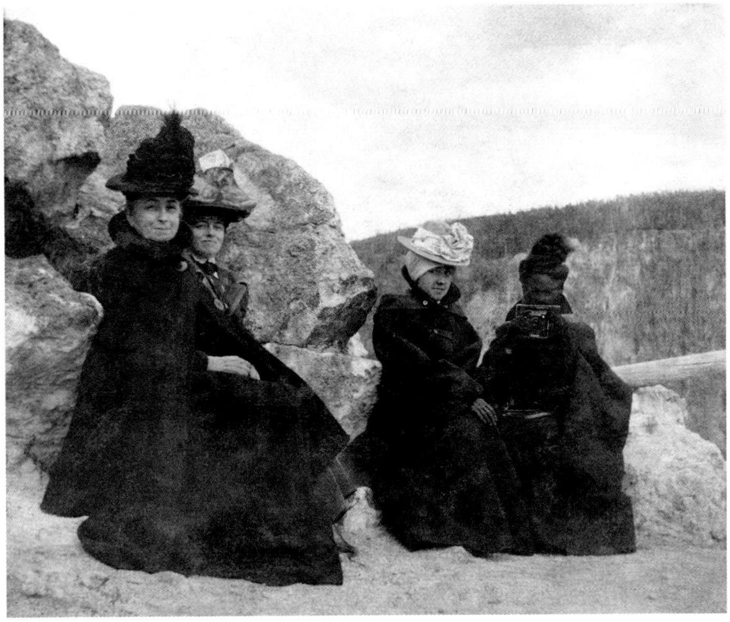

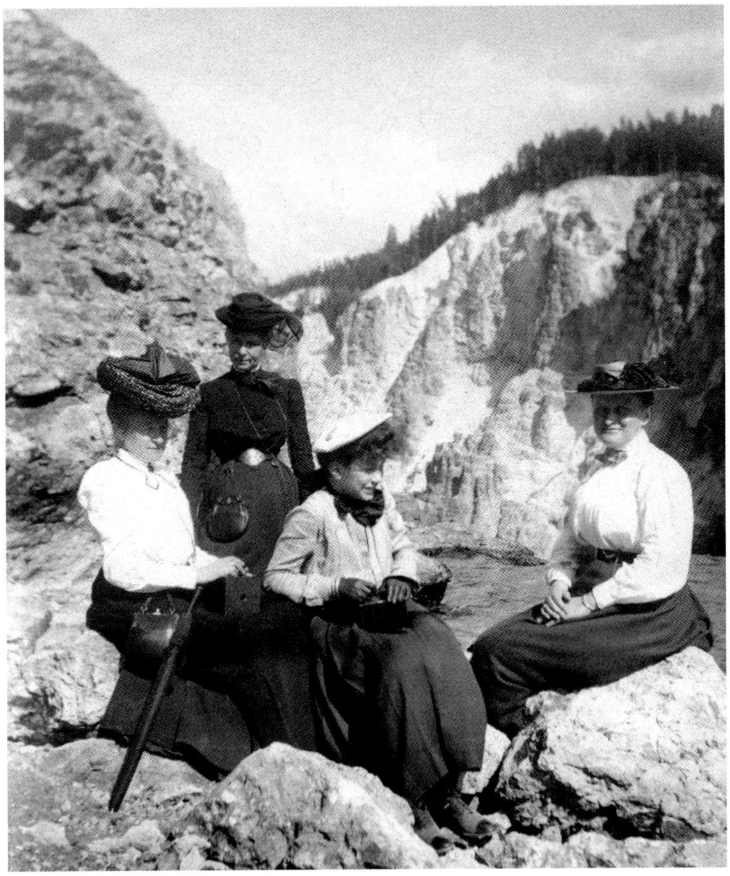

These images depict groups of ladies visiting the Grand Canyon of the Yellowstone roughly a decade apart. The older photo (top), likely taken in the 1890s, shows four heavily cloaked and gloved women seated near large rocks. The woman on the right is wearing a black veil, possibly a mourning veil following traditional Victorian propriety. Netting was also used as a defense against mosquitoes, making the intended purpose of this accessory unclear. She is holding an open, folding camera, which first reached the market in 1888. The second photo (bottom) shows four ladies posing on rocks just above the Lower Falls in 1903. The two women on the left have leather, Victorian Chatelaine bags attached to the waistbands of their skirt and dress, and the first woman has an umbrella leaning against her lap. Two of the ladies rest box cameras on their laps, probably to capture a photo of this exquisite area. Still popular in the early 1900s, the often leather-covered and simple box cameras were inexpensive and easy to use, making photography more accessible to everyone.

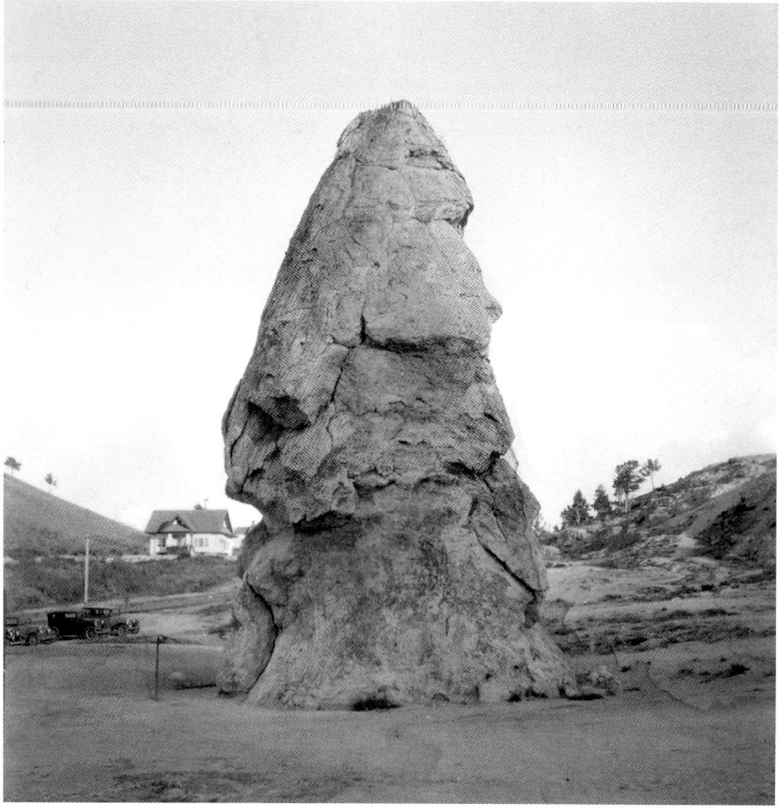

The distinctive Liberty Cap has long been a popular attraction in Mammoth, as evidenced by the row of automobiles parked at the far left. The vehicles indicate that this photo was taken in or after 1915, the first year autos were allowed in the park. Formed of travertine, the 37-feet-tall Liberty Cap started as a hot spring that bubbled water through an opening in its top, depositing the minerals as it grew. It gained the moniker "Liberty Cap" after noted mineralogist Albert C. Peale mentioned in his diary that Dr. Ferdinand Hayden of the 1871 Hayden Expedition said the formation reminded him of "the peasant caps worn during the French Revolution." Visible in the background, the frame-construction Commandant's House of Fort Yellowstone, built around 1904 or 1905, was used by the U.S. Army's acting-superintendents of the park until a stone building was constructed in 1909 near today's Albright Visitor Center. The Commandant's House remained until at least 1963.

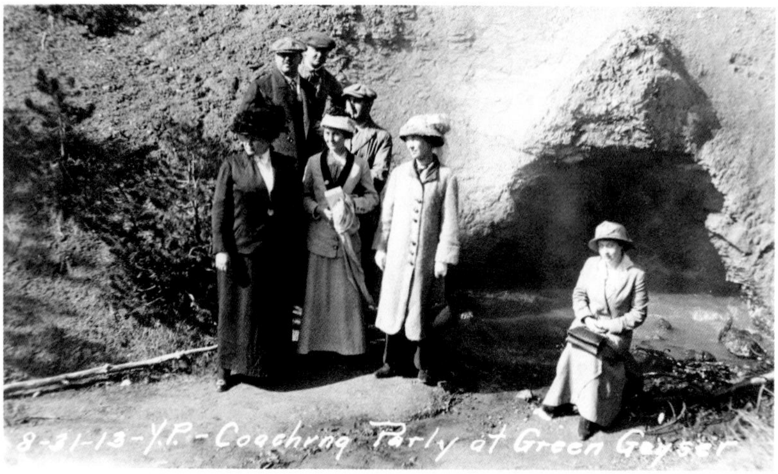

This well-dressed "coaching party," a group of guests traveling together via stagecoach, poses for a photo on August 31, 1913, at what is now called Dragon's Mouth Spring in the Mud Volcano area. The handwritten note on the photo calls it "Green Geyser," one of at least 17 names given to this growling hot spring. Records indicate that the Dragon's Mouth name, as it is known today and is fitting due to its rumblings and frequent spewing of hot water from the cavern, was mentioned the prior year. Currently, the boardwalk and platform bring visitors close to the spring, but not directly to its mouth as in this image.

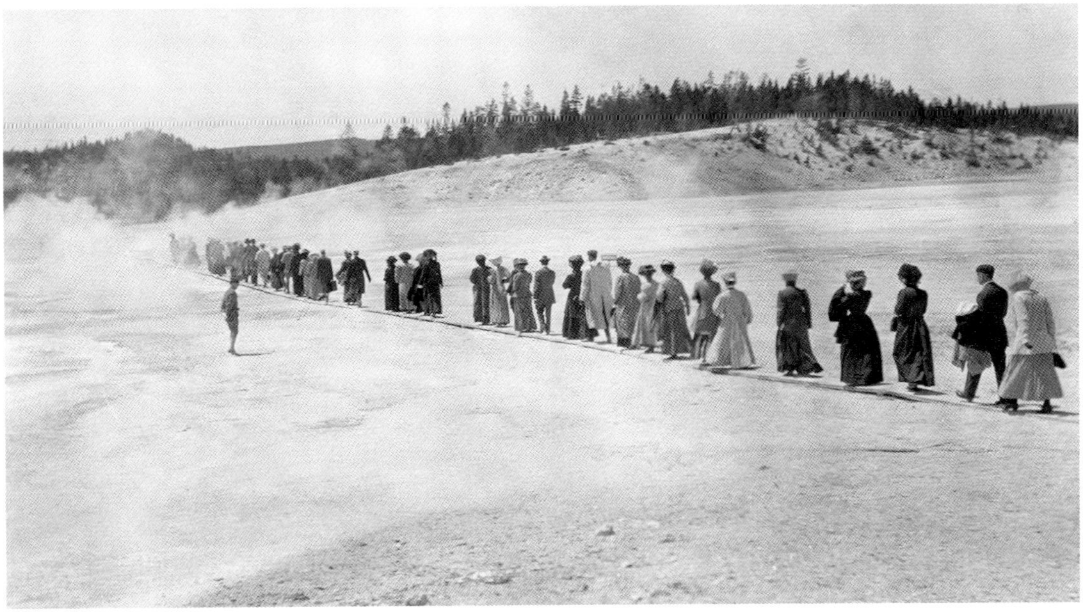

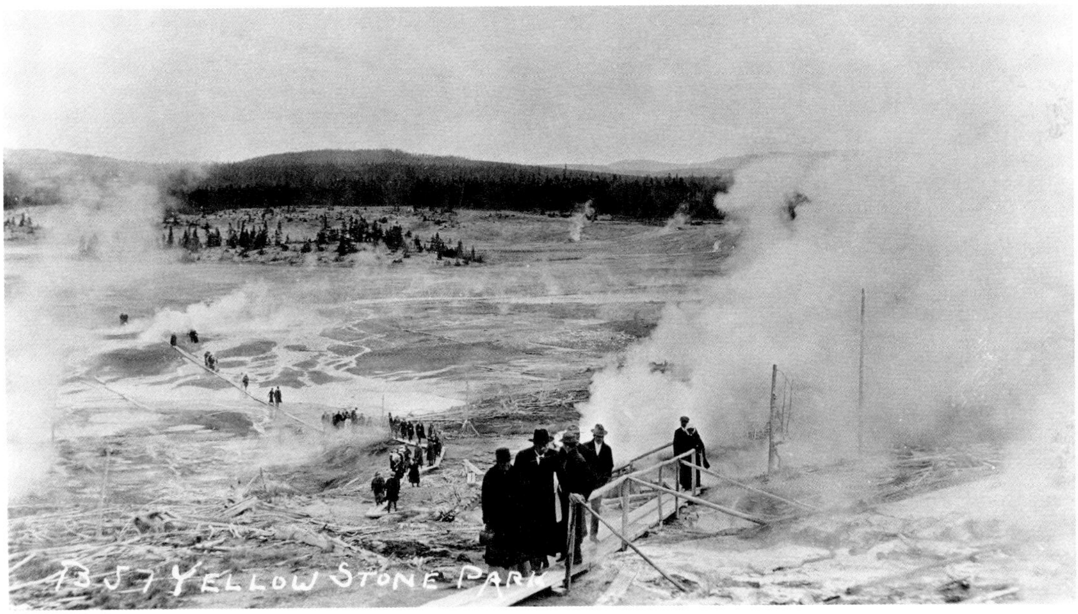

Visitors were naturally drawn to Norris Geyser Basin, the hottest thermally active region in the park, and they were commonly dropped off to explore the wide variety of geysers, spouters, and pools before being picked up again to continue their journey. The circa-1900 photo (top) shows a long line of visitors, mostly women, walking on a narrow boardwalk while a U.S. Army soldier stands off to the side. The narrow planks continued to suffice as a boardwalk into the 1920s, as indicated in the bottom photo, an expansive view of the basin and its early walkways.

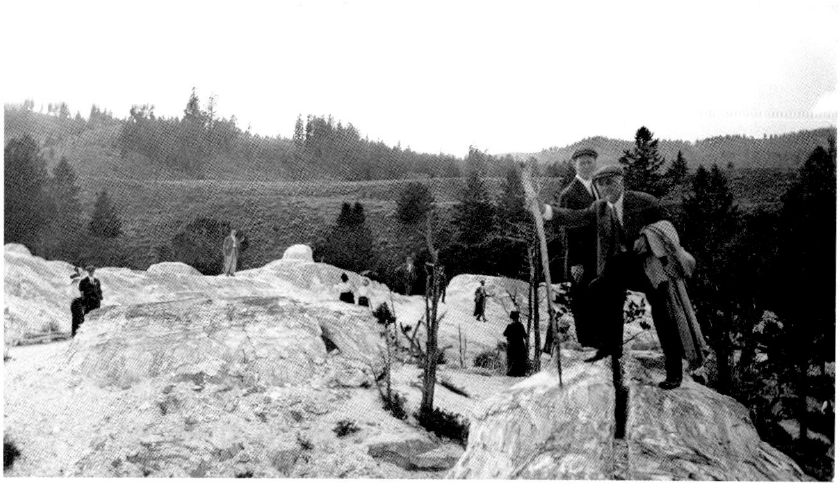

This photo shows visitors circa-1912 exploring the Glen Springs fissure ridge, a small, hidden thermal area north of Angel Terrace at Mammoth Hot Springs. The gentleman with the coat draped over his arm looks more likely to host a business meeting than to climb on top of a thermal feature, yet that clothing was the norm for male travelers at the turn of the century. Likewise, the women in the background wear floor length skirts or dresses that do not seem fitting to explore rugged terrain, yet they did so with style.

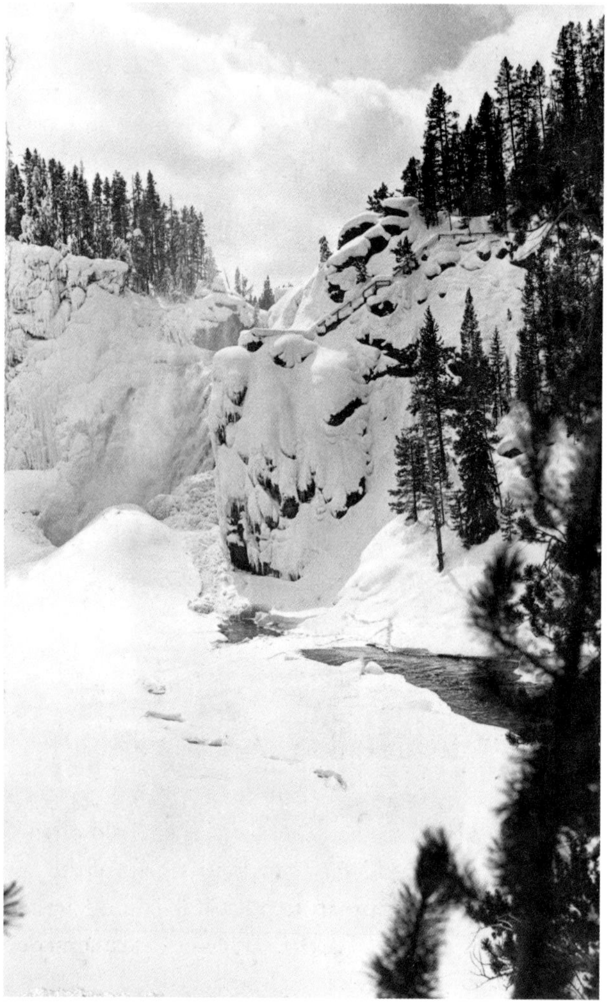

Equally dramatic in the winter, this photo shows the Upper Falls covered in snow, with the lower viewing platform visible to the right of the falls. This is a photo taken from park employee Lois Davis's Canyon Lodge album of 1934. It is interesting that the lower viewing platform appears in this photo, but it was eventually damaged, possibly by winter snows, and ultimately removed. While visitor accommodations at Canyon were not open during the winter, workers were still needed to clear heavy snow from the buildings' roofs. Otherwise, the buildings might collapse. ("Winter keepers" are still needed today for the same reason.)

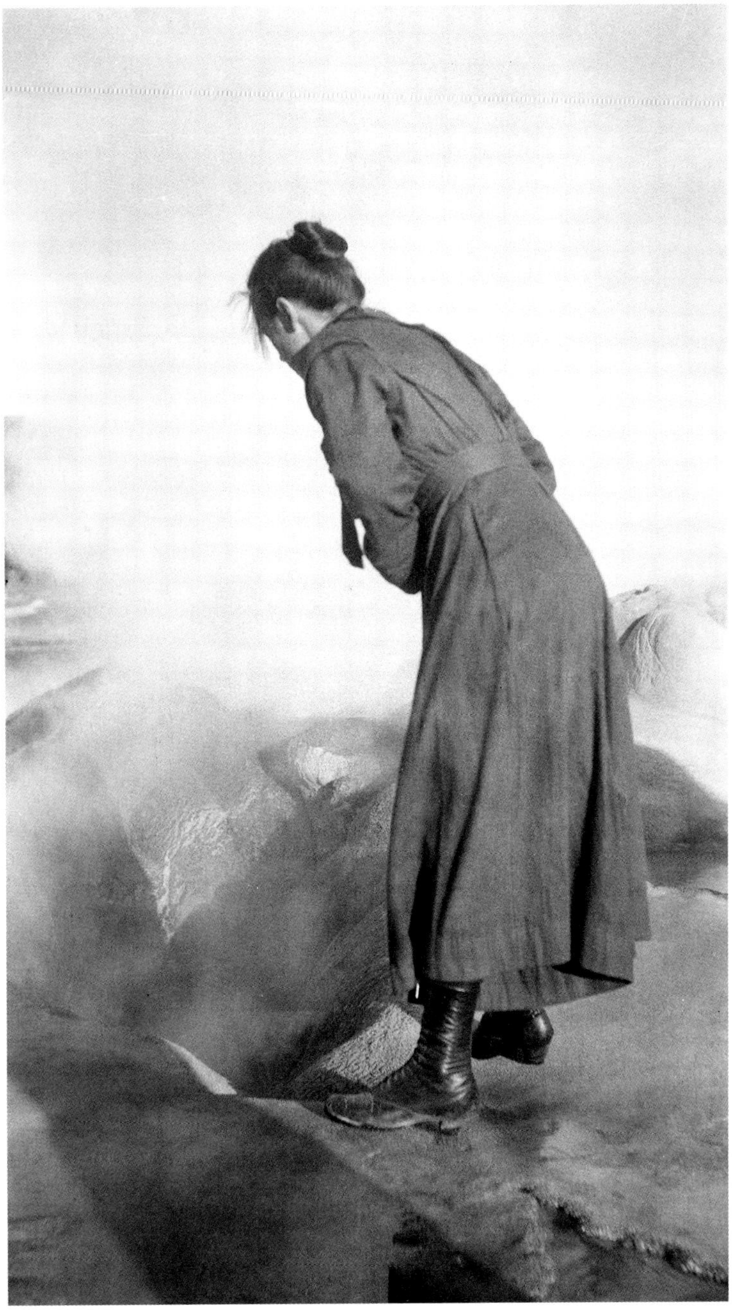

This circa-1910 image shows a woman standing on Old Faithful Geyser and peering into its crater. Visitors would often step close to the crater during an eruption to experience its full power, and the damage done by tourists was part of the reason the U.S. Army was sent to protect the park's resources from 1886 to 1918. The woman wears a simple, long dress, lace-up boots, and, notably, no hat. Since most women during this period wore hats, she possibly decided to have someone hold her hat, or she is holding it out of view of the camera, to avoid having it fall into the boiling water.

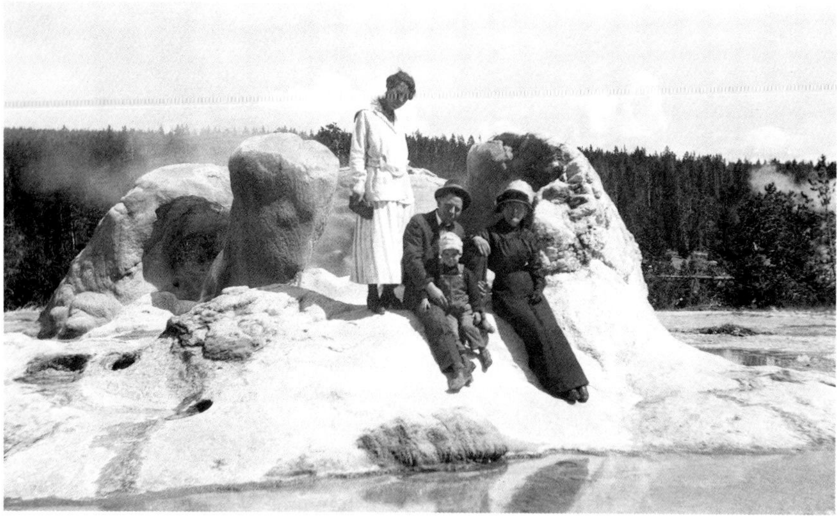

Probably taken around 1919, this family, which appears to be the mother, father, young son, and grandmother, poses on Grotto Geyser between eruptions that sometimes spouted water for more than ten hours. In the early days of the park, the road in the Upper Geyser Basin ran close to this popular attraction. The older woman wears full-length, all black clothing, possibly in mourning, while the younger woman wears more fashionable attire, including the slightly shorter skirt and a tuxedo sweater with a belt tie.

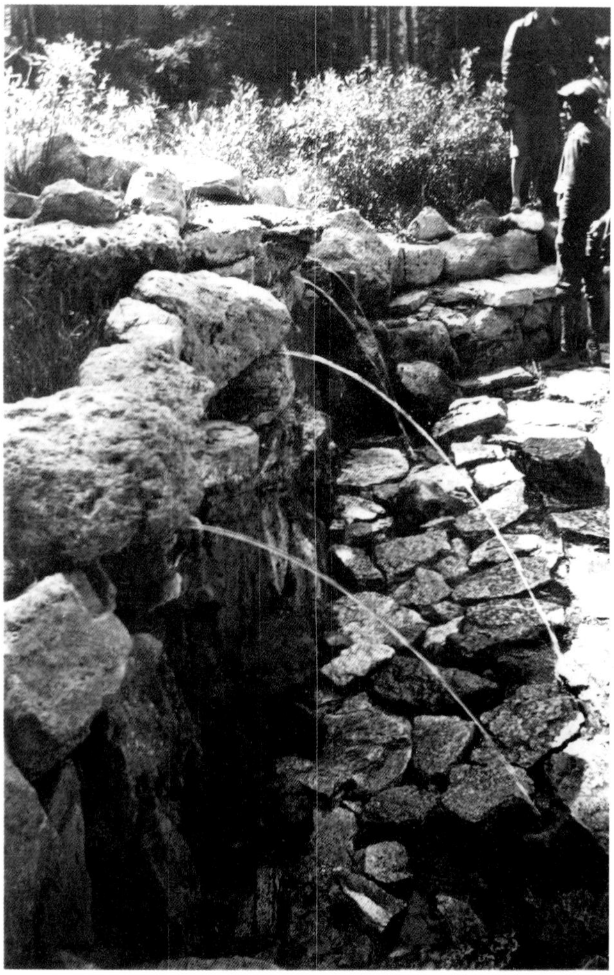

This is a July 1931 image of Apollinaris Spring with park visitors standing in the upper corner. As early as 1885, the springs were a popular stop between Mammoth Hot Springs and Norris Geyser Basin, where visitors enjoyed a drink of the naturally carbonated water. In 1925, the park made the area more visitor friendly, creating the travertine-flagstone platform and more accessible fountains, and it continued to be popular with visitors traveling via automobile. Because of potential contamination, it is no longer advisable to drink the springs' water.

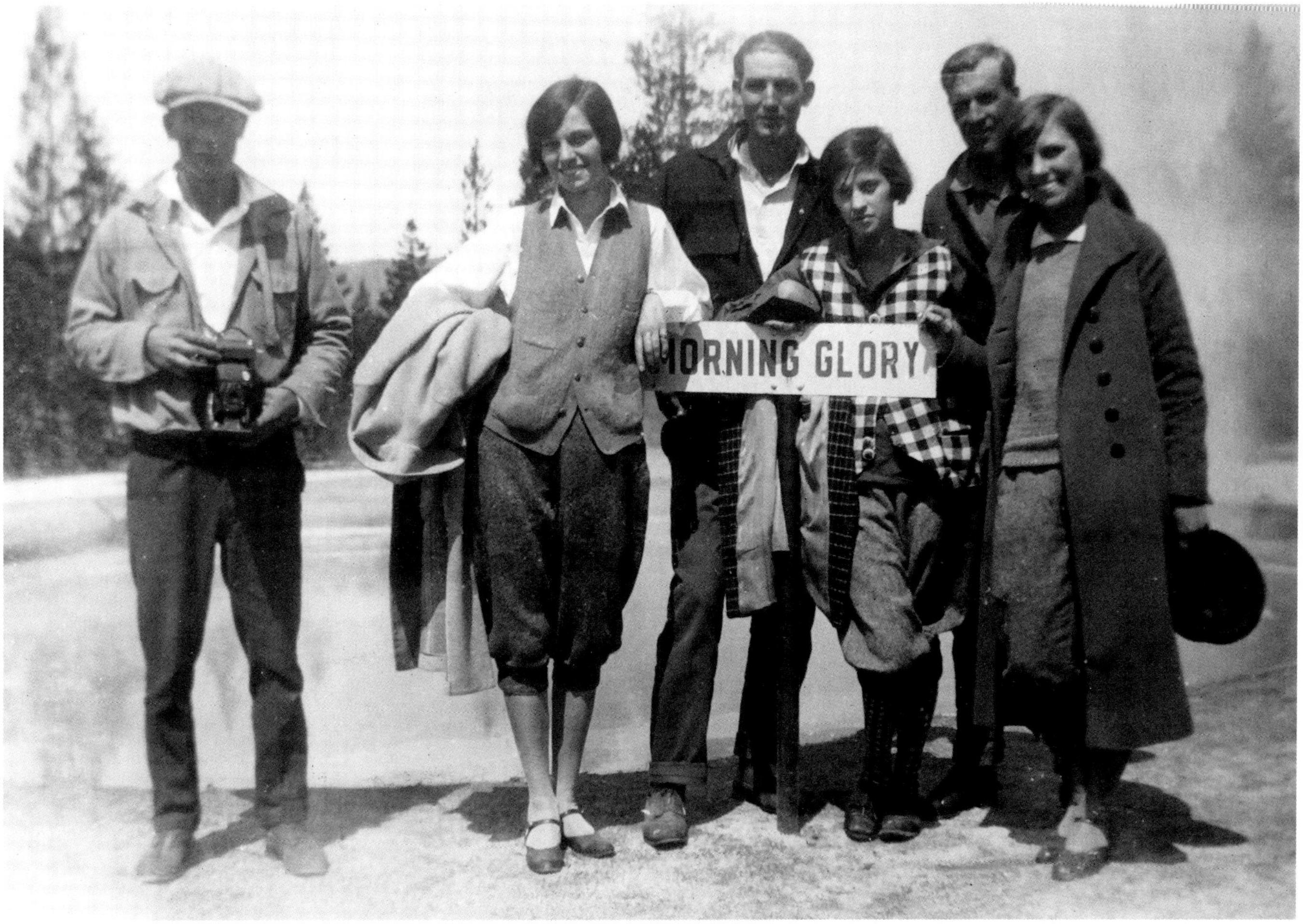

This fashionable group of park visitors circa-1925 poses at Morning Glory Pool in the Upper Geyser Basin. The "Roaring Twenties" ushered in a host of cultural changes across the country, including Yellowstone. All the women in this photograph appear to have "bobbed" hair, a new style, and they wear what appear to be wool knickers, which are cuffed just below the knees and often worn with knee-high socks or sometimes tall boots. This type of pants was far more functional than long skirts and dresses when it came to hiking and other forms of outdoor recreation. Vests for ladies were also popular, and it appears that each of these ladies was well-equipped for the fickle, Yellowstone weather with long coats, probably made of wool. Notice the gentleman on the left wearing a newsboy cap and holding a folding camera, possibly a Kodak Autographic Brownie. This rugged camera allowed the photographer to use a stylus to write comments on the back of the film, before it was processed. Later, when a print was developed, the comments appeared at the bottom of the print.

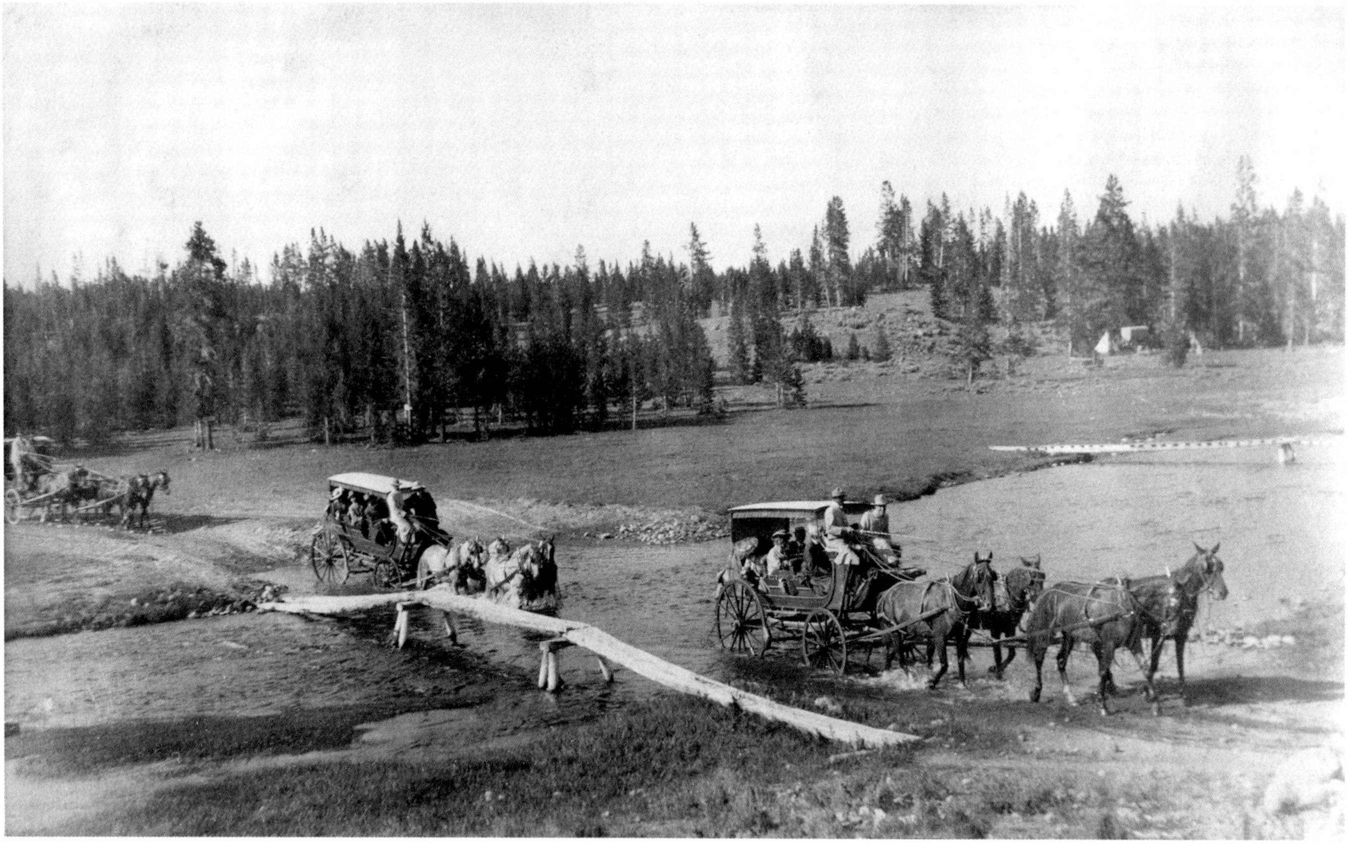

This 1904 photo shows three stagecoaches crossing and preparing to cross Nez Perce Creek in the northwestern region of Yellowstone. The creek was named to memorialize the flight of the Nez Perce Tribe in 1877. The four-horse stagecoaches, typically carrying 11 passengers, were the main mode of transportation for most pre-1916 guests. In this picture of the Oscar and Jeanette Law party, two plank bridges cross the creek for those traveling on foot, most likely on short excursions from the nearby Fountain Hotel or the U.S. Army's station at Lower Geyser Basin. It appears there is a small camp in the background, which might be a group of sagebrushers, tourists who traveled the park on their own and were not part of a guided tour.

CHAPTER 3

Getting Around Was Half the Fun

One of the greatest challenges for the newly created national park was to have a way for people to reach it, and then to explore its interior. Initially accessible only by horseback or a very rough wagon ride, it wasn't until 1878 that the first official roads in the park were created by Superintendent Philetus W. Norris. Roads were continually upgraded, and soon the "Grand Loop" became the standard touring route for park visitors.

Most early visitors rode stagecoaches to and through the park. Two- and four-horse stagecoaches dominated the dusty roads, shuttling visitors from one hotel to the next and taking them on daylong excursions of particular areas. To avoid stifling clouds of dust, stagecoaches had to travel far enough apart to allow the dust to settle before the next coach came. And sometimes, from 1887 to 1915, that separation was an invitation to "road agents." The worst day for hold-ups was July 29, 1914, when road agents stopped 25 stagecoaches near Shoshone Point east of Old Faithful. The thieves reportedly took approximately $1,000 dollars from 165 passengers, but they were apprehended and convicted because during one of the hold-ups a tourist took a photo that proved to be key evidence.

Some visitors skipped the long road around Yellowstone Lake by taking a steamboat between West Thumb and Lake Hotel. The trip cost a few dollars more, but passengers avoided the bumpy overland route and enjoyed the park from a different perspective.

Railroads were the lifeblood of early travel to the park. The Northern Pacific Railroad brought visitors within a stagecoach ride of the park's northern entrance, and later the Union Pacific Railroad disembarked passengers at the western entrance.

After the first automobile was permitted within Yellowstone in August 1915, the nature of park travel inevitably changed. Buses replaced stagecoaches in 1917, and soon private automobiles became the norm—if not always an easy way to travel. Roads were sometimes rough, dusty, and muddy, and automobile travelers had to know how to change a tire and fix mechanical problems.

Without question, traveling to and through the park was an adventure in and of itself.

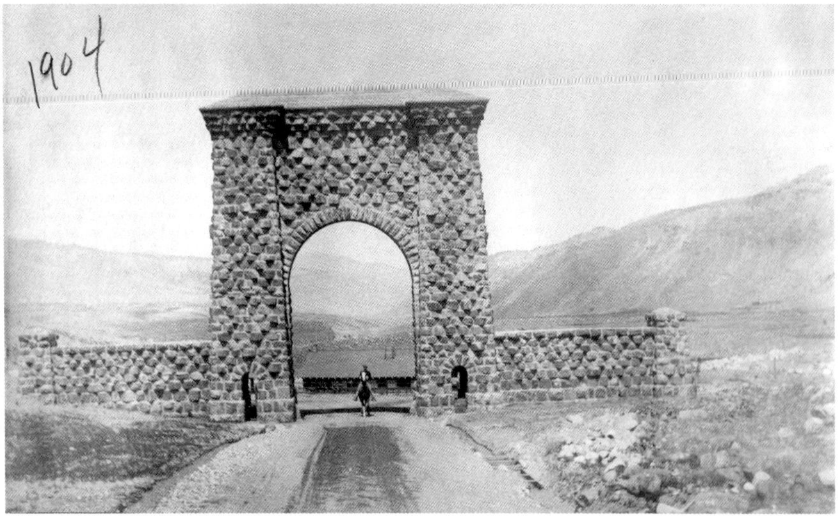

In 1904 a soldier on horseback posed for a photo beneath the Roosevelt Arch. Behind the soldier in the distance is the Northern Pacific Railroad Depot in Gardiner, Montana. Architect Robert Reamer designed the Depot, but the arch's creation story is more complicated. Because of the credibility of historian Aubrey Haines, Reamer has been partially credited, but from two local newspapers, historians also know that architect Nels J. Ness of Helena was involved. The arch was a vision of Captain Hiram Chittenden, who wanted to provide a dramatic entrance to the park. It was constructed from February 19 to August 15, 1903, and dedicated by President Theodore Roosevelt on April 24 when he vacationed in the park. The prior summer, the Northern Pacific Railway completed three miles of track from the previous terminus at Cinnabar to Gardiner, making that small community the terminus of the line and the starting point for many park visitors. Although a small depot sufficed in 1902 and 1903, the larger, rustic, peeled-log Depot was completed in 1904. It welcomed more than 14,000 visitors that same year. The National Park Service razed this architectural gem in 1954.

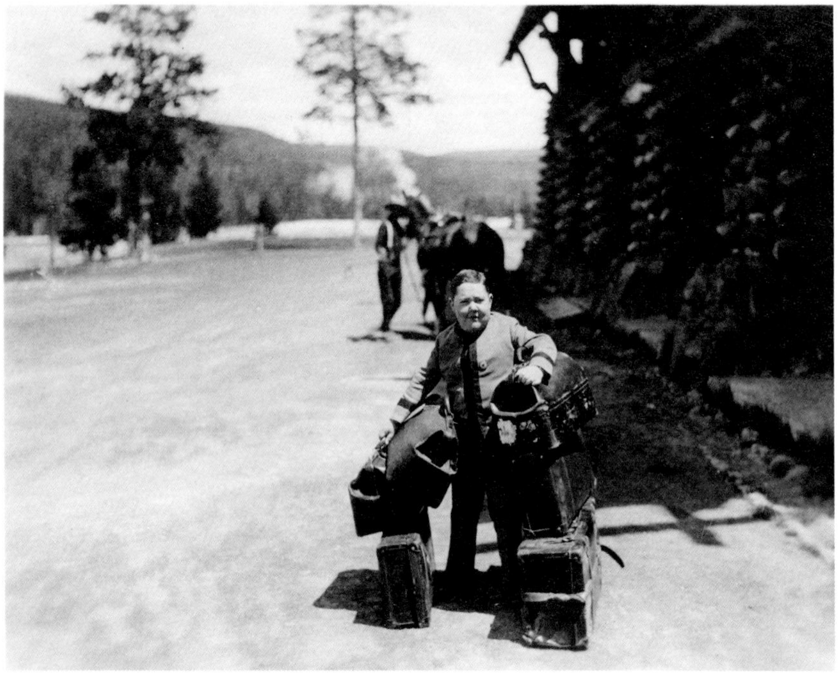

A hardworking bellhop at Old Faithful Inn, circa-1935, balances two stacks of luggage, possibly waiting for an automobile to arrive so he can load the gear and send off departing guests. He is wearing a "Yellowstone Park Hotels" button with the well-recognized image of the black bear in the center of the circle. Behind the bellhop, a cowboy stands next to his horse near the corner of the building. Horseback tours often left from the inn, so the cowboy may be a guide for the next group. The vapor rising behind the cowboy is from Old Faithful Geyser.

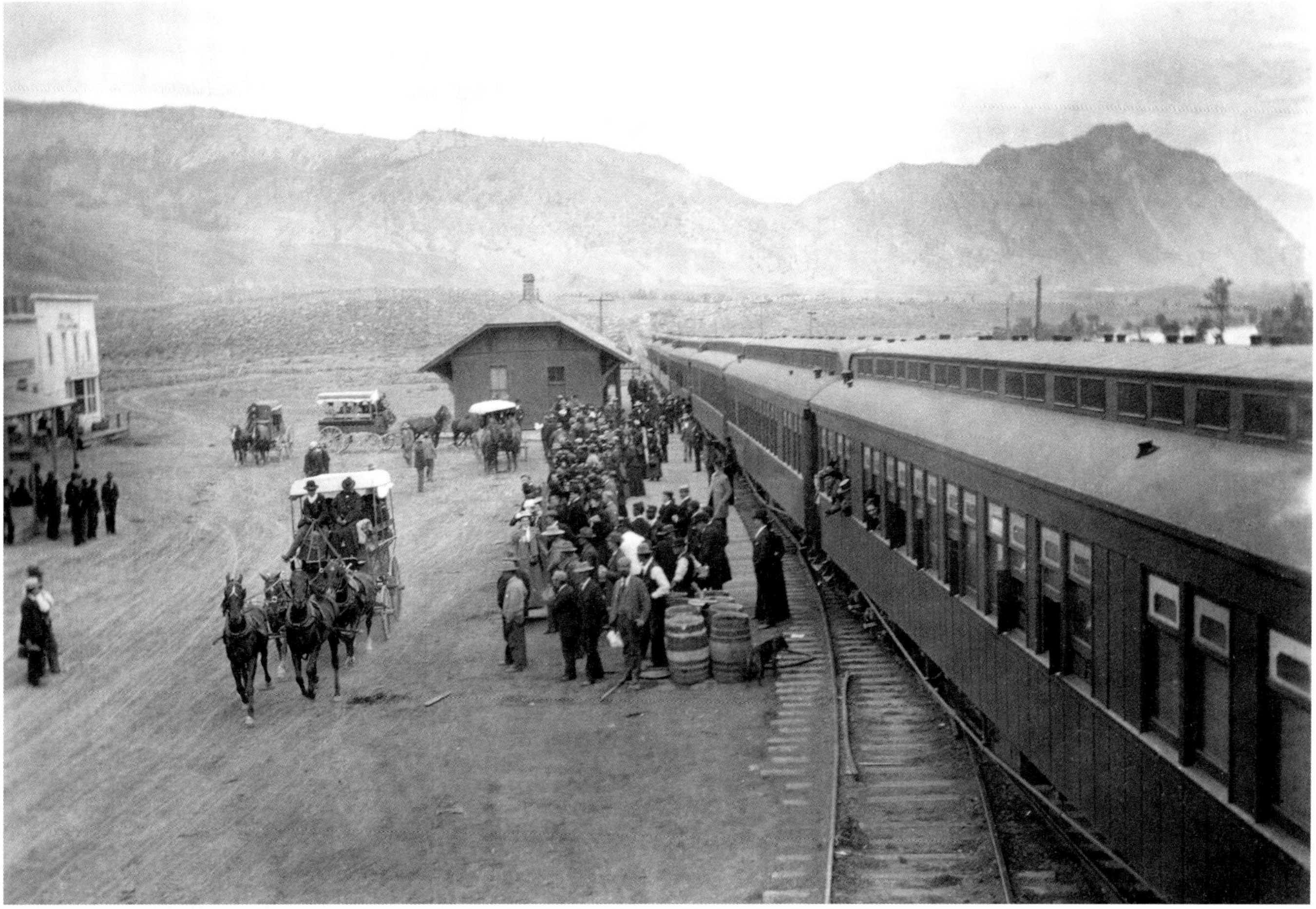

Beginning in 1883, Cinnabar was the southern terminus for the Northern Pacific Railroad and the starting point for a tour of Yellowstone. From here, stagecoaches whisked travelers and their luggage to Mammoth Hot Springs—and back to Cinnabar for those leaving the park. This photograph, taken in 1897, shows the train depot at Cinnabar, a passenger train several cars long, and a bustle of passengers, stagecoaches, wagons, and freight. Located on the Yellowstone River flats between Electric Peak and Sepulcher Mountain, Cinnabar was not the first choice for the railroad, but due to a property dispute with James "Buckskin Jim" Cutler, it was initially the most viable option. Early on, a post office added legitimacy to the notoriously raucous town, and other tourist-oriented businesses soon followed. The white building visible on the left is the W.A. Hall General Merchandise store. Constructed in 1891, the store provided the hardware, dry goods, and groceries any pioneer town needed, as well as housing the post office. After the property issues with Cutler were resolved in 1902, the railroad wasted no time in extending its rails to Gardiner. The presidential visit of Theodore Roosevelt in April 1903 gave Cinnabar a final moment of glory as the "temporary capital of the United States." During the visit, Roosevelt's staff occupied the Elysian, the presidential train car, while the U.S. Army took the president into the park for a week-long camping trip. On May 3, 1903, the railroad ceased operations at Cinnabar, and by June 15, the last mail arrived at the post office. After that, the town officially no longer existed. Although Cinnabar thrived for nearly 20 years, today there are little more than a few indentations in the soil where its buildings once stood.

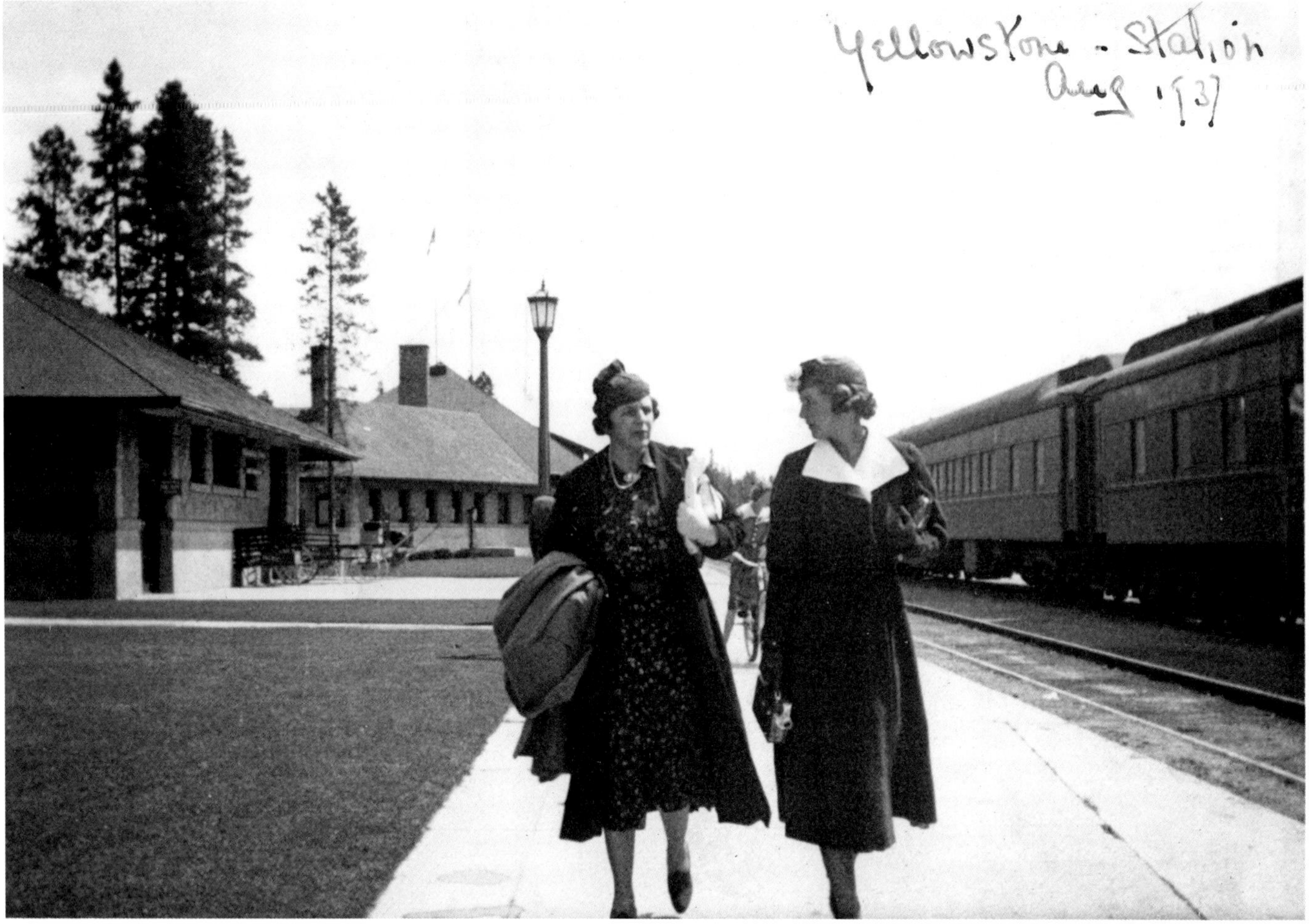

This August 1937 photo shows two women visitors walking on the sidewalk at the Union Pacific Depot at West Yellowstone, with the train's passenger cars off to their side. Prior to 1908, visitors traveling by railroad to the park's west entrance had to disembark at Beaver Canyon, Idaho, or Monida, Montana, and take a bumpy stagecoach ride the final eighty miles to the entrance. In 1908 the railroad completed the Oregon Short Line to the new town of "Yellowstone," which is now West Yellowstone. The depot, constructed in 1909, welcomed passengers until 1960, the final year for regular, passenger train service as rail travel declined. The single-story depot fit the "parkitechture" style with a hip-roof design and native, rhyolite stone quarried from the railway line. Inside, comfortable waiting rooms were heated by large fireplaces, and ticket counters provided fares for rail travel, as well as coach seats for the Monida and Yellowstone Stage Company. Wings on either side of the building offered men and women's showers for disembarking guests to freshen up before continuing into the park. Just as the railroads displaced stagecoaches, the increasing popularity of automobiles caused train ridership to decline. Although there was periodic passenger service and freight service throughout the 1960s and 1970s, the railroad tracks were removed in 1981. The Yellowstone History Center Museum now calls the depot building its home.

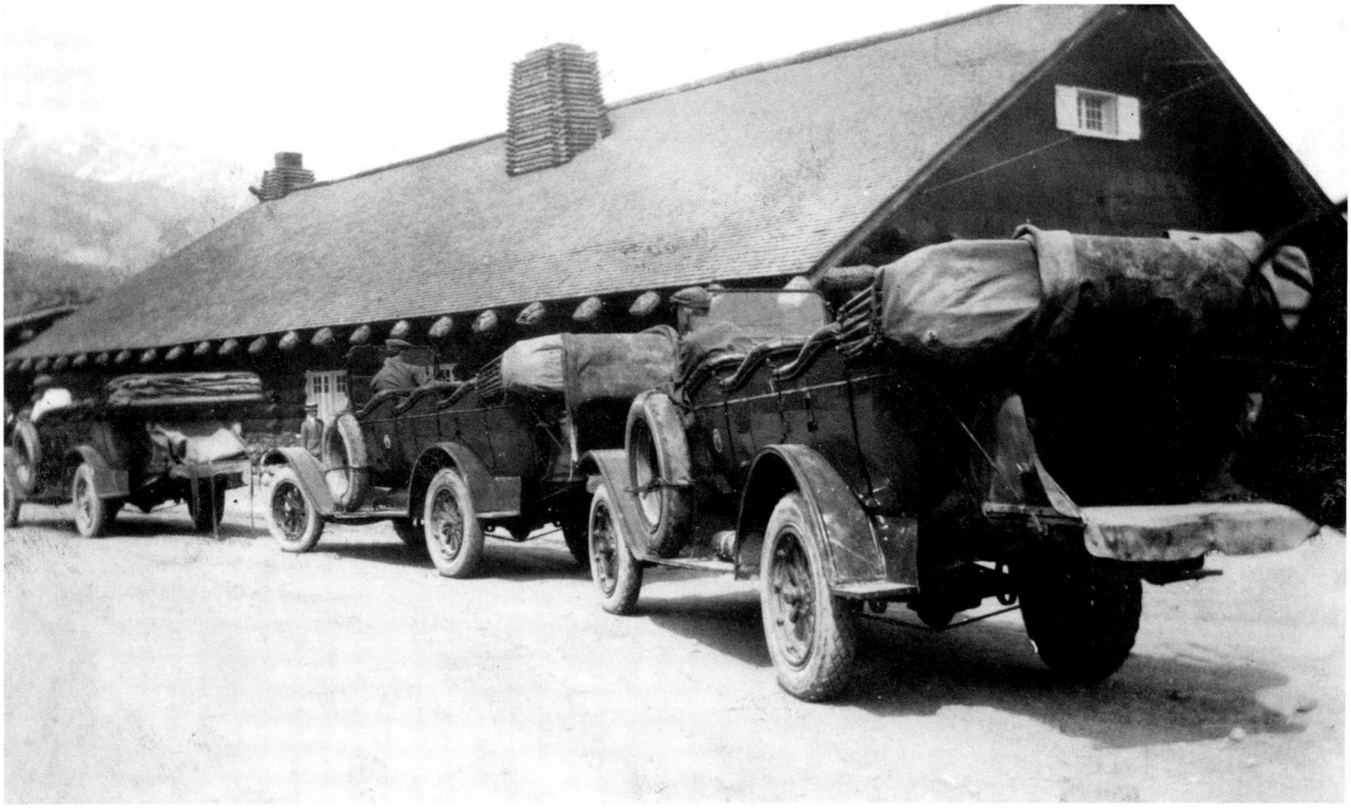

In this 1921 photo from park employee Hazel Jobb, three buses of the Yellowstone Park Transportation Company (YPT Co.) line up at the Northern Pacific Railroad Depot in Gardiner to take passengers into the park. By 1917, the YPT Co. had replaced its horse-drawn coaches with more than 124 new motorized buses and autos from the White Motor Company. Of these, 100 were the 11-passenger TEB buses (shown here). The buses, sometimes called "auto stages," were early "convertibles" because they had folding canvas roofs with celluloid windows for inclement weather. The headlights ran on acetylene gas, while kerosene fueled the running lights. Each bus was equipped with a rear platform for luggage. After these buses (along with additional buses and automobiles purchased through 1924) were lost in the 1925 Mammoth Transportation Building fire, they were replaced with model 15/45 buses that carried ten guests and a driver. The new buses boasted an improved motor that allowed them to reach the dizzying speed of 50 miles per hour.

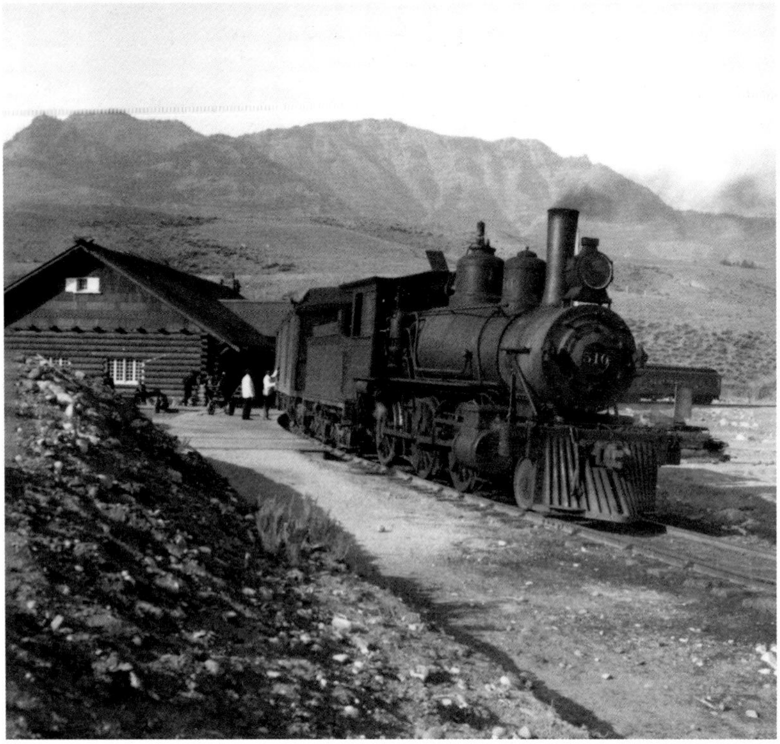

This post-1903 photo shows Northern Pacific Railway steam locomotive #510 stopped at the Gardiner depot. Porters stand on the platform, attending the waiting cars. The #510 was a 2-6-0 Mogul model of locomotive built in 1890. (The "2-6-0" designation meant two leading wheels on one axle, six powered driving wheels on three axles, and no trailing wheels.) Mogul locomotives were used after 1900 for mid- to lightweight work when heavier trains dominated freight runs. This photo shows the train wrapping around the end of the rail loop at the Gardiner station, preparing to either load or unload passengers.

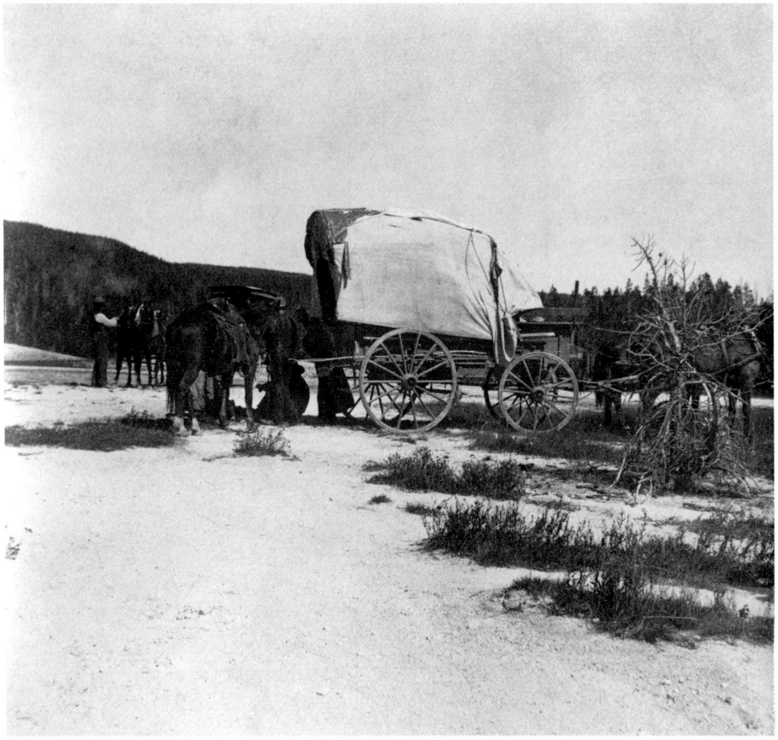

"Sagebrushers" were park visitors who explored the park on their own and were named as such because they often camped in the scrub brush and other off-the-beaten-path terrain. The independent campers in this circa-1900 photo, who either used their own equipment or rented gear from local suppliers, appear to be preparing their horses and baggage before venturing to their next adventure. Travel was far from easy during this era, as evidenced by the torn canvas on the top of the wagon, but it was far more economical for those of modest means.

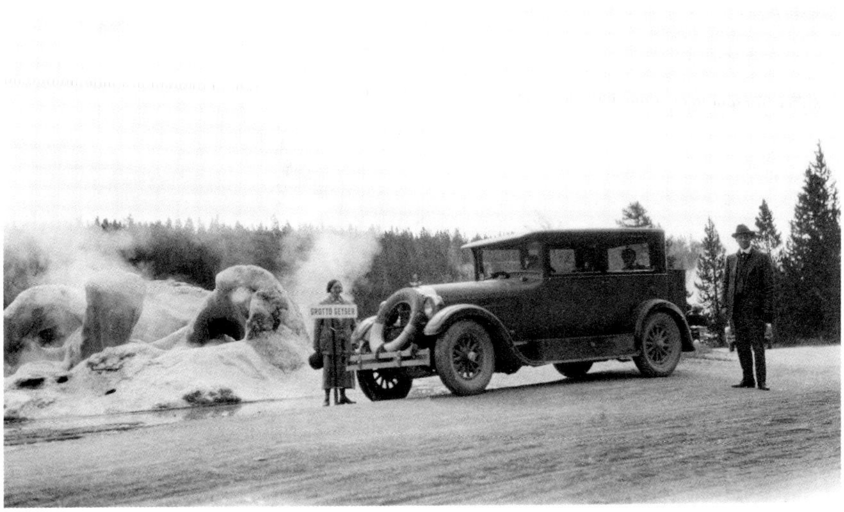

In this 1926 photo, a traveling couple stands near their Studebaker auto parked beside Grotto Geyser. This road past the Grotto Geyser was once the main road to Old Faithful and the Upper Geyser Basin; it was rerouted in the early 1970s. Notice the spare tire attached to the front grill, ready in the event of a flat tire.

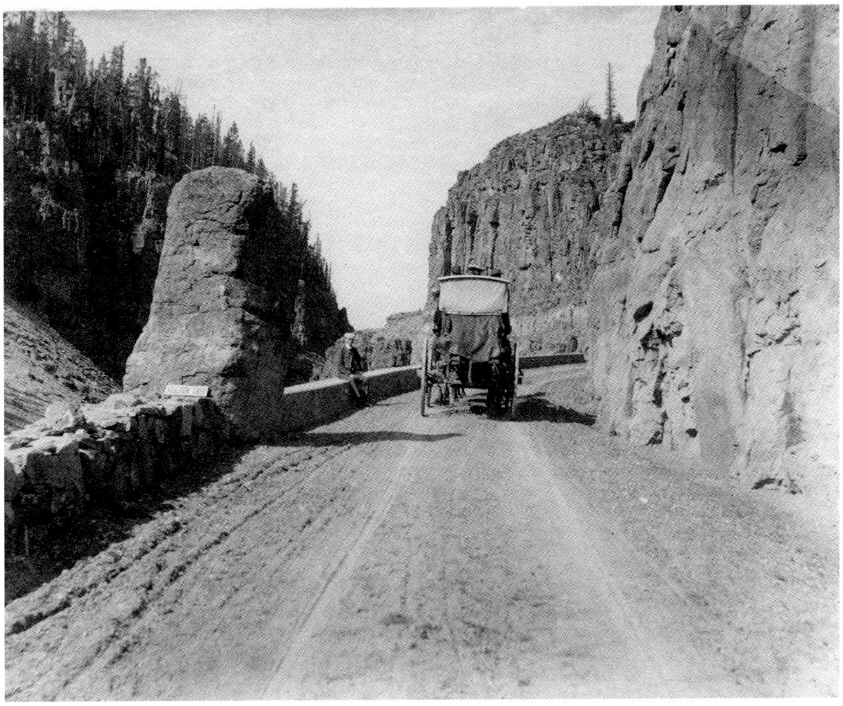

A 1901 or 1902 photo shows a stagecoach stopped near the Pillar of Hercules rock on the Golden Gate road outside of Mammoth Hot Springs. A passenger sits on the retaining wall. In 1900, park road engineer Captain Hiram Chittenden replaced the deteriorating wooden bridge (finished by Lieutenant Dan Kingman in 1885) that hugged 224 feet of the cliff through this scenic but precarious section. In its place, Chittenden built an expansive concrete structure supported by eleven arches. Road crews retained the conspicuous landmark, the Pillar of Hercules, that was initially at the edge of the wooden route. Although they kept it in the same general location, they moved it five feet over to the edge of the new viaduct so vehicles could pass more easily.

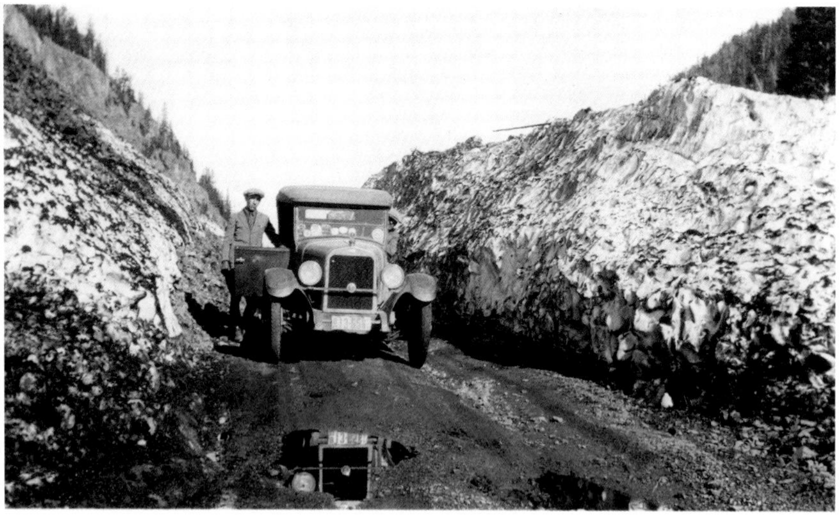

Park visitors pose next to their circa mid-1920s automobile, possibly an Oakland Motors model, between high snowbanks on the road from Sylvan Pass to Cody, the east entrance to the park. Notice the perfect reflection of the automobile's grill and license plate in the puddle in front of it.

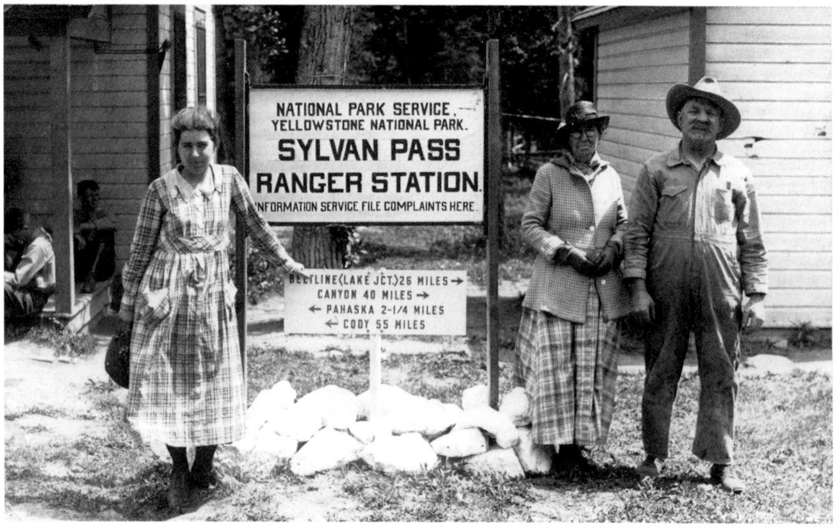

Park visitors stop at the Sylvan Pass Ranger Station near the park's east entrance for a photo at the sign, circa 1930s. Designed by Captain Hiram Chittenden, the road over the 8,530-feet-high pass went into construction in 1901, and visitors first traversed the route, a mere wagon road, in 1903. In 1905, a new corkscrew bridge climbed the steepest stretch, allowing coaches, wagons, and eventually automobiles on the road. Even though this was a challenging section to build, and not easy for horses or automobiles to climb, Chittenden felt Sylvan Pass was a more scenic route and easier to build than Jones Pass, the other proposed option.

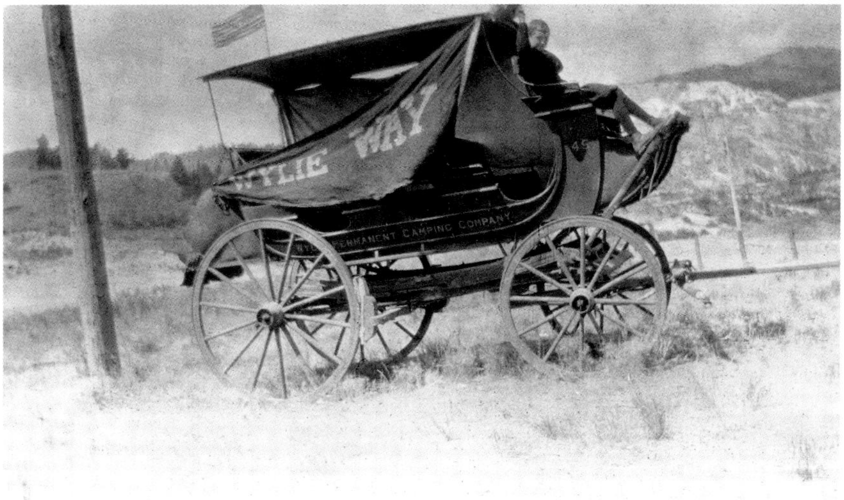

A park visitor poses in the driver's seat of the retired Wylie Permanent Camping Company Coach No. 45, displayed at Mammoth Camp (later Mammoth Lodge) in July 1921. Beginning in 1881, William Wallace Wylie, a Bozeman school superintendent who was enthralled with the new national park, created a more economical option for visitors wishing to experience Wonderland without the luxuries—and cost—of the hotels. As with the Yellowstone National Park Improvement Company and later the Yellowstone Park Association, Wylie's crews picked up guests via stagecoach at the railroad station to begin a park tour utilizing tent camps for a less formal, yet equally exciting, experience. After the park allowed automobiles, the tours continued with buses instead of horses.

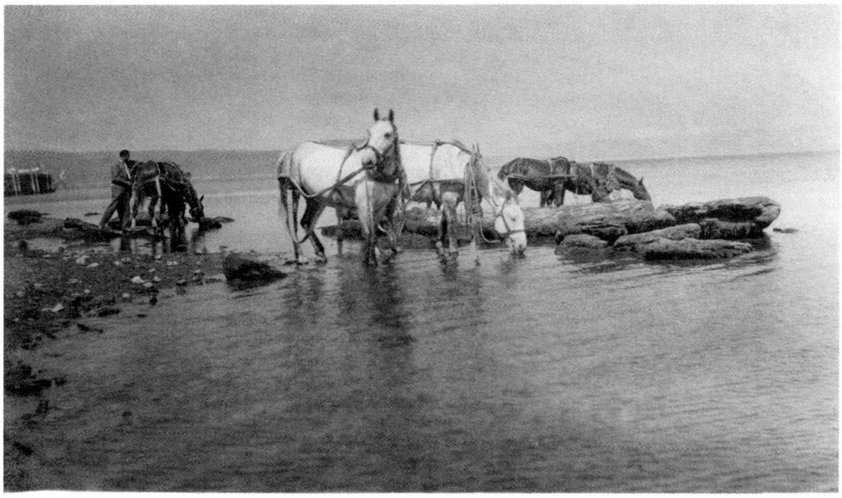

A cowboy waters six stagecoach horses at Winter Spring on Yellowstone Lake, near the West Thumb Geyser Basin, in 1911. Designed by Robert Reamer and built in 1903, the nearby Thumb Lunch Station catered to stagecoach travelers riding daily from the Old Faithful area to Lake Hotel. Once the automobile dominated park roads after 1915, the lunch station was no longer needed. The National Park Service shuttered it in 1917 and demolished the building a decade later.

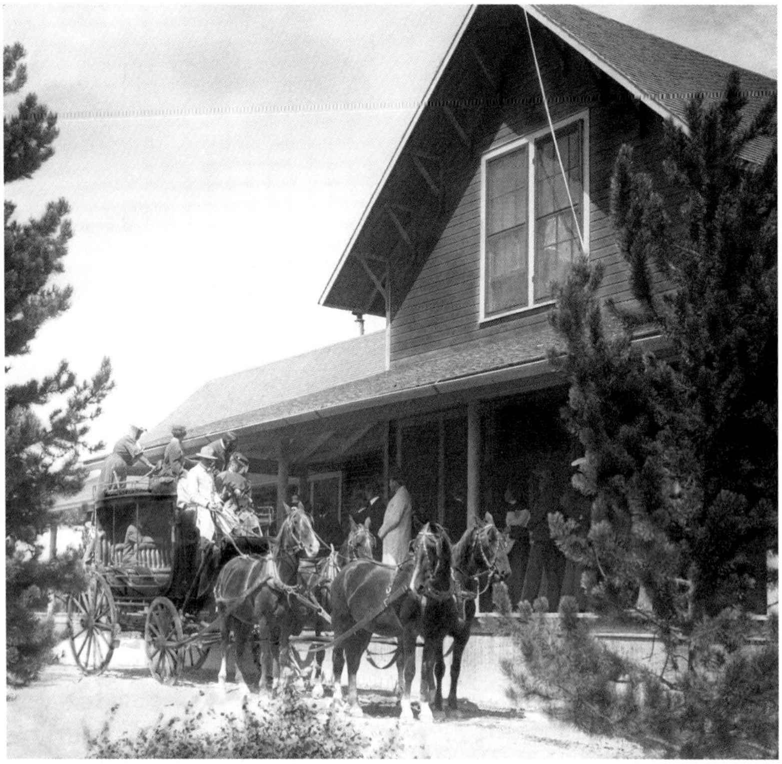

This four-horse coach of the Monida & Yellowstone Stage Company named "Montana" is pulled up in front of the fourth Norris Hotel in 1906. Instead of numbering its coaches like the Yellowstone Park Transportation Company, the Monida line gave their coaches names relevant to the park. In this photo, it appears the visitors are disembarking, possibly for lunch or to explore the popular Norris Geyser Basin. Renowned photographer Frank J. Haynes and William Humphrey started the Monida & Yellowstone Stage Company in 1898, picking up visitors from the Union Pacific Railroad in Monida, Montana, and bringing them through the west entrance. The two-, four-, or six-horse coaches were made by Abbot-Downing of Concord, New Hampshire, one of the most well-known and respected coach-building companies during this period. The Monida & Yellowstone coaches were painted red—and called the Red Line—to contrast with the bright yellow coaches of the Yellowstone Park Transportation Company. *Photo by Alvah C. Roebuck.*

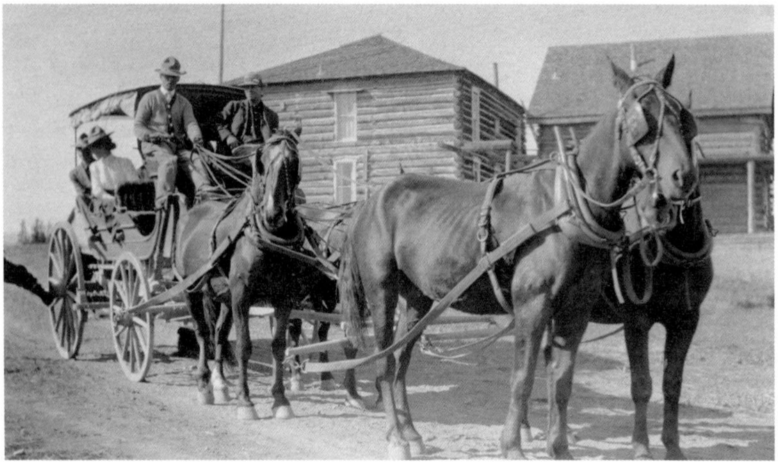

This is an uncommon photo of a four-horse Wylie Permanent Camping Company coach with park visitors at Riverside Station, just inside the park's west boundary, in 1911. Notice the "WC" (Wylie Company) initials on the front horse's blinders. Wylie guests' adventures began when they were picked up at the railroad station. If guests arrived on the morning train, the Wylie staff served them breakfast in one of these buildings or in the outdoor breakfast-camp before commencing their five- to ten-day tours, moving from camp to camp instead of shuttling between hotels.

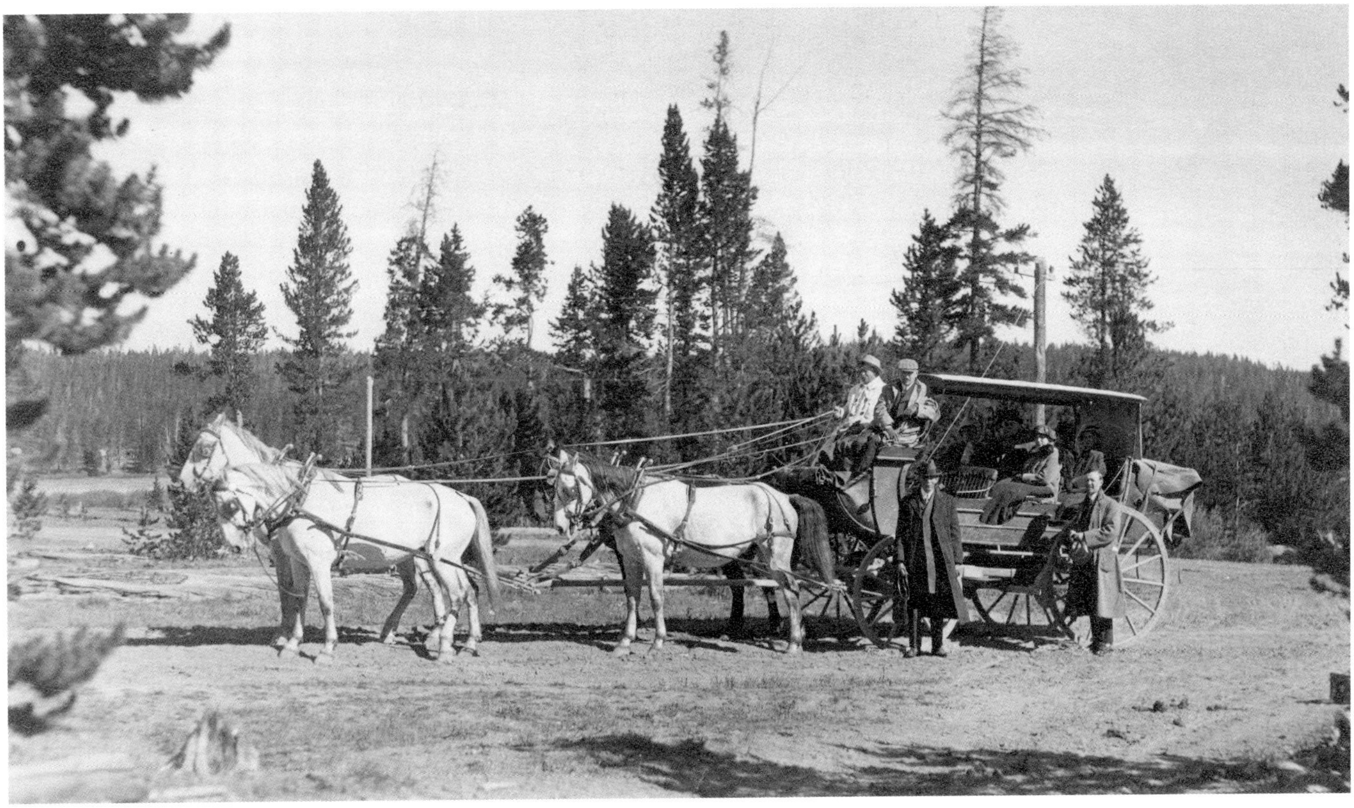

Although not obvious from this circa-1900 photo, the No.15 four-horse stagecoach sports the bright yellow paint of the Yellowstone Park Transportation Company (YPT Co.). The YPT Co. operated from 1898 to 1916 after Harry Child, an integral force in the transportation and lodging businesses within Yellowstone, along with Silas Huntley (Child's brother-in-law), and Edmund Bach (another relative through marriage) took control of the Yellowstone National Park Transportation Company (YNPT Co.), which ran from 1889-1898. Carrying seven guests—one of them riding with the driver "on the box"—on an outing probably along the Madison River, this stagecoach appears to sport a nearly matched set of white horses; only the manes and tails appear to be different colors.

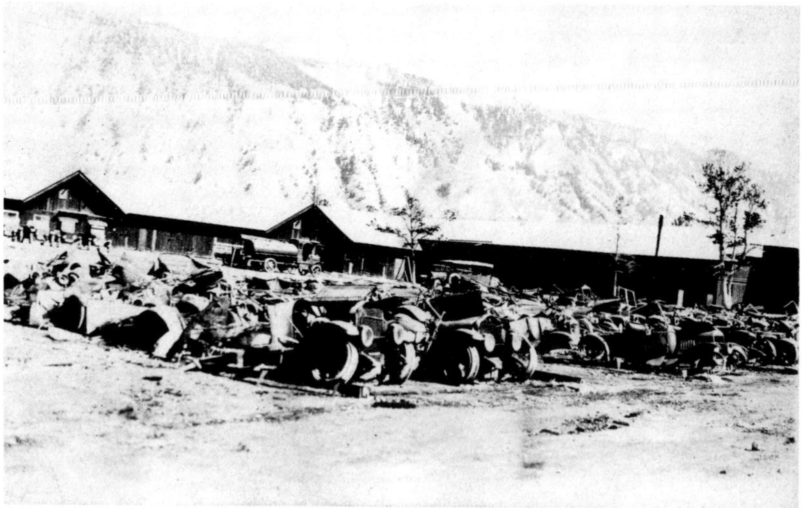

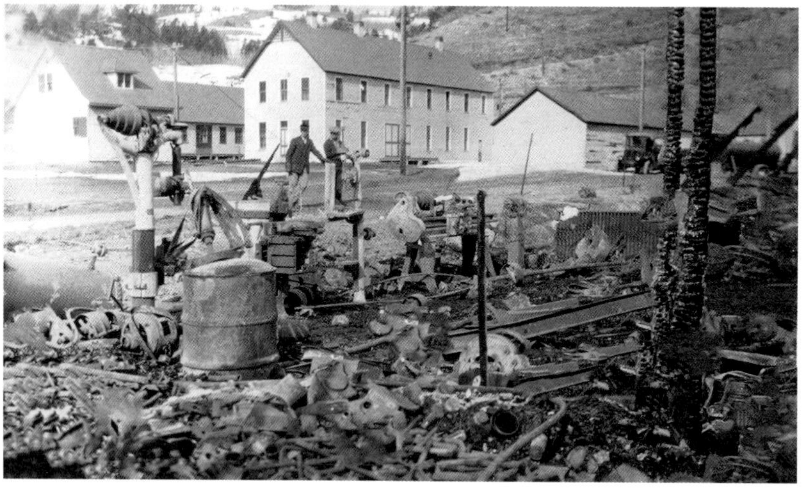

When an oil-fueled furnace exploded in the middle of the afternoon on March 30, 1925, at the Mammoth Transportation Building, the ensuing fire destroyed approximately 100 White buses, touring cars, and work trucks of the Yellowstone Park Transportation Co. (YPT Co.), as well as several other automobiles stored in the facility (top). Fortunately, 215 buses and automobiles were saved from another garage when it caught fire. The disaster damaged numerous other work buildings (the building in the bottom image appears to be a shop building or repair facility), as well as residences of some of the employees. Designed by architect Robert Reamer, sloping rooflines and steep gables made the "bus barn" an aesthetically pleasing, as well as a functional, structure. Even prior to the fire, the YPT Co. undertook the construction of a larger, more modern facility in Gardiner to handle the needs of the growing fleet. While it was not completed at the time of the explosion, by 1926 the enormous, brick structure housed more than 300 buses and automobiles. The building is still used today as operations for Xanterra Travel Connection, the company that currently operates many of the concessions within Yellowstone. Photo from National Park Service employees Joseph and Aleda Joffe's photo album when Joe Joffe was the assistant to the superintendent of the park, Horace M. Albright. *Compliments of Jay C. Lyndes Family Collection.*

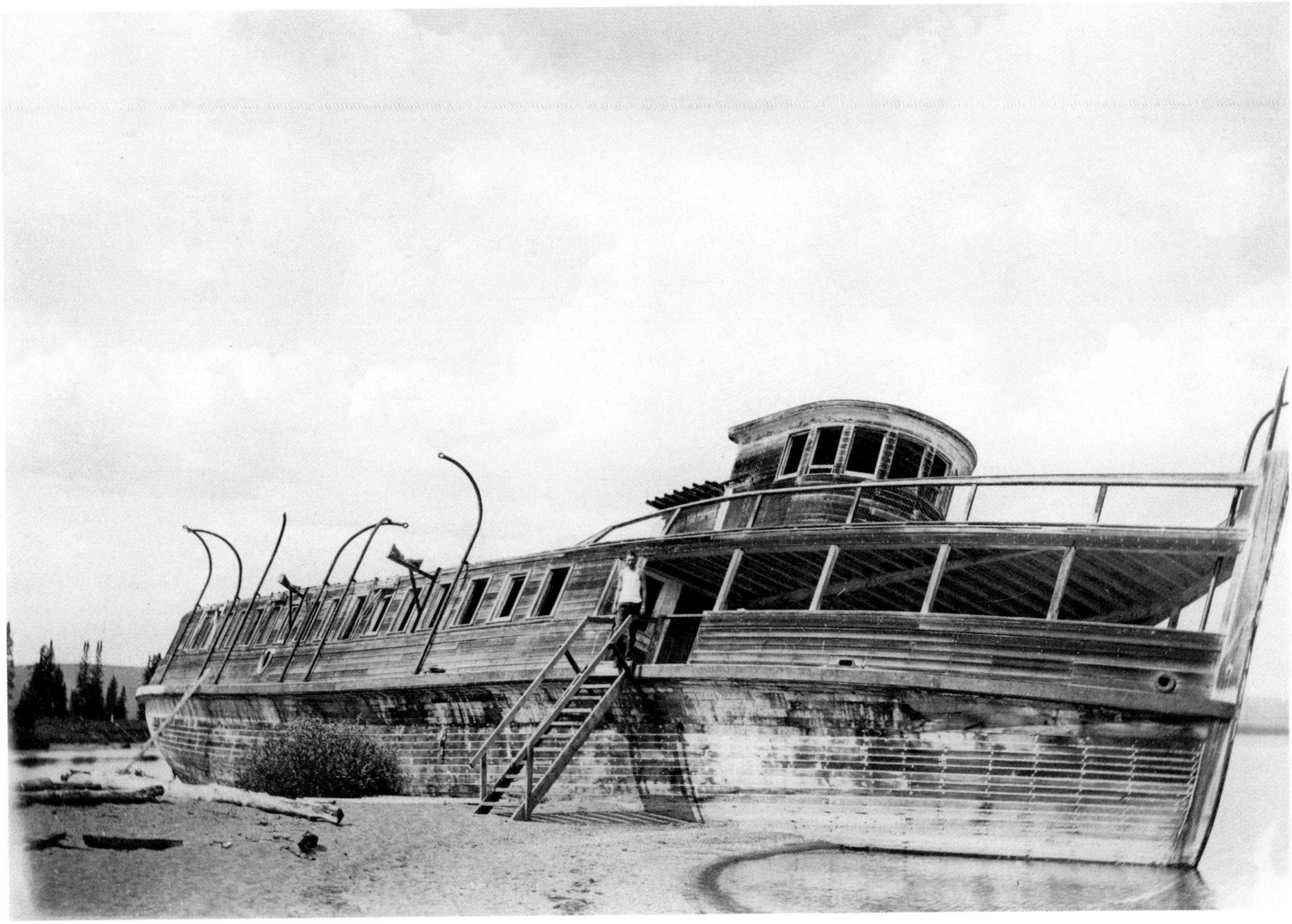

This photo taken prior to 1930 shows the leaning wreck of the E.C. Waters, the largest steamboat to grace Yellowstone Lake, in its final resting spot near Stevenson Island. Although the smaller steamboat *Zillah* was a popular and fairly lucrative attraction, the consistently over-ambitious E.C. Waters, president of the Yellowstone Lake Boat Company, spent nearly $65,000 to launch his namesake boat in 1905. The 125-feet long steamboat could carry up to 500 passengers. Yet, when the U.S. Steamship Navigation Service refused to grant Waters a permit to operate the boat, he moored it on the east side of Stevenson Island. After Waters was exiled from the park in 1907 because of unscrupulous business practices and immoral behavior (with reports of having to continually remove him as late as 1909), the E.C. Waters remained moored at Stevenson Island. In 1921, harsh weather pushed the boat onto the beach. The steam-boiler was removed in 1926 to use at Lake Hotel. Because some considered the wreck to be an eyesore, it was torched in 1930.

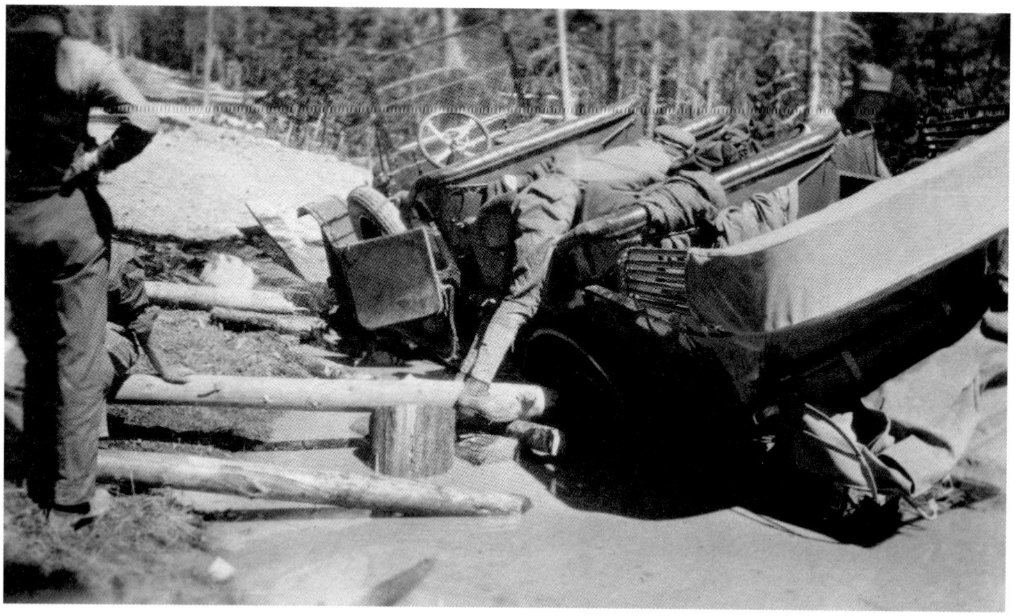

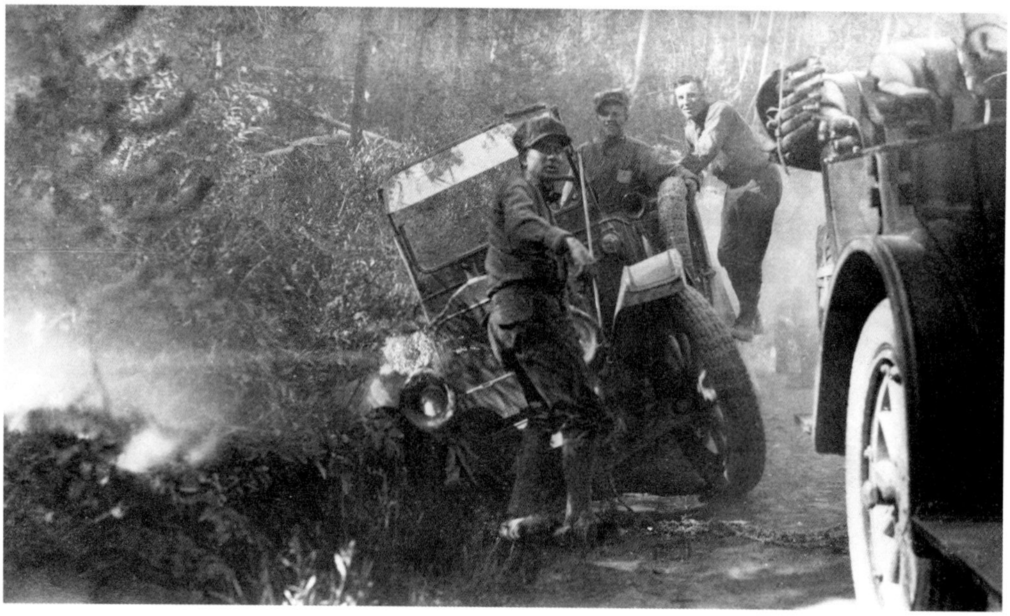

Roadside auto repairs were part of the job for the bus drivers of the Yellowstone Park Transportation Company (YPTCo.). Roads were rough, rutted, and often muddy, particularly early in the season, requiring drivers to be proficient in changing tires and extracting stuck vehicles. The YPTCo. utilized the White Motor Company's TEB "Auto Stage" bus beginning in 1917, followed by the Model 15-45 from 1920 to 1925. The top photo shows a bus bogged down in a mud hole as the driver and helpers try to extricate it with planks and poles, including one pole used as a lever.

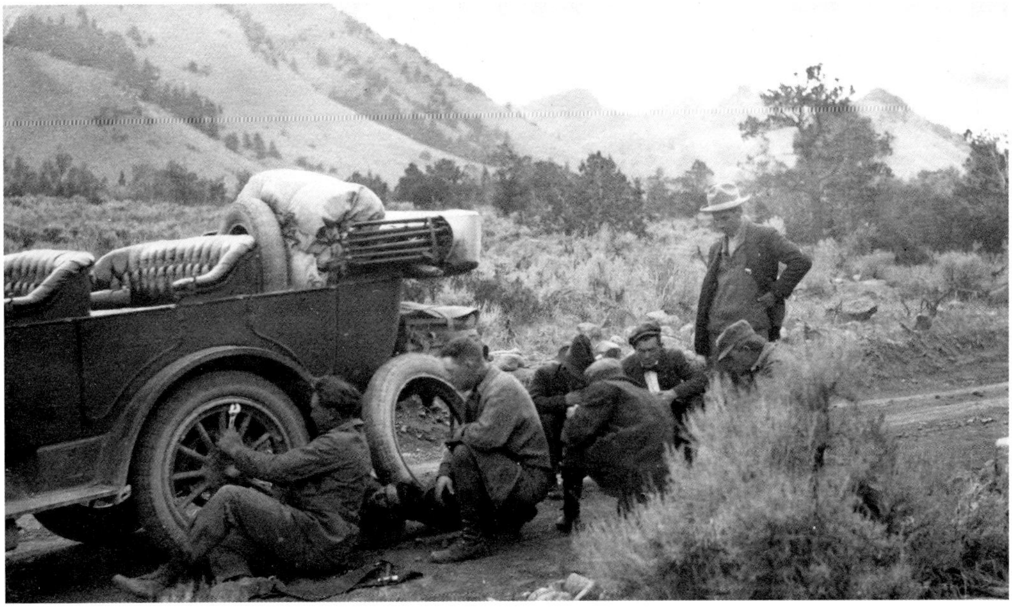

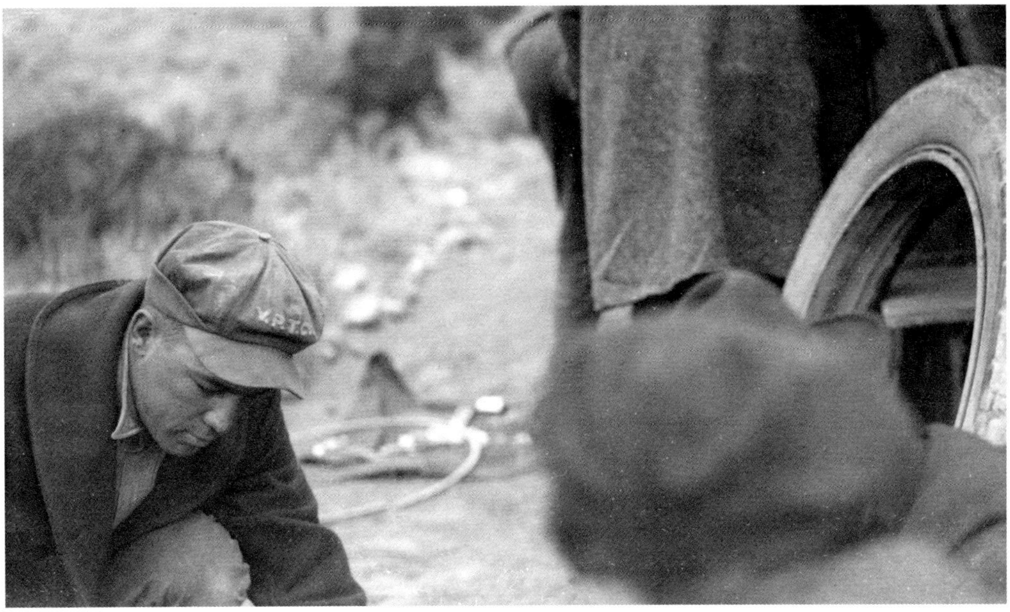

(Opposite, bottom left) This car apparently got too close to the edge of the road and tipped over. The helpers are all smiles, but the man in front, possibly the driver, doesn't appear so cavalier. A heavy chain lies between the stuck vehicle and what appears to be a bus, apparently to pull the vehicle onto the road. (Top) Changing a tire was not as simple as today. The spare tire had to be mounted onto the wheel on the spot. Here the man at the tire wields a wrench while two men look on—note one man's head between the tires as he lies beneath the vehicle. While they wait, the group to the right appear to be playing a game, probably dice, as another employee looks on. Note the man's YPTCo. cap in the bottom photo.

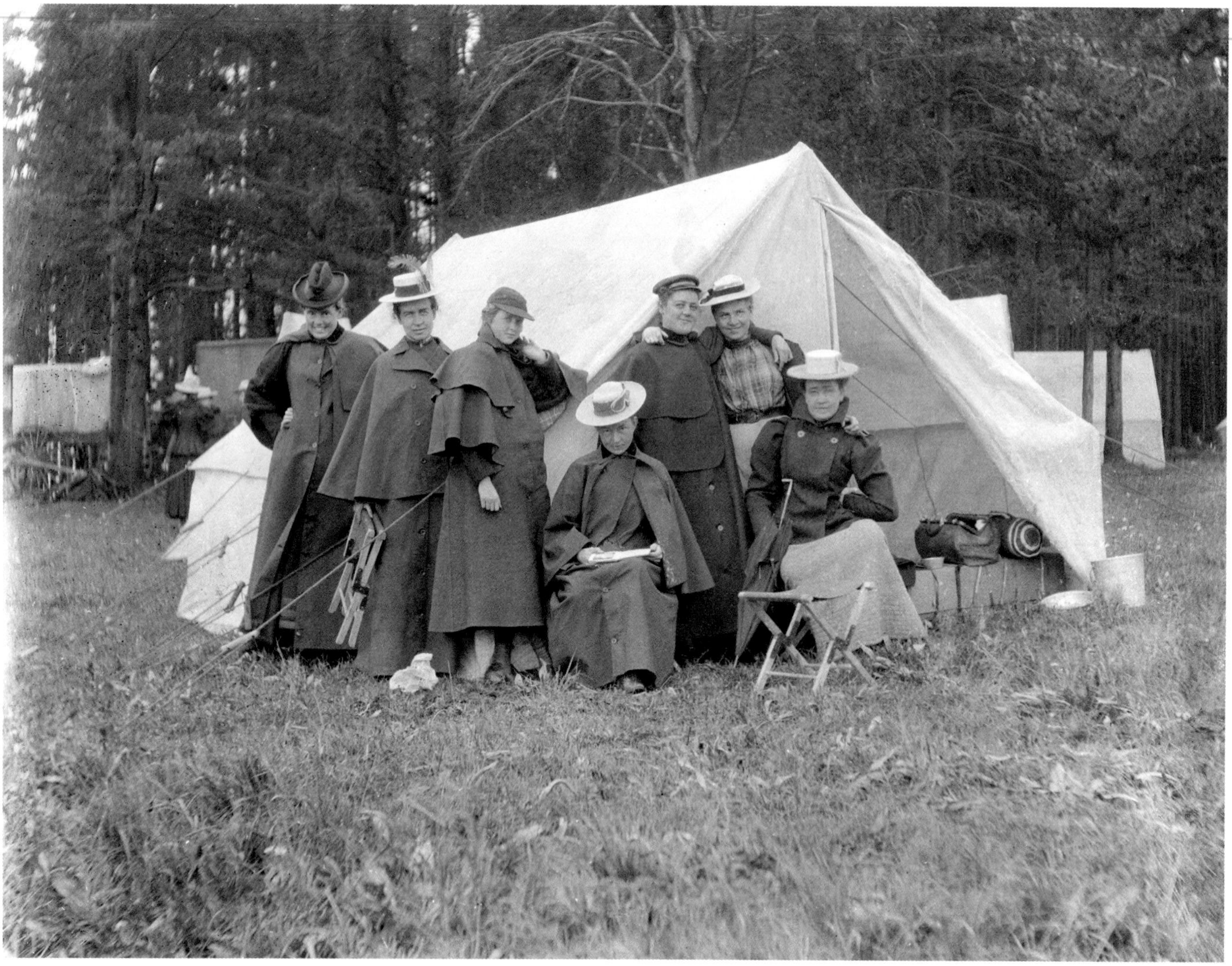

In the park's early days, it was not common for women to travel on their own or even in groups of women, making this an unusual image of seven ladies posing at their tent-camp in 1898. Two or possibly three more women are visible in the left background. Based on the numerous tents, it appears they were traveling with a camping company. The women appear well outfitted with practical clothing, such as the long, outer coats. Most of the women wear wide-brimmed hats to shade their faces from the sun, but one seems to be wearing a long-billed cap and another wears a Greek fisherman's hat. The lady seated in the middle has a park guidebook open to a photo of a geyser. Note the folding stools—a camp comfort—and travel bags inside the tent door.

CHAPTER 4

The Evolution of Camping

While the hotels catered to wealthy clientele, organized camping groups offered a more economical experience. The Wylie Camping Company, Shaw & Powell Camping Company, and numerous other operations provided visitors with creature comforts combined with friendly and knowledgeable staff.

In the early days, a camping company picked up guests at the train stations, then traveled via stagecoach from camp to camp. With snug sleeping quarters, high-quality meals served on china, and ample cooks, wranglers, and guides, the experience was the "glamping" of its day.

Automobile visitors set their own schedule, yet many still wanted a rustic experience. This inspired park officials to consolidate the camping companies and create the lodge system. In the 1920s, lodges replaced camps, cabins replaced tents, and camp life centered around a central lodge building.

All the while there were those independent souls, affectionately called "sagebrushers" in the early days, who camped on their own. This type of camping became more popular as people traveled in their own cars, so the park established auto campgrounds. In 1916, the first free automobile campground opened. By 1919, two-thirds of Yellowstone's visitors camped, at least at some point during their vacation, motivating Superintendent Horace Albright to build more and better-equipped campgrounds.

The beauty of camping, whether with an organized group or on your own, is personal immersion into the landscape. At any time, campers could step out of their tents and cabins and experience the park at its most intimate level.

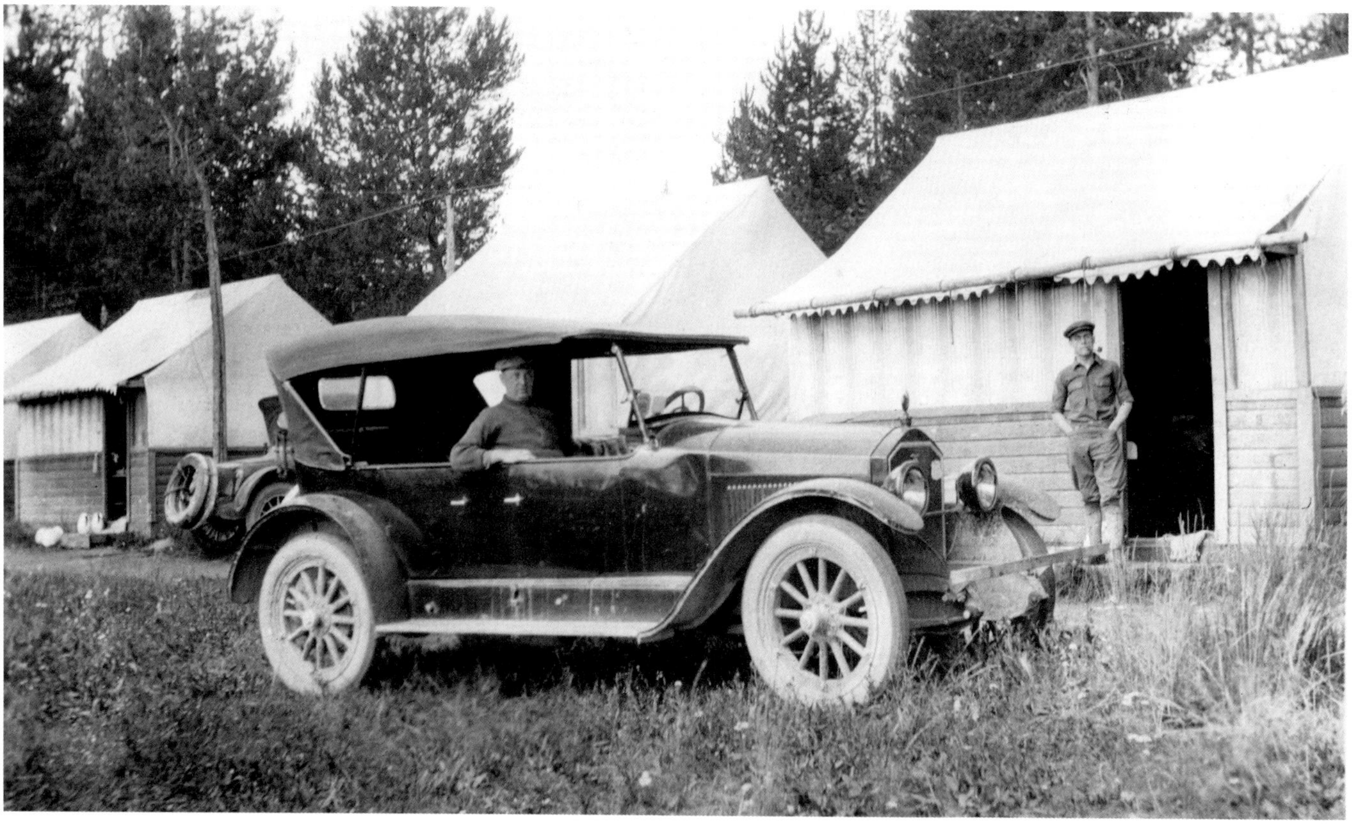

In this 1921 photo at Lake Camp, a pipe-smoking gentleman stands in the doorway of a signature-striped, formerly Wylie Camping Company tent, while another male visitor sits in the passenger seat of a Stearns-Knight touring automobile, built by the F.B. Stearns Company of Cleveland, Ohio. Established in 1898 as part of the Wylie Camping Company's locations, Lake Camp allowed travelers to explore the Yellowstone Lake region until moving on to the next location. In 1905, after a couple of decades of strife with park officials and the Department of the Interior, William Wylie sold his beloved enterprise to businessman A.W. Miles, and, unknowingly, to Miles's silent partner Harry Child, president of the competing Yellowstone Park Association—and general thorn-in-the-side of Wylie for years. The new owners renamed the outfit the Wylie Permanent Camping Company. This title remained until 1917 when park officials consolidated all camping companies into the Yellowstone Park Camping Company (later Camps Company), once again headed by Child. This area of the original Lake Camp is now the current site of Lake Lodge.

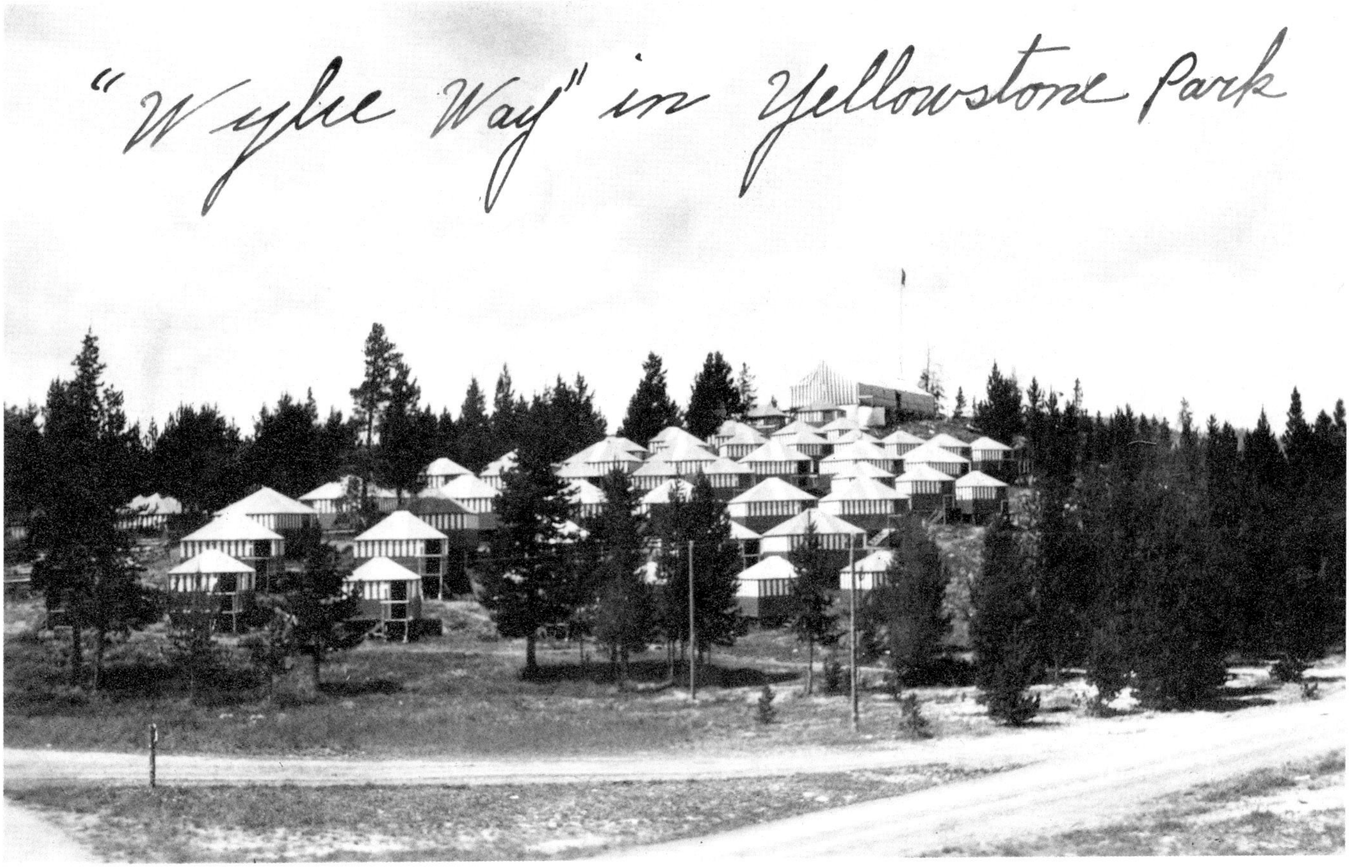

The neatly tiered tents of the Wylie Permanent Camping Company adorn the hillside at the Upper Geyser Basin in this 1916 postcard found in a Wylie Permanent Camping Company trip album. Located near the Daisy and Grotto Geysers in the Upper Geyser Basin on Wylie Hill, this camp was organized by William Wylie in 1898. All the tent-cabins sported striped-canvas upper halves with wooden-framed low walls and wood floors. Small woodstoves for heat and beds with mattresses and warm blankets ensured that guests slept comfortably. Some tent-cabins were single open spaces with one bed, while others were much larger units featuring up to four rooms. This location was abandoned after park officials consolidated all the camping operations within the park in 1917, the year after this photo was taken.

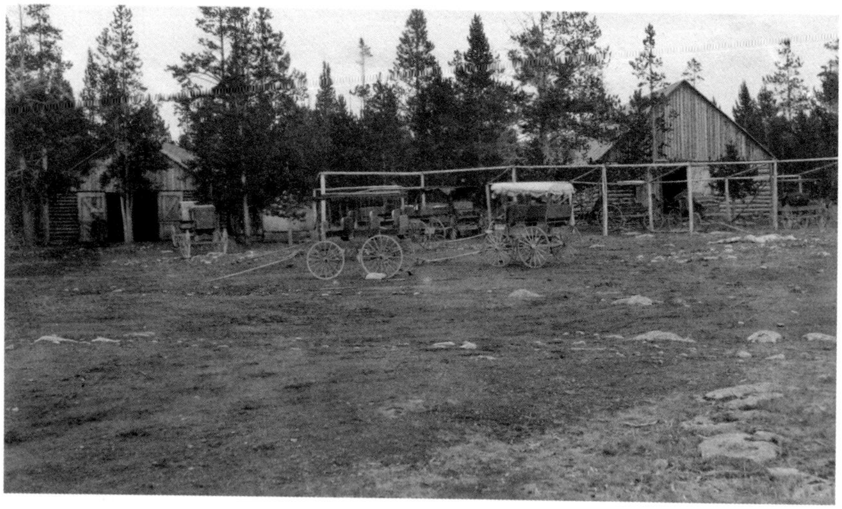

This is a rare, behind-the-scenes glimpse of the barns and the rear section of the Wylie Permanent Camping Company at Swan Lake Flat, south of Mammoth Hot Springs and the Golden Gate Canyon, taken in 1911. It is unusual to see where the camp stored the coaches and wagons, along with where they were repaired after days on the dusty—and rutted—roads.

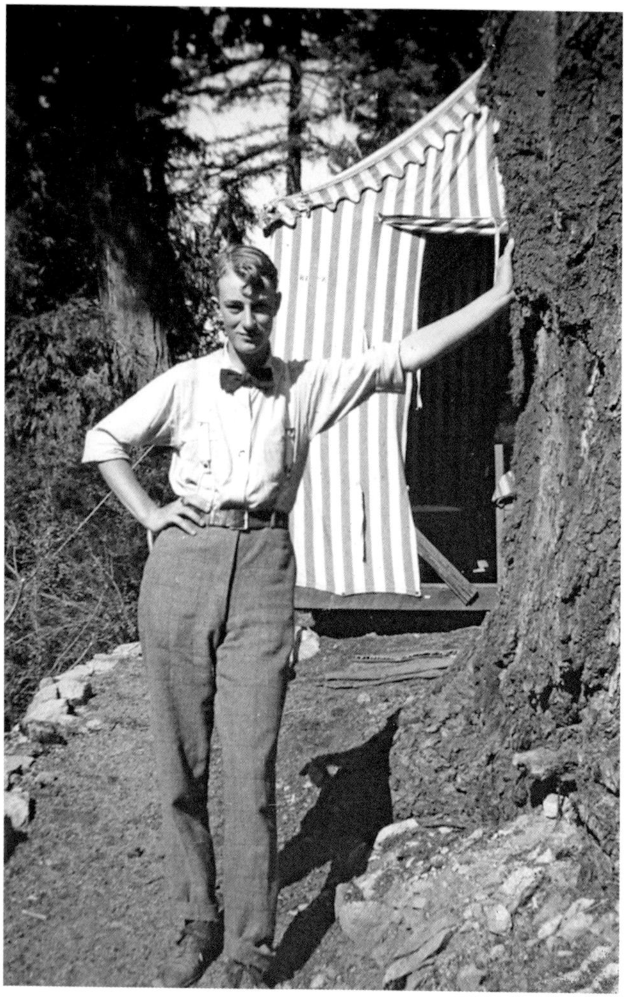

The back of this photo identifies this young man as Harold, who is posing at one of the distinctively striped guest tents of the Wylie Camping Company in 1901, probably near Tower. In 1883, William Wylie, a teacher from Iowa who moved to Montana in 1880 as the superintendent of the Bozeman schools, launched a mobile camping option for Yellowstone guests three years later. His operation was a more economical way for visitors to experience the park. By 1898, he set up semi-permanent camps along the Grand Loop, offering a seven-day tour for $35 instead of the $50 for those staying in hotels. Guests moved to another camp every day, enjoying the sights of each location.

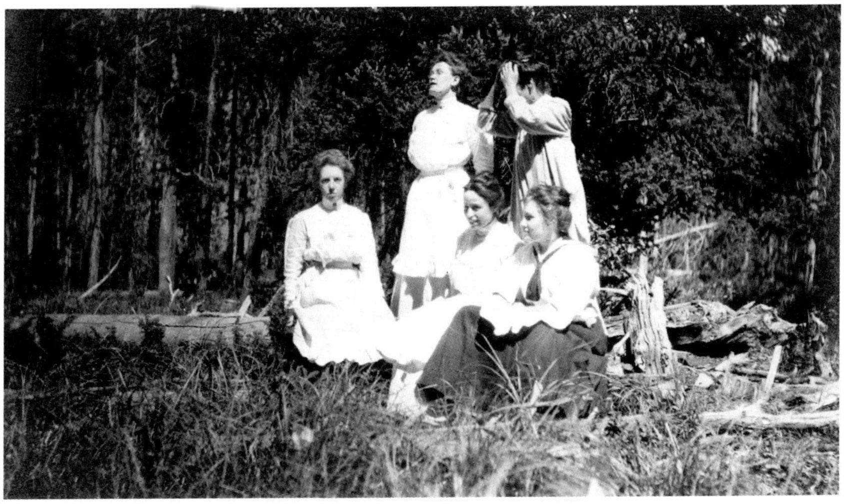

Women were an important aspect of the success of the Wylie Permanent Camping Company. The five ladies in this 1911 photo were typically responsible for serving as tent maids—making beds or changing linens—along with emptying chamber pots, serving the meals, and socializing with guests who stayed in camp during the day. In the evenings, the "savages," as the summertime concessioner employees were generally known, put on performances and often danced around the campfire with guests and fellow savages. Most of the women employees were from working class households, yet many sought college educations, and a good number of them thoroughly enjoyed the freedoms and independence gained during the summers.

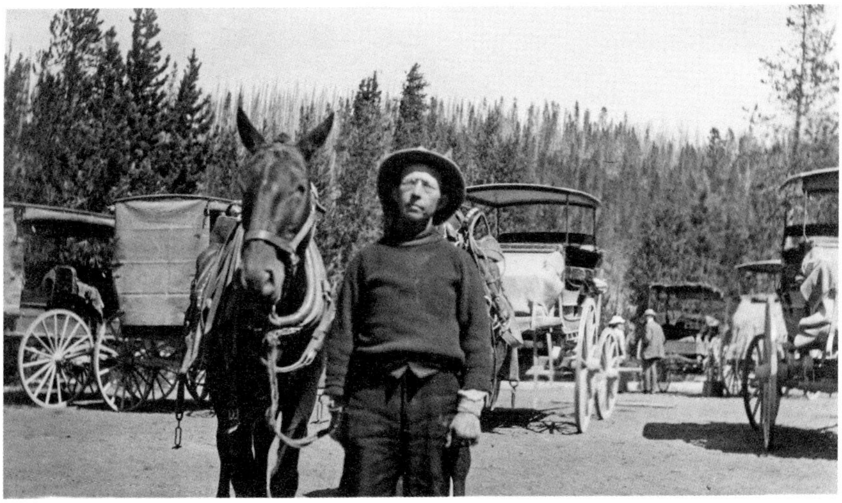

For the first 43 years in the park, traveling through Yellowstone was all about horse power, whether seeing the wonders from the saddle or riding in a coach. This tacked-up horse and male "hand" pose in front of the coaches of Wylie Permanent Camping Company at Swan Lake Flat in 1911. After the consolidation of all the camping companies in 1917, the National Park Service ordered many of these semi-permanent structures removed in favor of lodges having a main, central building surrounded by tent-cabins—and eventually wooden cabins. The following season, the Yellowstone Park Camping Company improved the facilities throughout the park.

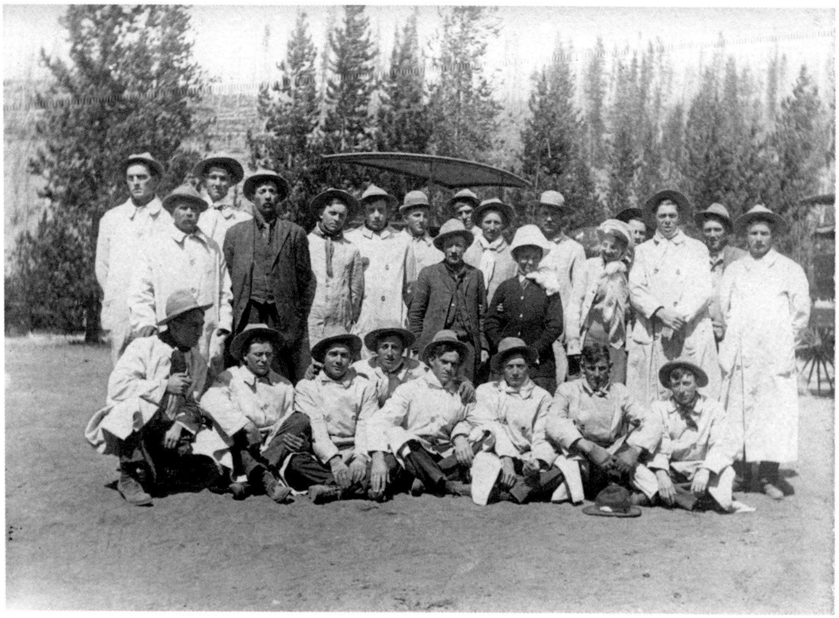

This 1911 photo shows a group of coach drivers. The drivers all wear the long dusters to prevent being covered in the dust and dirt of Yellowstone's early roads.

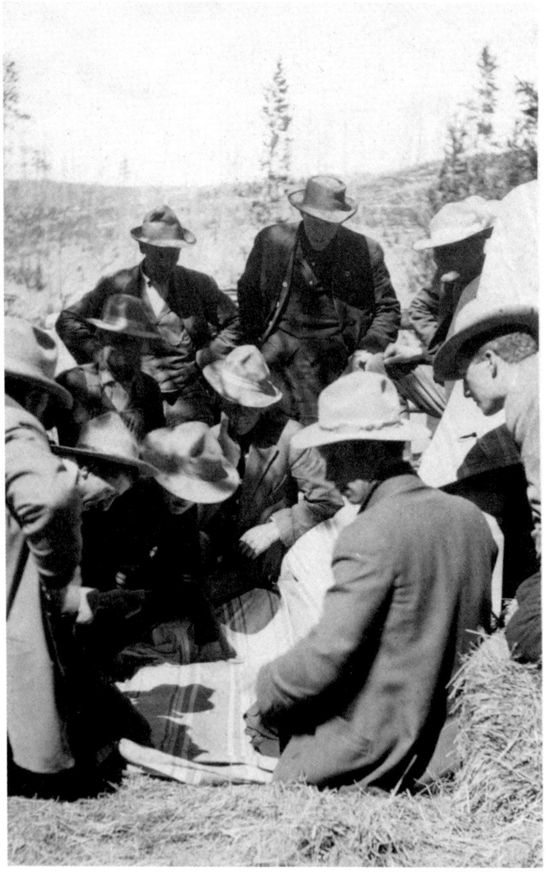

Even the employees needed to have fun once-in-a-while. It is difficult to see what they were playing, but it appears the coach drivers are focused on some sort of dice game, using a blanket to throw the dice on. The crouching man, second from the left, appears to be ready to throw dice from his closed hand. The men are at the Wylie Permanent Camping Company at Swan Lake Flat in 1911.

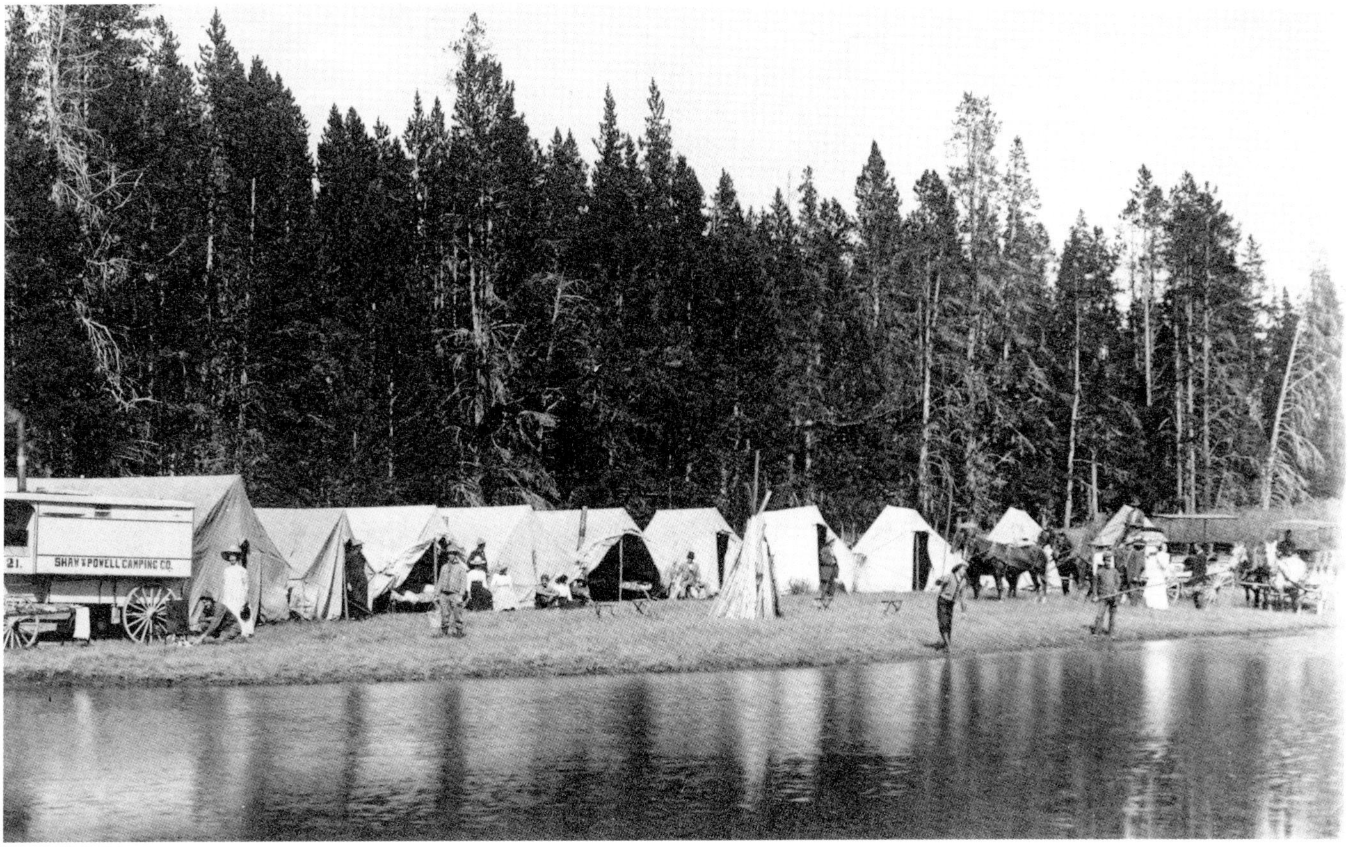

The tidy tents of the Shaw and Powell Camping Company are lined up along the Yellowstone River at Paradise Glen in this circa-1910 photo. Notice the chuck wagon with Shaw & Powell Camping Co. painted on the side and a smoking chimney, indicating meal preparation was under way. It appears that a large, tipi-shaped stack of wood, with stools around it, was ready to be lit for the evening's campfire. This company, based in Livingston, Montana, was founded by Amos Shaw and John D. Powell in 1898. In the beginning, they brought guests through the north entrance for five- to seven-day journeys. In 1908, they added travelers arriving through the west entrance at the town of "Yellowstone," which became "West Yellowstone" in 1920.

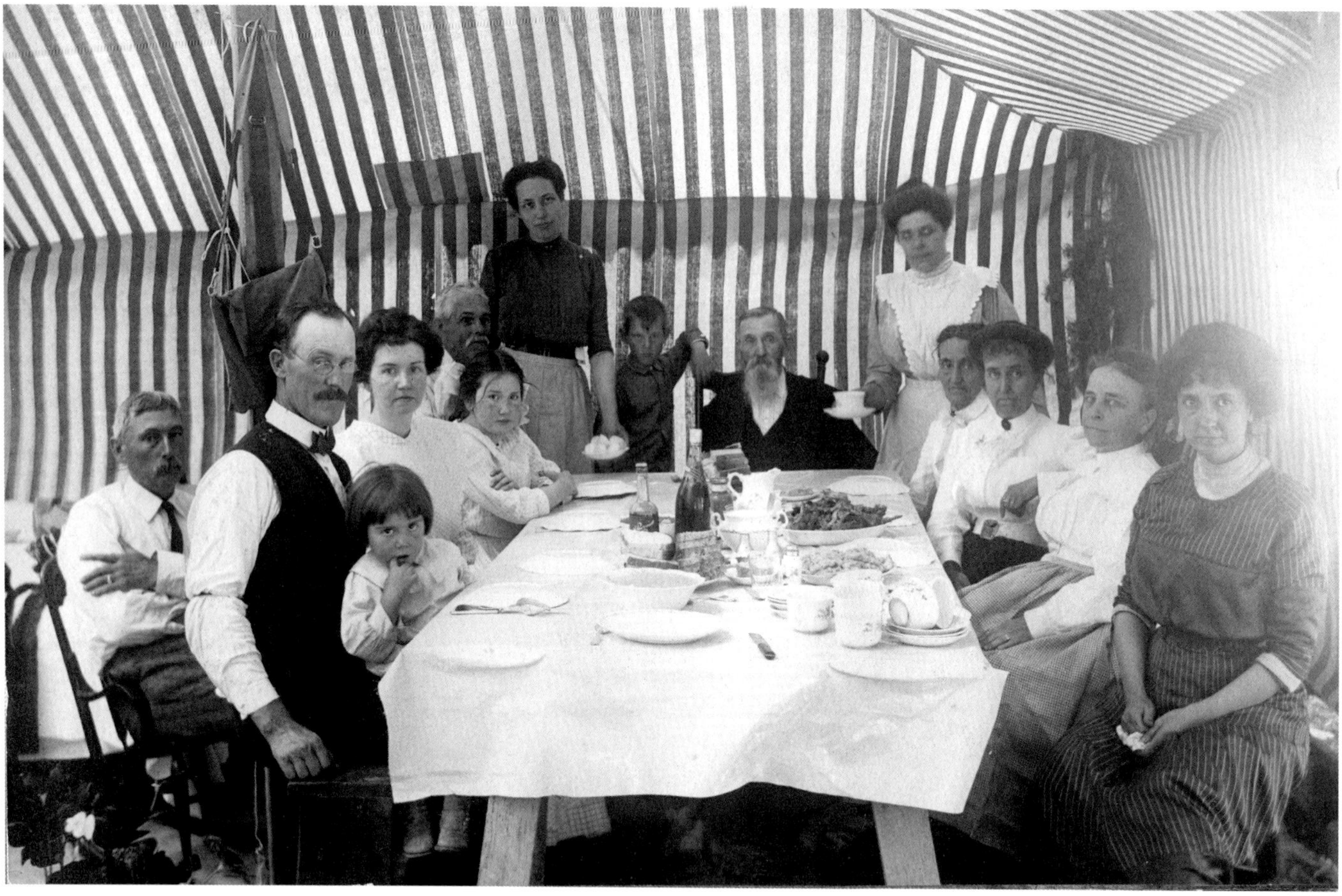

It was far from roughing it with the Shaw and Powell Camping Company, as demonstrated in this August 1911 photo of a meal being served. Guests were treated with a level of refinement, including china dinnerware, tablecloths, good food, and attentive servers. In pleasant weather, tables were set up outside. Although camping was considered "roughing it" versus staying in one of the hotels, Shaw and Powell took great pride in the quality of the food built around their exceptional cooks, fresh vegetables grown in their own truck gardens, and local dairy products. In this photo, plates are stacked high with bread probably baked in camp. Other dishes may be fried chicken and maybe fried fish, along with bowls filled with side dishes. It is difficult to tell what the tall bottles hold in the middle of the table, although the one on the far right appears to be Heinz Ketchup, which was developed in 1876 by Henry John Heinz.

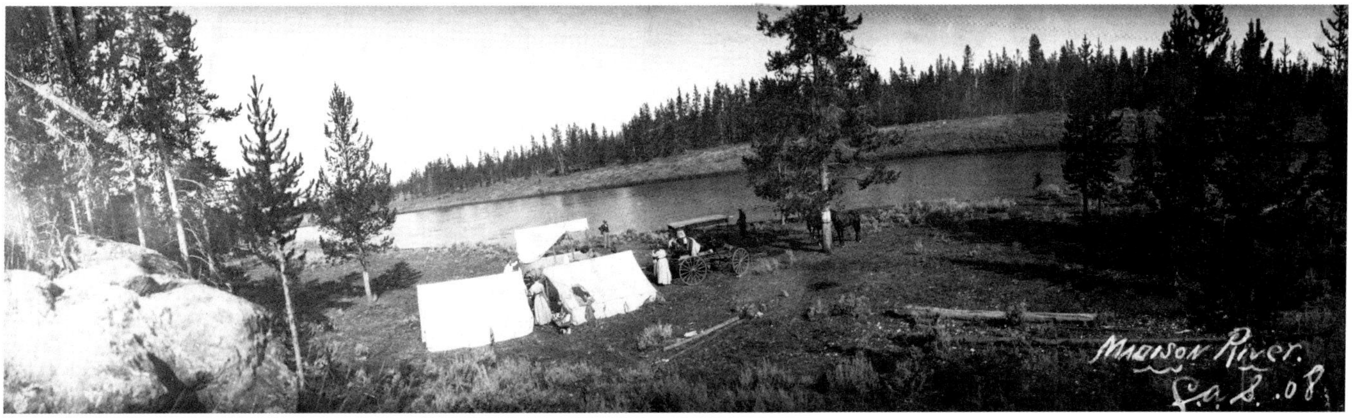

Yellowstone is steeped in the camping tradition, as exemplified by this group of park visitors with tents set up along the Madison River in 1908. While many people hired the services of one of the camping or guiding operations, there have always been independent souls who preferred to explore the park on their own (or did not have enough money for a tour), hauling their gear with their own coaches and horses, or with an outfit rented outside of the park. These campers were informally known as "sagebrushers" because they often camped in open sagebrush areas.

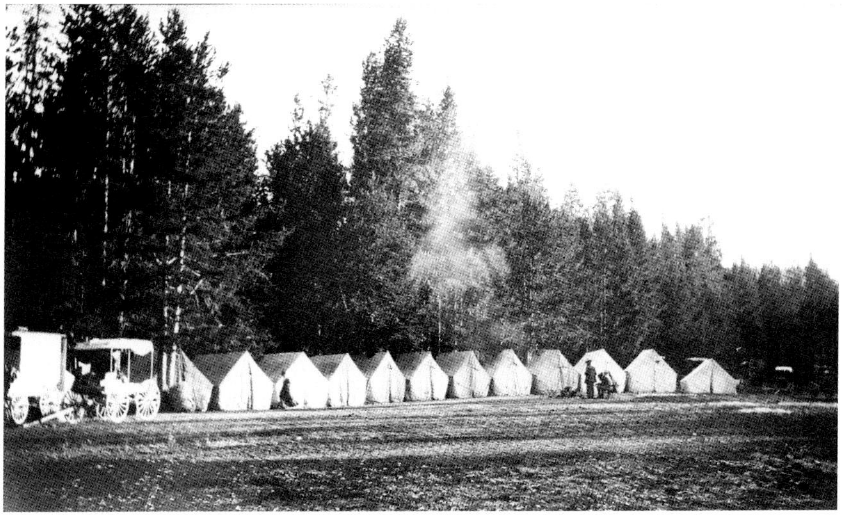

This 1911 image shows the Shaw and Powell Camping Company at DeLacy Creek, north of Shoshone Lake. In the early days of the company, they used moveable canvas tents, but they switched to semi-permanent camps with wood-bottomed and canvas-topped tents beginning in 1912 at their Willow Park location. Like the Wylie Camping Company, Shaw and Powell took guests on multi-day tours following the Grand Loop route. The DeLacy Creek camp was part of a five-day tour heading from there east to Yellowstone Lake. In 1917, park officials consolidated the various park camping companies into the Yellowstone Park Camping Company; the consolidation eliminated some camping locations, including this one at DeLacy Creek.

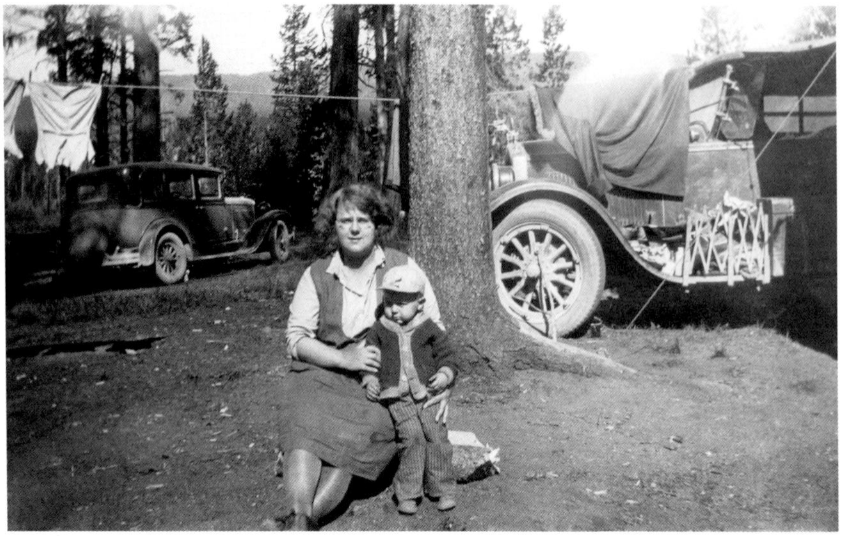

A mother holds her young child while sitting on a log at the Lake Junction auto campground in July 1928. Laundry, including a couple of shirts and an overcoat, is hung to dry from lines strung between the trees. After establishing the initial auto campgrounds in 1916, the year after automobiles were first permitted in the park, the National Park Service saw a growing need for services to accommodate the two-thirds of park visitors who were now car camping. Superintendent Horace Albright improved the Lake auto campground with bathhouses and cooking areas in 1921 as part of his effort to create a "motorist's paradise" in the park. This campground was in the forest behind Lake Hotel, close to the present ranger station. The forest is now gone, and the hotel's yellow cabins took the place of the campground.

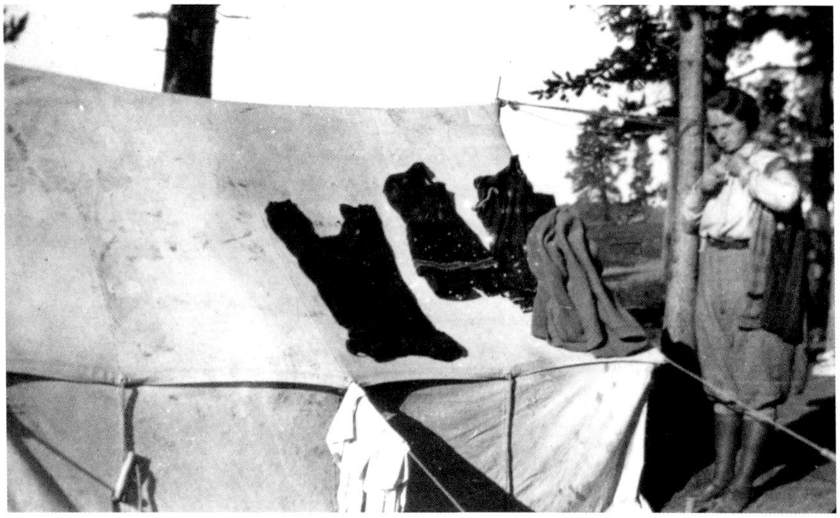

Even on vacation, the laundry did not wait. This female park visitor at Grand Canyon Auto Camp in 1925 is drying clothes on the tent-line and draping them on the tent itself. She wears wool knickers, one of the few pants options acceptable for women to wear in public at this time. This photo is from the Big Timber family photo album.

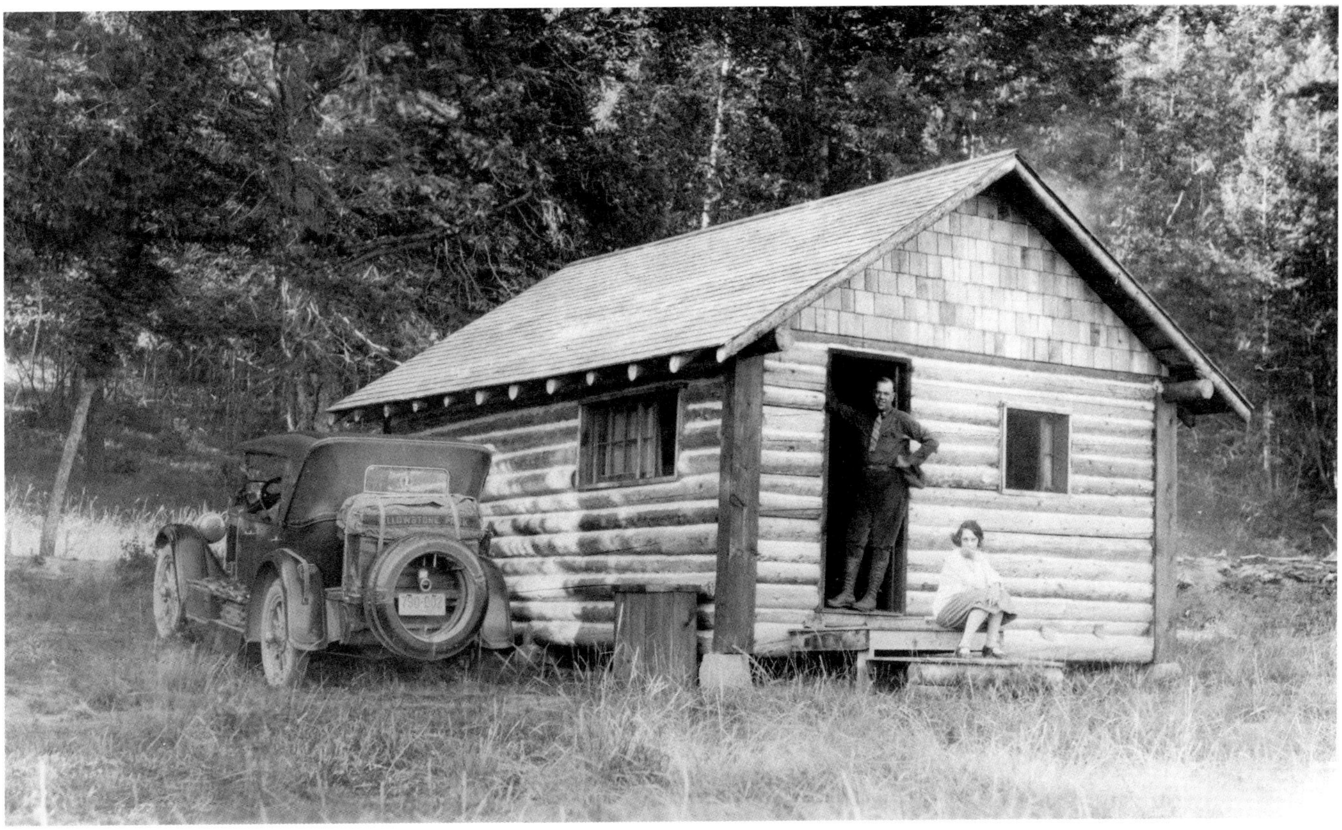

A husband and wife pose at the entrance of one of the Camp Roosevelt cabins in the 1920s. Notice the "Yellowstone Park" felt banner strapped to the stowed gear on the rear of the automobile. This beautiful location, nestled in a meadow surrounded by aspens and firs, was a popular stop between Mammoth Hot Springs and Canyon. President Chester Arthur camped in this location during his 1883 visit, and in 1906 it became home to a tent-camp of the Wylie Permanent Camping Company. As part of transitioning the permanent camps into a lodge-system, in 1919 the Yellowstone Park Camping Company (YPC Co.) built a rustic, central log building that featured two large fireplaces and a spacious dining hall. In the 1920s, the YPC Co. constructed 37 cabins, such as the one in this photo, along with 26 tent-cabins to keep up with the needs of the new automobile-traveling visitors.

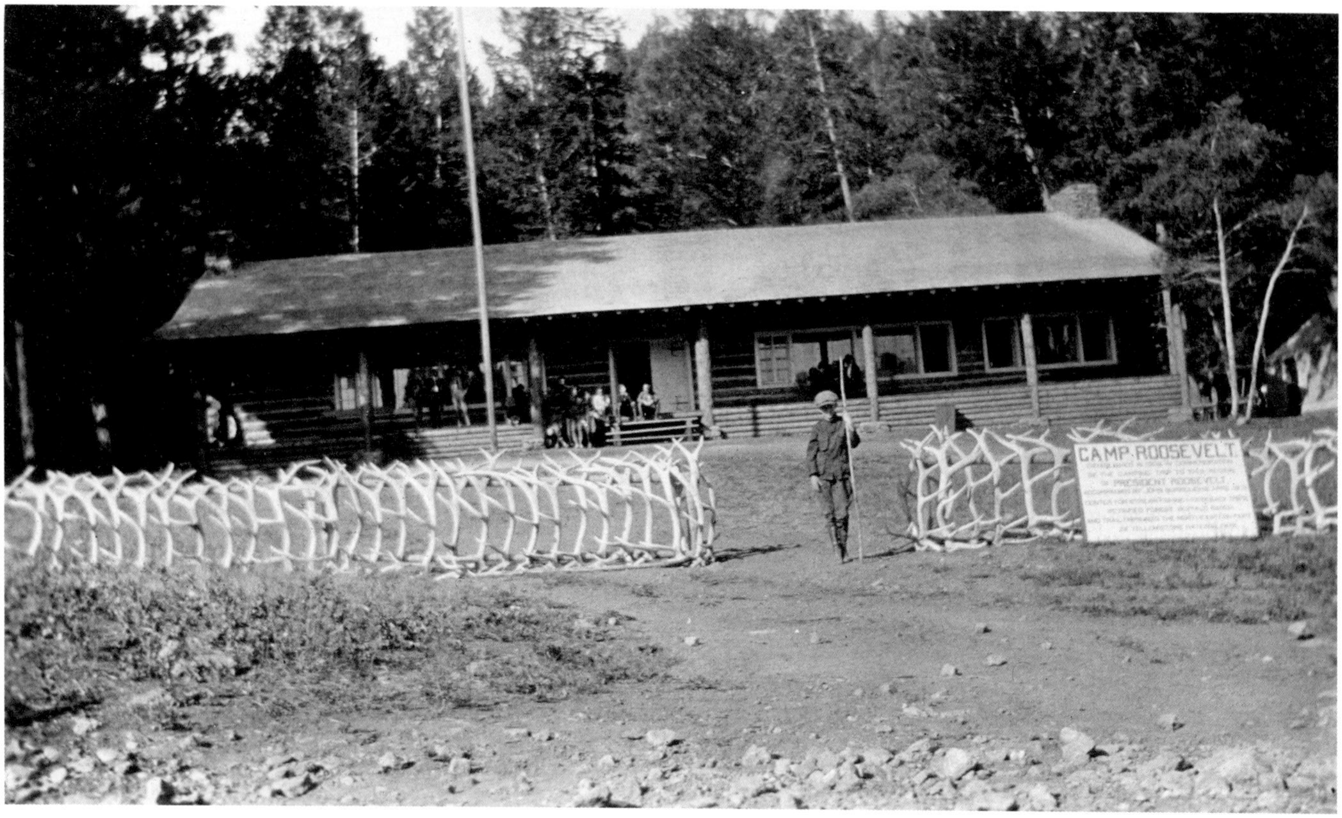

Visitors in this July 1921 photo pose at the "Camp Roosevelt" main lodge with its elk-antler fence and a sign indicating that President Roosevelt camped in this spot during his 1903 trip. "Roosevelt camped here" was good publicity for the new lodge, but, unfortunately, it was not true. Roosevelt himself stayed a mile to the south at the Tower Soldier Station, while his entourage camped at Rainy Lake, a quarter mile southeast of present Roosevelt Lodge. This main building at "Camp Roosevelt," built in 1919-1920, measured 50-feet by 90-feet, with an additional 29-feet by 59-feet extension off one side, and was the first, yet the smallest, of the new lodge buildings created in the existing camps.

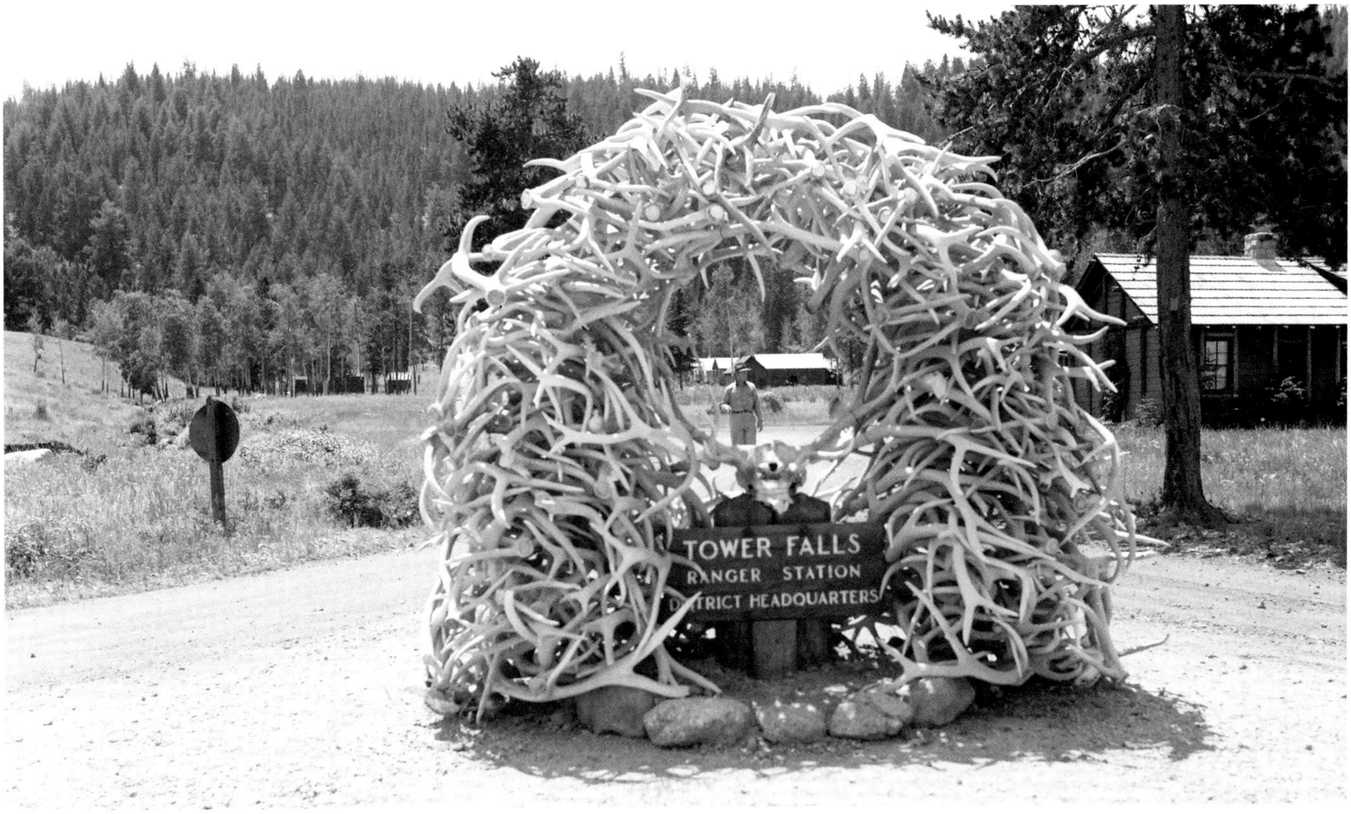

This photo of the Tower District headquarters in 1940 shows an impressive arch of elk antlers with a male visitor standing in the background. The first structure built at Tower Junction near Roosevelt Lodge was constructed as a soldier station in 1907, followed by a ranger station in 1923. During this period, collecting and stacking antlers to create an impressive display such as this was popular with staff. There are no other known photographs of this antler creation, indicating that it most likely did not last very long. The building to the right of the antler arch still stands as a ranger's residence, and the government structures in the background are used today to house National Park Service employees.

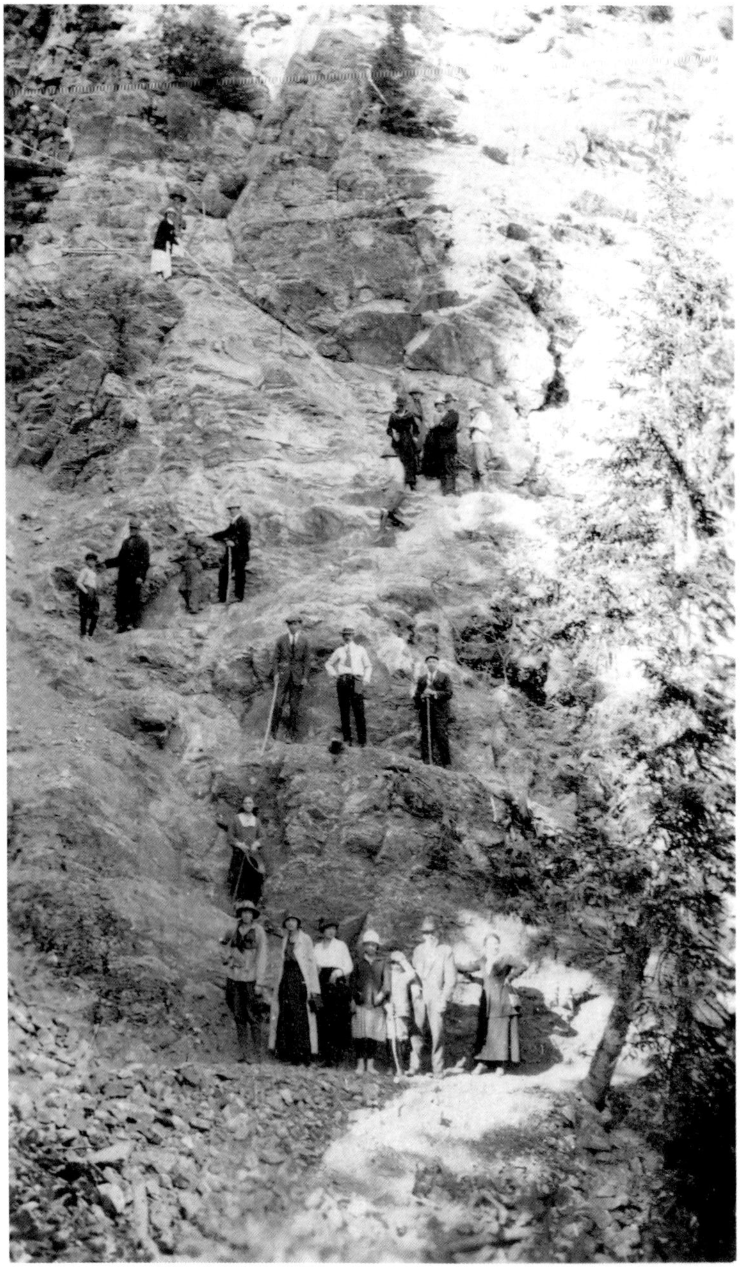

Only hearty souls braved the rickety railings, snaking cables, steep switchbacks, and cobbled system of ladders to descend roughly 500 feet on the Uncle Tom's Trail to the base of the Lower Falls of the Yellowstone, as shown in this photo taken between 1917 and 1920. In 1896, H.F. "Uncle Tom" Richardson created this trail along the south side of the canyon. For a dollar a person, he boated his guests across the Yellowstone River above the falls and guided them down the steep terrain—often providing pins for ladies to pin up their long dresses and skirts to make it easier to descend and climb back up the steep terrain.

CHAPTER 5

Activities Abound

Geysers, hot springs, wildlife—including begging bears—and natural beauty drew people to Yellowstone to witness these wonders for themselves. As visitation increased, so did guest activities. These photos give us a look some of the most popular experiences, whether they were natural wonders or manmade attractions.

Even after the appearance of automobiles, visitors still sought a "western" experience on horseback, and day rides became popular. Hiking grew in popularity because it required minimal gear and was suitable for nearly everyone. Fishing was an enormous draw for many guests who did not have the opportunity to catch the same species of fish, or in the same numbers, as was possible in Yellowstone, and Yellowstone Lake appealed to anglers, private boaters, and water-loving sightseers.

Surprisingly, there were swimming pools for guests in the early part of the century. Located at Mammoth Hot Springs and Old Faithful, these pools used hot water from nearby thermal features.

There was never a lack of ways to make a Yellowstone trip memorable. It is obvious from these photos that back then, as now, guests enjoyed adventures they would never forget.

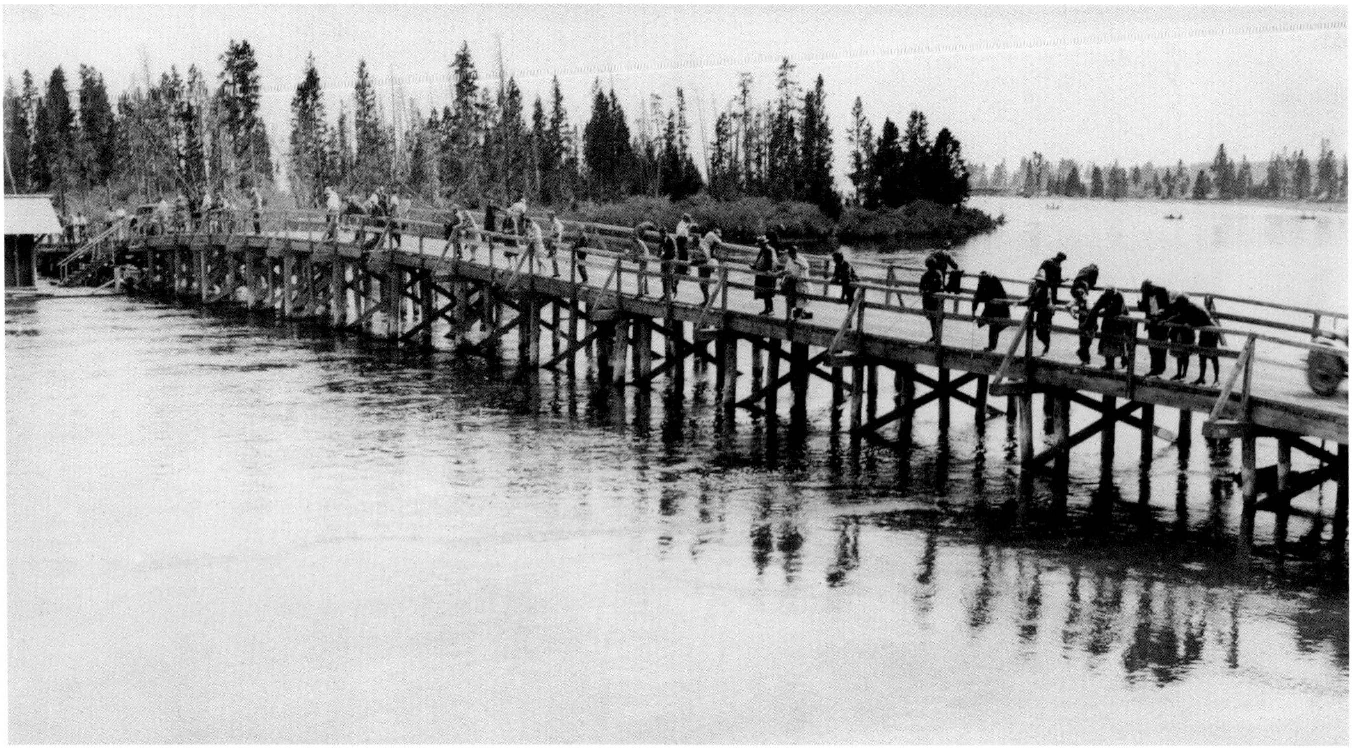

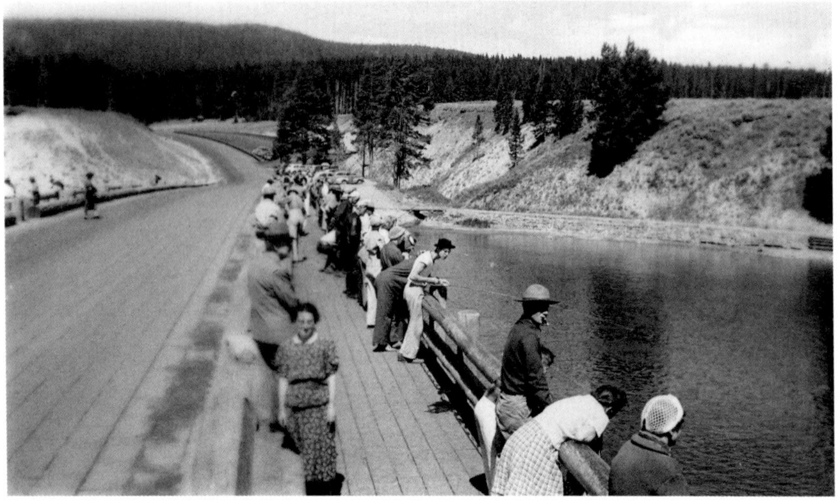

From these photos, it is obvious that Fishing Bridge was a popular attraction for park visitors. Located over the Yellowstone River at the outlet of Yellowstone Lake, the first bridge was designed by Captain Hiram Chittenden and finished by park engineers in 1902. It was officially dubbed "The Fishing Bridge" by 1914. After significant damage from ice and flooding, the National Park Service rebuilt the bridge in the design of the 1928 photo (top), which served enthusiastic anglers until 1937 when a wider bridge was constructed. The new bridge is shown in the bottom image, dated July 31, 1940. Standing shoulder to shoulder, guests sometimes hooked their neighboring anglers while trying to catch Yellowstone cutthroat trout.

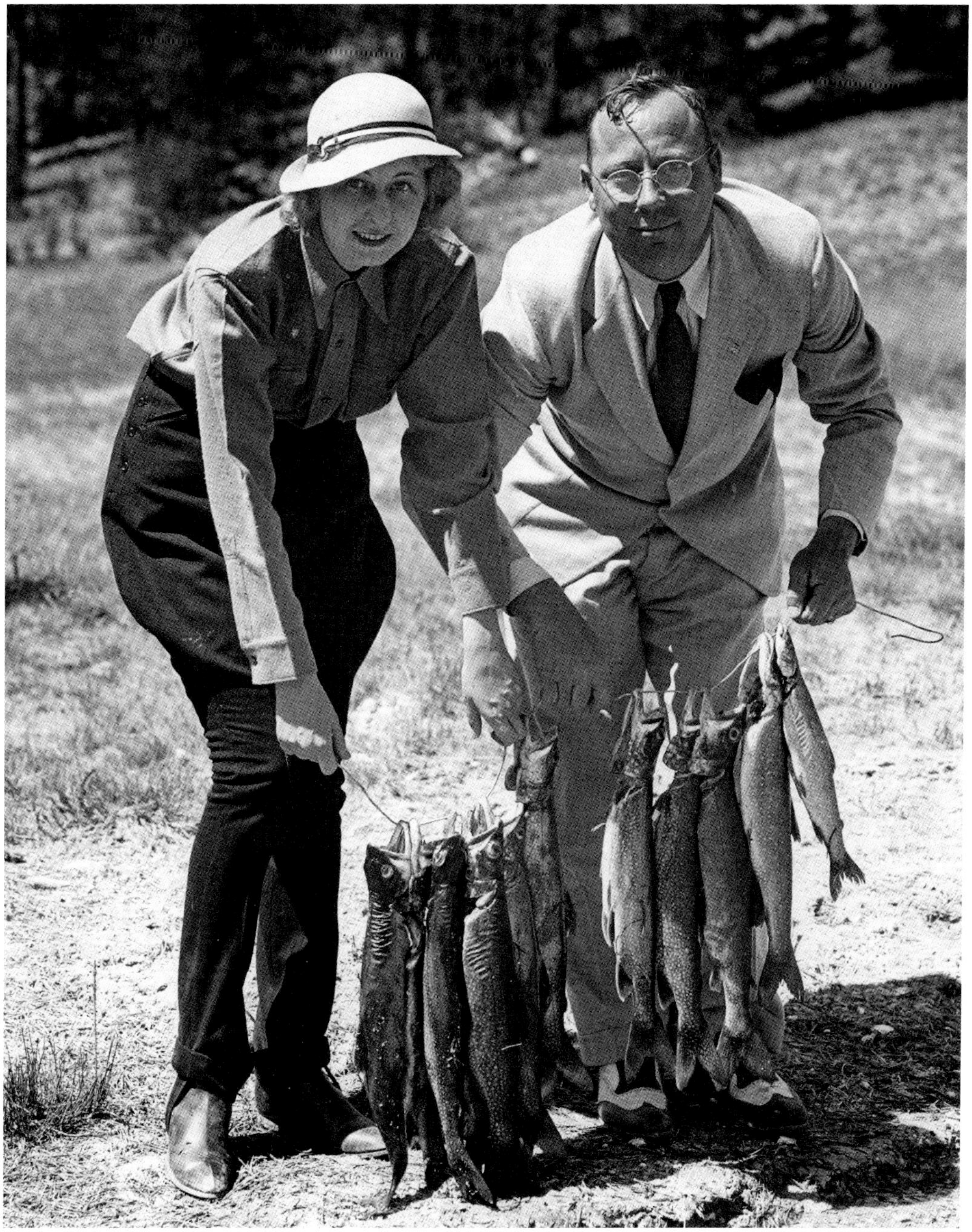

A well-dressed couple shows off their catch of lake trout at Shoshone Lake in this photo dated June 3, 1936. Non-native species, including lake trout, were transplanted into many Yellowstone lakes in the early 1900s. Unfortunately, officials at the time did not realize the harm that such introductions could have on native populations. For example, when lake trout were illegally introduced into Yellowstone Lake in the early 1990s, the voracious predators decimated native Yellowstone cutthroat trout. The collapse of the cutthroat population affected the entire lake ecosystem, from grizzly bears to ospreys.

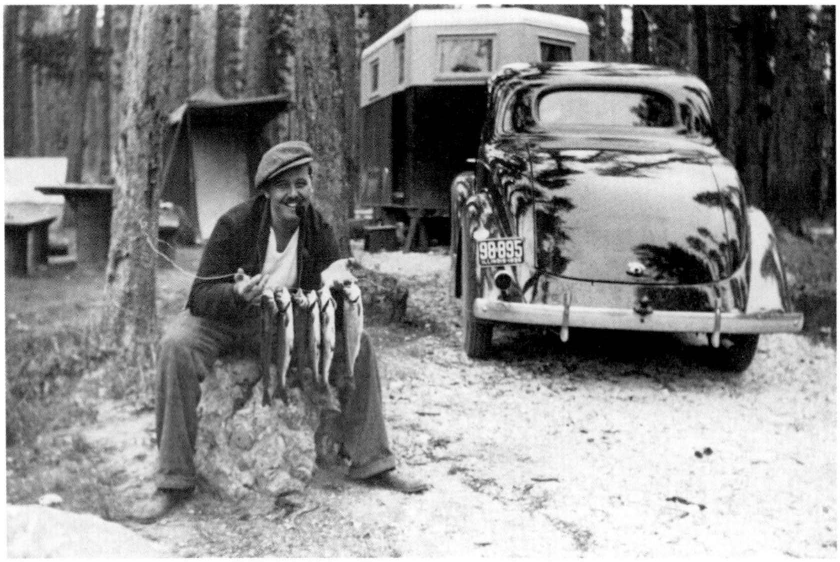

This smiling, pipe-smoking fisherman wearing a newsboy cap presents his stringer of Yellowstone cutthroat trout at one of the campgrounds in this 1936 photo. Notice the camping trailer parked in front of the car, which has a ball hitch on the bumper. In the 1930s, camping trailers, or travel trailers as they were also called, exploded in popularity despite, or possible due to, the economic woes of the Great Depression. Many families were forced to take up residence in these mobile, albeit tiny, homes. One of the most successful models was the "Covered Wagon" designed by George Sherman of Detroit, Michigan. In 1930, he debuted his model at the Detroit Auto Show, and the camping trailer industry was born. The "Covered Wagon" featured an ice box, stove, cupboards, and built-in furniture. The trailer in this photo appears to be a "Covered Wagon" model, although the precise year is unknown.

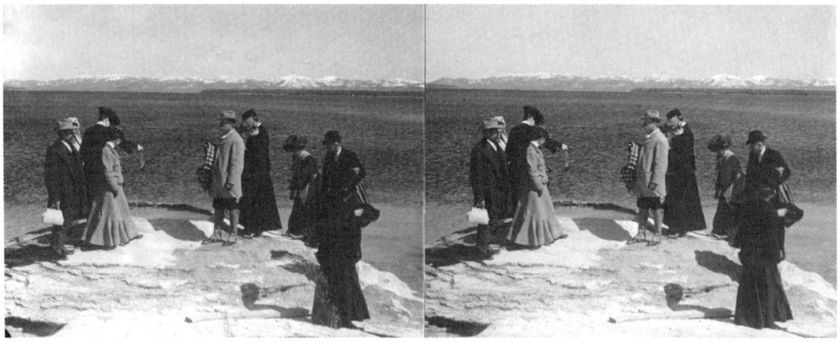

A circa-1900, black and white stereo view of Fishing Cone at West Thumb Geyser Basin shows park visitors ready to lower a fish into the thermal feature. Since the Washburn Expedition of 1870, the Fishing Cone has earned the fascination of visitors who, longing for the freshest dinner possible, submerged a freshly caught fish into the near-boiling waters without even removing it from the hook. In three to five minutes, the fish was cooked. This feat was so popular that Superintendent Philetus Norris routinely showed this unique feature to guests during his tenure, 1877-1882. Thankfully, this inhumane practice was prohibited in 1911, although people still reportedly cooked killed fish in the heated waters.

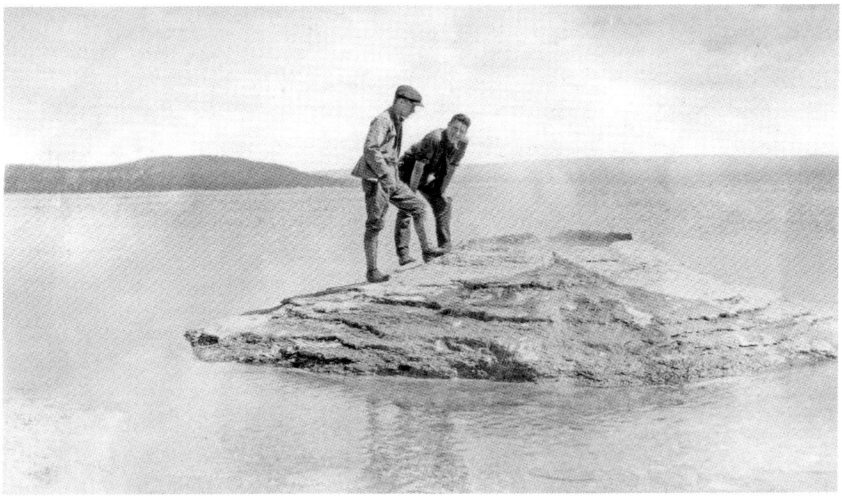

Two young men stand near the crater of the Fishing Cone hot spring in this photo taken in August 1921. It is difficult to see, but the path from the edge of the lake leading to the cone is at the right of the photo, although, due to the changes in the lake's level, the cone is today often cut off from land.

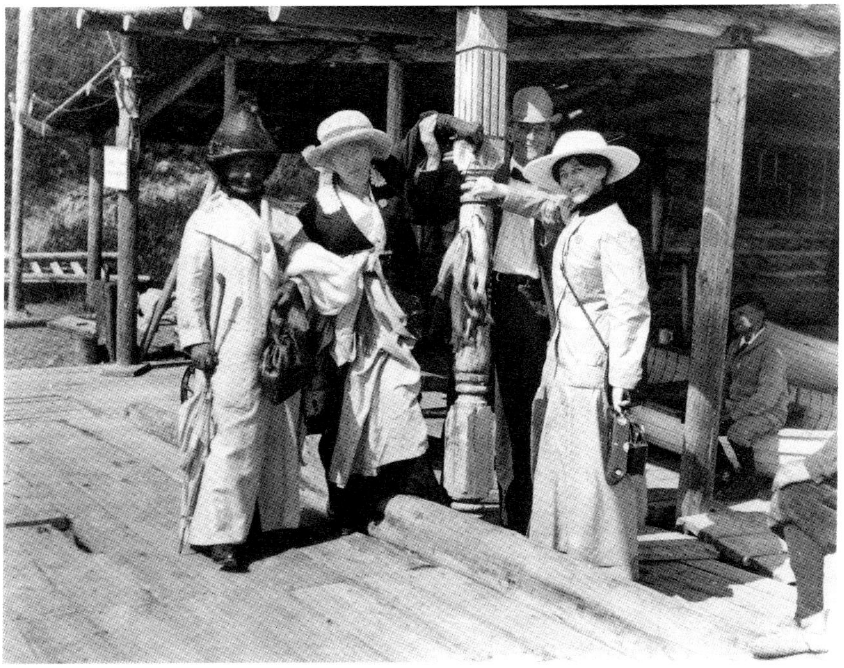

Although not wearing typical attire for fishing, these lucky park visitors pose with their freshly caught catch on the Yellowstone Park Boat Company dock at Lake in 1911. The smiling gentleman behind the post supports the arm of the woman wearing black so she can hold the fish high enough for the photo. The wide-brimmed hats worn by these ladies are typical of Edwardian fashion. It was also common for women to wear lightweight veils around their hats and over their faces when they spent time outdoors. The woman on the right holds a folding camera.

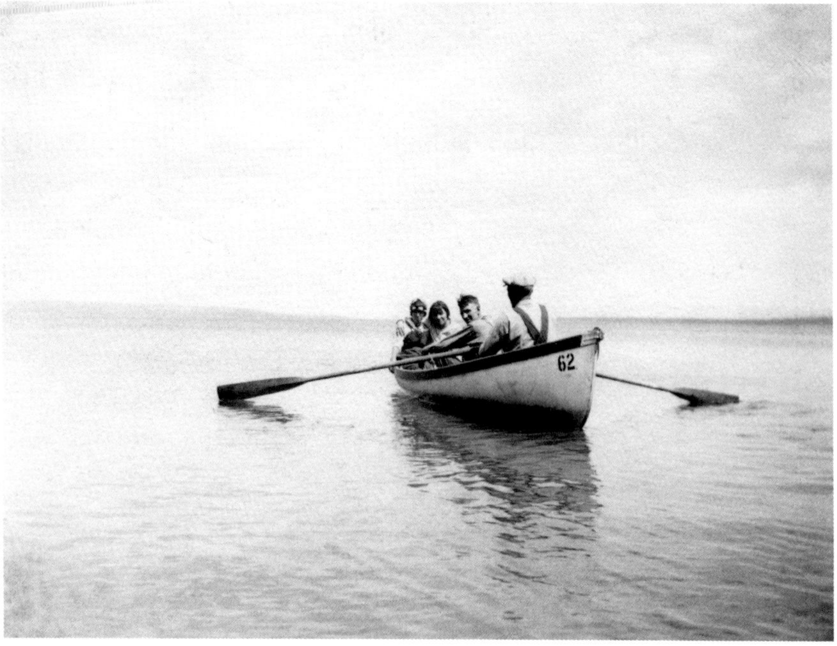

The man wearing suspenders provides the manpower to take three passengers, who are possibly all family members, for a boat ride on Yellowstone Lake in rental boat No. 62. Although steamboats gave passengers a unique view of the lake's lengthy shoreline, guests could also rent their own watercraft to explore on their own or to go fishing. Boat rentals were available as early as 1891.

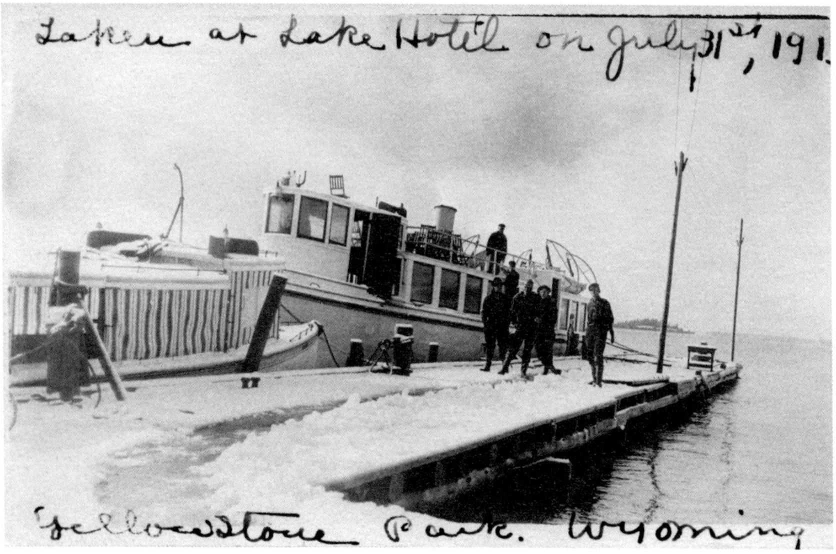

Summer snow covers the dock at Lake Hotel in this photo dated July 31, 1913. The gasoline-powered *Jean D* and a smaller boat are moored here, probably waiting for better weather. The *Jean D* is one of the smaller crafts that replaced the steamboat *Zillah* in 1909. This photo is a keen reminder that Yellowstone weather can change dramatically from hour to hour, regardless of the season, and especially on Yellowstone Lake, the largest high elevation lake (7,733 feet) in North America.

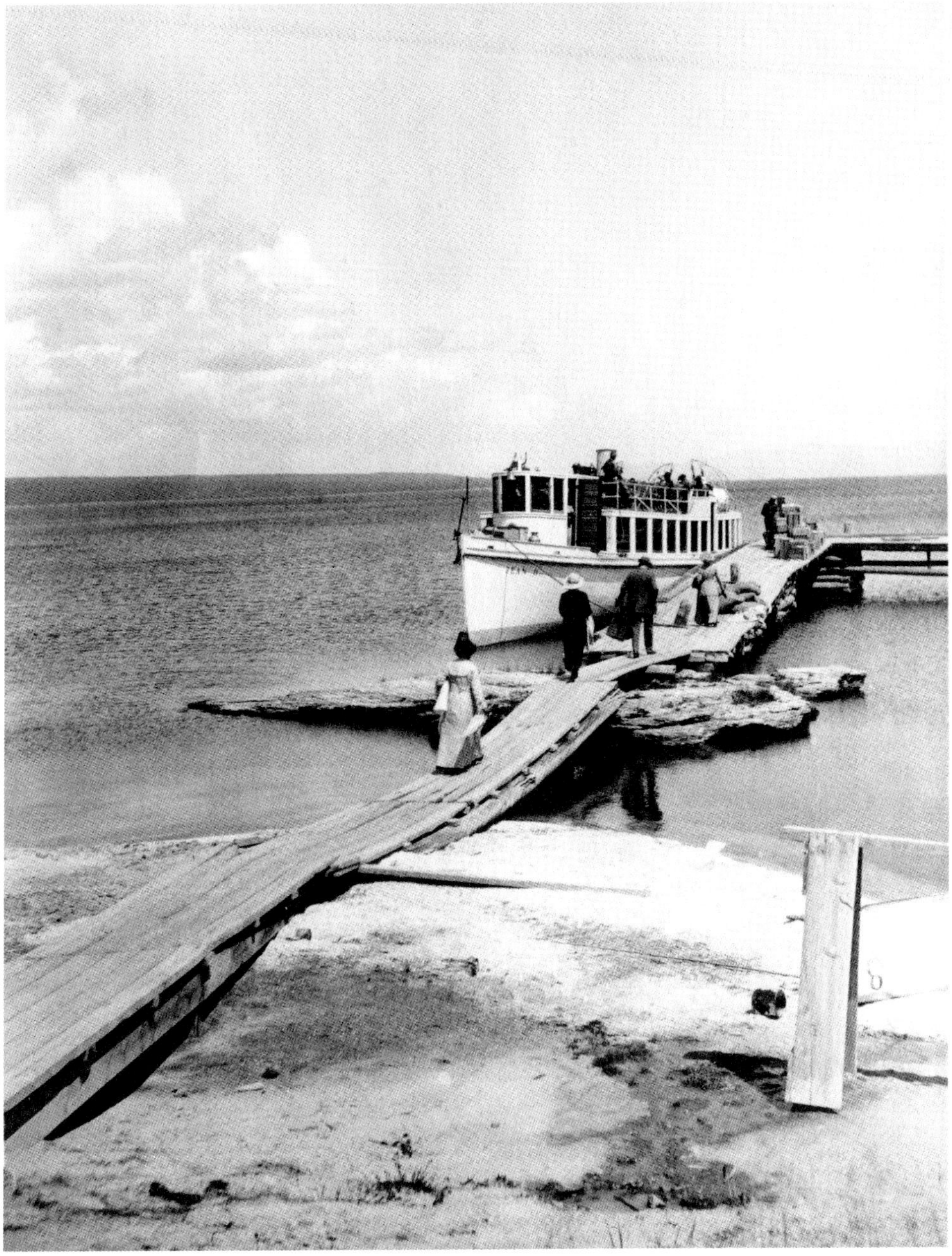

At West Thumb on Yellowstone Lake, visitors traverse the rickety-looking, sagging plank walkway to board the *Jean D* for a trip to the dock at Lake Hotel, circa-1911. After taking over the lake's boating contract when E. C. Waters was in banned from Yellowstone in 1907, Thomas Elwood "Billy" Hofer created the T. E. Hofer Boating Company. He replaced the *Zillah* with the 120-horsepower, gasoline engine *Jean D.* Beginning in 1909 or 1910, this smaller boat shuttled up to 150 passengers per trip back and forth from West Thumb to Lake Hotel for over a decade. Hofer did not last long in the boat business. By May 1911, the Yellowstone Park Boating Company had taken over the operation.

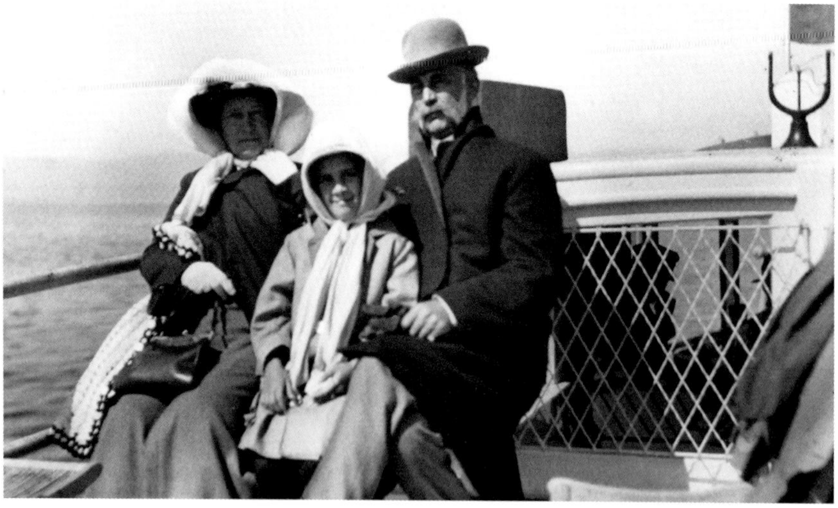

In this photo, a young girl's grandparents sit with her aboard the steamboat *Zillah* on Yellowstone Lake, circa-1900. The grandfather wears a classic bowler hat, popular since the mid-1800s, with a heavy, wool, button-up coat to brace against the cutting breezes. The grandmother and granddaughter use scarves to keep their hats firmly in place, and they are equally well-dressed for a scenic, yet most likely cold, tour of the lake. Brought to Yellowstone from Minnesota in 1889, the *Zillah*, named for the daughter of the president of the Northern Pacific Railroad, was a wildly popular attraction. Used primarily from 1891 to 1907, the *Zillah* disappeared except for a brief appearance in a photo in 1920. Its fate is unknown. *Photo by Chas Beseler Company.*

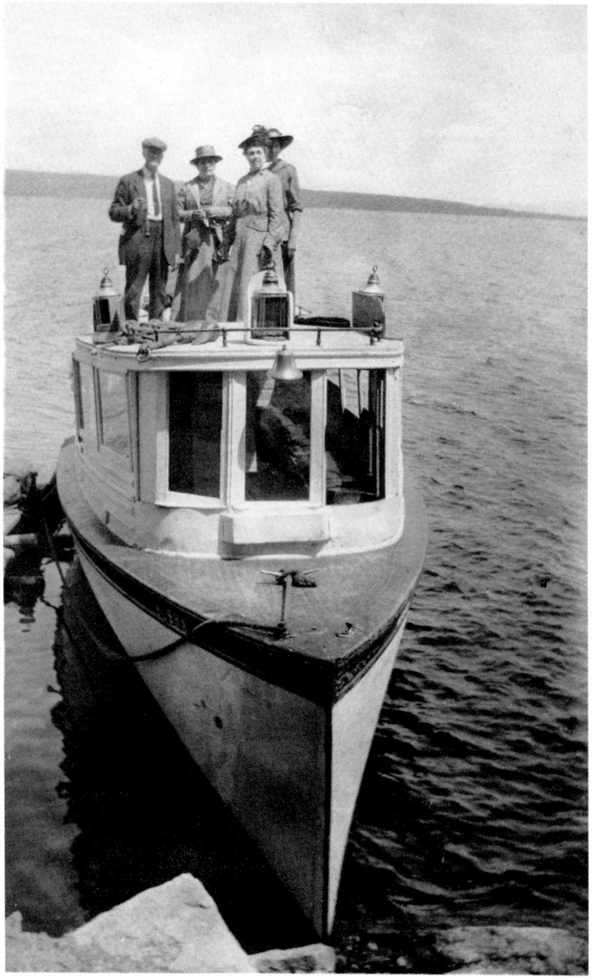

Three women and a man stand atop the *Busha*, docked at West Thumb on Yellowstone Lake in this 1916 photo. As guests of the Wylie Camping Company, they opted to boat across the lake instead of riding in the stagecoach. The *Busha* was one of the gasoline-fueled boats brought to Yellowstone Lake by the T.E. Hofer Boat Company, which operated from 1908-1911. The Yellowstone Park Boat Company acquired the Hofer company in 1911.

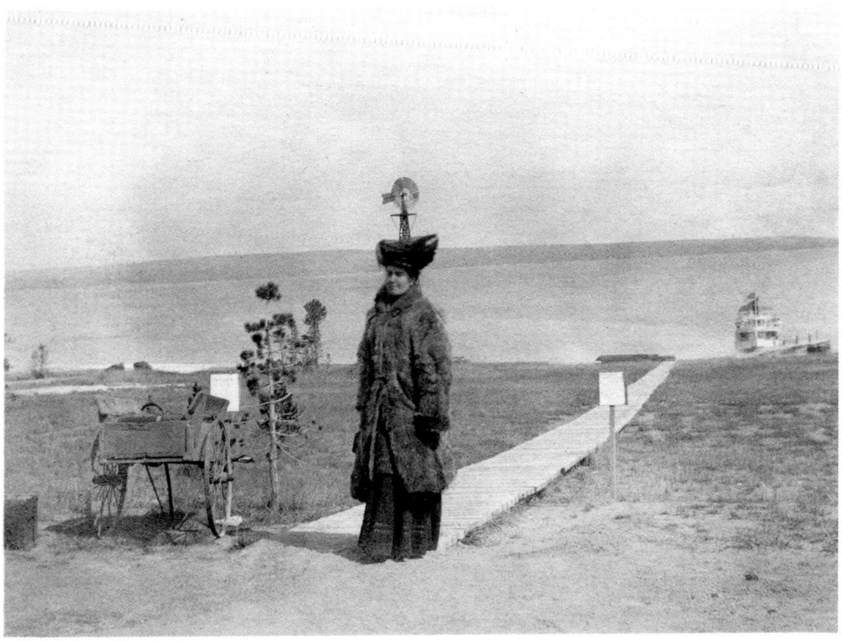

A woman warmly dressed in a three-quarters-length fur coat stands at the walkway to the West Thumb dock in 1904. A two-wheeled luggage cart is next to her. The steamboat *Zillah* is docked behind her. The windmill directly behind her, which looks like it is emerging from her hat, was used to pump water from Yellowstone Lake. Unfortunately, the signs on each side of the walkway are not legible.

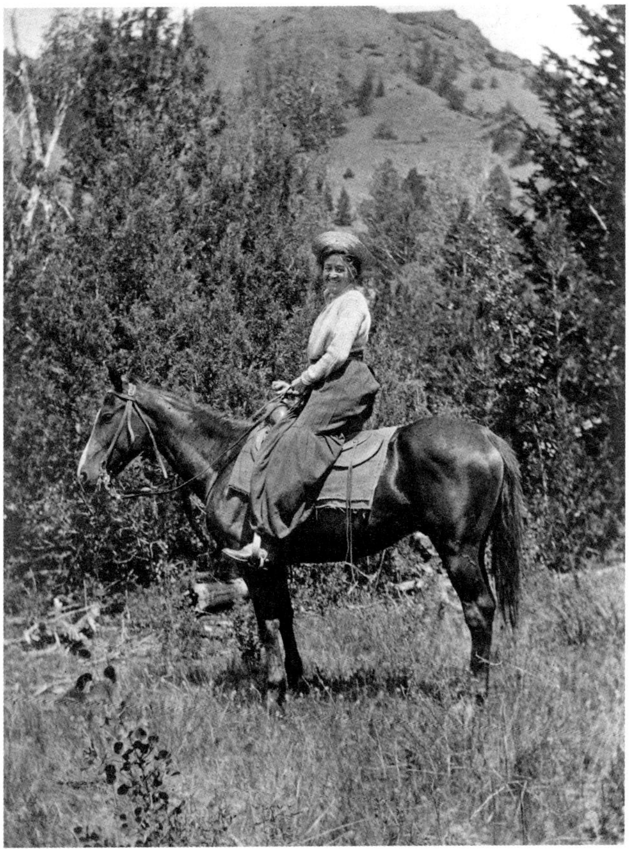

Obviously enjoying her time on horseback, a smiling visitor wears a turned-up straw hat as she rides astride, instead of side-saddle, in Yellowstone in 1906. Around the turn-of-the-century, riding side-saddle diminished in popularity, particularly in the American West where riding astride was far more practical—and safer—in rugged terrain. She is most likely wearing a type of split skirt to accommodate the riding style, along with short-heeled boots. The young lady wrote a friendly note on the photo: "Hello Emma—Do you recognize this? It is taken at Yellowstone National Park where I spent my vacation. E.G.D. The original of it."

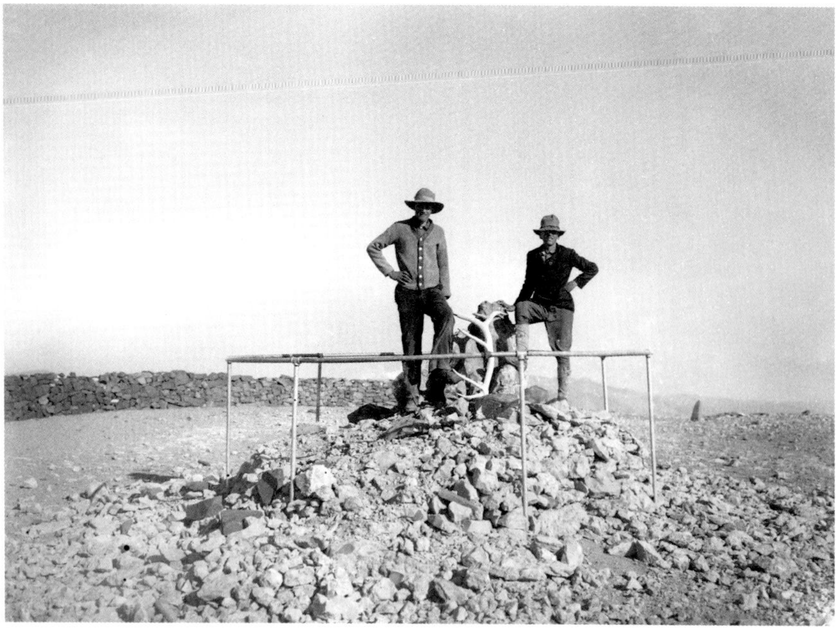

Park visitors pose on a pile of rocks adorned with an elk antler on the summit of Mount Washburn. This photo was most likely taken in 1918 or 1919 when the National Park Service identified the spot (indicated by the pipe fencing) as a strategic area for a fire lookout. Named for Henry Washburn, leader of the Washburn Expedition of 1870, the 10,243-feet-high mountain was popular before the completion of its beautiful stone building lookout in September of 1921. Mount Washburn was a side trip between Mammoth and Canyon; for an additional $2, a bus guide would drive visitors to the summit for a stunning view of the area.

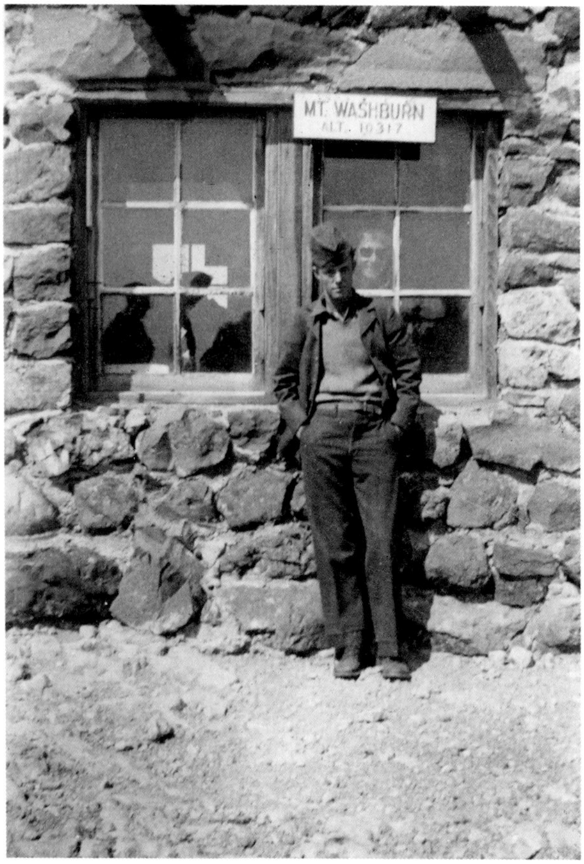

During their time off, Civilian Conservation Corps workers often explored the park. In this 1934 photo, two workers, one standing outside while the other inside wears sunglasses and peers through the window, pose at the Mount Washburn fire lookout. When the stone building began failing, the National Park Service razed it and built a concrete replacement in 1940. *Photo from Warren A. Brown of Pickerington, Ohio; Civilian Conservation Corps, Company 581 YNP 2.*

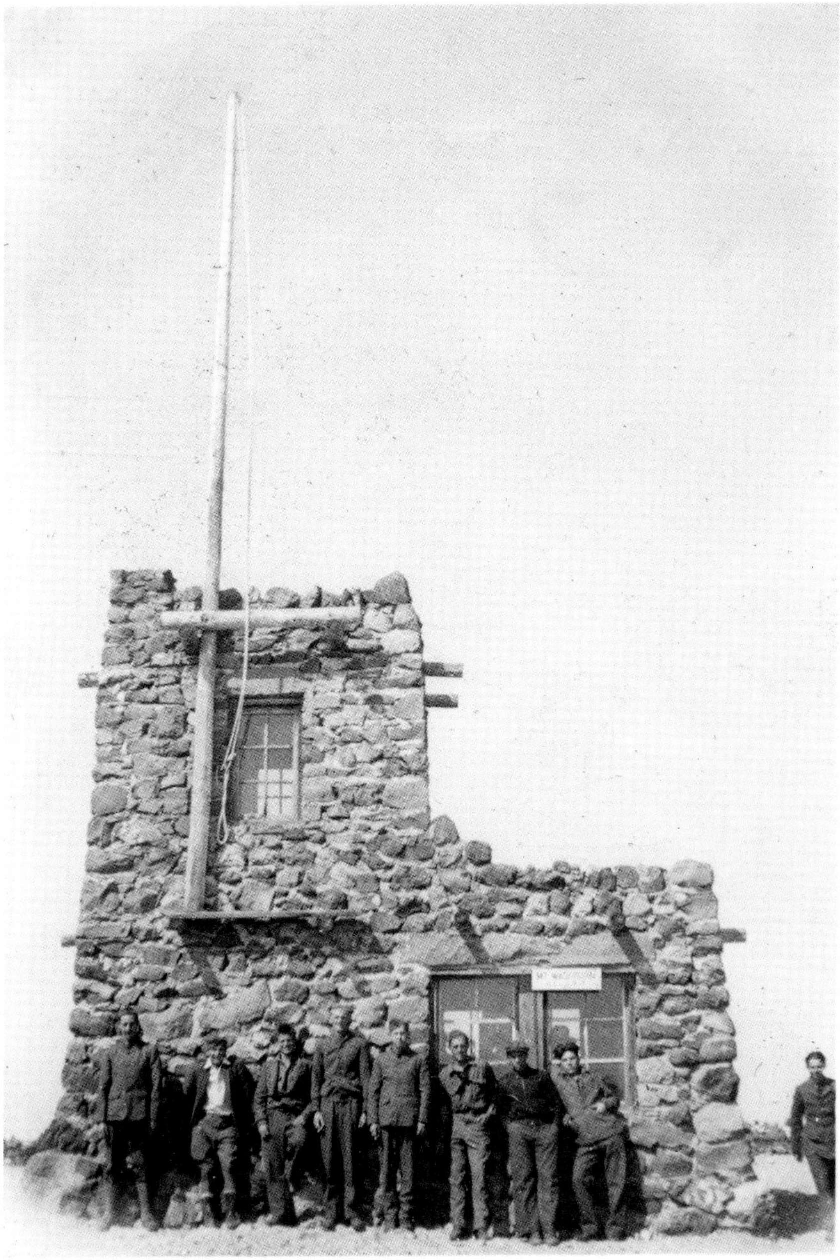

This group photo of Civilian Conservation Corps workers provides a full view of the stone fire-lookout on Mount Washburn in 1934. The structure was built in 1921 with concrete mixed by the workers of the Landscape Engineering Department of the National Park Service, who melted snow to mix it for the two-foot-thick stone and mason walls to erect the square structure with 16-foot-long sides, whose fire lookout was situated on the second floor. Most years from 1922 to 1940, a ranger stationed at the lookout served as interpreter and fire watcher, welcoming guests to see the park from a new perspective. Note the flagpole firmly attached to the side of the building. *Photo from Warren A. Brown of Pickerington, Ohio; Civilian Conservation Corps, Company 581 YNP 2.*

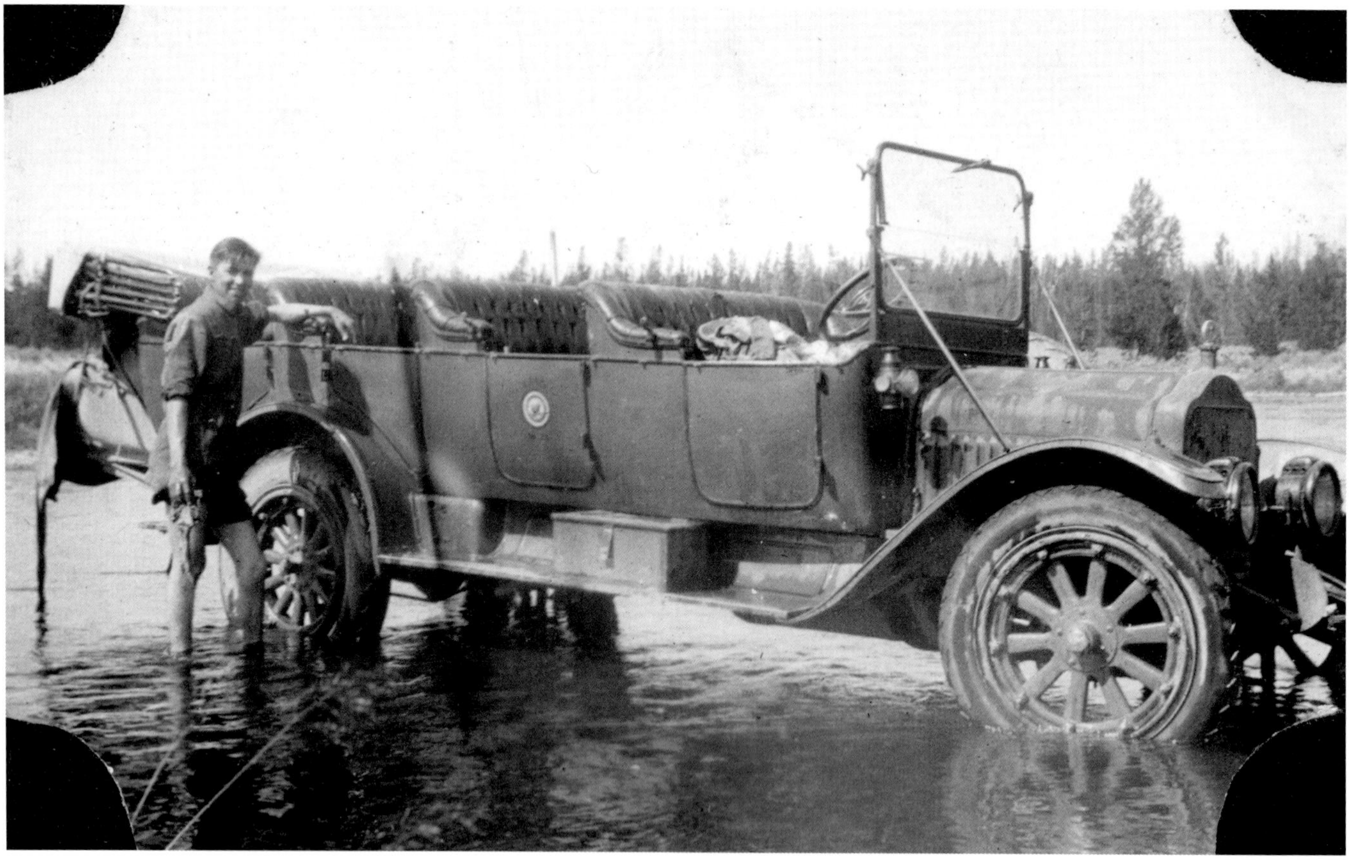

It took frequent washings to keep the fleet up to standards in both the stagecoach and the bus eras. In this 1924 photo, Yellowstone Park Transportation Company driver John Hawkins uses a shallow spot in a stream to spiff up the White Motor Company TEB bus #21. The 10-passenger TEBs were the first buses used in the park, beginning in 1917. They were later replaced with Model 15/45s, which featured a more powerful engine and a more comfortable chassis. One distinguishing characteristic between the two was the windshield. The TEB's windshield was divided horizontally, while the Model 15/45 was divided vertically. It is likely that this particular bus burned in the 1925 Mammoth Bus-Barn fire that destroyed much of the fleet. Courtesy of Bob Reynolds Collection.

CHAPTER 6

Hard Work and Lots of Play

Looking at these photos, one wonders if park employees had more fun than visitors because they seem to be smiling in every photograph. The summer was busy, and the work was hard, but employees had the whole season to make the most of a unique opportunity.

Many employees at the hotels and lodges took care of the behind-the-scenes tasks of cooking, cleaning, and stocking cabins with wood, but they also sang, acted in skits, and played music to entertain guests.

These images provide a glimpse of daily work and moments of relaxation. The camaraderie is obvious, and it is no wonder that lifelong friendships—and marriages—often developed during these memorable summers.

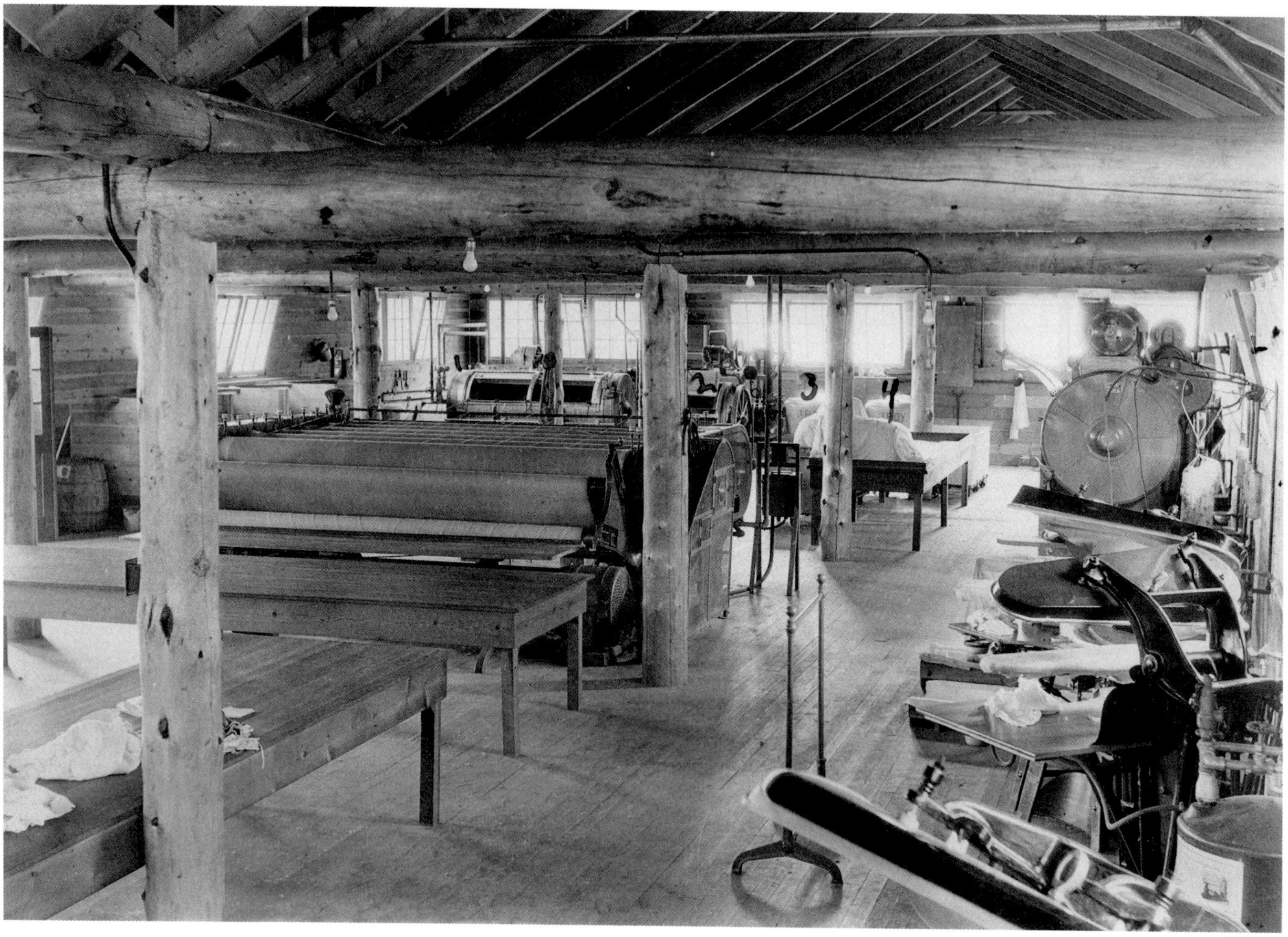

This photo shows the laundry facility at Lake Lodge in 1930. Towels and bedding were washed in the large cylindrical washers at the far end of the building. From there, they were moved to industrial extractors. Then workers fed the damp sheets, pillowcases, and hand towels through the rollers of the mangles or ironers to wring out as much water as possible. The bath towels went into commercial dryers. The smaller presses along the sides were used for employee uniforms and guest clothing. Considering there were 233 cabins at Lake Lodge by 1930, along with all the rooms at Lake Hotel, one can imagine the number of linens laundered every day in this facility.

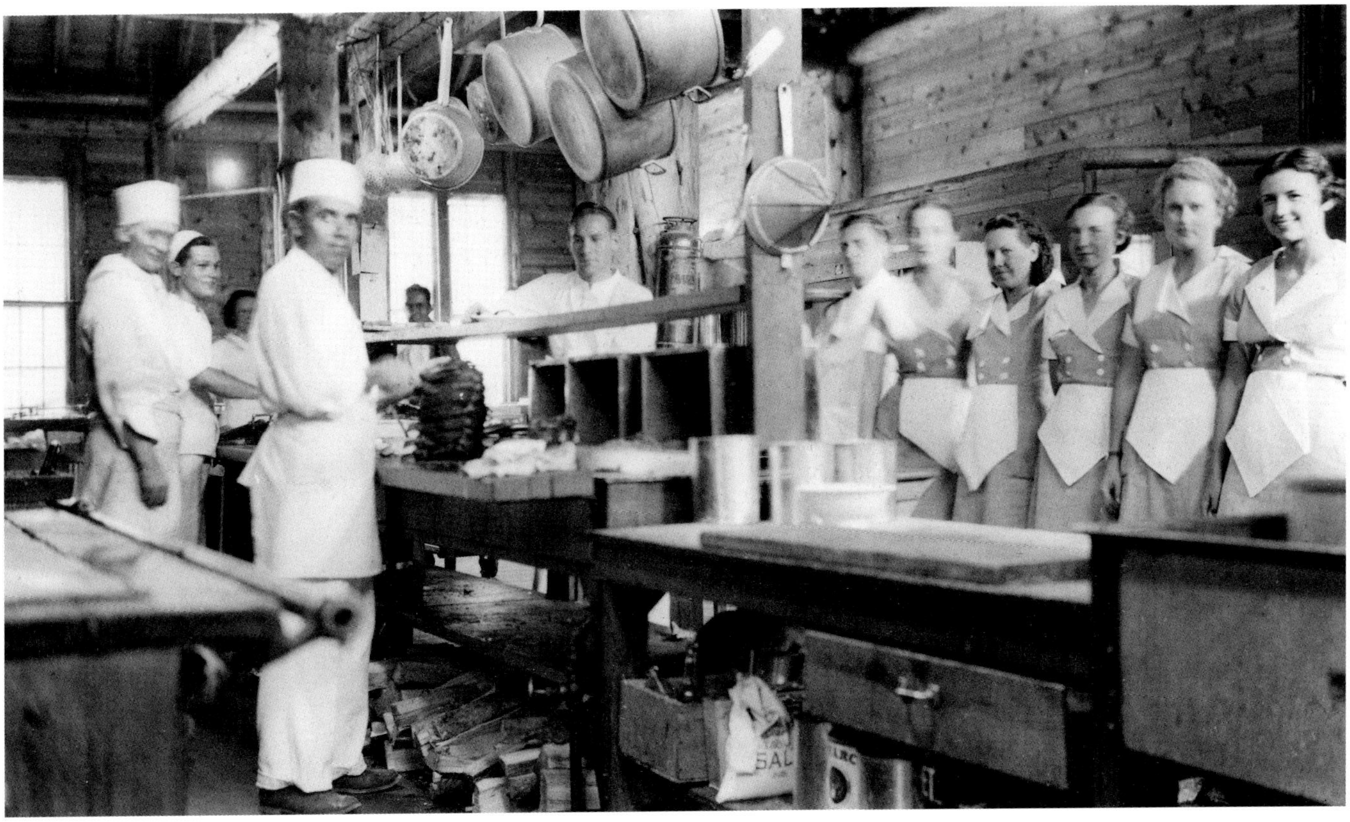

This 1936 photo taken in the kitchen at Lake Lodge shows the female wait-staff dressed in identical uniforms as they pose prior to their shift, along with the cooks and other members of the kitchen staff. With Lake Hotel closed for its fourth year in 1936 due to the financial devastation and subsequent, decreased visitation from the Great Depression, the more economical lodges, such as Lake Lodge, were in greater demand. The modestly priced cabins provided convenient and comfortable sleeping accommodations, while giving visitors the option of cooking their own meals or utilizing the dining facilities.

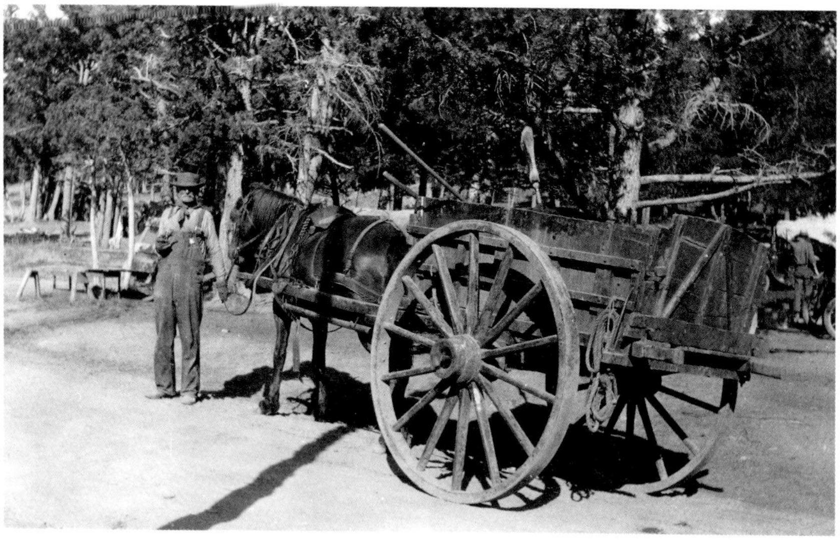

A weathered janitorial worker stands next to his work-cart at the Mammoth Auto Camp in 1921. A broom and other tools stick up from the cart. Established in 1916, the Mammoth Auto Camp was one of the first free campgrounds in the park. It was opened the year after the first automobiles were permitted into the park. Just as today, keeping campgrounds tidy was a non-stop task.

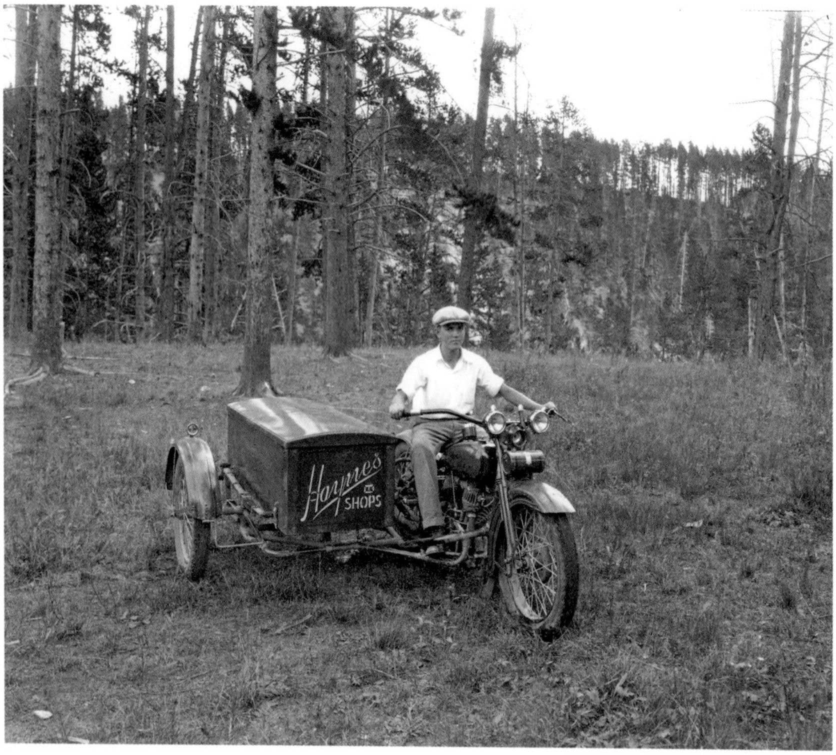

While it does not deliver the instant gratification of today's digital images, next-day film processing was a reality in Yellowstone as far back as 1929. To meet the needs of visitors, Jack Haynes purchased five, Harley Davidson JDH motorcycles with sidecars, and employed five young men to pick up film every day from his various Haynes's Photo Shops and take it to the processing lab at Old Faithful, then return it to the appropriate shop the next day. In this photo, employee Don DeVore of Billings, who worked at Montana Cycle and Supply where Haynes purchased the motorcycles, poses during one of his daily deliveries. When the unassembled bikes arrived at the shop, Haynes hired 18-year-old DeVore to assemble the bikes, train the other drivers, and shuttle film and photos for him for that summer.

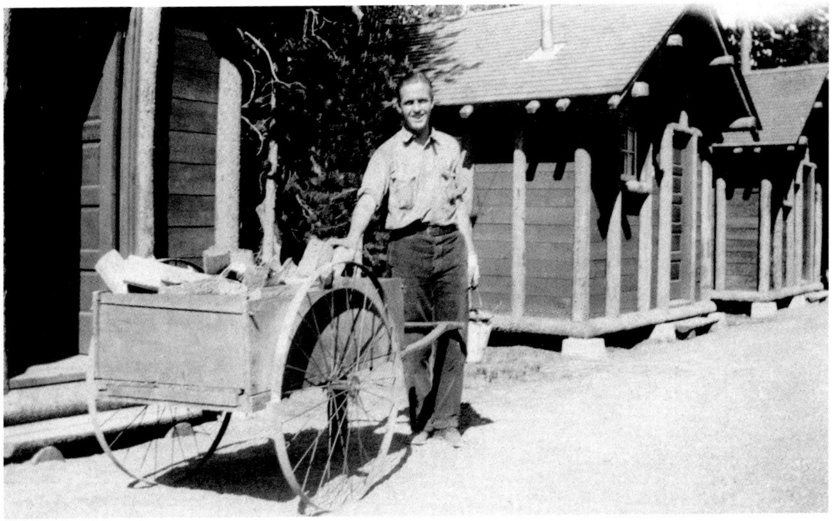

This male park employee uses a pushcart to deliver wood to the cabins at Old Faithful Lodge in 1925. The cabins had small, heater stoves. The employee appears to be holding a bucket, possibly to collect ashes from the stoves. Cabins at the lodges were popular because visitors traveling by automobile had a warm, weather-proof place to sleep. The small stoves in each cabin provided warmth on chilly evenings and a place to cook.

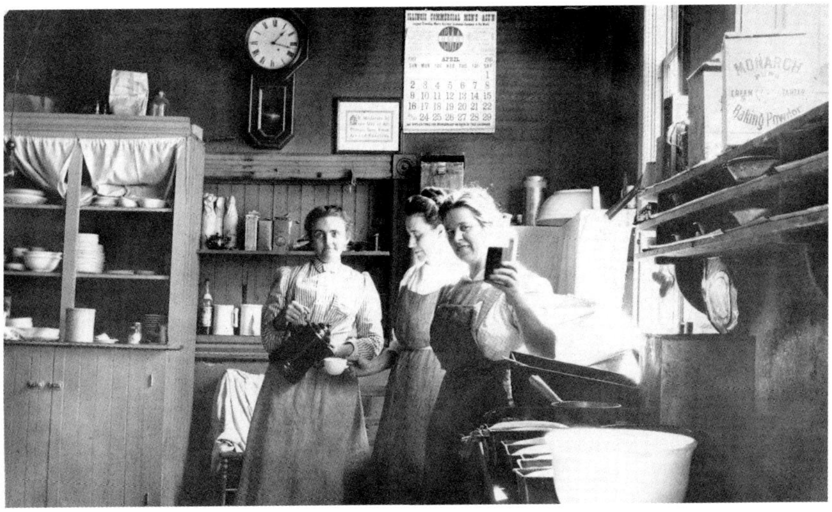

This photo dated May 9, 1911 (even though the calendar on the wall reads April) is a rare glimpse into what is thought to be the kitchen of the Mammoth Hot Springs Hotel. Judging by the time of 1:17 on the wall clock behind them—and the woman pouring a cup of coffee for her co-worker--these ladies could be enjoying a brief rest after serving lunch. The large box of Monarch Baking Powder on the upper shelf (right), along with what appear to be loaves of bread rising in pans behind the white bowl, indicates they baked breads and desserts between meals.

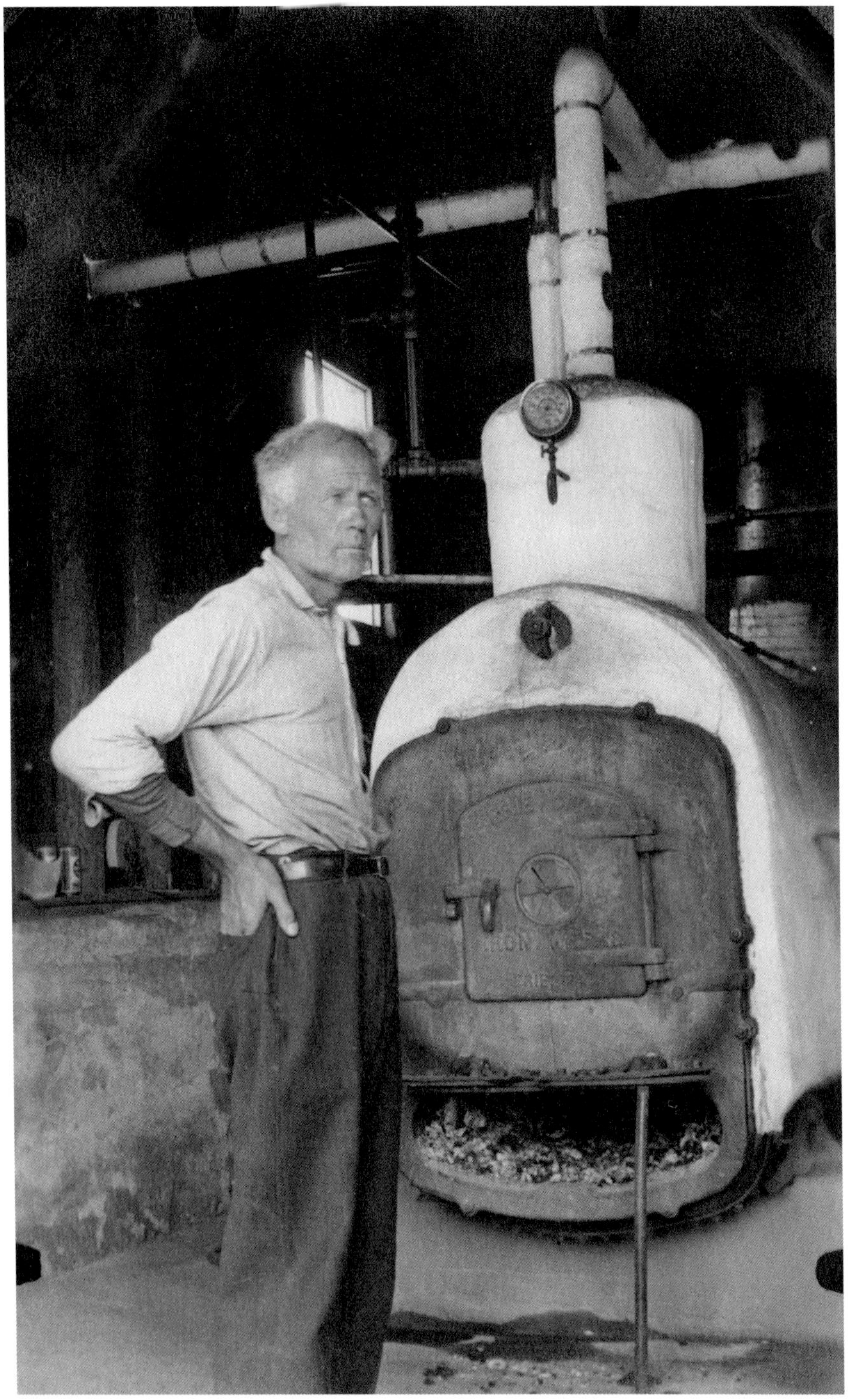

Many employees worked behind the scenes to keep the visitors' vacations running smoothly, although it is rare to find images of them in action. In this 1922 photo, Harry Hawks, the Mammoth Camp boiler-plant engineer, stands near one of the wood-fired boilers used to heat the lodge. This is from the park employee album of Matte Kincaid at Mammoth Hot Springs.

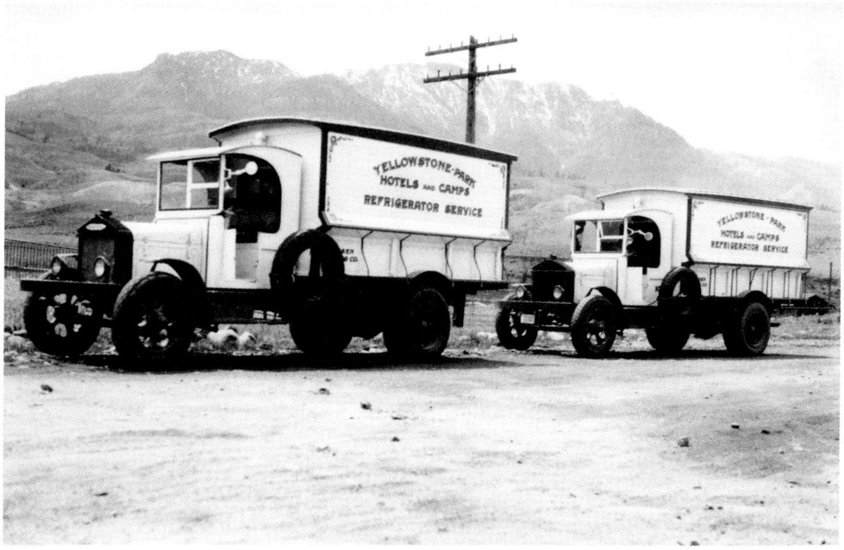

This is a rare photo (circa 1925 to 1927) of two Yellowstone Park Hotels and Camps Refrigerator Service trucks made by Pierce-Arrow. In 1911 the Pierce-Arrow Motor Car Company of Buffalo, New York, expanded from building what were reportedly the world's most luxurious automobiles to building heavy trucks, and these are most likely either the XA or XB five- to seven-ton models. Because mechanical air-conditioning for trucks was not invented until 1939, it is likely that these well-insulated trucks were cooled by large blocks of ice. The refrigeration service typically hauled fresh and possibly frozen or refrigerated foods to hotels and camp delicatessens throughout the park.

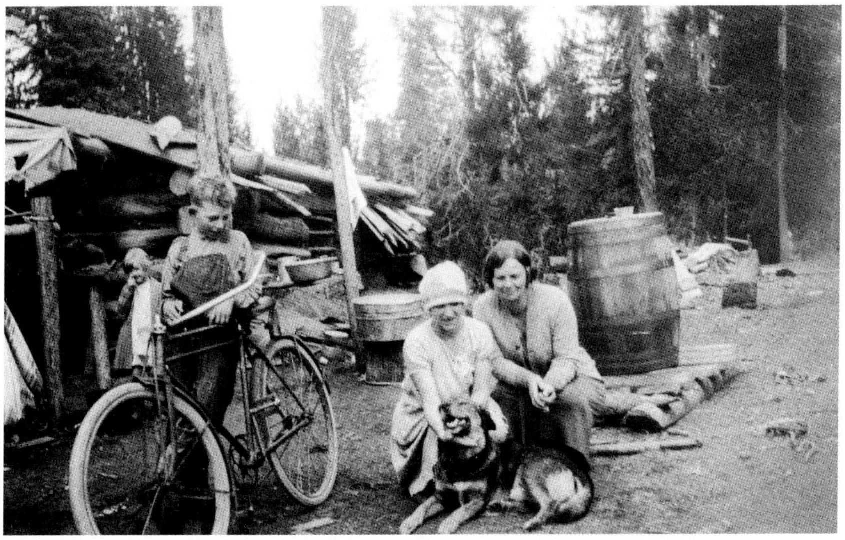

Providing wood for cabin heaters and wood-fired boilers in the hotels and lodges was a constant task requiring many hands. This 1927 photo shows a "wood camp" where logs were brought in to be cut and split. It also indicates that entire families, including children and pets, spent the summers at wood camps in the park. This mother with her children apparently stayed in the small cabin behind them. This photo was found in an Old Faithful Lodge employee's album.

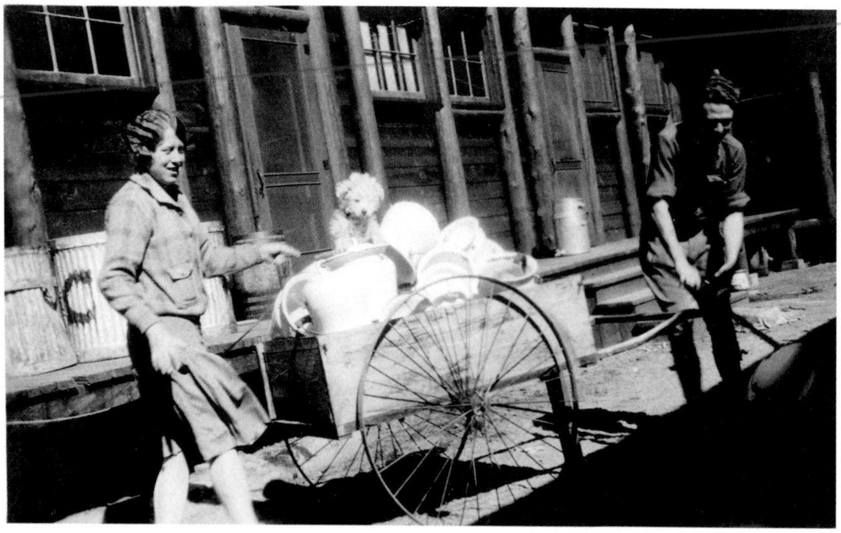

Working in housekeeping was far from glamorous, yet these employees at either Old Faithful Lodge or Old Faithful Camper Cabins are smiling for the camera. Their small dog rode on top of the pile of cleaned chamber pots as they returned them to the cabins. Because there was no indoor plumbing in the cabins when this photo was taken in 1927, staff collected the nighttime toilet facilities every morning, cleaned them, and returned them before evening. This photo is from an Old Faithful Lodge employee's album.

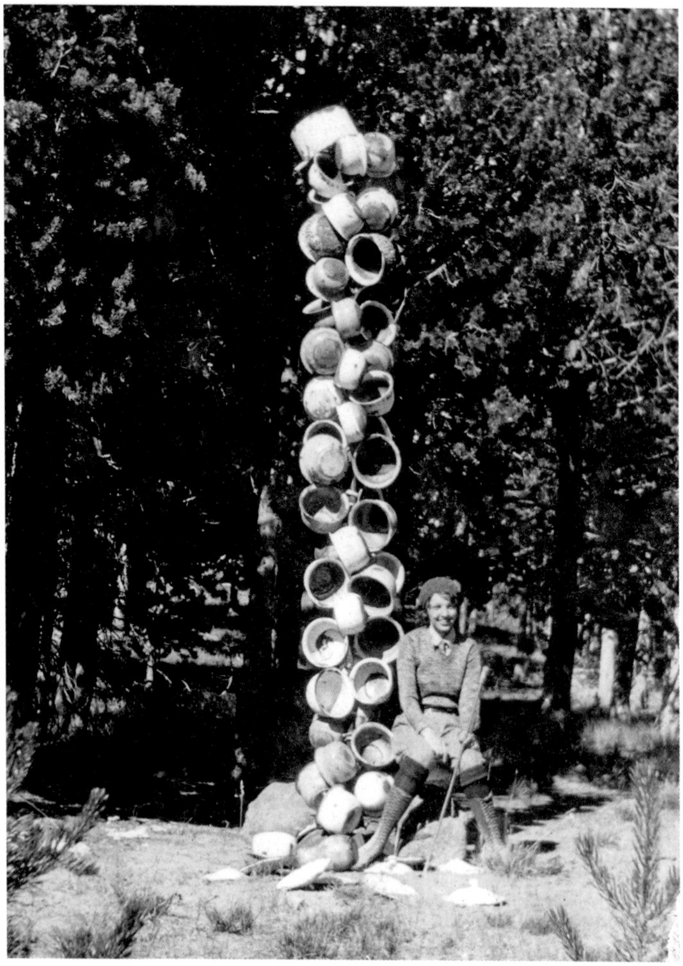

A smiling female employee sits beneath the "duck tree" at the Old Faithful Lodge in 1931. In employee parlance, chamber pots were "ducks," and the duck tree probably was a visual joke. Chamber pots were a necessity in the days before indoor plumbing, and employees made the unpleasant task of cleaning them a running joke. Sometimes chamber pots were illegally tossed off the edge of the Canyon Lodge abyss or pitched into the woods at Old Faithful. The tosser would then obtain a clean, replacement "duck" for the requisite cabin. This photo is from park employee Lois Davis's Old Faithful album.

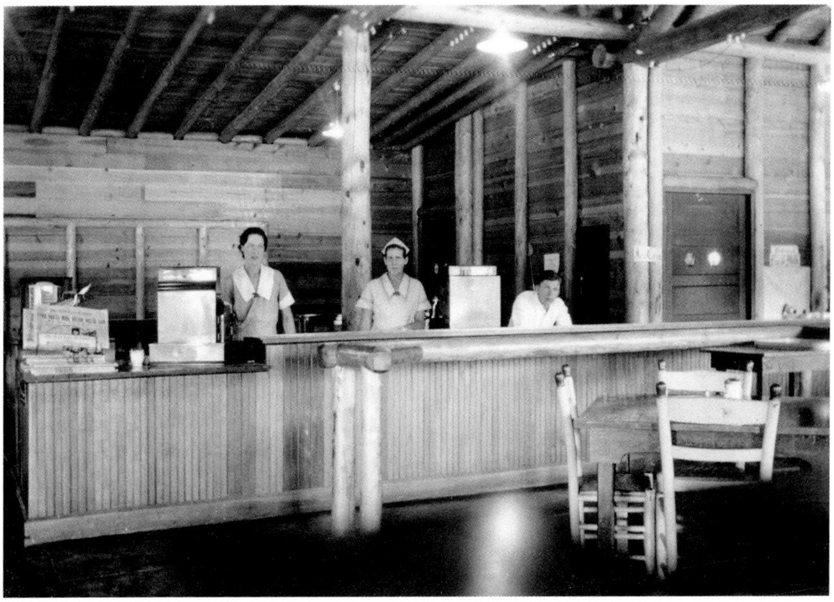

Two women and one male employee wait for hungry customers at most likely either the Old Faithful Lodge or Old Faithful Camper's Cabins cafeteria in this 1935 photo. During the Great Depression, the lodges fared better financially than the hotels (some of which were closed anyway) as travelers preferred the more economical cabins. Even so, being able to pick up quick meals at the cafeteria was a welcome change to camp fare for many visitors. This photo is from an Old Faithful employee album.

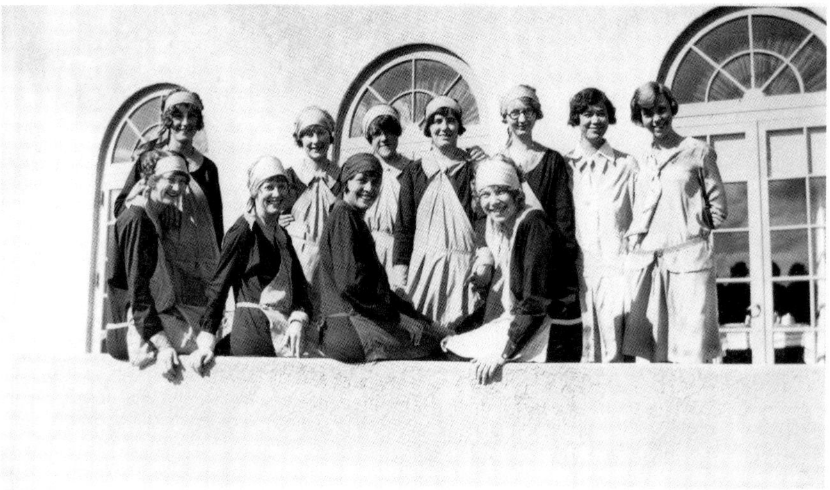

A group of the female staff poses on the balcony outside the dining room of the Gallatin Gateway Inn in the summer of 1927. The inn, approximately 76 miles north of West Yellowstone, was constructed from February to June 1927 by the Chicago, Milwaukee & St. Paul Railway. Designed in a Spanish Revival style, the grand structure was an impressive introduction to the area. It offered only 26 guest rooms, which were primarily used for visitors arriving from the northwest, but the inn was a popular transfer for other travelers. The dining room seated 186 people and served visitors arriving on the trains before they traveled to their next destination, along with dinner, breakfast, and lunch for overnight guests who took the *Olympian* streamliner, which arrived in the evening. The railroad spent a half-million dollars to build the inn and another $100,000 to upgrade the tracks from Three Forks, Montana, to the small town of Gallatin Gateway, which was originally named Salesville.

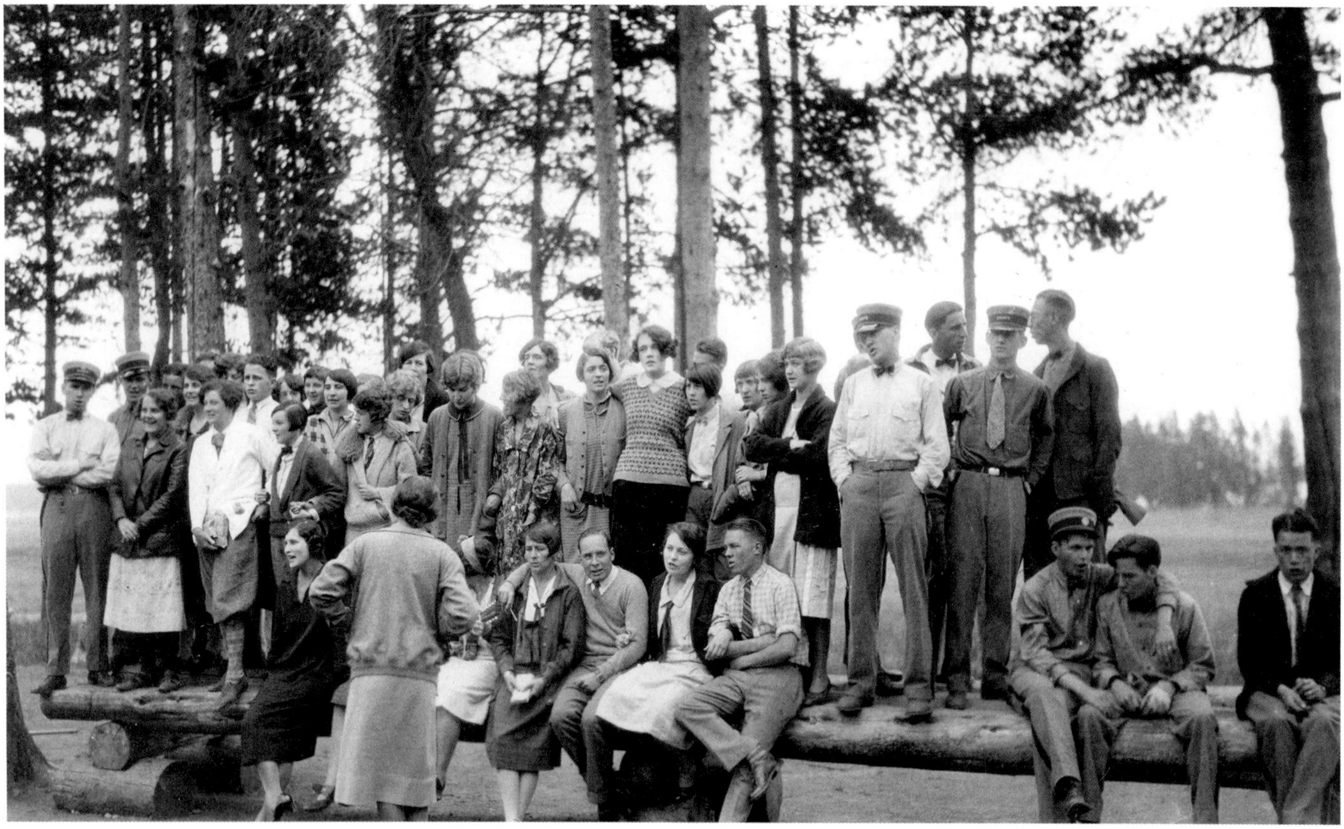

In this 1926 image, a large group of employees gathers at Lake Camp to sing a welcome, or a goodbye, to their guests. Notice that many of the young men wear the same hats. Located northeast of Lake Hotel in what was formerly one of the Wylie Camps and designed by Robert Reamer, the main Lake Camp (later Lake Lodge) building was erected by the Yellowstone Park Camping Company (YPCC) in 1918, but it did not open until 1920, under the new leadership of Howard Hays. Wings were added to the structure in 1926, including the recreation hall where employees regularly put on performances to entertain the guests. *Compliments of Jay C. Lyndes Family Collection.*

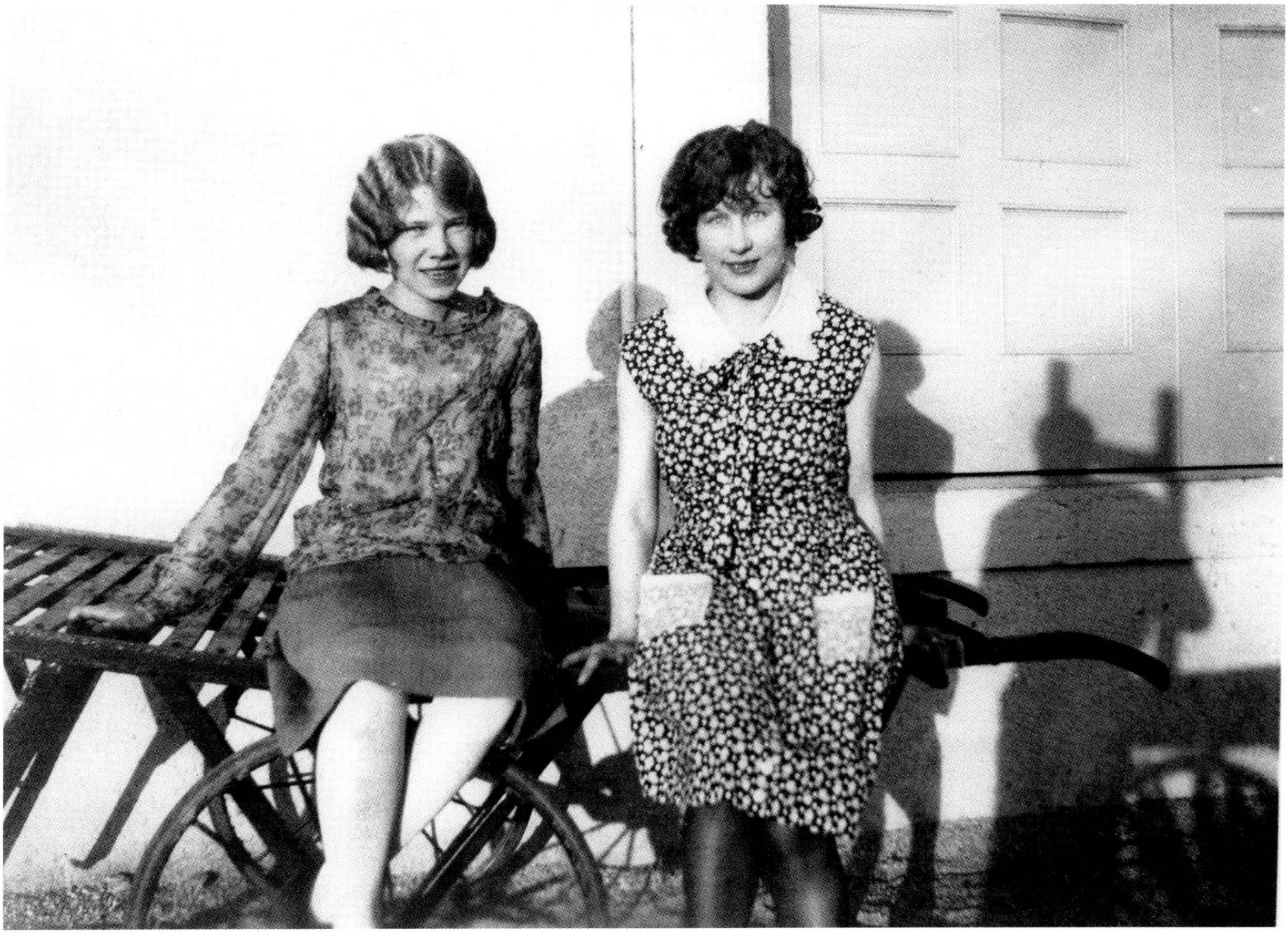

These bright-eyed female employees of the Gallatin Gateway Inn sit upon a luggage cart in this 1927 photo, the same year that the grand facility opened. Serving as a luxurious hub for Yellowstone guests traveling via the Chicago, Milwaukee, & St. Paul Railway, like the facilities within the park itself, the restaurant and hotel employed many young people, many of whom experienced their first taste of independence.

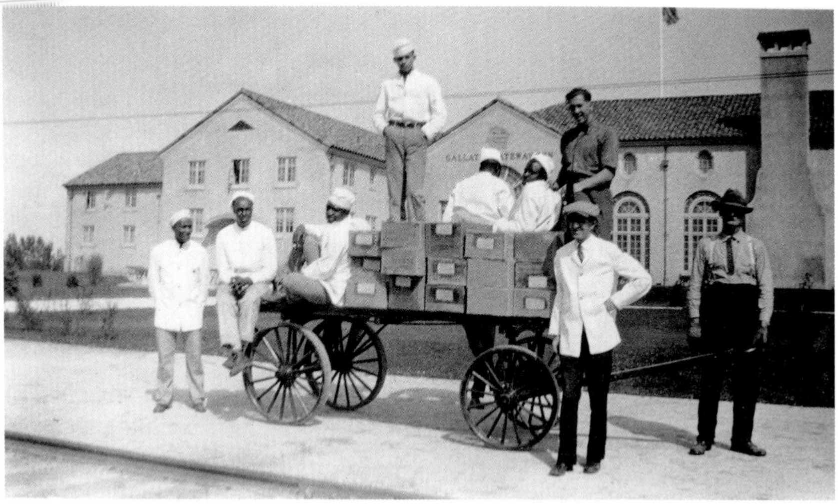

This photo taken in 1927 shows a group of the Gallatin Gateway Inn kitchen staff, including six African American men, posing on a wagon full of supplies. The inn was intended as a jumping-off point for Yellowstone visitors who took the Chicago, Milwaukee & St. Paul Railway to the park. After disembarking at Three Forks, Montana, they took an electric train roughly 30 miles to Gallatin Gateway to enjoy lunch before riding a bus another several hours through Gallatin Canyon to the west entrance of the park. While the intention to create a luxurious hub northwest of the park seemed viable at first, the railroad, and subsequently, the Gallatin Gateway Inn, struggled for many years. It was never expanded as originally planned, and it changed hands multiple times through the decades. The inn was listed on the National Register of Historical Places in 1980, but it was closed to the public in 2013.

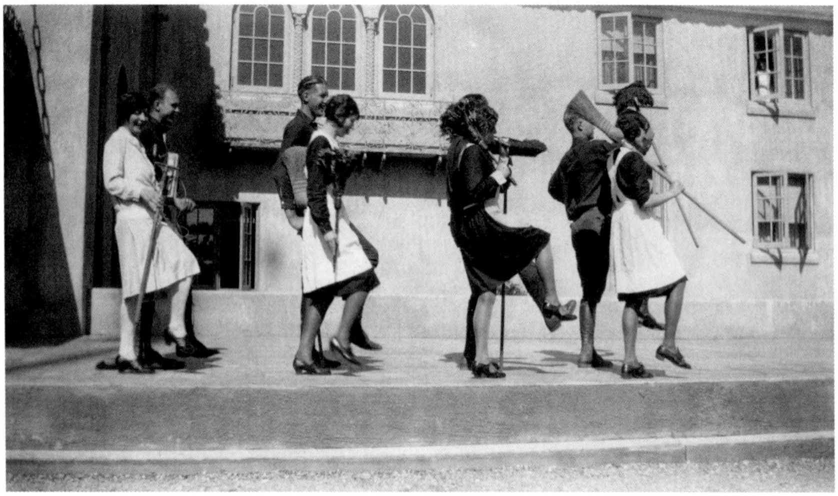

In many of the Gallatin Gateway Inn photos, including this one taken in 1927, the employees obviously delight in their duties, particularly when it comes to entertaining guests. This image from the Louise Crain employee album shows a laughing troop of eight employees, including three women who are apparently members of the housekeeping staff, marching with brooms and feather dusters.

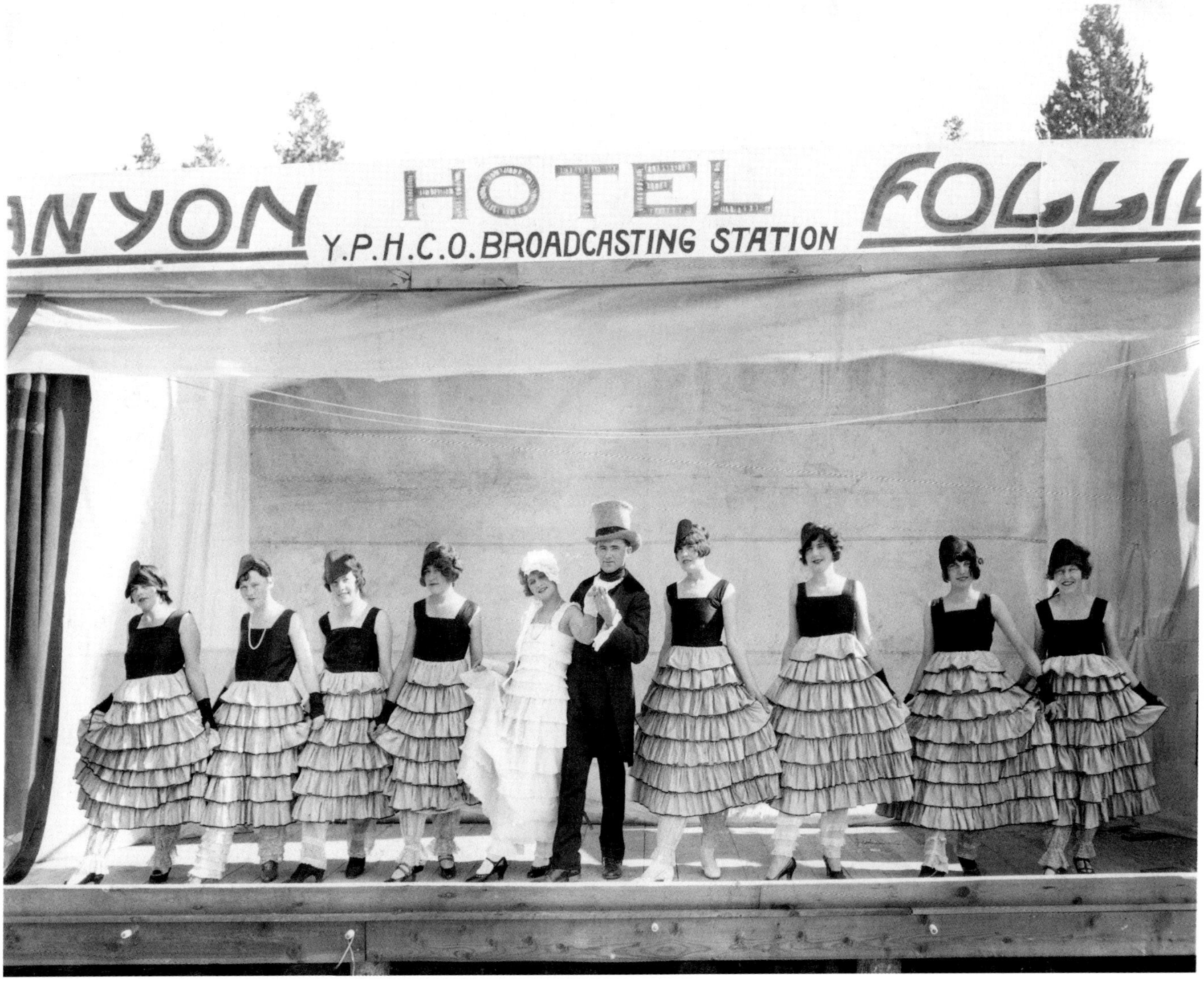

Everything about the Canyon Hotel was top notch, including entertainment provided by its talented and enthusiastic employees. In this 1926 photo of the Canyon Hotel Follies, sponsored by "Y.P.H.C.O. Broadcasting Station" (Yellowstone Park Hotel Company), employees delighted guests with elaborate skits and handmade costumes for their singing and dancing routines. In this performance, it appears the couple in the center played a husband and wife, flanked with a full line of bridesmaids on either side. It makes one wonder what hilarity and drama surrounded the "wedding" in this play.

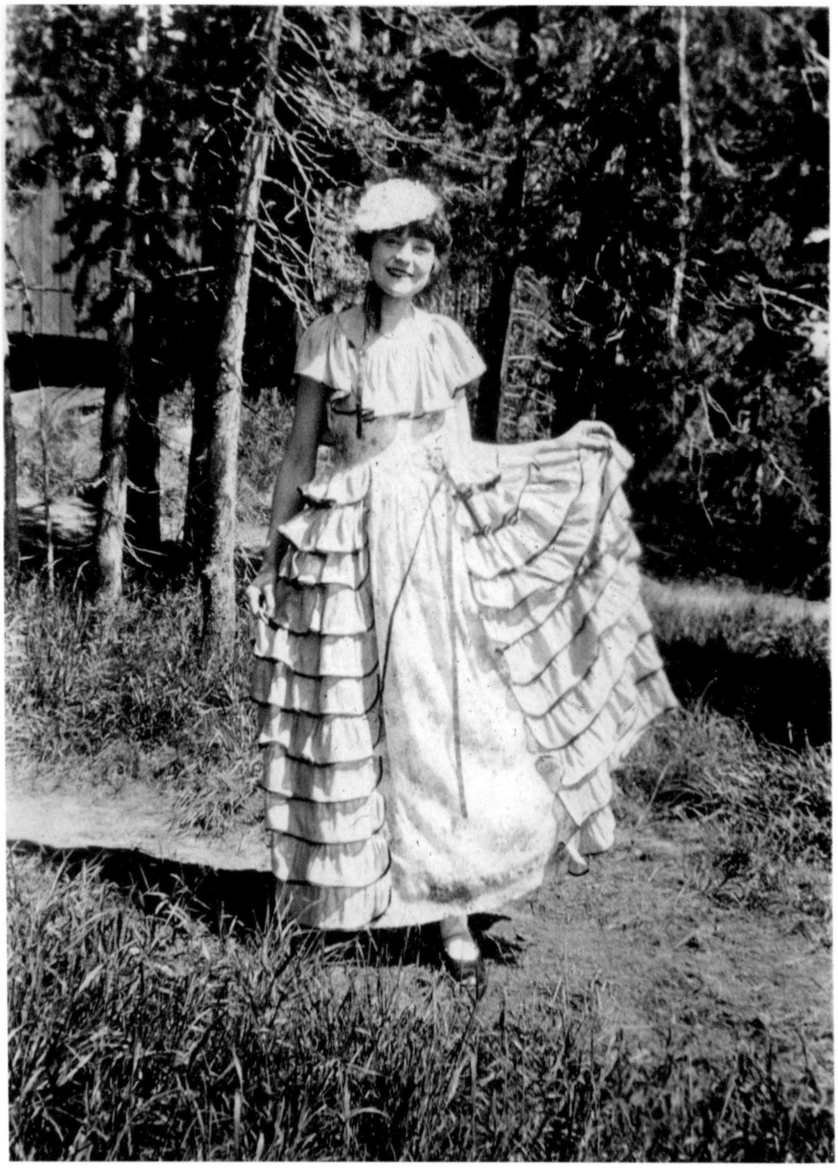

A smiling female concessioner employee shows off her costume for the nightly skits at Camp Roosevelt in 1927. Besides serving meals, handling the laundry, or cleaning cabins, possessing "show-biz" talent and being willing to participate in song and dance routines for the guests were considered relevant parts of employment. Each evening the summer "savages," as they were affectionately called, performed shows and skits at both at the luxurious hotels and the more rustic lodges.

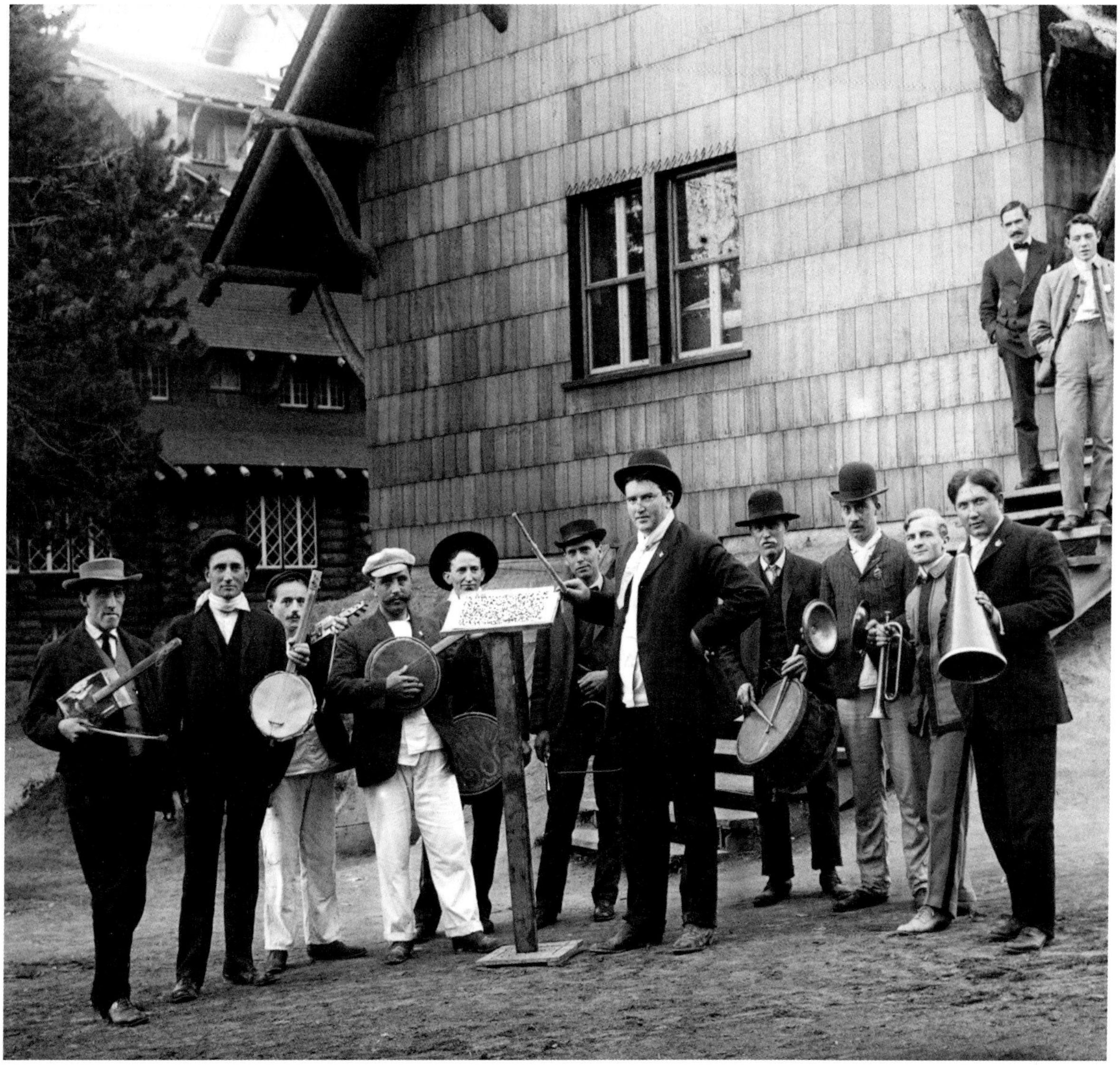

Music was an important part of the Yellowstone experience for employees and guests. Even in the earliest days, string musicians seated in the balcony of the Old Faithful Inn filled the interior with music. In this circa-1920s photo, the Old Faithful Inn's kitchen employee orchestra displays a unique array of instruments. The gentleman on the far left and the third man from the left both hold single-string, cigar-box fiddles, which were simple, homemade instruments popular since the mid-1800s. The second and fourth men from the left (the latter sporting an impressive handlebar mustache) played four-string banjos. Other instruments include simple drums, what appears to be a homemade triangle, cymbals made of pot lids, and a bugle. The man on the right is an apparent crooner who holds a megaphone, which was "all the rage" during the jazz-age of the 1920s and 1930s. The conductor wields an uncommonly thick baton; perhaps it is just a tree branch. No matter, this ensemble undoubtedly enjoyed playing in this vaudevillian style for fellow employees—along with any guests lured by their merry sound. *Photo by E. B. Thompson.*

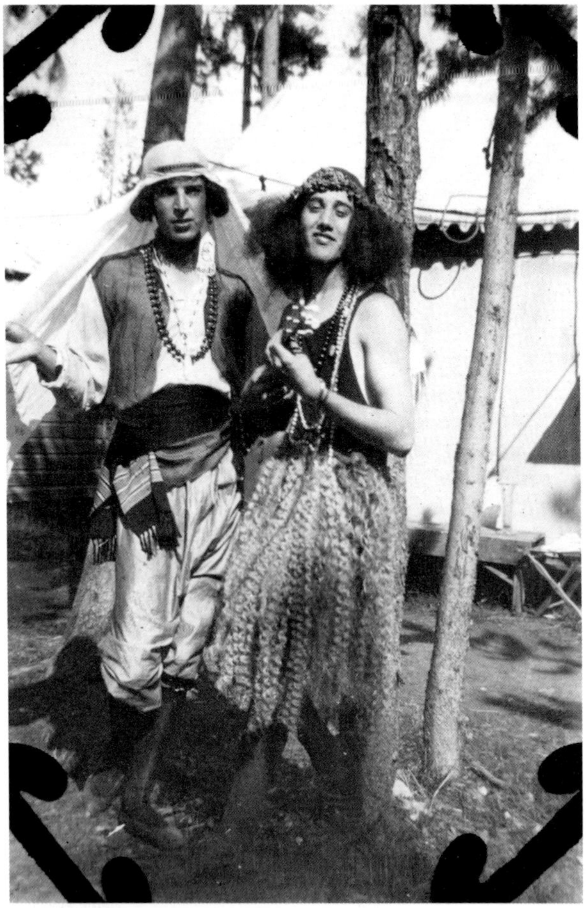

Even before screen star Rudolph Valentino thrilled movie-goers in the 1921 silent movie *The Sheik*, Middle Eastern dress had caught the attention of a young and curious generation. In this circa-1920s photo from Old Faithful Camp guide Elton E. Singletary's photo album, the young man looks the part of the iconic movie star while his female counterpart (or female-impersonating counterpart) is equally exotic in her frayed-cord skirt with bare arms.

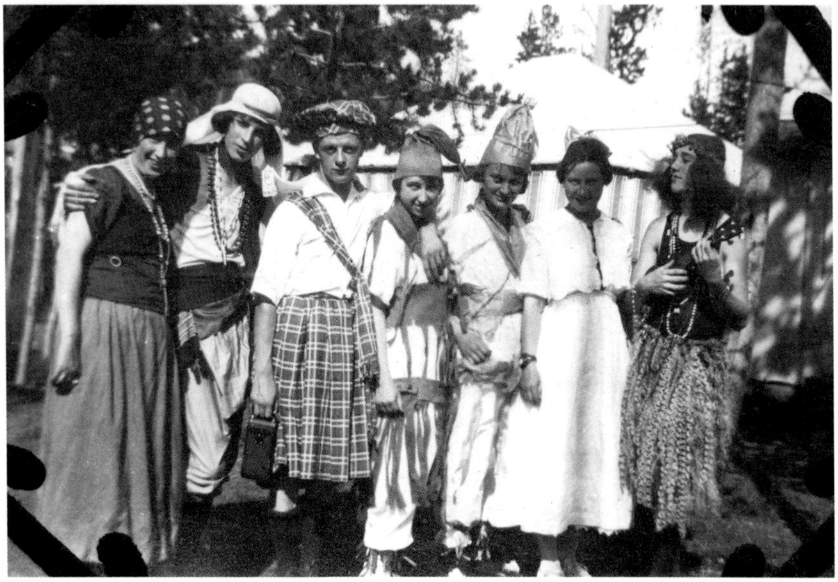

In this 1920 photo from concessioner employee Elton E. Singletary, a guide at Old Faithful Camp, seven employees in eclectic and apparently Middle Eastern-styled costumes—although one holding a folding camera wears a makeshift Scottish kilt and Balmoral cap—pose prior to the night's performance.

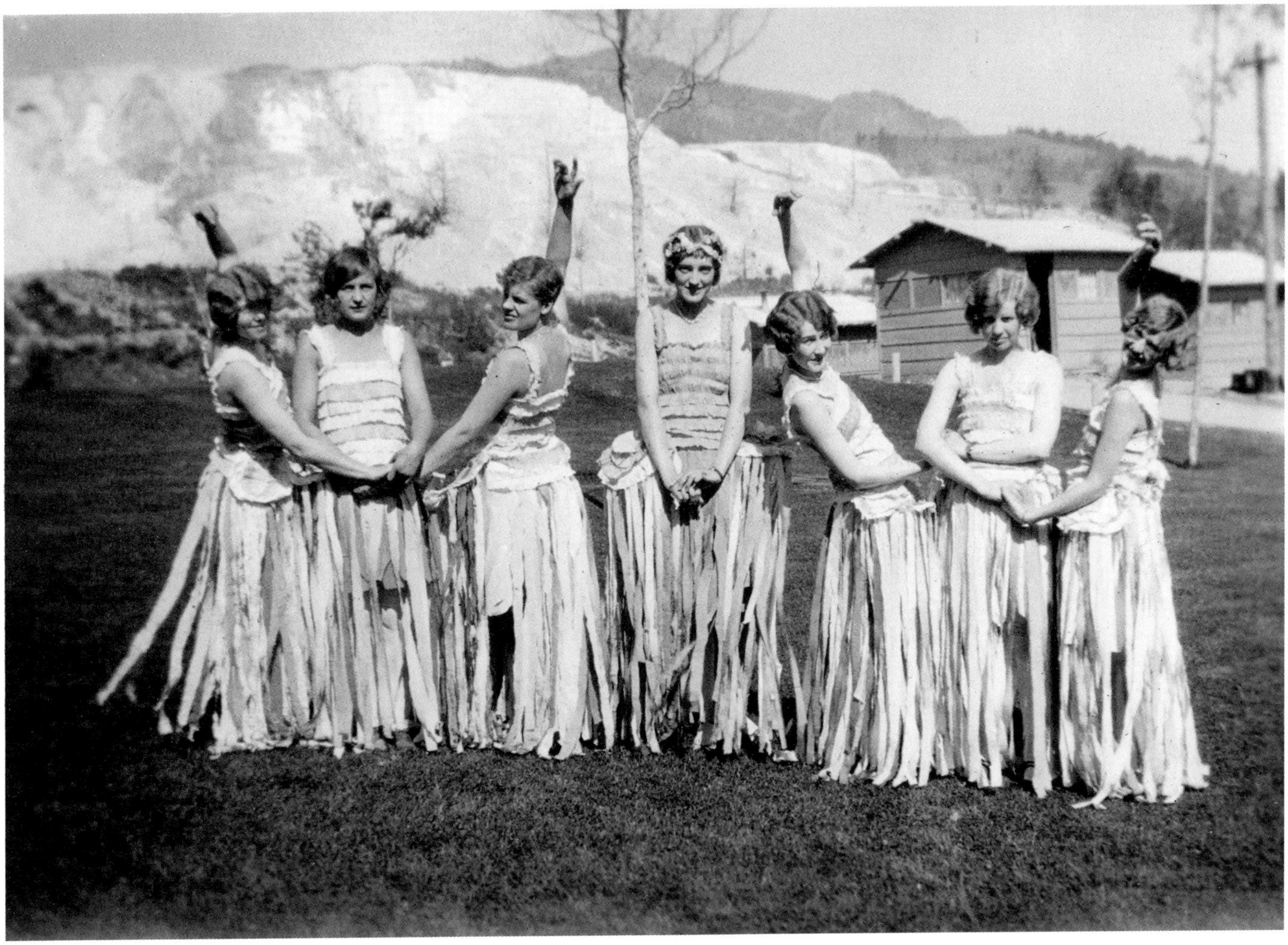

Seven young women employees at Mammoth Camp pose in hand-created costumes of shredded-rag skirts and tiered, flouncy tops in 1927. It is not known for what show or skit the costumes were made. Besides their ability to serve guests, park employees were hired based upon their entertainment skills, or at least a willingness to perform, to enhance guests' experiences during their tours of the park. This photo is from park employee Garnet Alder's Mammoth Camp album.

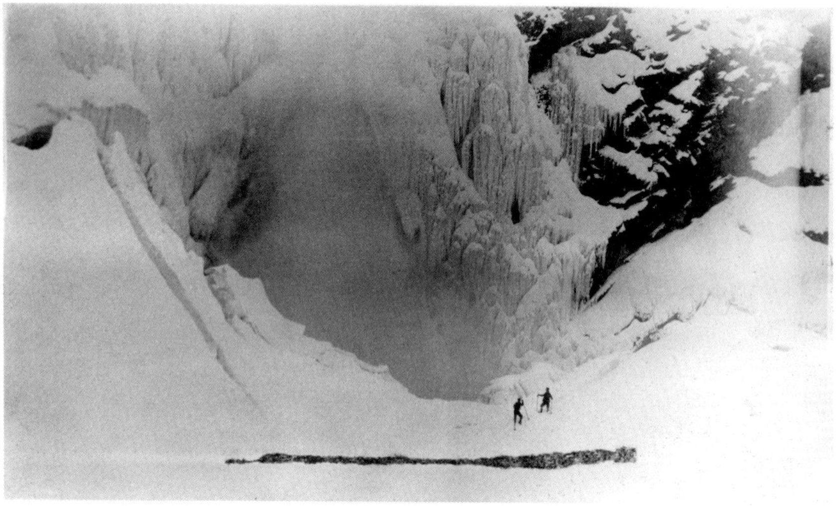

The ice-encased base of the Great Falls (now known as the Lower Falls of the Yellowstone River), dwarfs two park employees traveling on snowshoes or cross-country skis in 1927. These intrepid explorers, including the third person who took the photo, might have been winter-keepers at Canyon, or friends of the winter-keeper, who chose to do this on their time off. Owing to possible avalanches (as evidenced by the long crack in the snow at left) and thin ice over sections of river, this excursion was particularly dangerous. It is no longer allowed by the National Park Service.

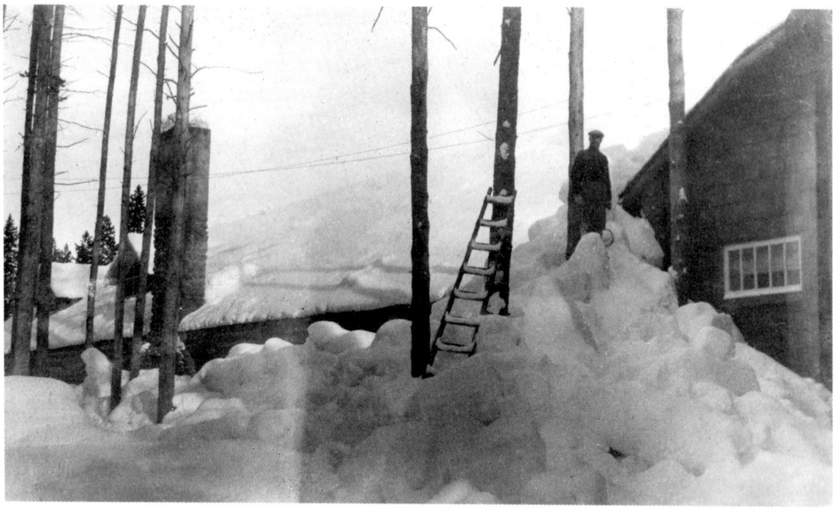

After apparently shoveling it from the roof, an employee stands on a pile of snow at Canyon Lodge in 1927. The Canyon region is the highest elevation in the park with buildings; consequently, buildings there receive more snow than other locations. To prevent damage to the buildings and possible collapse, a hardy group of workers remains all winter to saw and shovel the snow off the structures.

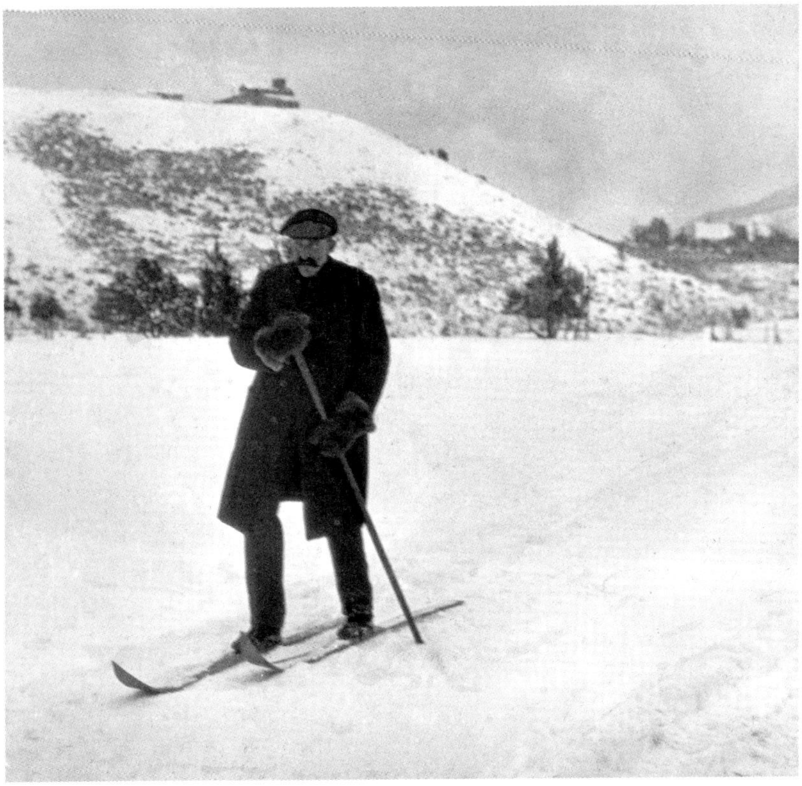

A man wearing a newsboy-style hat—that must have left his ears cold—and fur mittens poses on wooden skis at Mammoth Hot Springs in this circa-1905 photo. At the turn of the century, cross-country skiers utilized a metal-tipped, five- to six-foot-long pole for balance, as well as to help them turn and stop. Cross-country skiing became popular in northern areas of North America in the 1890s. The Norris blockhouse, the first administration building in the park, is visible on Capitol Hill in the background. In light of previous conflicts with native tribes, Superintendent Norris built the two-story, defensible structure in 1879. It had a log turret that was 12 feet in diameter. In less than a decade, the building was turned into housing for three or four lieutenants from Camp Sheridan. Park officials razed the structure in 1912, reportedly utilizing some of the logs for the Buffalo Ranch in Lamar Valley.

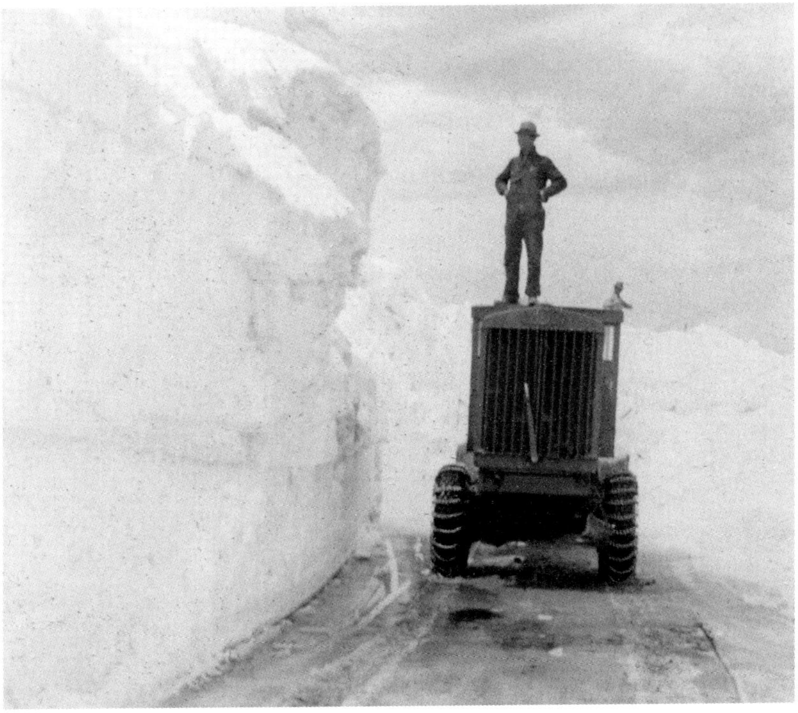

Yellowstone's high elevations means snow sticks around well into springtime. This road clearing crew tackles a snow drift much taller than their Snogo rotary snowplow—even with a man standing on its hood--in this early 1940s photo, probably taken in 7,700-feet-high Hayden Valley. Park visitation dropped precipitously after the United States entered World War II (from 581,761 visitors in 1941 to 191,830 in 1942), but roads still needed clearing by early June so plowing had to begin in April. Photo from Lena Eggleston park employee album.

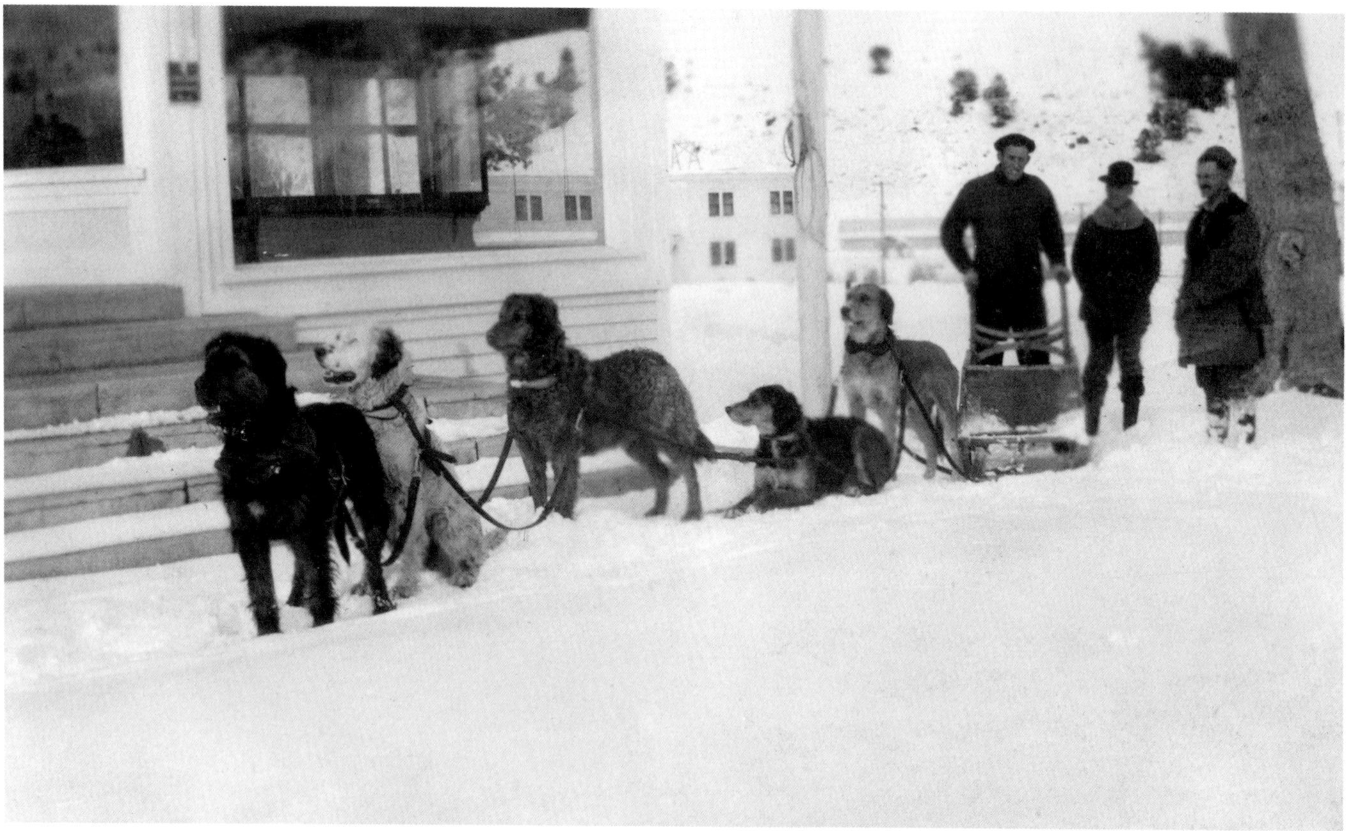

A mixed team of sled dogs rests alongside the Yellowstone Park Store in Mammoth Hot Springs in 1922, with three park employees standing next to the empty sled. The men might have been government employees who lived at Mammoth, or they could have sledded in from Gardiner just to enjoy a beautiful winter's day. Photo from the Matte Kincaid park employee album, Mammoth Hot Springs.

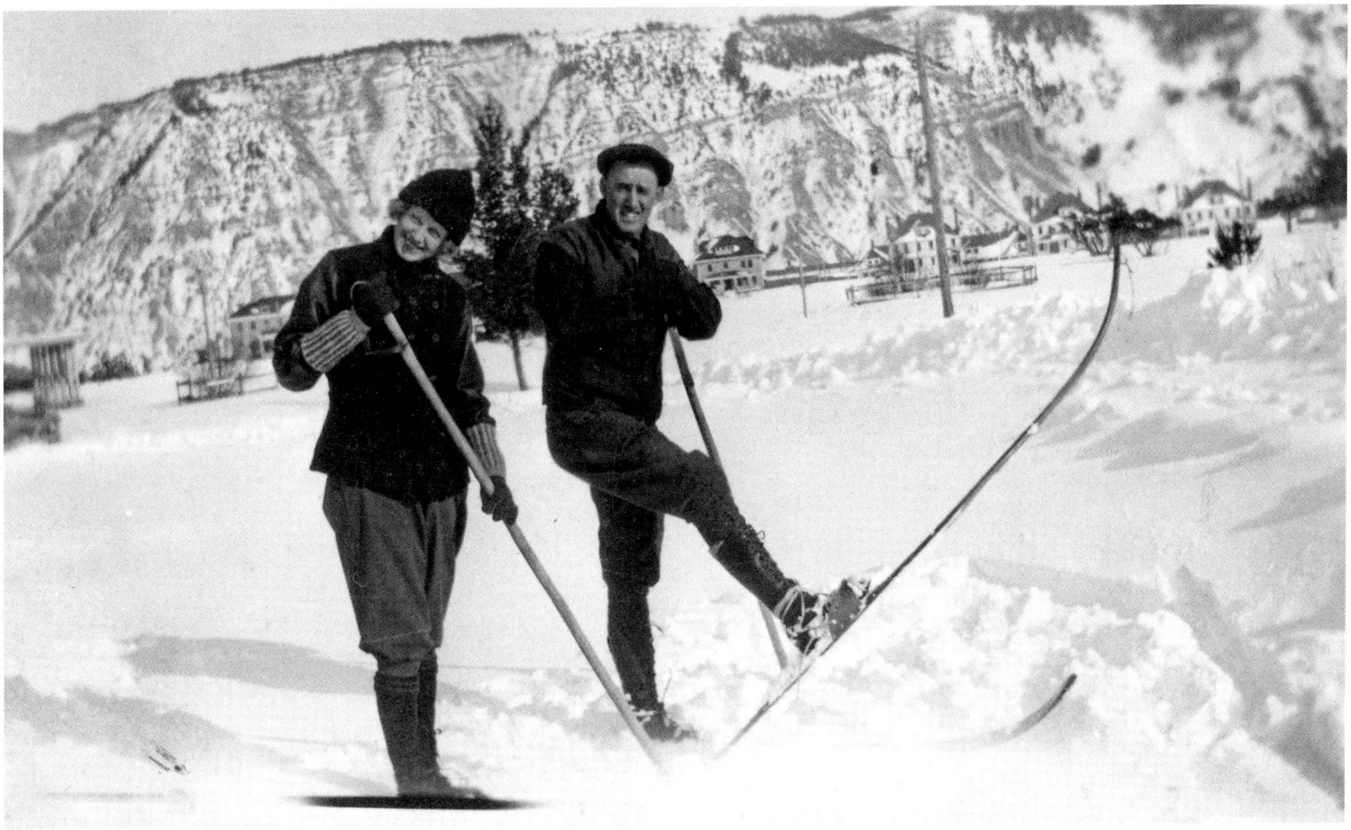

A pair of park employees show off their skis in the winter wonderland of Mammoth Hot Springs in 1922. This duo is utilizing the traditional single ski pole instead of the shorter and lighter dual-pole system that became popular as cross-country skis became shorter and lighter. Notice the slip-in binding with cables that hold the man's foot to the ski. This photo is from the Matte Kincaid park employee album, Mammoth Hot Springs.

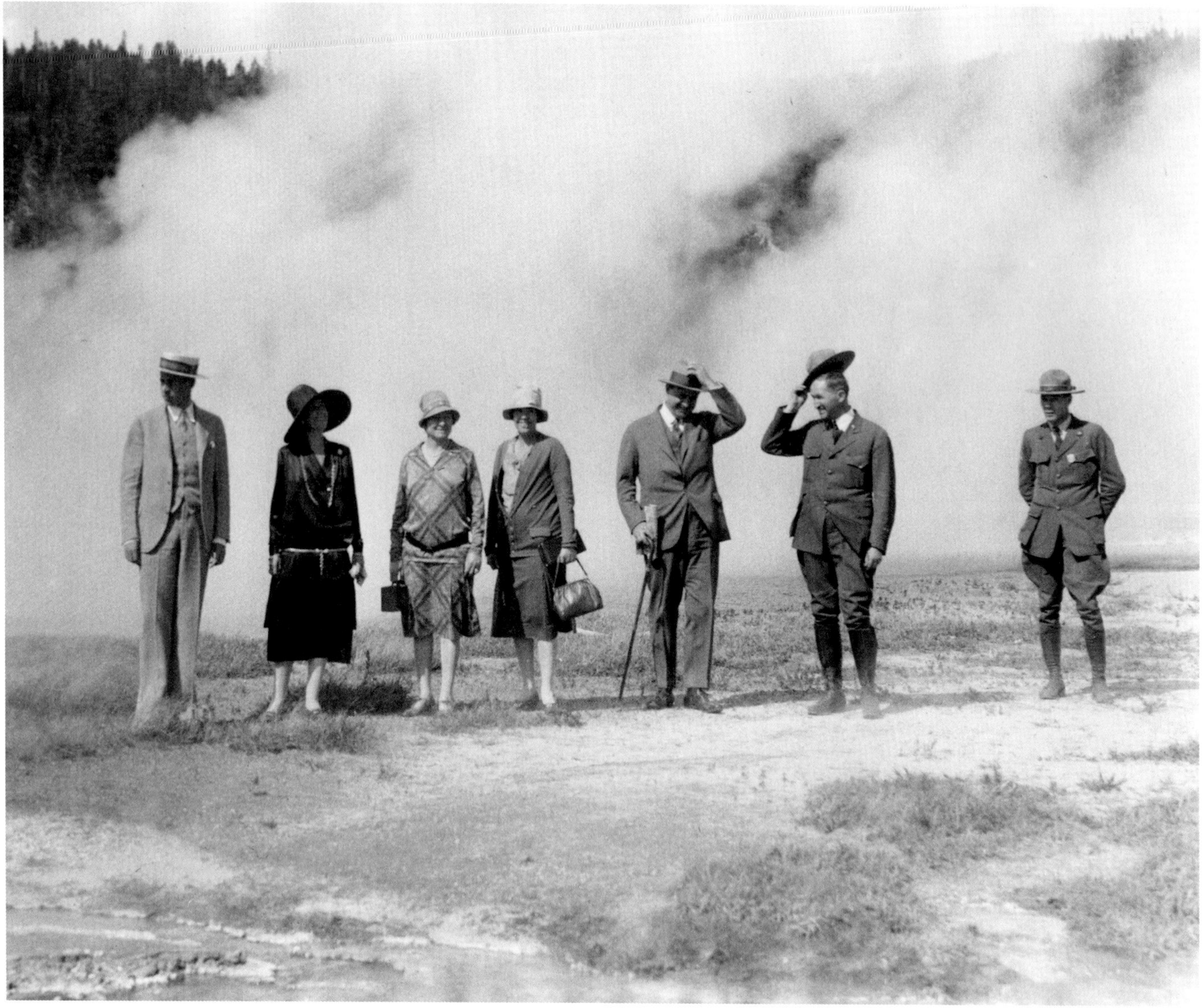

During their visit in August 1927, Superintendent Horace M. Albright, along with his wife Grace, President Coolidge's Presidential secretary Everett Sanders with his wife Ella, accompanied First Lady Grace Coolidge and her son John on their tour of the park. In this photo, the first lady is wearing the black outfit with the large-brimmed hat and her son John stands next to her in the left of the photo. In the center-right, Superintendent Horace M. Albright tips his hat to Everett Sanders, and it is most likely Grace Albright and Ella Sanders posing in the center. Grace Albright may be next to Grace Coolidge and Ella Sanders to the right of her husband. An unnamed ranger accompanying the group stands attentively at the far right.

CHAPTER 7

Famous Figures

Yellowstone has long attracted all types of people from all walks of life. Presidents, actors, and foreign officials all visited the park, and Yellowstone boasted its own collection of memorable, perhaps eccentric, characters.

Five U.S. presidents spent time in the park before World War II. Most notably, President Theodore Roosevelt dedicated the cornerstone of the Roosevelt Arch outside of Gardiner in 1903. The vibrant outdoorsman spent two weeks touring the area.

Lesser-known presidential visits included Chester Arthur in 1883 and Warren Harding in 1923. President Calvin Coolidge, his wife, Grace, and their son, John, toured the park in 1927. In 1937 Franklin Delano Roosevelt broadcast one of his "Fireside Chats" from the park after seeing the hard work of the Civilian Conservation Corps.

Actors have worked in Yellowstone ever since the silent films of the early 1900s. In all, the park has been a production location for more than 150 films and television programs.

Yellowstone also had homegrown celebrities. Most were charismatic entrepreneurs who made as much of an impression on guests as did the natural wonders.

While the general public did not travel to Yellowstone to see the stars, at least not the human kind, interacting with or just noticing these personalities made visitors' and employees' time in the park even more memorable.

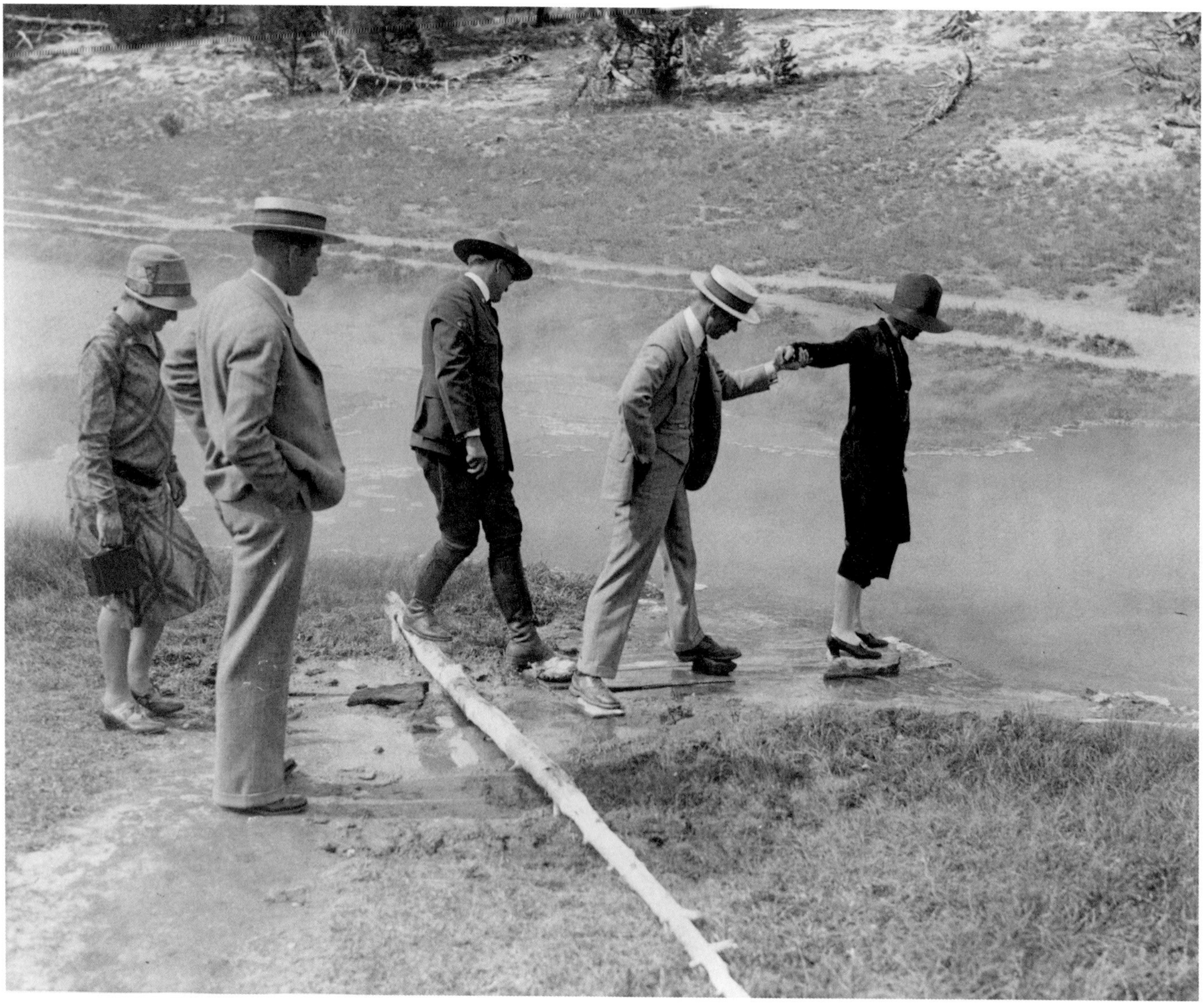

In August 1927, President Calvin Coolidge, First Lady Grace Coolidge, and their grown son John visited Yellowstone after a lengthy stay in the Black Hills of South Dakota. While President Coolidge accompanied the group on several sight-seeing excursions, he also took time for himself, fly-fishing as much as possible, often joined by Superintendent Horace M. Albright. In this photo the First Lady carefully steps near the edge of Firehole Lake with John holding her hand for support. Superintendent Albright (in uniform) stands behind them, watching their footing. The president is not in the photo.

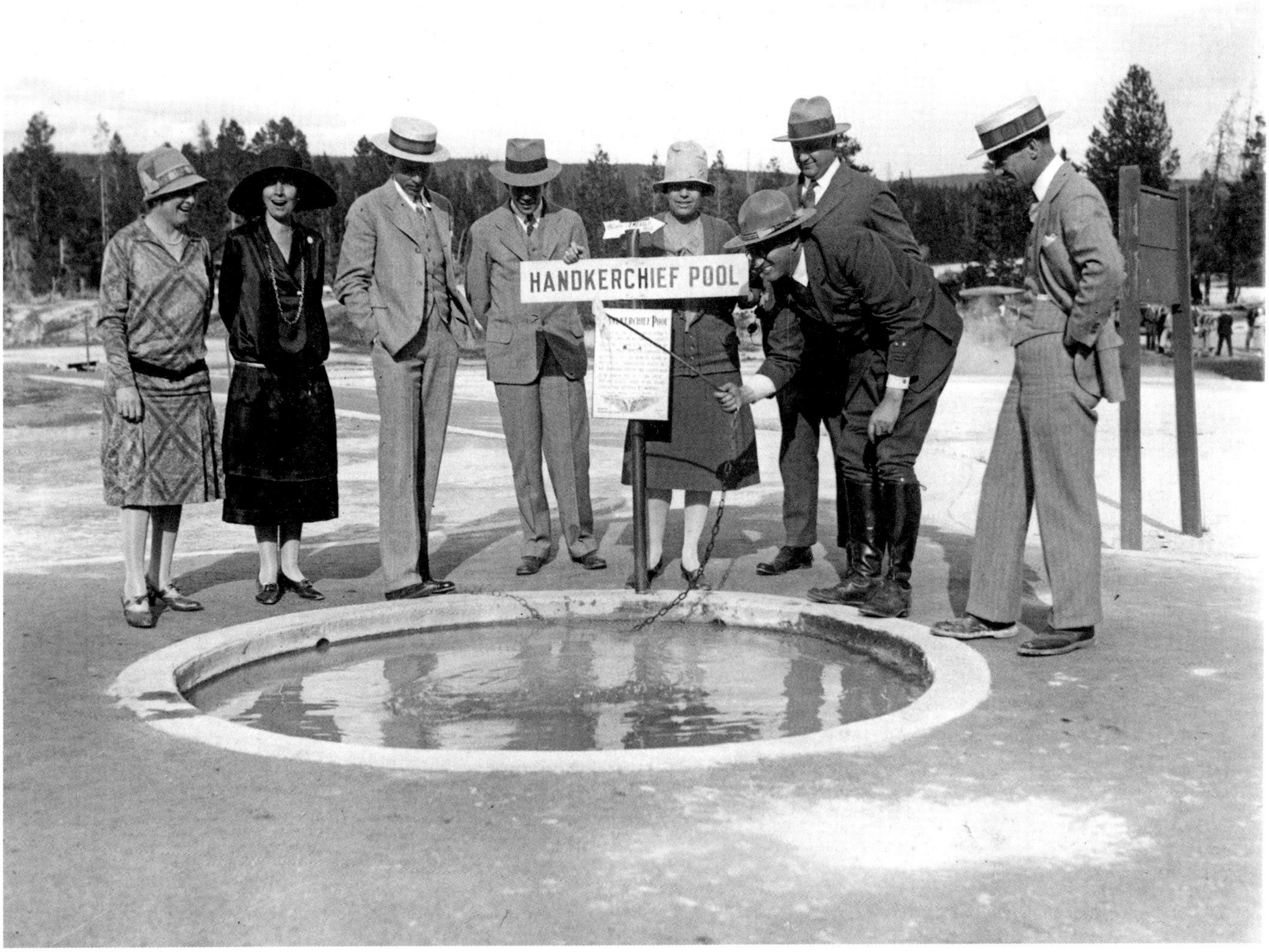

When President Coolidge and his group visited Yellowstone National Park in August 1927, Handkerchief Pool in the Black Sand Basin was as popular as Old Faithful Geyser. In this photo, Superintendent Horace M. Albright lifts a handkerchief that circulated through the thermal feature before floating to the top of the pool, much to the delight of smiling First Lady Grace Coolidge, second from left. The First Lady is flanked by Grace Albright, the superintendent's wife (far left) and her son, John Coolidge. The man beside John is unknown, as is the man directly behind Albright. Presidential secretary Everett Sanders stands far right, and his wife stands behind the sign. Albright is lifting the handkerchief with a metal rod attached to a chain, apparently placed there for park visitors to use. Due to the debris tossed into its waters over the years, Handkerchief Pool went dormant by the late 1920s.

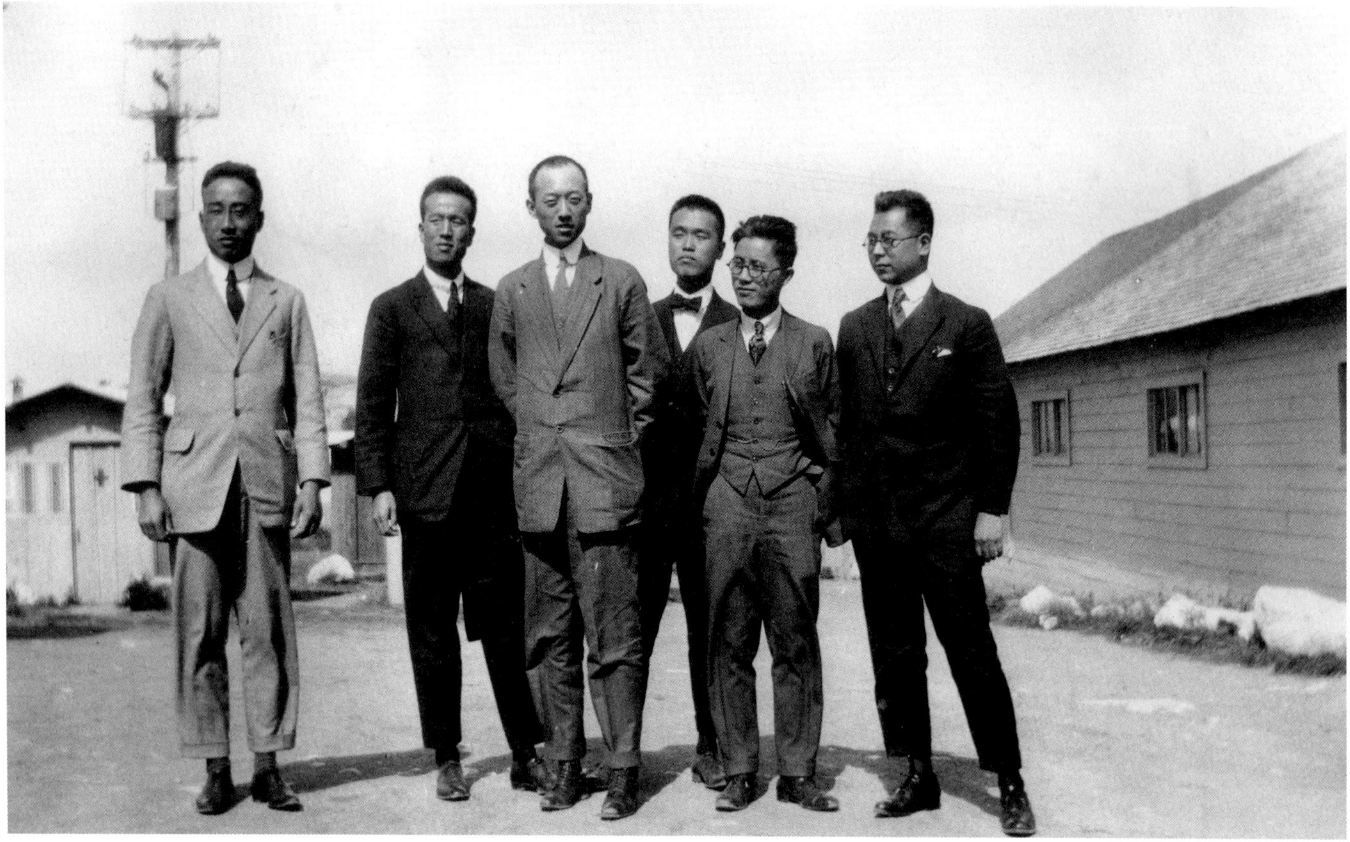

As the world's first national park, Yellowstone attracted world-wide attention. These Chinese officials were probably touring the park on their own because they are staying at Mammoth Camp instead of one of the finer hotels in this circa-1922 photo taken by Matte Kincaid, a park employee at Mammoth Hot Springs. Their visit to Yellowstone may have been independent of their primary duties.

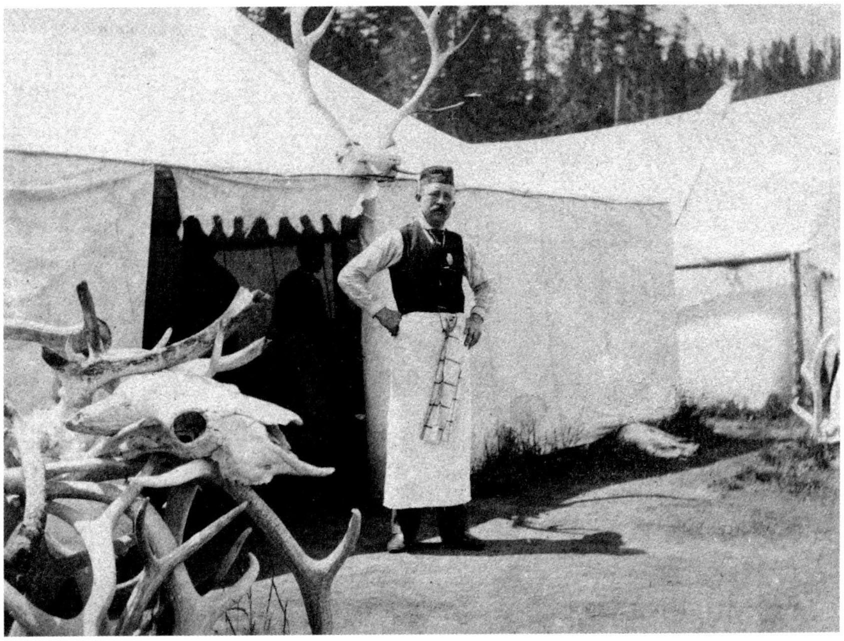

This is a rare cyanotype taken some time from 1888 through 1891 which was converted to a black and white image. It shows the vivacious Larry Mathews posing at Larry's Lunch Station at Trout Creek. Fitting to the rustic atmosphere, although frowned upon today, skulls and antlers served as decorations. Larry Mathews was an entertaining Irishman who worked for the Yellowstone Park Association from 1887 to 1904, often managing similar tent camps, and serving as the first manager of the new Old Faithful Inn in 1904. This Trout Creek location, situated between the Fountain Hotel and the road to Canyon and Yellowstone Lake, was the first of several lunch stations. Only a few images are known of the Trout Creek Lunch Station.

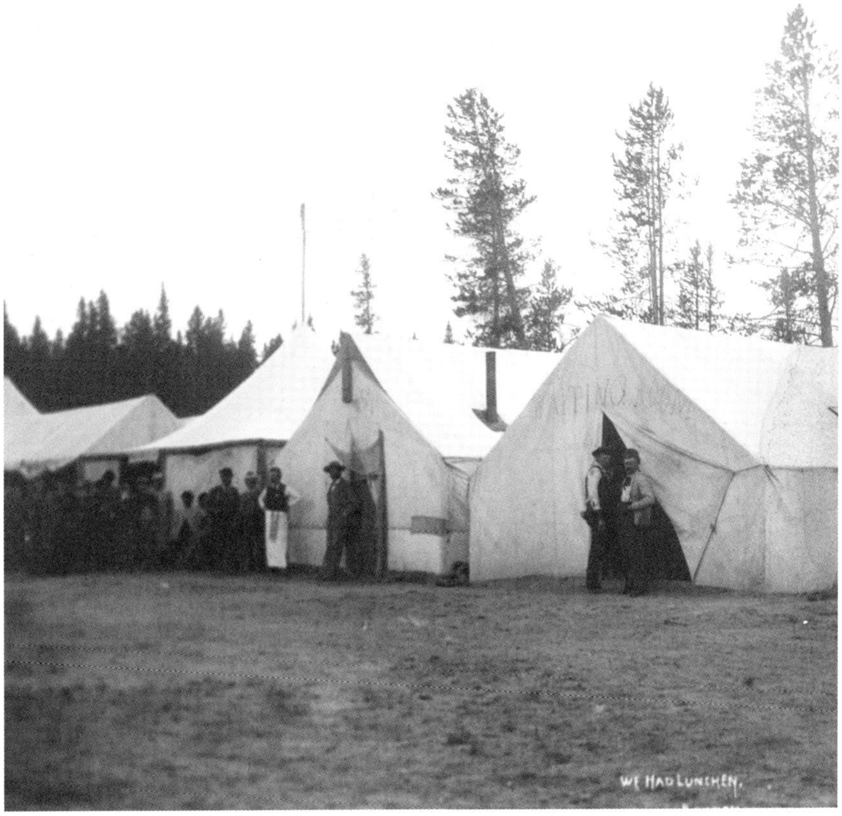

Larry's Lunch Station at Norris is shown in this black and white, Magic Lantern glass-slide by an unknown photographer. The period is 1893-1900, after the first and second Norris hotels burned. Even though there are few, high-quality photos of owner Larry Mathews, his reputation as jocular host of the operation is well-known. In this photo he stands in front of the second tent from the right. He wears a white apron, with his hands on his hips. The tent on the far right, where two male guests look toward the camera, has "Waiting Room" written on the canvas above the doorway. Larry and his staff served visitors to the popular thermal area, and while the food was not haute cuisine, Larry's sharp wit and friendly personality usually made the meal a memorable experience.

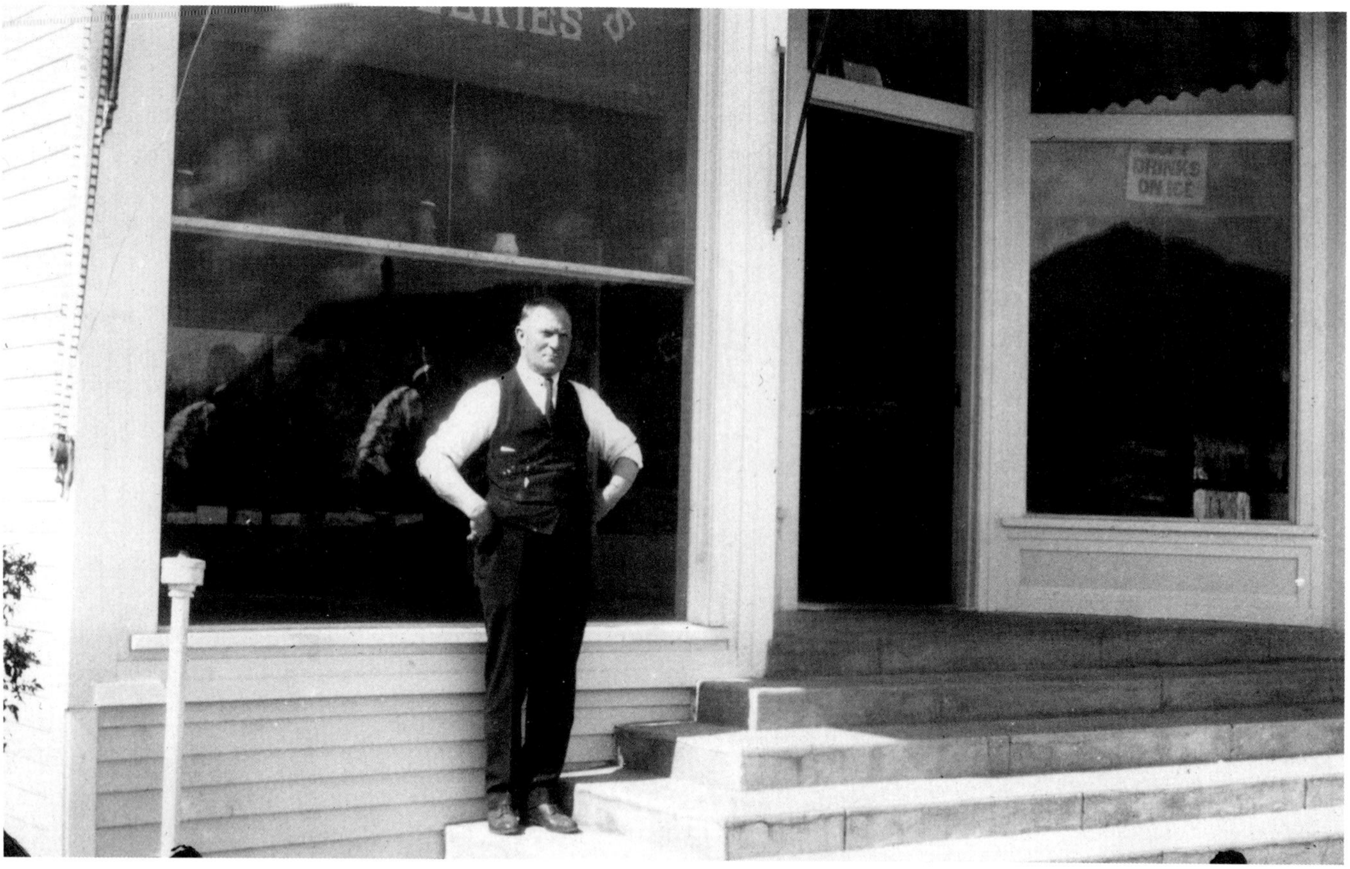

This is a rare photo of George Whittaker, who is standing on the steps of his Yellowstone Park Store in 1900. Between serving in the U.S. Army at Fort Yellowstone for five years, and afterwards working for the Yellowstone Park Transportation Company, George Whittaker boasted a long history in Yellowstone before becoming proprietor of the Yellowstone Park Store in Mammoth Hot Springs. Built by Jennie Henderson Ash, daughter of George L. Henderson, and her husband George Ash in 1895, the "Ash and Henderson" served as the post office and a place to buy dry goods and tourist supplies. In 1906, Jennie's brother-in-law, Alexander Lyall, husband of her sister Barbara, became postmaster and a partner in the store. Two years later, Jennie sold her share to Alexander and her brother, Walter Henderson. They changed the name to Lyall-Henderson. George Whittaker purchased the store in 1913 and renamed it the Yellowstone Park Store. He operated it for nineteen years before selling it to sisters Anna Pryor and Elizabeth Trischman in 1932. Now known as the Mammoth General Store, visitors still purchase gifts, supplies, and ice cream there. This photo is from a Mammoth Hot Springs park employee album.

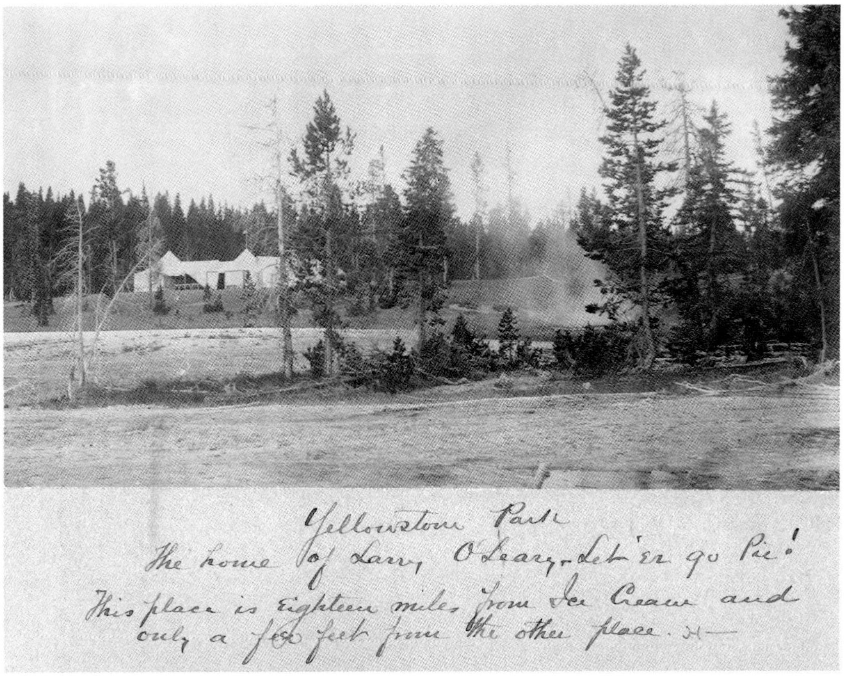

A guest made interesting observations about Larry Mathews's Lunch Station at Norris in this circa-1895 photo, writing below the photo: "The home of Larry O'Leary & Let 'er go Pie! This place is eighteen miles from Ice Cream and only a few feet from the other place, H –." From this report, it sounds like the pie was a big hit; unfortunately, the pie's recipe is not known. The charismatic Larry Mathews was the face of hospitality for the Yellowstone Park Association's Larry's Lunch Stations, including this tent set-up at Norris 1893-1900. *Photo courtesy of Jay C. Lyndes Family Collection.*

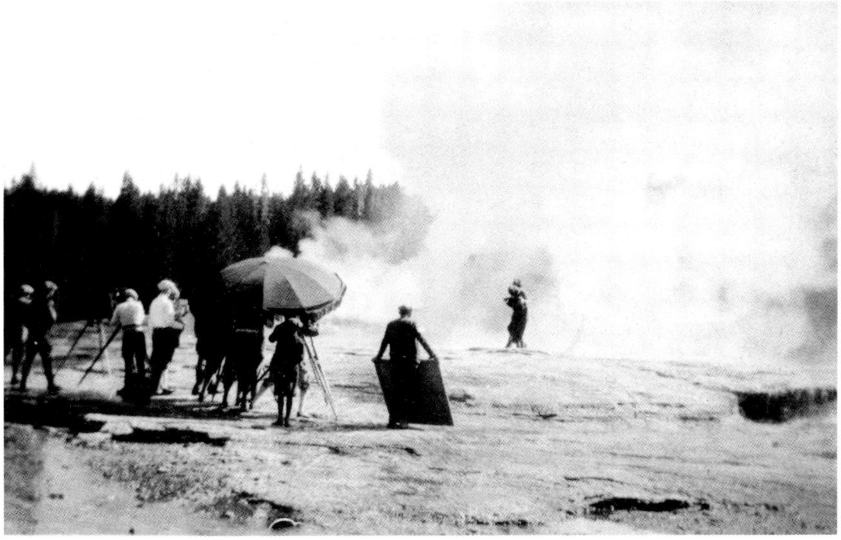

A film crew shoots at Giant Geyser in the Upper Geyser Basin in 1923. They were shooting the climactic scene in the silent film *Reno*. Produced by Samuel Goldwyn, *Reno* was a satirical film highlighting the mess of quickie marriages and divorces. In the overly dramatic plot, when Emily (Helene Chadwick) stole back her children from her ex-husbands' aunt, she and her new husband, Walter Heath (George Walsh), fled to Yellowstone Park. When her ex-husband, Lew Cody (Roy Tappan) found the family, Lew and Walter fought. Walter ultimately threw Lew into a geyser, which erupted and shot Lew into the air. His body was crushed upon the rocks as he fell back to the ground.

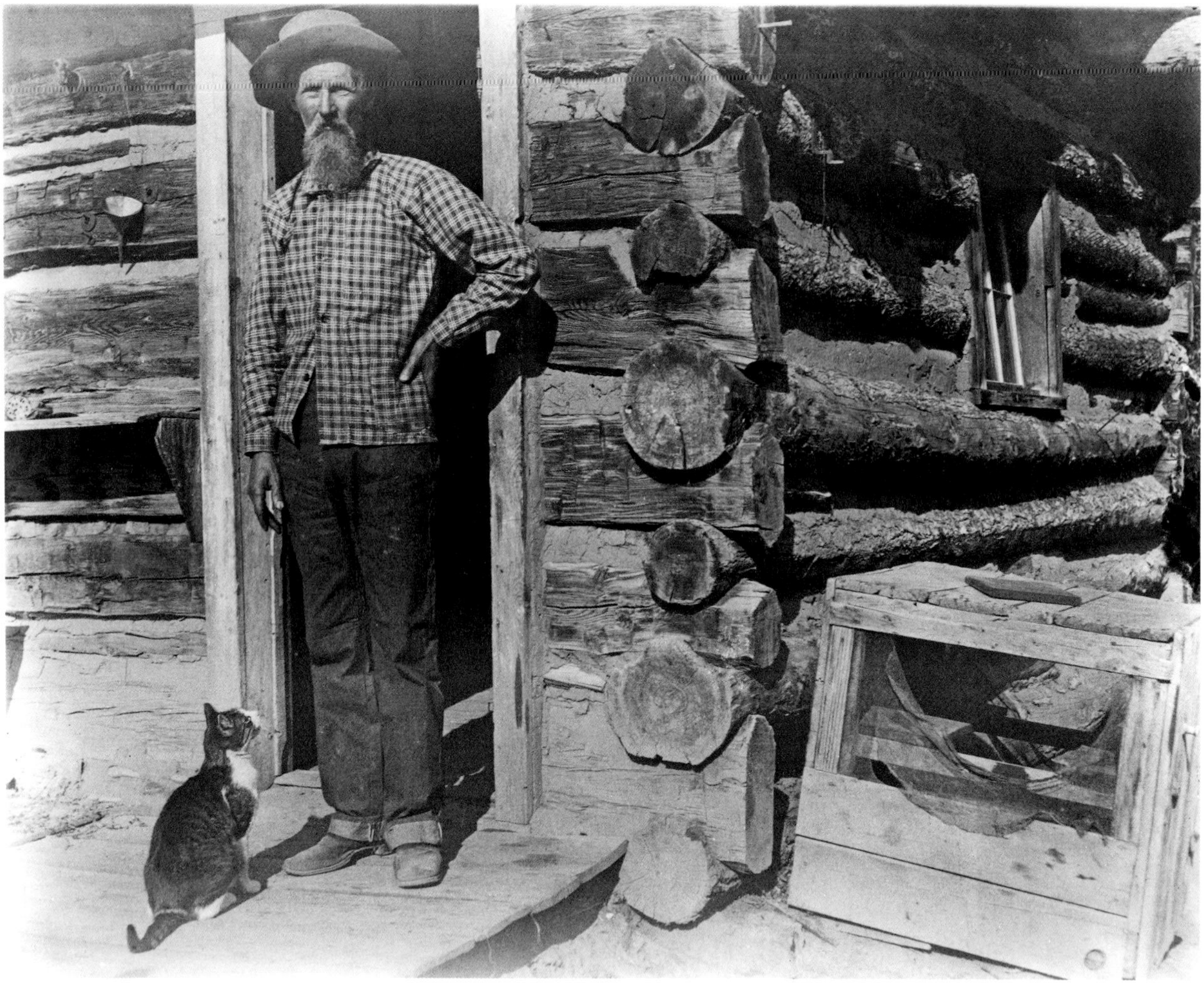

Yellowstone attracted colorful characters, including James George, better known as "Yankee Jim." The lure of gold in 1863 brought the Vermont-born pioneer, probably in his twenties, to Bannack, eventually moving closer to where Livingston is now and working as a meat hunter and trapper for the Crow Indian Agency. In 1873 he acquired property along the rugged canyon stretching along the west bank of the Yellowstone River north of Gardiner. A road ran through the property, and although he did not build the road, he collected tolls from travelers heading between what became Livingston and Mammoth. He was known as a spinner of tales—or an outright liar—and dispenser of valuable fishing advice, and many visitors, including touring British author Rudyard Kipling, were enthralled by his stories. Kipling even wrote about Yankee Jim in his 1899 book, *From Sea to Sea*. In this 1898 photo, Yankee Jim's cat intently looks at him while he stands in the doorway of the cabin. After years of legal squabbles with the Northern Pacific Railroad, which wanted to build a rail line through his property, Yankee Jim sold his remaining section of the road to Park County in 1914. By 1922, heavy drinking and old age wore on Yankee Jim, and his brother took him to California, where he passed away in 1924 at the apparent age of 85 years old. The area along the Yellowstone River where he lived is now named Yankee Jim Canyon.

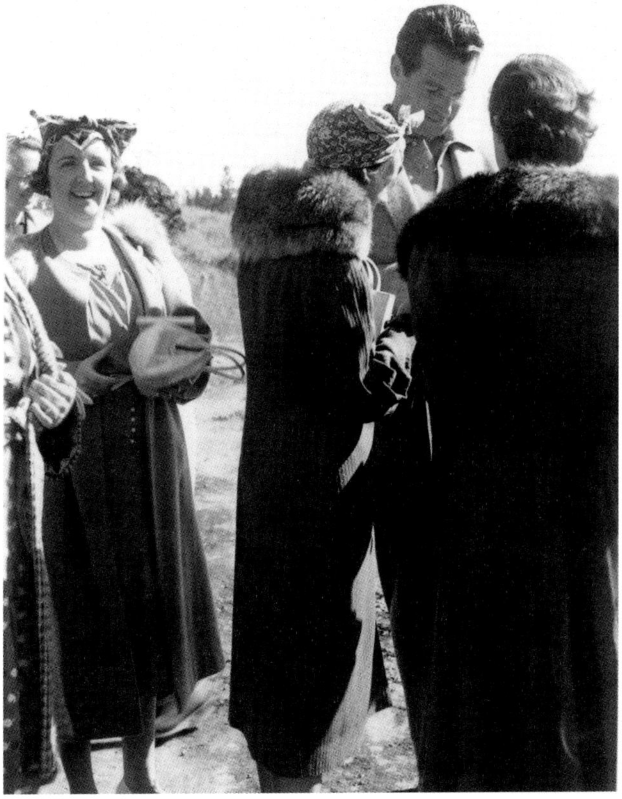

The lady at left is all smiles as she and other female park visitors ask American actor Frederick Martin "Fred" MacMurray to sign autographs at Canyon in 1938. Launching his career in the 1930 Broadway production, *Three's a Crowd*, MacMurray ultimately performed in more than100 films and television series, including his well-known role as widowed father Steve Douglas in the popular television series *My Three Sons*. There is no record of MacMurray filming in the park, so he was probably in Yellowstone as a tourist.

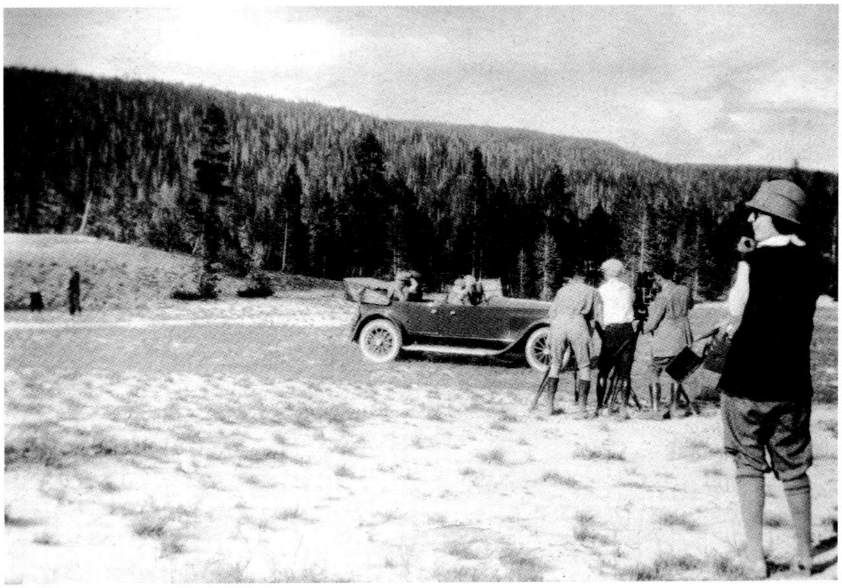

A film crew sets a scene for the silent movie *Reno*, which was written and directed by Rupert Hughes in 1923. Four actors are in the automobile. *Reno* was one of many silent movies, including *Seeing America* (1916) and *Cupid Angling* (1918), filmed within Yellowstone during the early years of motion pictures.

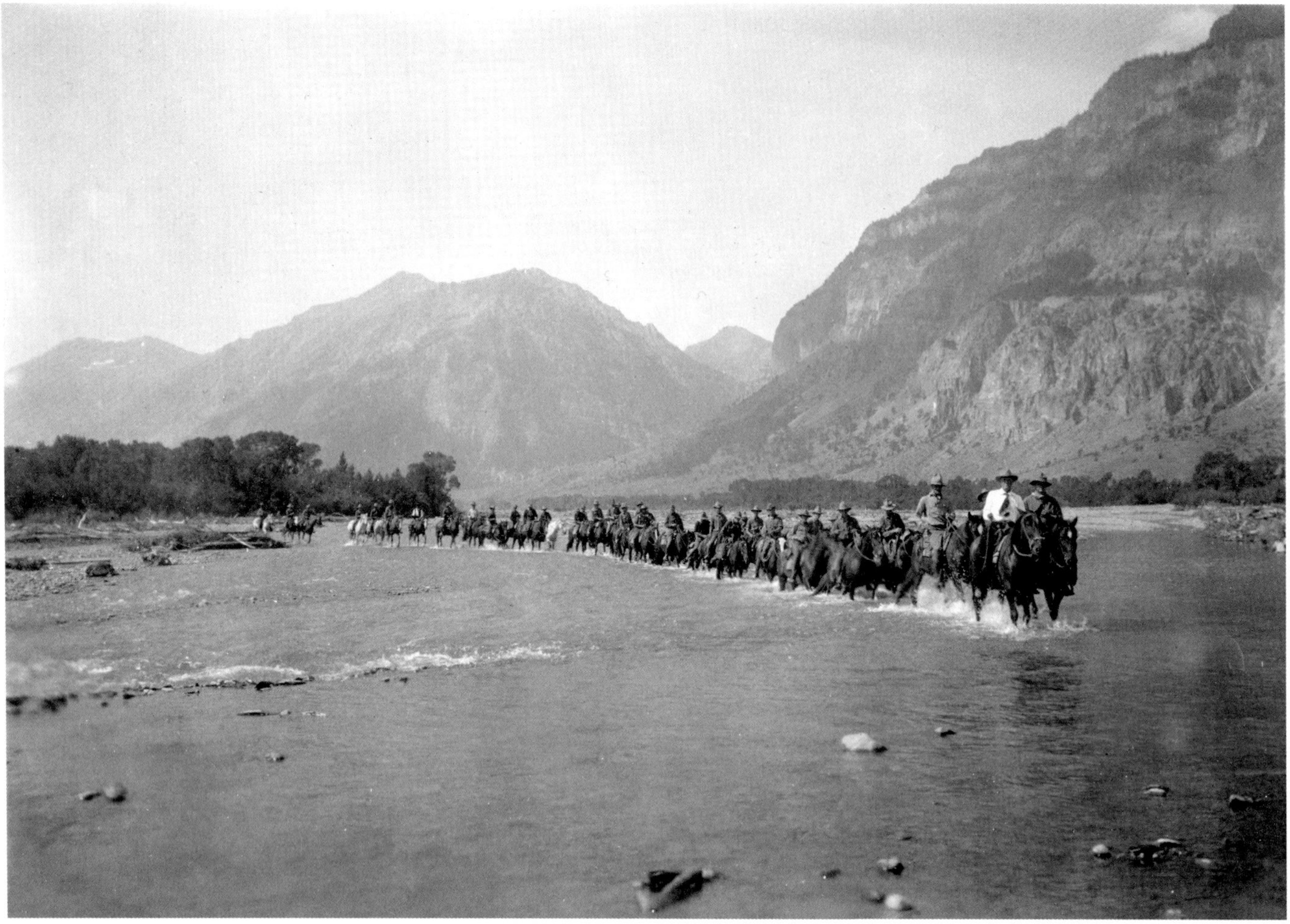

A large group from Valley Ranch crosses the North Fork of Shoshone River on horseback circa-1925. Raised in New York and educated at Princeton, Larry Larom became enthralled with the West after experiencing Buffalo Bill's Wild West Show in Madison Square Garden in 1910. After staying at Jim McLaughlin's Valley Ranch for four summers, he pivoted from his, or most likely his parents' intended life path to forge his own future in the area he loved. In 1915, he purchased the Valley Ranch with his friend and business partner, Winthrop Holley Brooks. The men tapped into the deep well of Eastern wealth and created a thriving venture. In 1919, Brooks left the ranch to join the family business, Brooks Brothers, but Larom expanded the ranch business, eventually becoming a founding member and president of the Dude Ranchers Association. *Photo courtesy of Jay C. Lyndes Family Collection.*

CHAPTER 8

Exploring Yellowstone Dude Ranch Style

Dude ranches gained popularity in the early 1880s, beginning with the Eaton family's first dude ranch in North Dakota. By the turn of the century, dude ranches were established in the Yellowstone area, outside of the park.

The heart of the dude ranch was the main lodge, usually a log building. From this home base, guests visited the park. Many guests rode their own horses, although wagons were available for those who had no desire to spend a day in the saddle. The groups stayed in well-appointed camps, either in permanent locations or tent camps. Dude-ranch trips were known for good guides, high-quality food, and entertaining camp life. Many outfits were so popular that guests returned year after year, practically becoming family to the ranch owners.

Yellowstone was uniquely situated to be an integral part of this American style of vacationing. Whether or not the dude ranches in these photos are still operating, all of them were important because they were born out of a desire to give guests an experience like no other, in a place like no other.

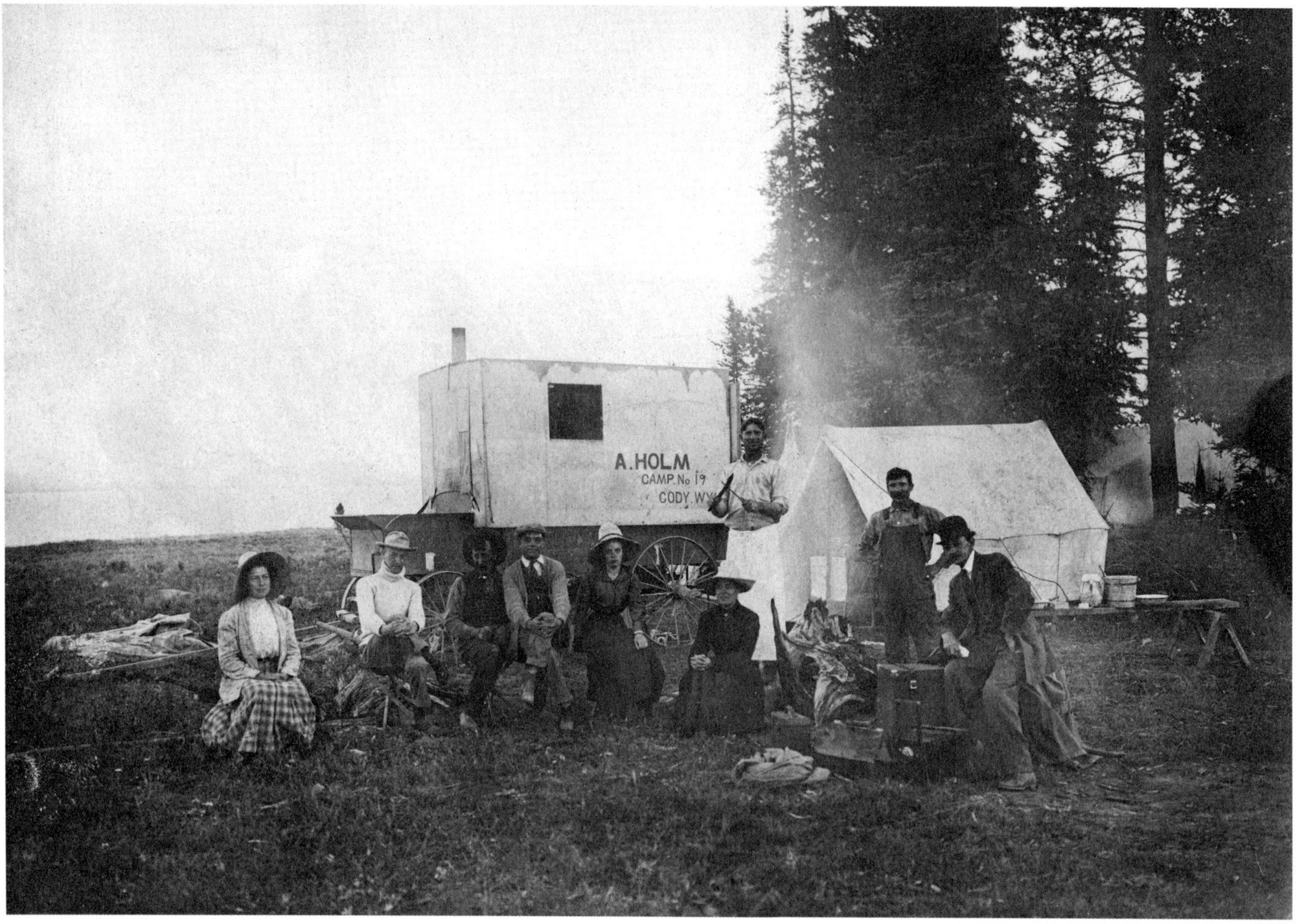

This circa-1905 photo shows the Aron "Tex" Holm Camp No. 19, complete with horse-drawn chuck wagon, tents, men and women campers, and the camp cook, wearing an apron. Beginning in 1901, when the Chicago, Burlington, & Quincy Railroad arrived in Cody, Wyoming, "Tex" Holm picked up his guests and transported them to Holm Lodge, roughly seven miles from the park's east entrance. In 1910, he built a rustic log lodge at his headquarters outside of the park. It housed a dining hall and amusement room for guests who stayed in the surrounding tent-houses. The following year, the Holm Transportation Company increased operations within the park, having its guests stay in hotels as well as in the Wylie Permanent Camps.

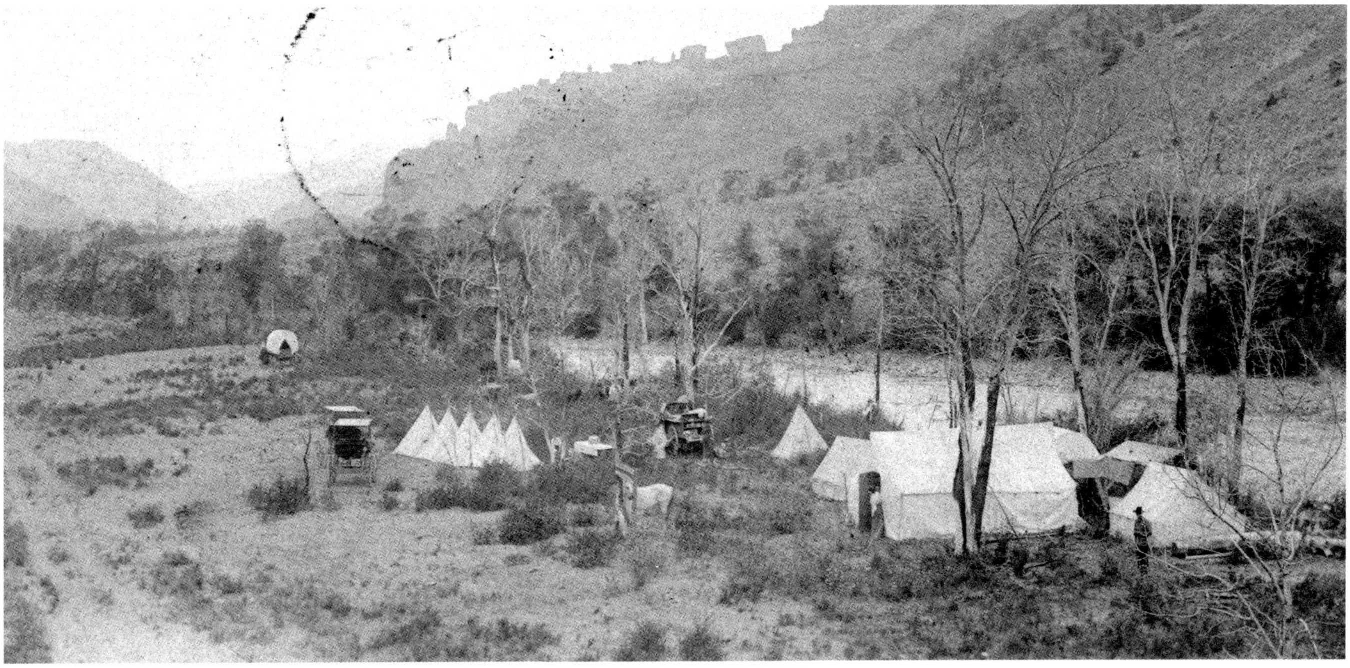

This postcard, postmarked May 4, 1906, shows the "Tex" Holm Camp on the North Fork of Shoshone River west of Cody, Wyoming. The famous "Holy City" rock formation is visible on the skyline. The scene shows the sleeping tents, cook tents, stagecoaches, and the chuck wagon parked away from the group. The large wall tent probably served as the dining room. Holm took guests on extended trips often lasting ten days or longer for those wanting a truly Western, and somewhat gritty, experience. Holm accommodated his guests at permanent cabins such as at Sylvan Lake, Grand Canyon, Norris, Upper Geyser Basin, and Yellowstone Lake, as well as more mobile tent-camps.

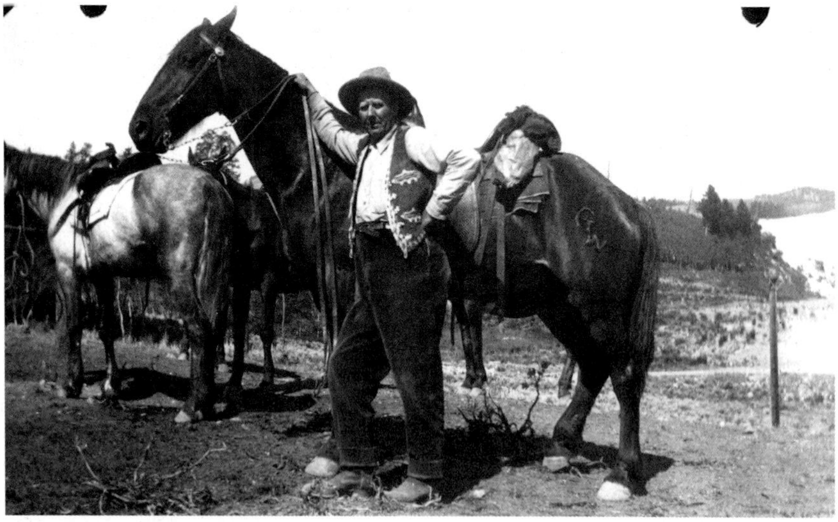

The renowned cowboy and guide Aron "Tex" Holm stands with his horses at "Mammoth Camp" in this 1922 photo from park employee Matte Kincaid's personal album. "Tex" was born in Sweden, but he looked like the iconic American cowboy and spent his life showing guests places in Yellowstone not seen on standard tours. After selling his lodge property outside the east entrance following a devastating fire in 1913 that destroyed the log-lodge, Holm turned his attention to the transportation aspects of his business. In 1911, he increased his automobile fleet, including buying four, 12-person, Stanley Mountain Wagons, which were powered by steam and did an admirable job of "powering up" the mountain roads. Unfortunately, the Holm Transportation Company went bankrupt in 1915. At the time of this photo, Tex Holm was guiding tours for the Yellowstone Park Camping Company.

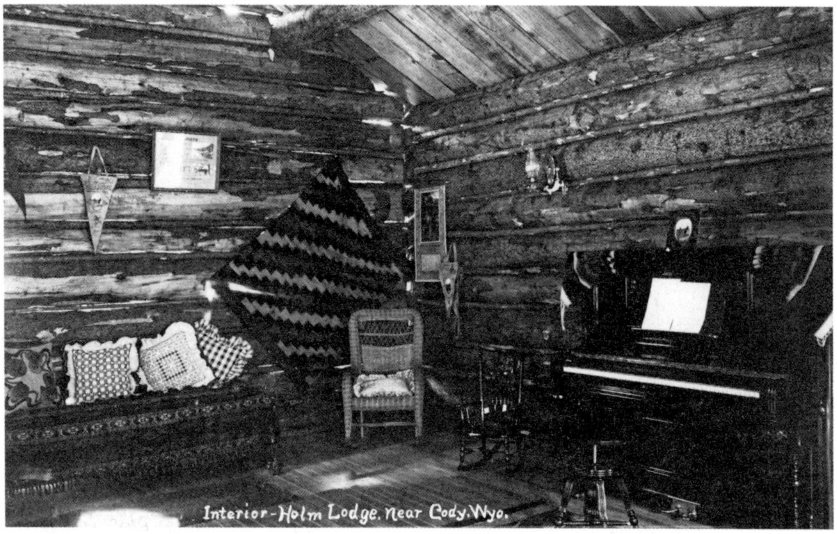

The piano shown in this postcard, dated August 8, 1910, was undoubtedly the hub of entertainment in the main building of the Holm Lodge, seven miles from the east entrance of Yellowstone National Park. One can imagine the gaiety of singing guests gathered in the room. This log-lodge was the heart of "Tex" Holm's operation. When the building burned in 1913, much of the furniture was saved, but the structure was a total loss. Probably due to financial struggles, Holm sold it to one of his shareholders and guides, J.W. "Billy" Howell, who rebuilt and operated it until 1947.

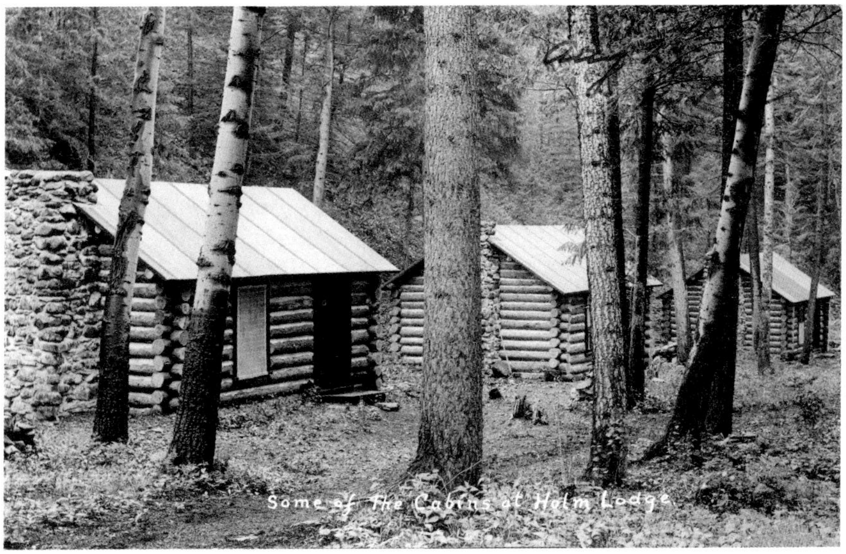

This is an August 25, 1916, photo of a few of the cabins at Holm Lodge, west of Cody, Wyoming. After taking the reins of the operation from Aron "Tex" Holm, Billy Howell rebuilt the main lodge and improved the facilities with log cabins containing stone chimneys for their guests, many of whom returned annually for decades.

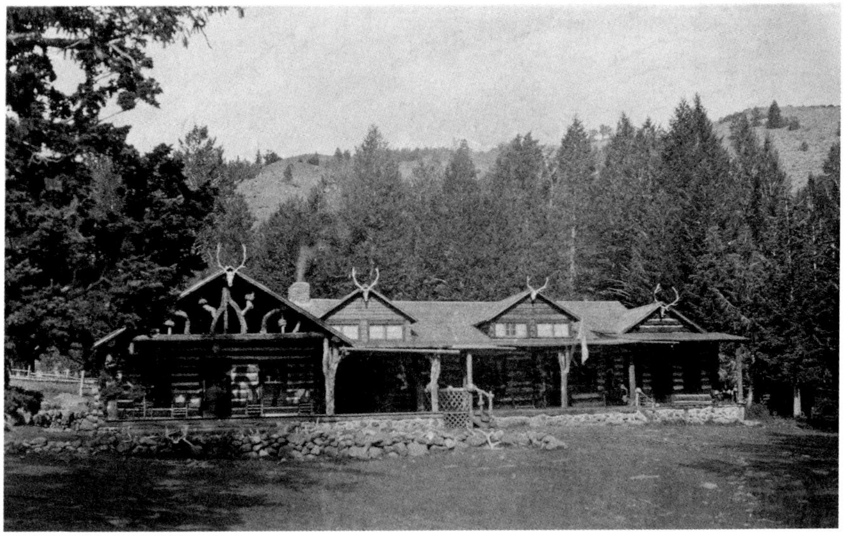

When Billy Howell purchased Holm Lodge from "Tex" Holm in 1913 after a fire destroyed the original log-structure, Howell began using his brand, the Crossed Sabres, on his stock, which became identified with his operation until he sold the iconic ranch in 1947. The Holm Ranch was renamed Crossed Sabres Ranch in 1972, giving a nod to that history. This postcard, postmarked in August of 1935, shows the reconstructed, main log building that welcomed guests for more than fifty years.

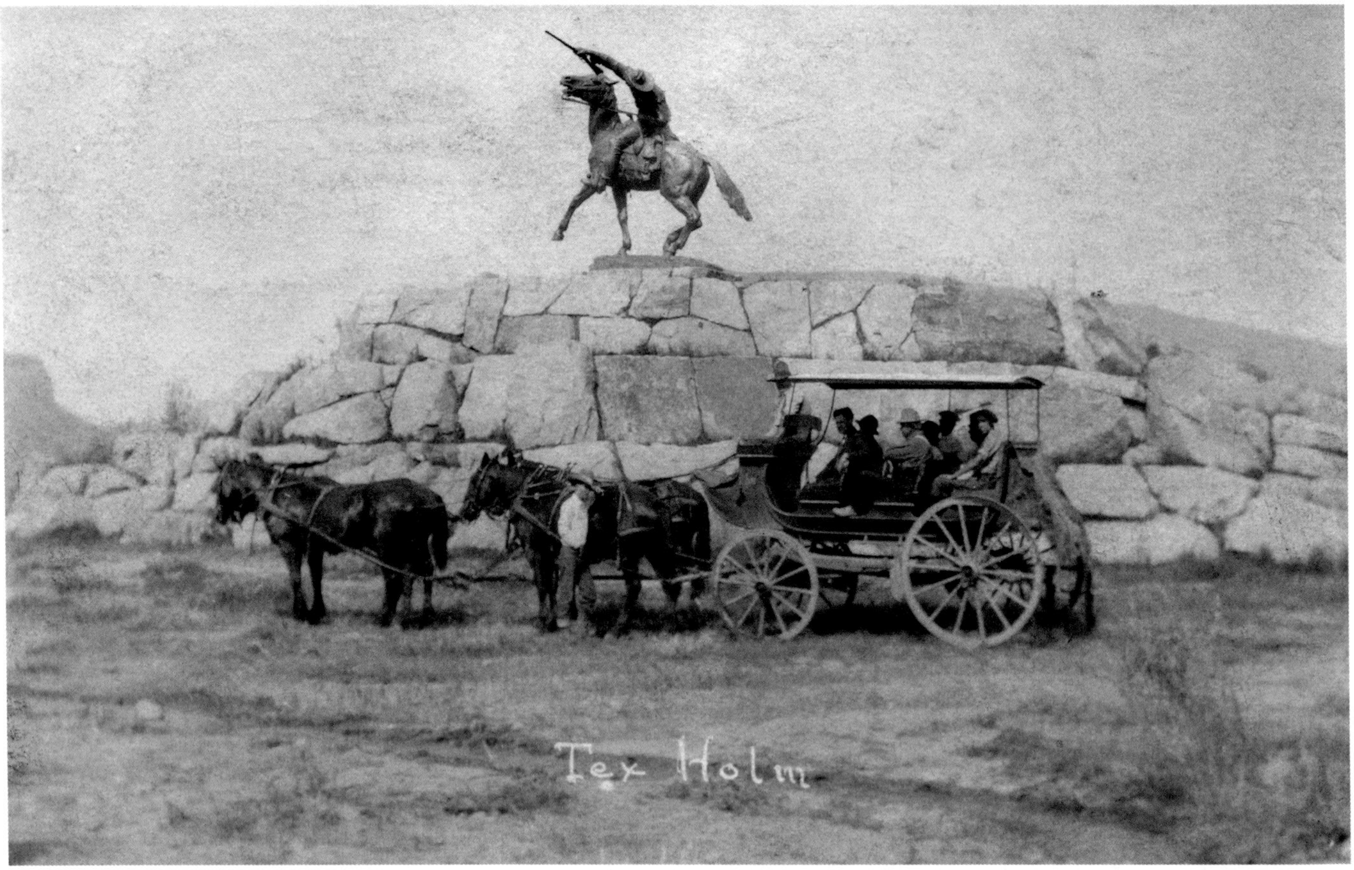

This 1924 photo shows Aron "Tex" Holm standing next to the horses with members of a camping party in a horse-drawn coach. They are parked in front of the "Buffalo Bill - The Scout" statue in Cody, Wyoming. Inspired by Mary Jester Allen, the niece of William F. "Buffalo Bill" Cody, her idea for this sculpture had to wait for seven years while she convinced the Buffalo Bill Memorial Association to commission the statue by Gertrude Vanderbilt Whitney, a respected sculptor and art patron, who not only donated her bronze sculpture to the association but also forty acres of adjacent land for it to stand on. For thirty years, the life-size memorial stood alone, until a $250,000 donation by Whitney's son, Cornelius Vanderbilt Whitney, allowed the association to build the Whitney Gallery of Western Art with a large, front window facing the bronze that his mother created. The gallery is now named the Whitney Western Art Museum.

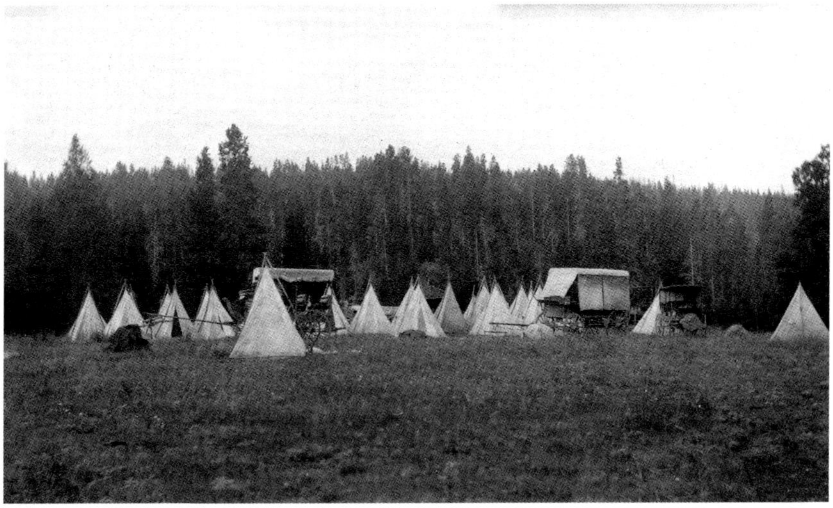

In this pre-1916 photo, the Holm Camp No. 4 consists of a tipi-style encampment with wagons and coaches near the park's Lower Falls of Yellowstone River. The wagons hauled the gear while the coaches, called "wagonettes," were outfitted with a more durable undercarriage to offer a more comfortable ride for guests who did not wish to ride a horse.

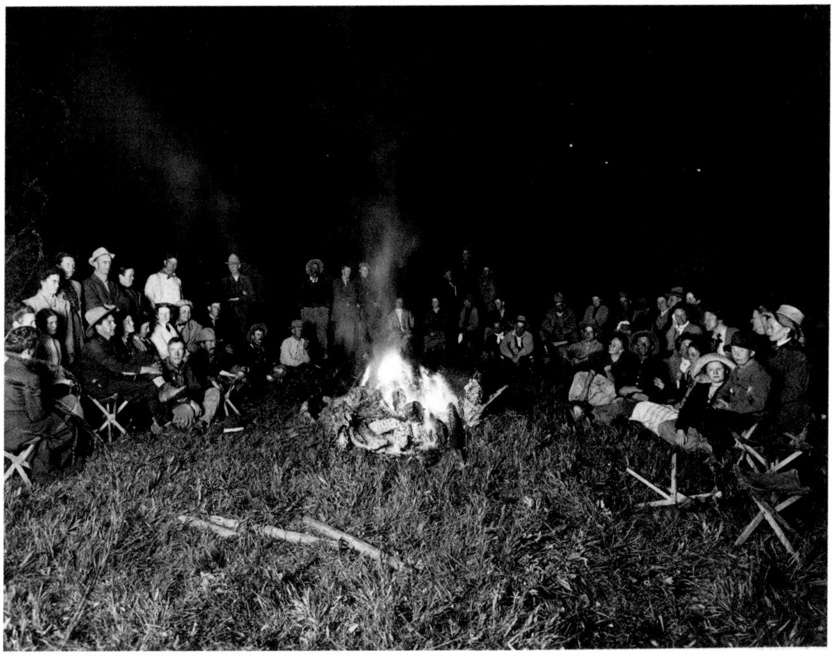

The camping life was as much a part of the Tex Holm experience as touring the sites of Wonderland. After a hearty evening meal prepared by talented camp cooks, guests often gathered around the fire to share the day's stories, sing songs, and perhaps hear tales from Tex himself. In this photo, everyone is dressed for the trail, making it difficult to differentiate between the dudes and the wranglers. These uncommon, numbered images may have been given or sold to guests.

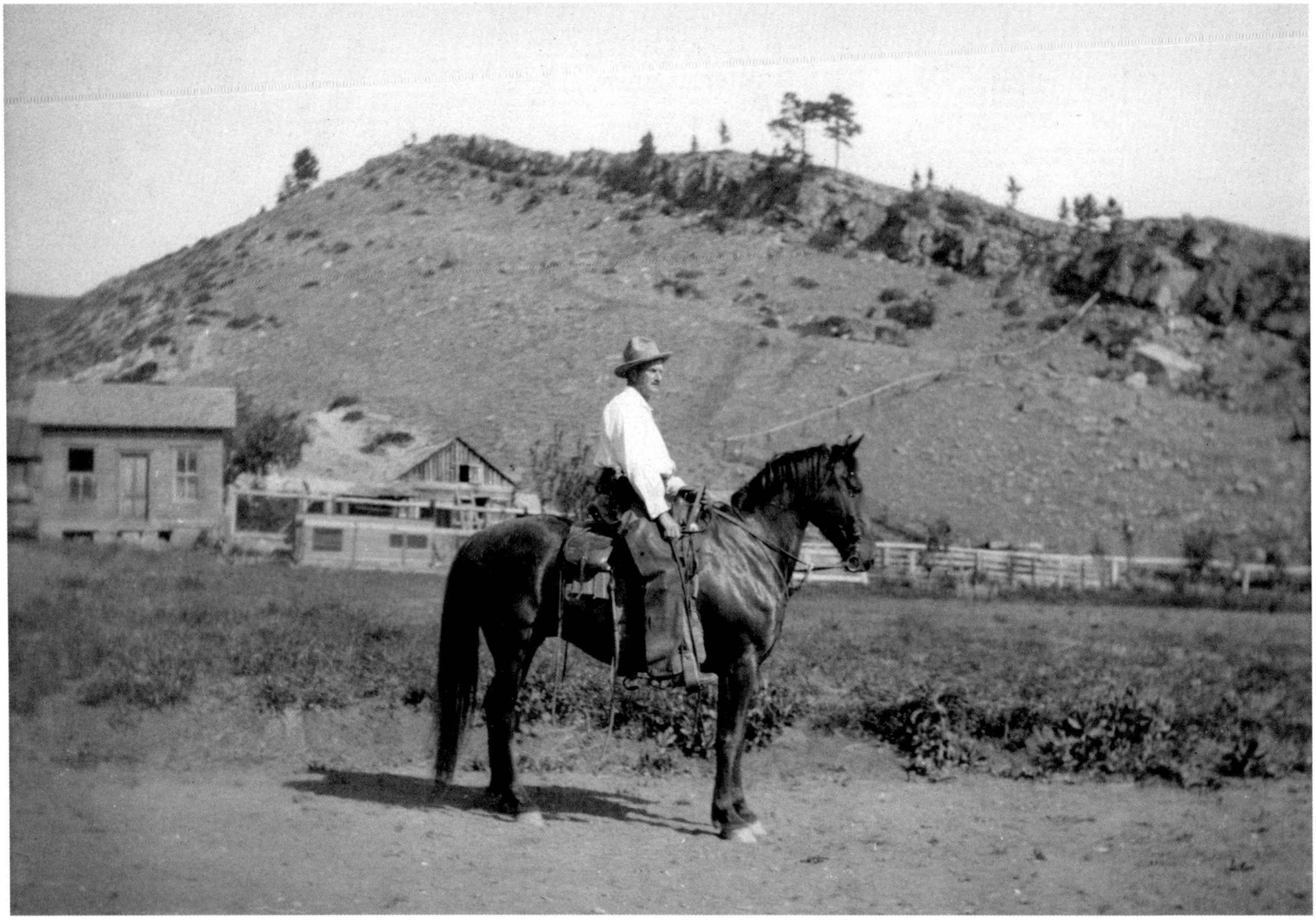

A photo from the Eaton photo album shows Howard Eaton posing atop a fine-looking horse, most likely a Morgan-Standardbred cross, between July 3-8, 1906, at the Eaton Ranch in Wolf, Wyoming. The brothers Howard, Willis, and Alden Eaton established the first dude ranch in America in 1870 near Medora, North Dakota, and became well-acquainted with President Theodore Roosevelt during his frequent trips to the region. Howard Eaton led his first pack trip into Yellowstone in 1883, and in 1904, recognizing the economic potential of the young national park, the family relocated their operation to Wolf Creek, outside of Sheridan, Wyoming. Most of their guests were wealthy travelers from the East Coast who were seeking outdoor experiences. They wanted to ride horses and sleep in a tent. Yet with all the amenities and care Eaton bestowed on his guests, the experience was more like modern-day "glamping." As a popular and politically well-connected figure in Yellowstone for more than thirty years, who was one of the park's strongest advocates, Howard Eaton's untimely death in 1922 inspired naming a 157-mile hiking trail and bridle path in the park after him. After several reconfigurations over the decades, particularly because the trail passed through sensitive, geothermal areas, the National Park Service ceased maintaining the trail in 1970. *Photo courtesy of Jay C. Lyndes Family Collection.*

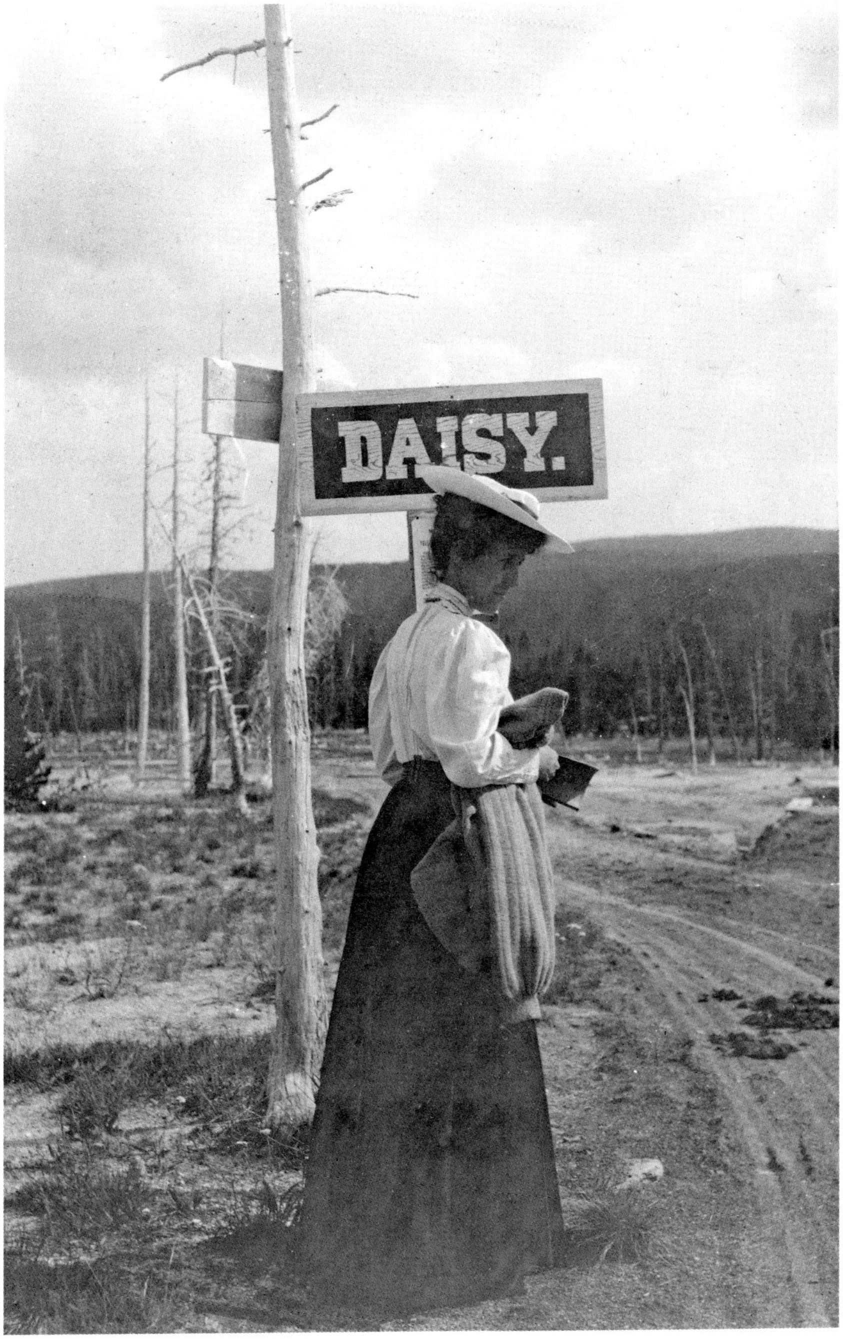

A female guest of Eatons' Ranch, circa-1906, waits by the sign for Daisy Geyser in the Upper Geyser Basin. From 1883 to 1922, Howard Eaton guided groups of up to sixty guests at a time for two to three-week tours, camping in style while seeing Yellowstone from a perspective not found from a stage-coach or automobile. This was also the time of the Women's Suffrage Movement, and Eaton encouraged women to "ride astride" instead of side-saddle. He probably surmised that his camping trips attracted forward-looking, independent-minded ladies who would do so, in contrast to the women who stayed in hotels. It is difficult to tell whether this lady was wearing a pair of pants below her ankle-length skirt, which was an option before split skirts or trousers were acceptable. *Photo courtesy of Jay C. Lyndes Family Collection.*

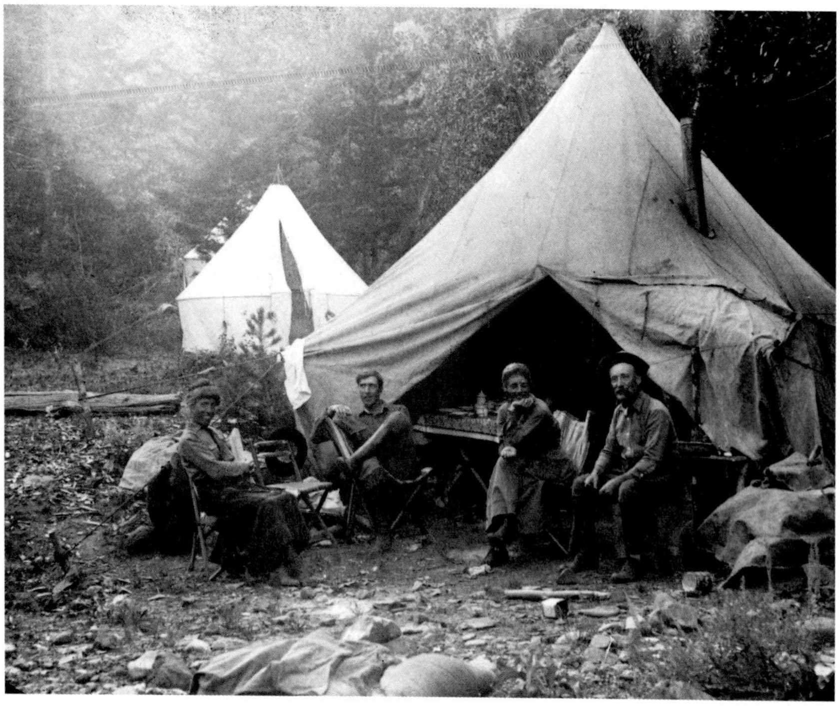

Smiling visitors Mrs. Merrill and Miss Harper relax at the cook tent with J.C. Harmon and their guide, Monte Jones, who is most likely the gentleman smoking the pipe, at the Majo Ranch camp on Ishawooa Creek in 1916. Although this location is in Wyoming beyond the eastern boundary of the park, the Majo Ranch, established in 1911, was an excellent home base for many travelers visiting Yellowstone. It reportedly was Buffalo Bill Cody's favorite lodging in the area. *Photo courtesy of Jay C. Lyndes Family Collection.*

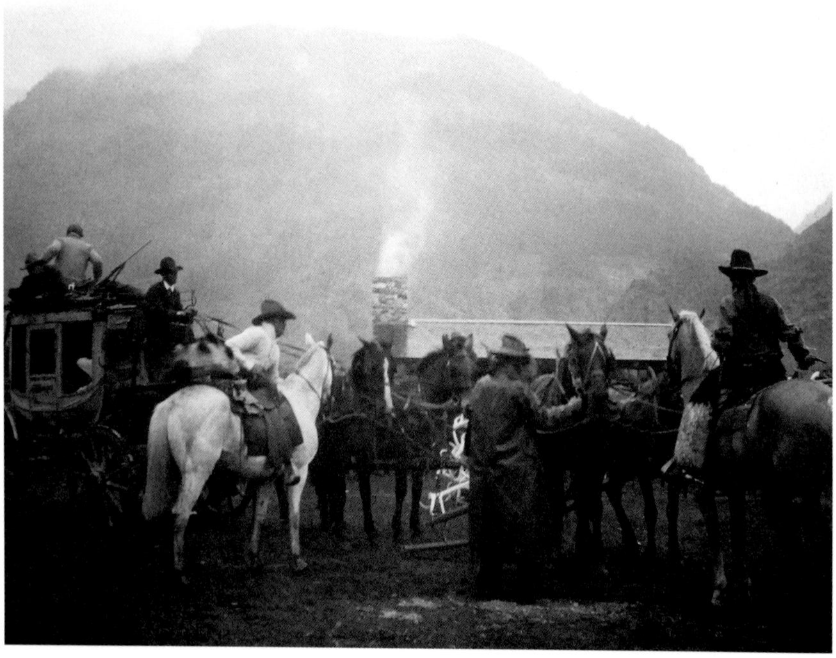

In the 1880s, stagecoach robberies truly happened within the park, but in this 1916 photo, the Valley Ranch performs a mock hold-up for its guests, complete with a stagecoach and "bandits." The Valley Ranch offered multi-week outings that were often large affairs involving dozens of guests. Larry Larom and his business partner, Winthrop Holley Brooks, purchased the ranch in 1915. At that time, Europe was fighting World War I, making Yellowstone an ideal travel alternative for wealthy Easterners. *Photo courtesy of Jay C. Lyndes Family Collection.*

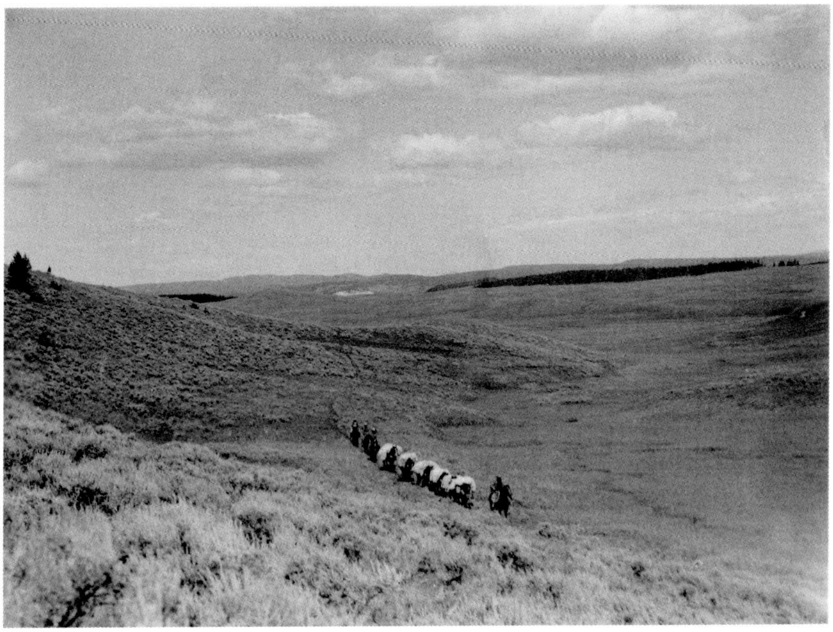

It was never an easy endeavor to organize a couple of dozen dudes, tents, chuck wagons, guides, and gear, as evident in this circa-1925 photo. The wide shot shows wranglers leading pack mules through Hayden Valley to the next camp, with Forest Springs in the background. Typically, "hired hands" broke down the camps, moved them, and set them up again while the dudes rode off with their guide to see the sights of Wonderland.

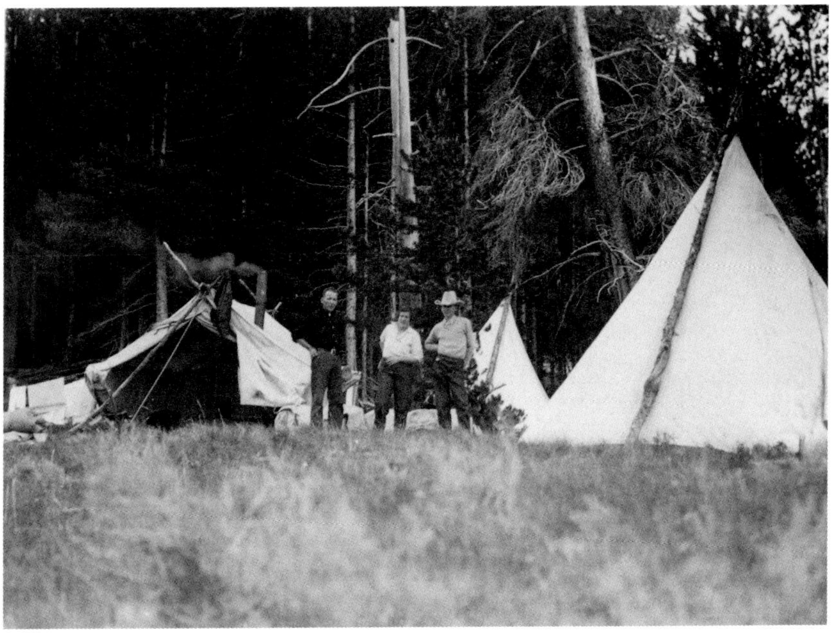

In this circa-1925 photo, three people, most likely guests, stand next to the pyramidal tents that were common in mobile camps because they were easy to set up and break down. The smoking chimney in the wall tent indicates that cooks were busy preparing meals. Wall tents, named for their low vertical sides (walls), were roomier and better suited for cooking and dining.

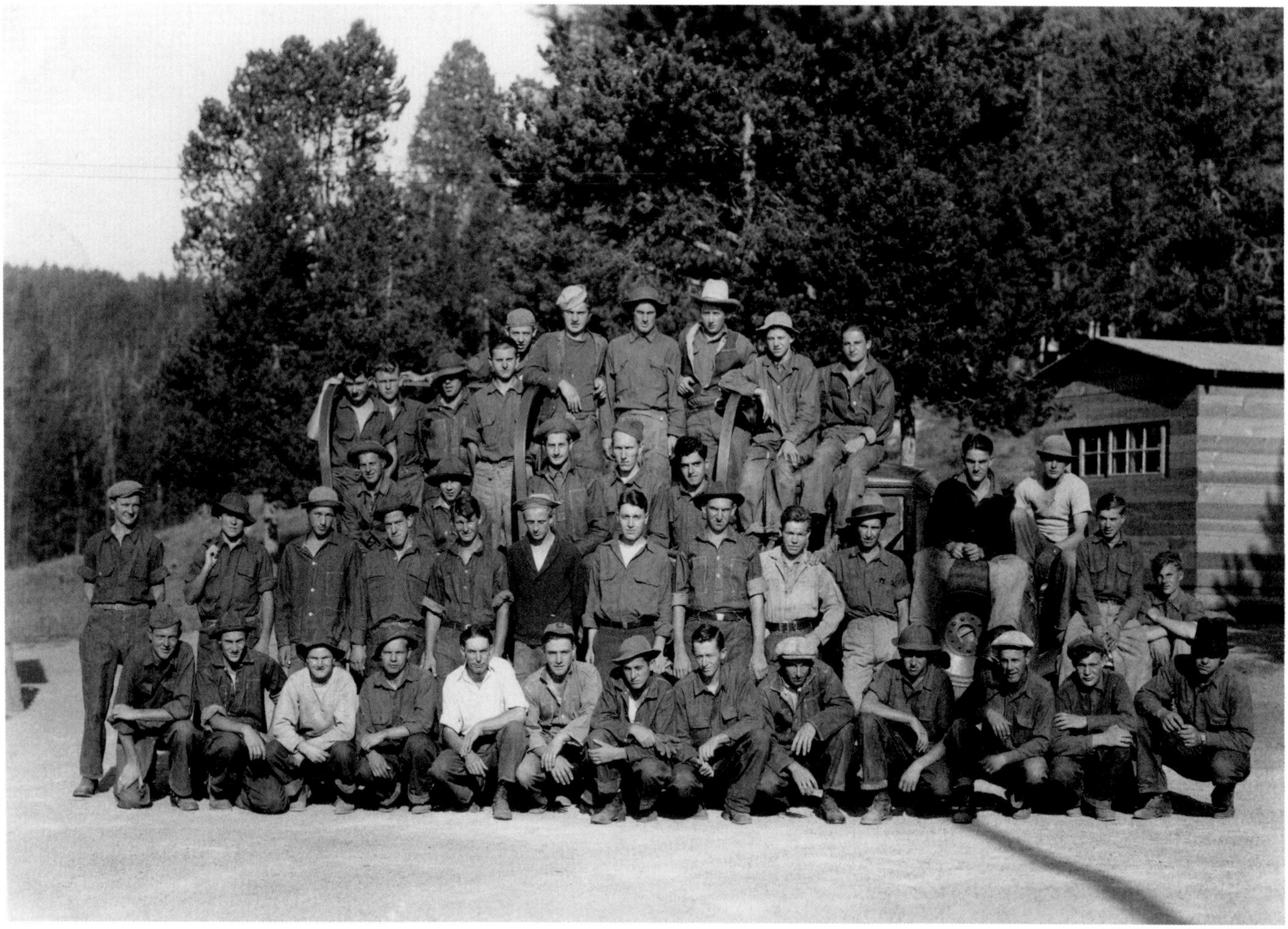

Created as part of President Franklin Delano Roosevelt's "New Deal" program during the Great Depression, the Civilian Conservation Corps offered a way for young men to support their families who remained back at home. Enrollees were unmarried men between the ages of 18 and 25, each earning a dollar a day, with most sending $25 home every month. In Yellowstone, they were critical for fire suppression, including fighting active wildfires and building preventative measures such as fire caches and fire breaks. A typical camp averaged 200 men, but they often broke into smaller groups to tackle specific projects. This photo shows 42 members of CCC Company 58, YNP 2, Group 3 at Canyon Camp in July 1934. They are posing on the camp truck, most likely before heading out to daily tasks. Note the brand-new cabin at the right. Photo from the Warren A. Brown album, Pickerington, Ohio.

CHAPTER 9

Time Well Spent: Civilian Conservation Corps

During the Great Depression, President Franklin Delano Roosevelt created "New Deal" programs to provide work—and hope—to millions of Americans. One program was the Civilian Conservation Corps (CCC), which employed thousands of young men to work on conservation projects.

The CCC lifted many young men out of poverty. They were able to send money home to their families. Some even got an education by taking CCC classes.

In Yellowstone, there were around a half dozen CCC camps from 1933 to 1941. The men built and improved trails, roads, and structures that benefited the park's infrastructure and improved the visitor experience. They were an important part of fire prevention and firefighting.

Their hard work was integral in developing many of the park amenities that visitors still enjoy today. It was a noble project that made a lasting impact to the men and the park.

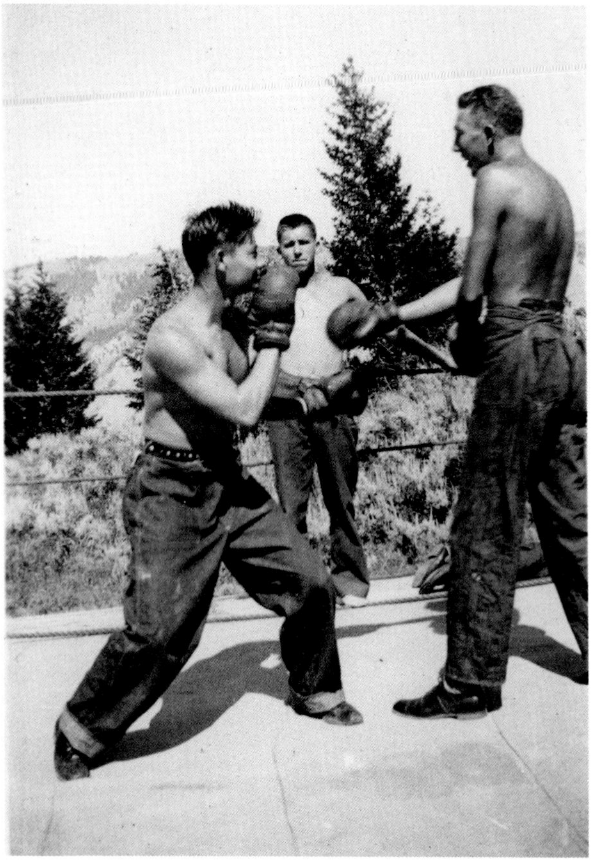

Two men from the Civilian Conservation Corps test their physical prowess sparring in an outdoor ring at Mammoth Hot Springs in this photo taken in the mid-1930s. The CCC worked within Yellowstone National Park from 1933 to 1941, constructing trails, buildings, and bridges to make the park "more comfortable and attractive to visitors" as part of President Franklin Delano Roosevelt's Emergency Conservation Work Act of 1933, more commonly known as the "New Deal." Recreational activities, including basketball, baseball, and boxing, gave these young men an opportunity to blow off steam from what could be mundane jobs.

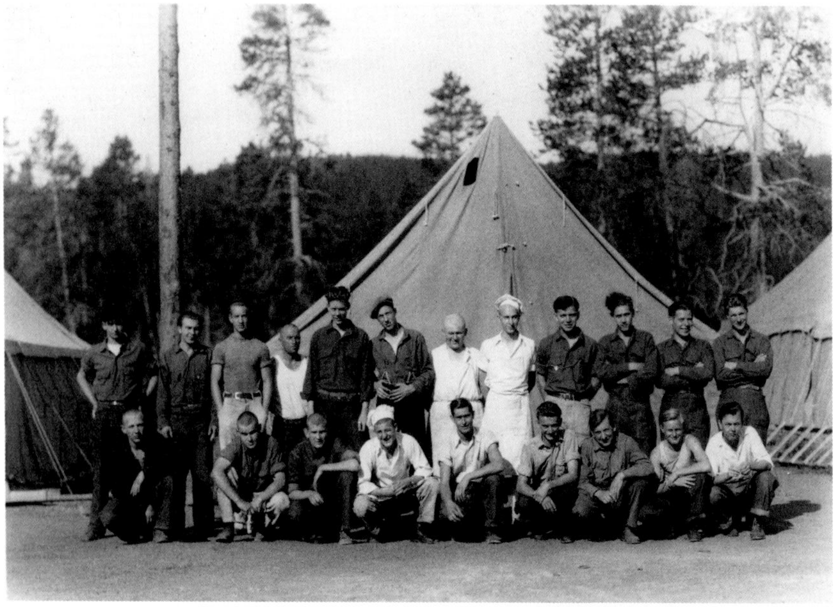

It took many hands to feed the hungry workers of the Civilian Conservation Corps Company 581, YNP 2, at Canyon Camp in July 1934. The cooks, including some apparent additional kitchen staff, made sure everything ran smoothly in the mess. Organized in a similar fashion as a military encampment, the camp fed an average of 200 men three high-calorie meals each day. Malnutrition was a significant problem in some regions during the Great Depression, so for many of the enrollees, even the basic CCC fare was more than they received at home. *Photo from the Warren A. Brown album, Pickerington, Ohio.*

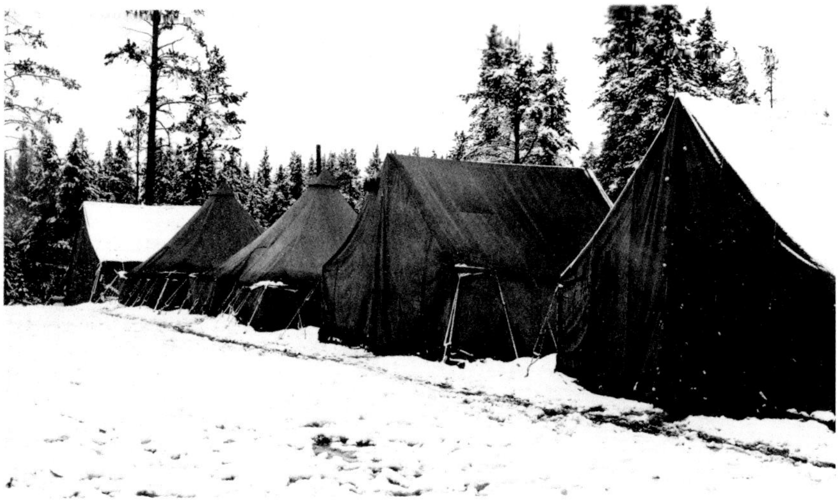

Even though the Civilian Conservation Corps operated during the summer in the park, snow falling during any month was a chilly reality. These soggy-looking tents in 1934 most likely kept the young men dry, but whether they stayed truly warm was another matter. *Photo from the Warren A. Brown album, Pickerington, Ohio, of the CCC Company 581, YNP 2 at Canyon Camp.*

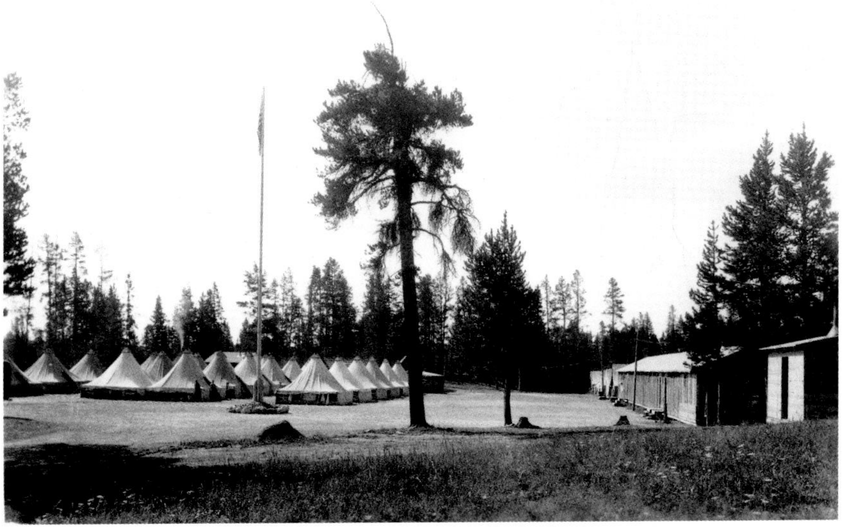

Mobile and efficient Bell tents house the men of the Civilian Conservation Corps Company 581, YNP 2, at Canyon Camp in this photo dated July 1934. The simple, wooden-frame buildings (right) housed the mess hall, canteen, and an area where the enrollees, some of whom did not have more than a sixth-grade education, took reading, writing, and arithmetic classes. Nationally, it was estimated that 57 million illiterate men learned to read through the CCC. *Photo from the Warren A. Brown album, Pickerington, Ohio.*

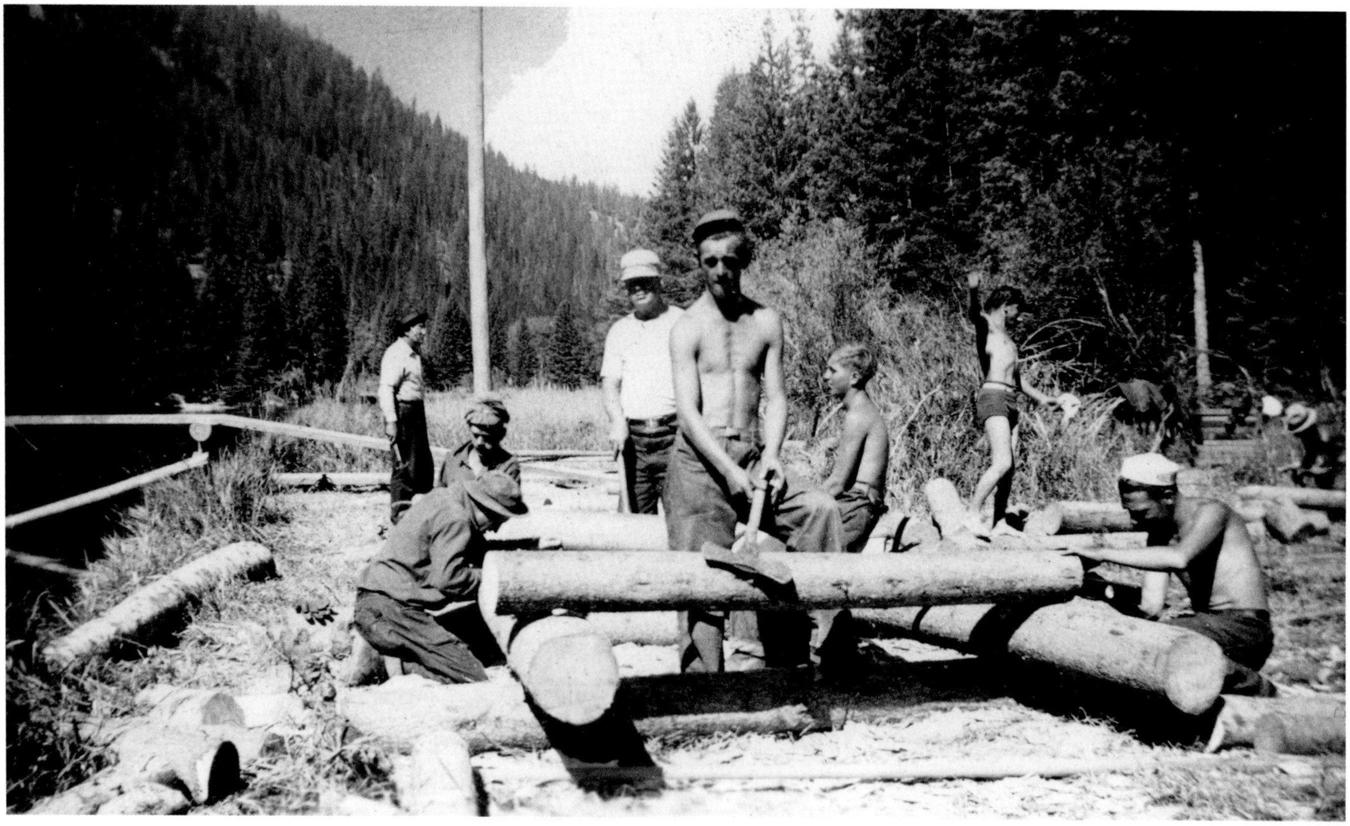

A CCC work detail builds a bridge in Yellowstone in 1935. During the CCC's nine years in the park, it accomplished much of the construction and maintenance work the park needed, particularly because National Park Service seasonal staffing was limited. Among numerous projects, the Corps' young men built trails and improved roads, assisted with revegetation for elk habitat, and constructed the facilities at the Lamar Buffalo Ranch. *Photo from the Warren A. Brown album, Pickerington, Ohio, of the CCC Company 581, YNP 5, at Camp Old Faithful.*

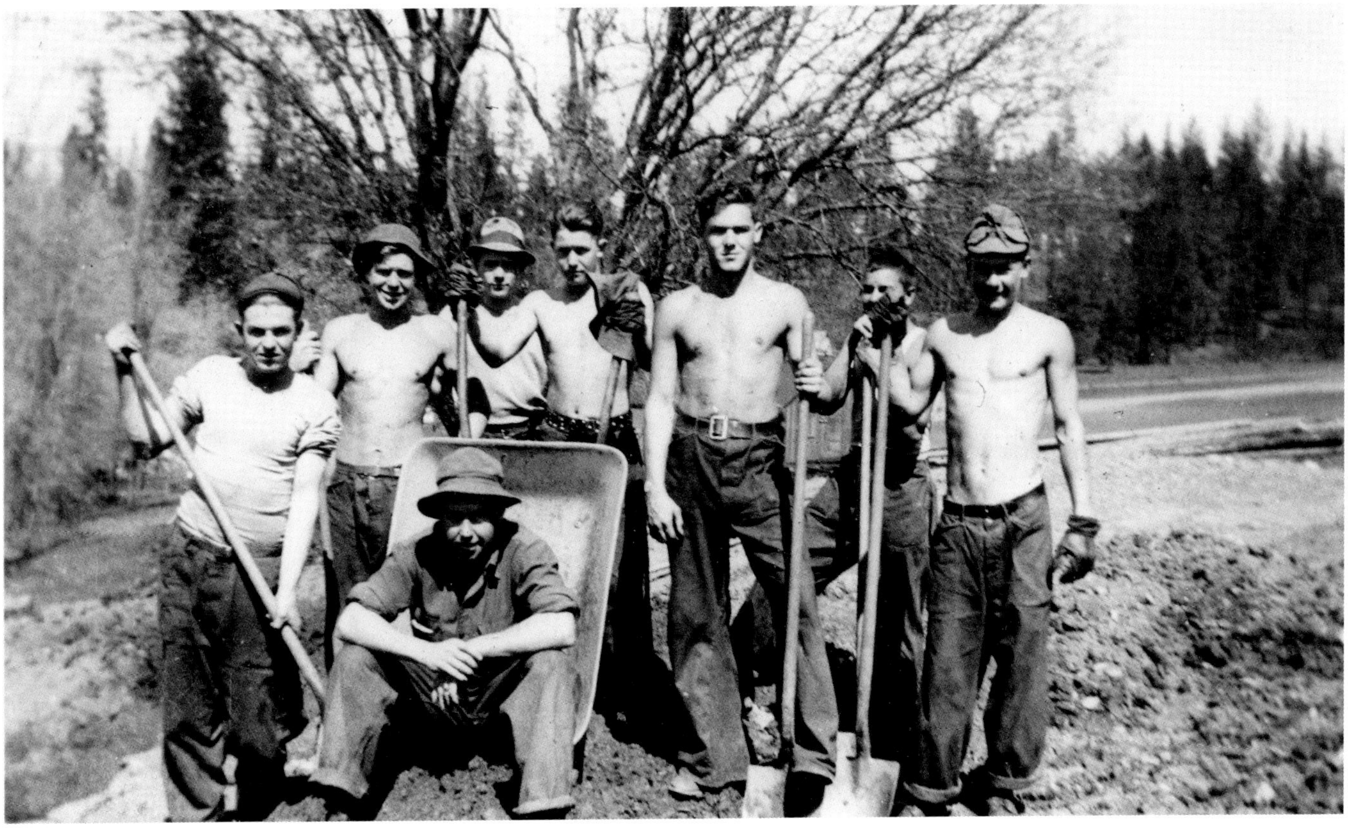

Shovel work was part of many CCC projects. Here a group of enrollees takes a break from the work to pose for the photo. These young men were part of the Civilian Conservation Corps Company 581, YNP 5, at the Camp Old Faithful, in the summer of 1935. CCC workers built or improved many of the park's roads and bridges, and cleared or constructed hundreds of miles of trails, during the worst years of the Great Depression. *Photo from the Warren A. Brown album, Pickerington, Ohio.*

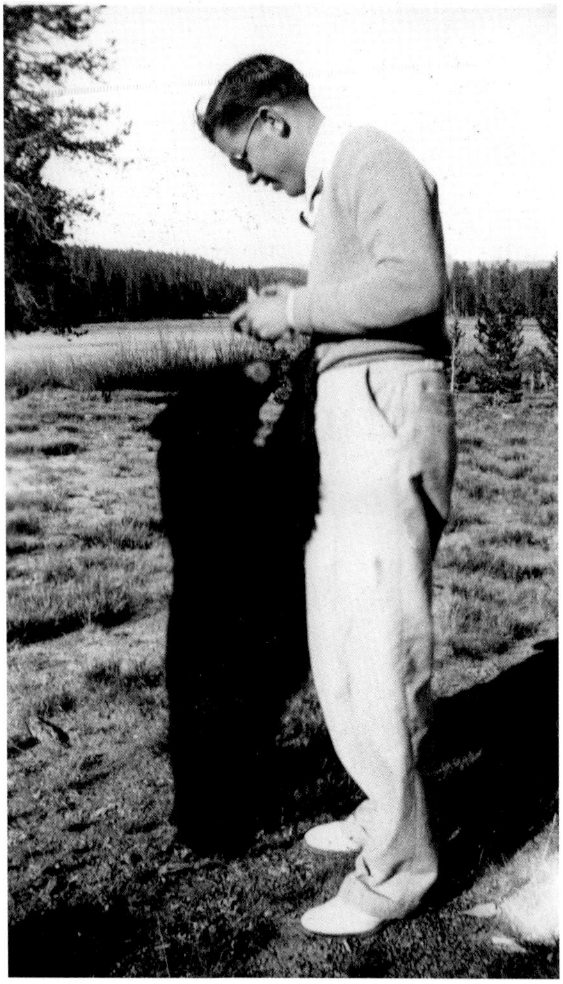

Like other visitors and employees of the park, the Civilian Conservation Corps men often interacted with the park's bears. In 1935 a member of CCC Company 581, YNP 5 at the Camp Old Faithful lets a black bear cub put its front paws on him while the cub stands up and begs for food. Such contact—and feeding—has long since been prohibited in the park. *Photo from the Warren A. Brown album, Pickerington, Ohio.*

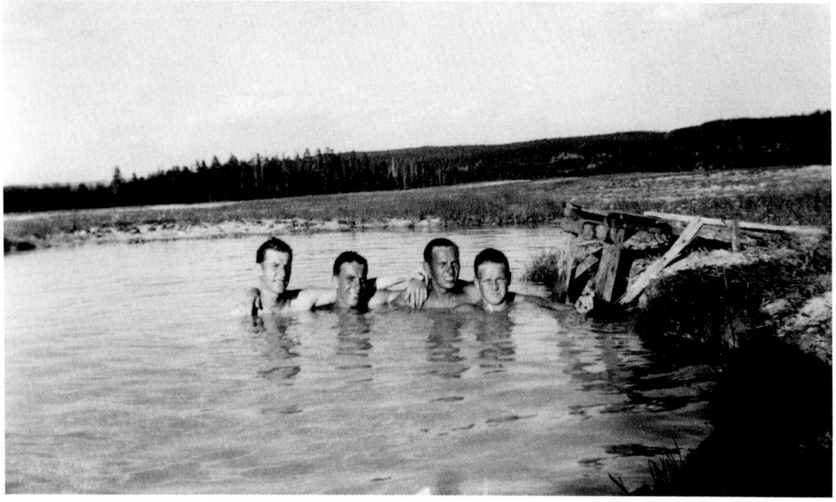

The CCC was not all work and no play, as demonstrated by these four enrollees swimming in a small pond. They were members of the Civilian Conservation Corps Company 581, YNP 5, at the Camp Old Faithful in 1935. Besides swimming when they could, the enrollees played pool in the recreation hall, had a library at their disposal, and took classes to improve their educations. *Photo from the Warren A. Brown album, Pickerington, Ohio.*

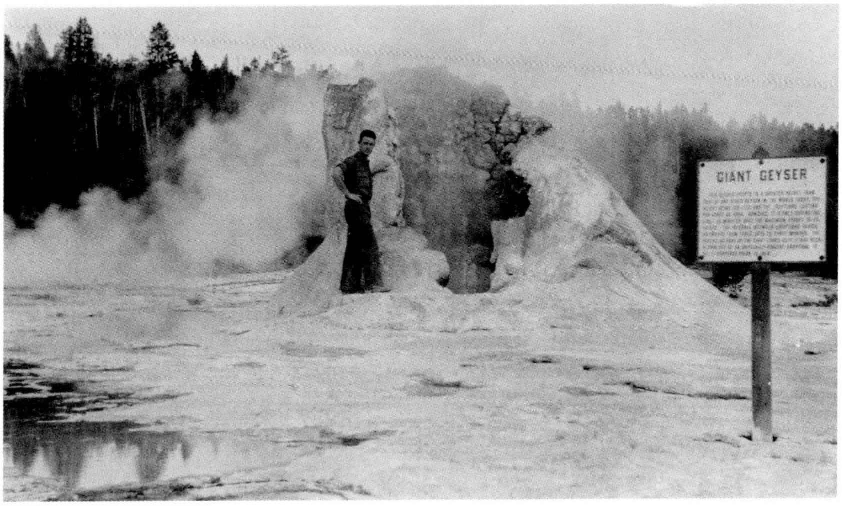

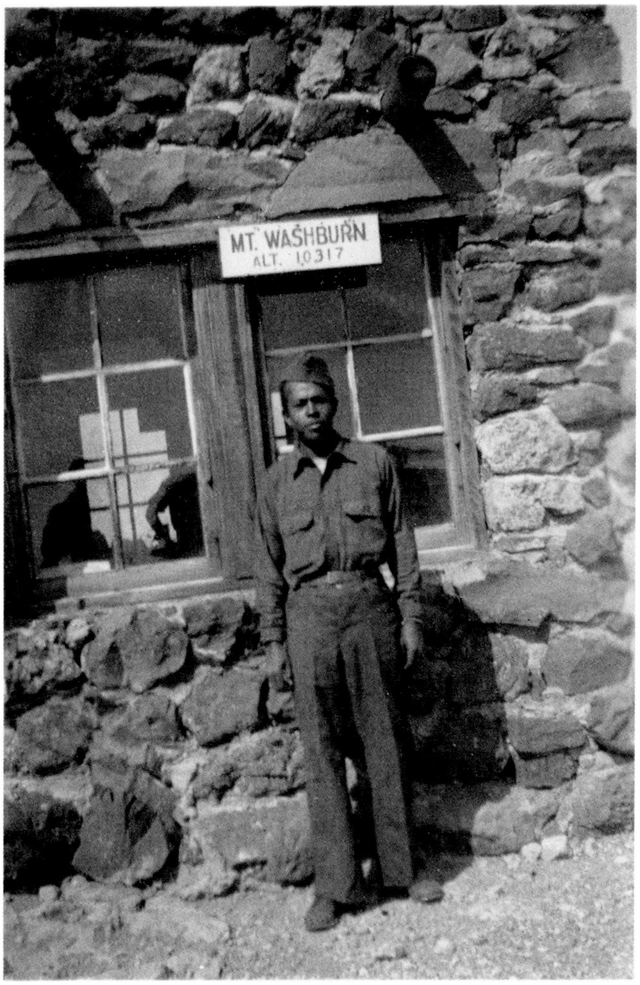

An enrollee of Civilian Conservation Corps Company 581, YNP 2 at Camp Canyon stands on the cone of Giant Geyser near the interpretive sign of this impressive feature. Giant Geyser, located within the Upper Geyser Basin, had the second tallest eruptions of any geyser in Yellowstone, spraying water over 250 feet high, but yielding the primary title to Steamboat Geyser. One of the benefits of living and working in the park for the CCC enrollees was experiencing these thermal features that were unlike anything they had ever seen near their homes. While standing on or close to thermal features was not technically against regulations during this time, it was illegal to purposefully damage them. Such closeness is prohibited today. In the bottom photo, an African American CCC enrollee from Company 581, YNP 2, Canyon Camp, poses in his uniform at the Mount Washburn fire lookout in 1934. One provision within the law that created the CCC specified no discrimination based upon race, color, or creed, but in 1935, only ten percent of CCC members were African American. *Photos from the Warren A. Brown album of Pickerington, Ohio, of Civilian Conservation Corps Company 581, YNP 2, at of Canyon Camp.*

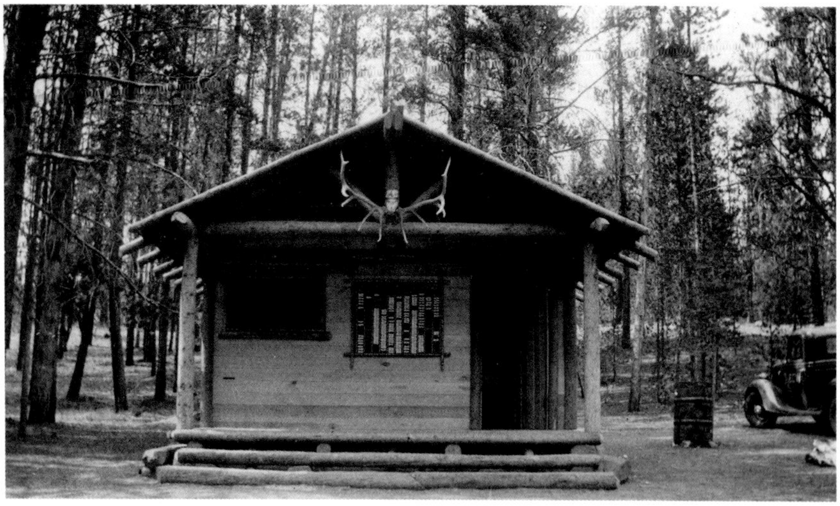

This newly constructed, duty-assignment cabin decorated with antlers was built probably at Old Faithful in 1935. Notice the slotted assignment cubby on the front wall. It held work instructions for enrollees to pick up each day. *Photo of CCC Company 581, YNP 5 at Camp Old Faithful from the Warren A. Brown album, Pickerington, Ohio.*

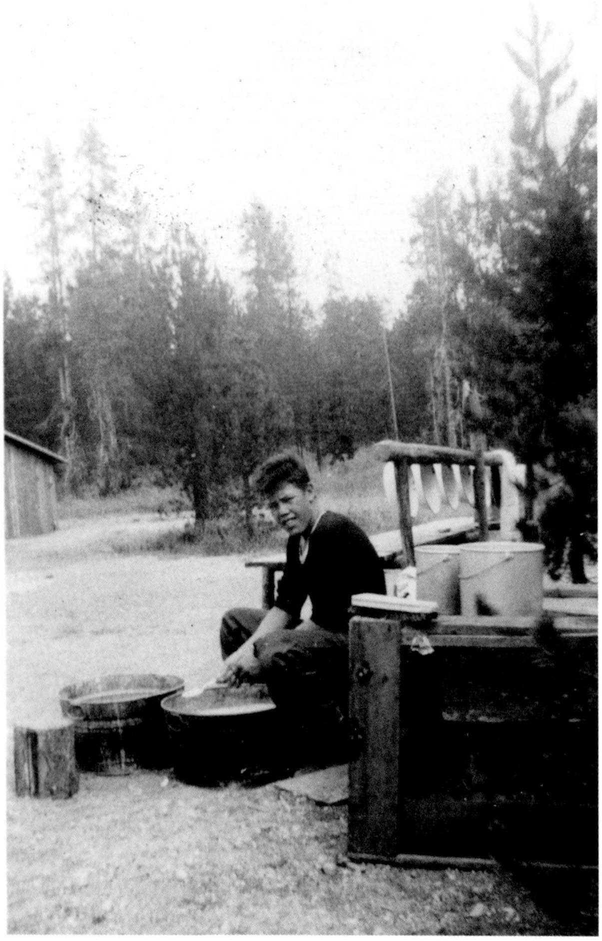

Scrubbing pots is not glamorous work, but it has to be done. This photo shows a Civilian Conservation Corps enrollee doing his "kitchen patrol" (KP) duty at CCC Company 581, YNP 2, at Camp Canyon in 1934. Many of the young men arrived underweight from the lean years of the Depression. The quality of meals varied from camp to camp, but the men required high calorie nutrition, and consequently substantial food preparation was required on the part of the kitchen staff. Reportedly, the men enrolled in this program gained an average of 12 pounds by the end of their terms. *Photo from the Warren A. Brown album, Pickerington, Ohio.*

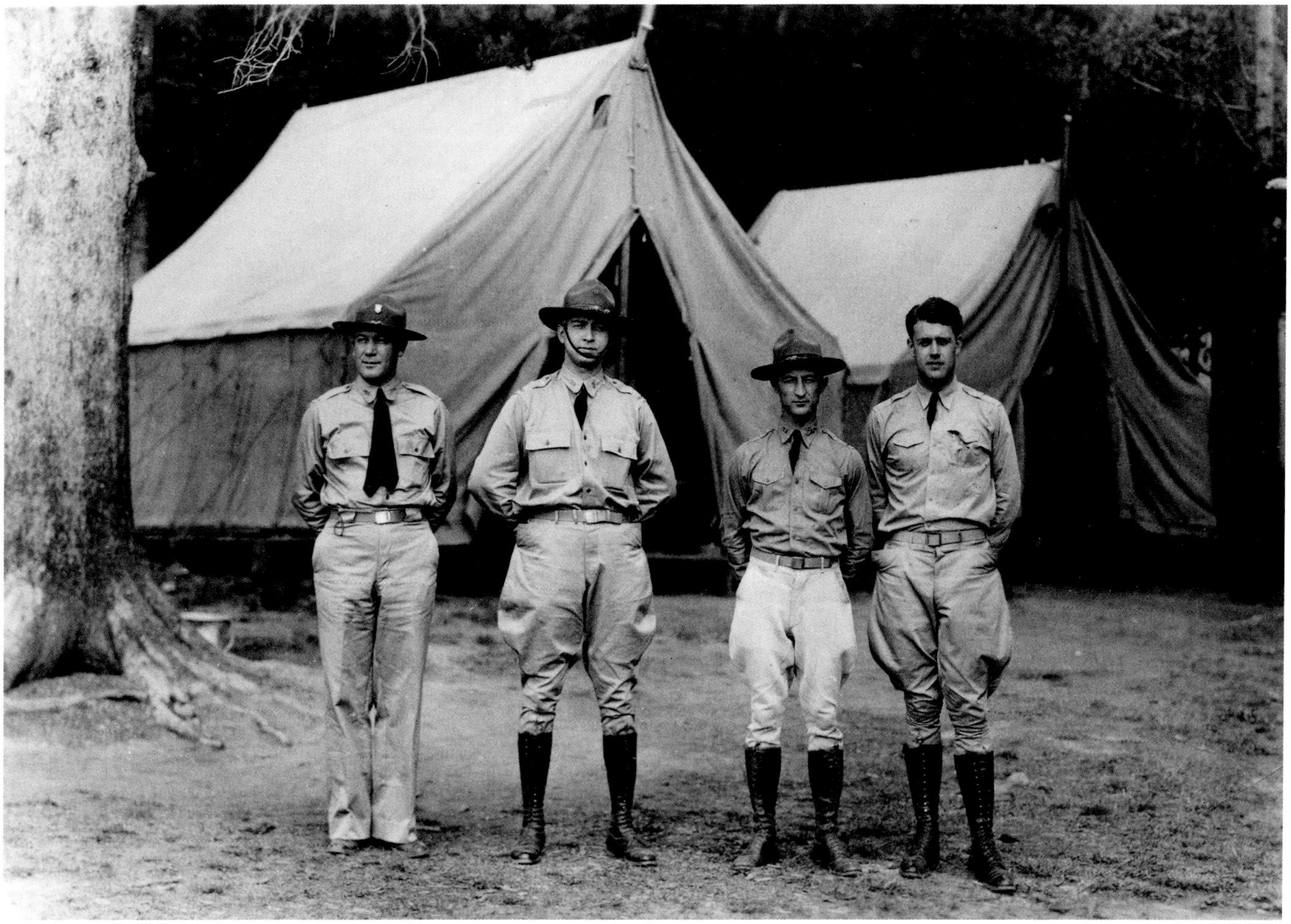

The Civilian Conservation Corps was set up in a military fashion to maintain order within the camps and provide structure for the young men. These CCC officers pose in front of the tents at the Canyon Camp of the CCC Company 581, YNP 2, in July 1934, possibly during a day off. *Photo from the Warren A. Brown album, Pickerington, Ohio.*

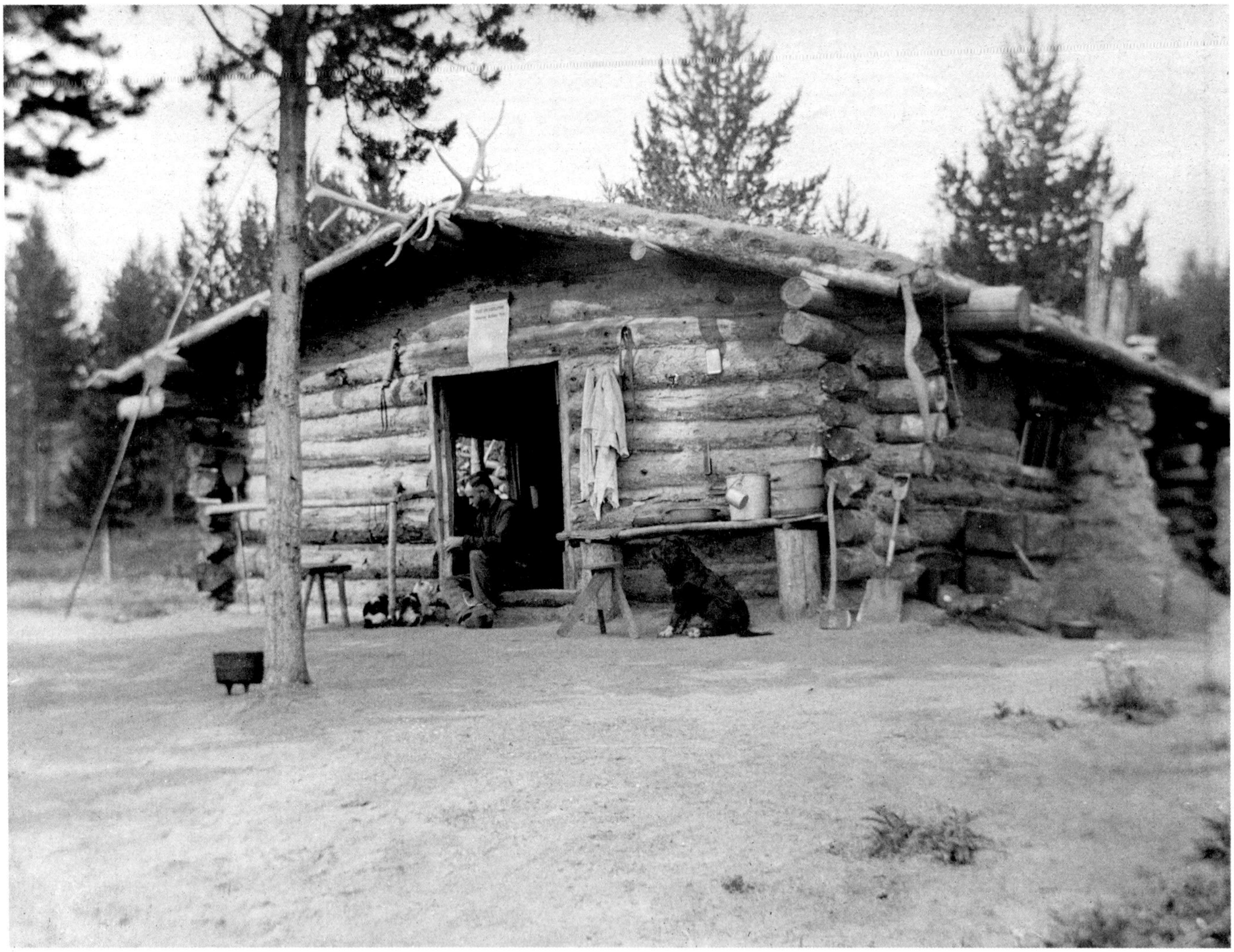

This is the only known photo of the Mud Geyser Soldier Station. Elk antlers decorate the roofline on the front and a sign above the door states, "Rules and Regulations, Yellowstone National Park." A soldier sits in the doorway, flanked by his dog and cats. The animals provided company at the lonely outposts, and the cats were useful in keeping mice at bay, since one mouse could wipe out supplies that were not easily restocked during the middle of winter. A pan and bucket of fresh water, with the drinking cup attached, sit on the bench along the front of the cabin, and a shaving mirror hangs at face height. Towels also hang within arm's reach. It is unknown why the Dutch oven is set by the tree. This station was built in 1895 and repaired two years later. When the Army took over administrative duties of Yellowstone in 1886, Captain Harris constructed six soldier stations. By the time the military left thirty-two years later a total of sixteen soldier stations housed troops in locations where they could best fulfill their duties: preventing the destruction of natural objects, fighting fires, keeping the peace with visitors, and patrolling the area in the winter to thwart poachers. While some men thrived in these rugged and remote places, others found the solitude, particularly during the long winters, disconcerting. As a result, "cabin fever" was a valid concern.

CHAPTER 10

The U.S. Military to the Rescue

For many years after Yellowstone was created in 1872, the few park officials there watched with frustrating helplessness as souvenir hunters broke off hunks of thermal features, poachers decimated the wildlife, outfits cut timber, and rogue entrepreneurs set up illegal businesses. Finally, in 1886, Congress sent in the U.S. Army to bring order and protection to the park.

Captain Moses Harris and approximately 60 men of Company M, First Cavalry, spent their first five years in frame buildings at the base of the Mammoth Terraces. In 1890, Congress allocated $50,000 for permanent structures, and by the following year, the first stately buildings were completed in Fort Yellowstone. More buildings followed as troop numbers increased to more than 300 soldiers (and some officers brought their families) by 1910.

The troops took their post seriously. They kept a watchful eye on geysers and prominent thermal features, patrolled the park on horseback, and built patrol cabins in several locations. In 1894 soldiers were integral in arresting poacher Ed Howell for killing some of the last remaining bison in the park. The notoriety of his capture created a public outcry and pressured Congress to pass the Lacey Act, which made it illegal to kill or capture wild animals in the park.

The U.S. Army watched over Yellowstone for 32 years, turning over control in 1916 when the National Park Service took the helm, and ultimately wrapping up its duty in 1918. Today, the 35 remaining buildings of Fort Yellowstone serve as a reminder of the decades the U.S. Army protected the park when nobody else could.

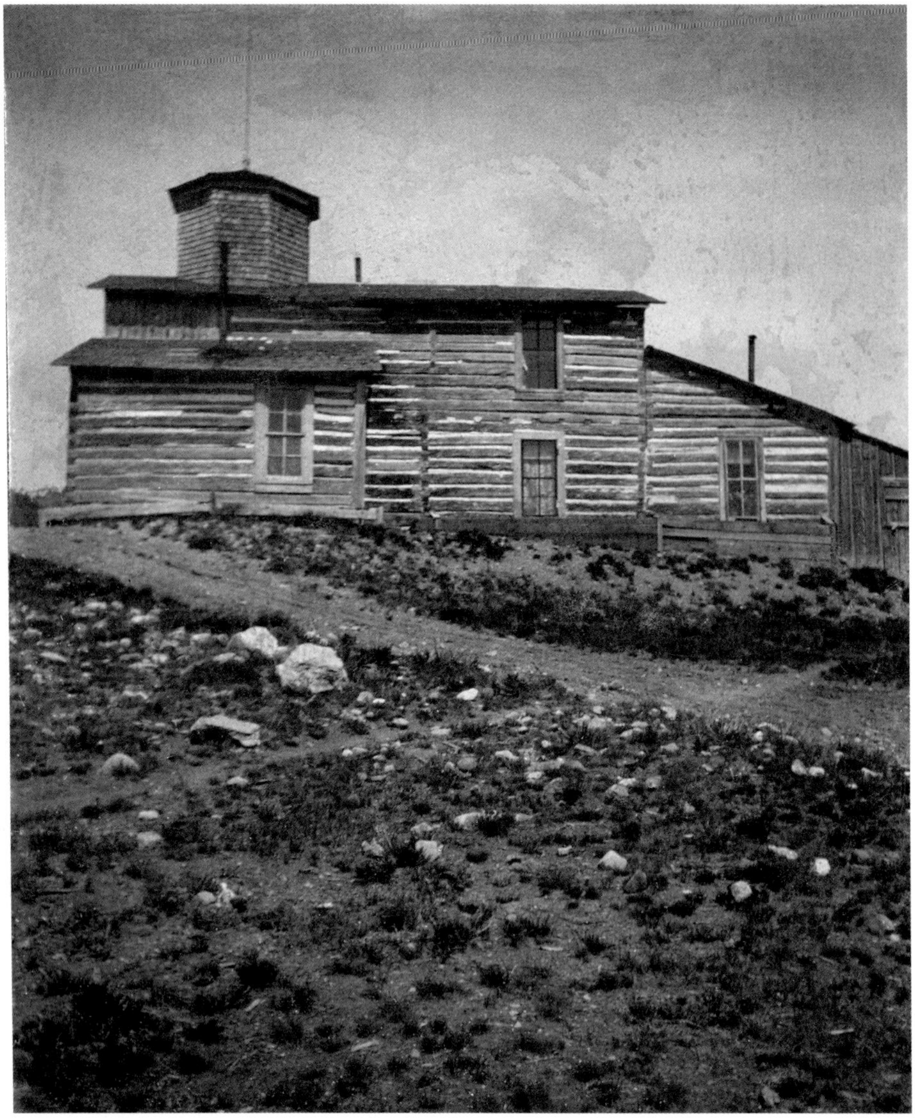

During the Nez Perce War of 1877, Chief Joseph led his tribe through Yellowstone as they fled from the U.S. Army. In case there were future hostilities, Philetus Norris, Yellowstone's second superintendent and ardent supporter of the park, decided to construct a defensible building. In 1879, he built what was ultimately called the Norris Blockhouse on top of Capitol Hill. The location provided a 360-degree view of the Mammoth Hot Springs area. The building also became the rudimentary park headquarters until the U.S. Army created Camp Sheridan at the base of Mammoth Terraces. This is an unusual side view of the building; it shows the road leading to it, the building's thick, hewn-log walls, and the formidable hexagon turret. The structure was razed in 1912, having outlived its purpose.

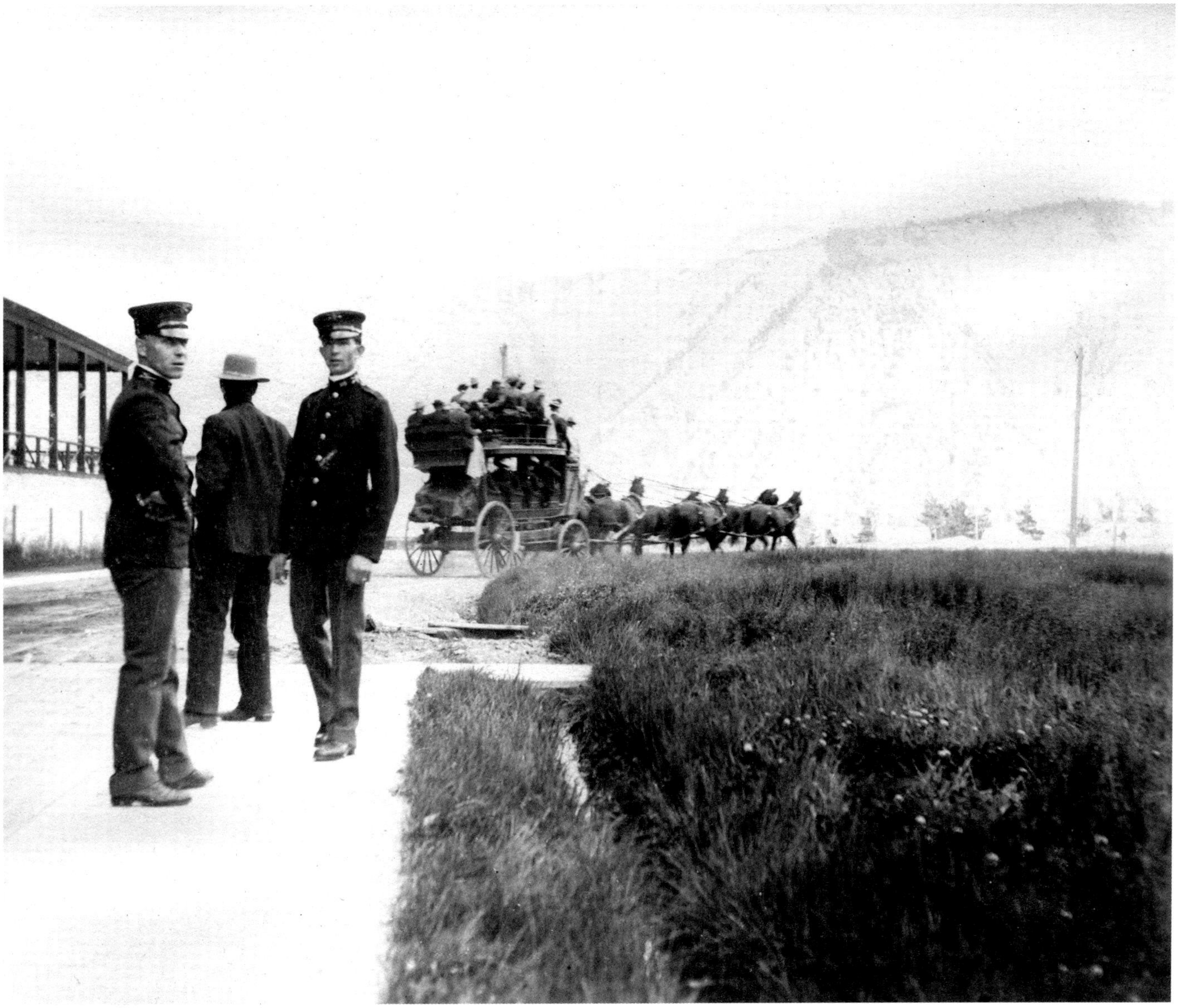

This circa-1890 to 1903 photo shows a fully loaded, six-horse, tally-ho stagecoach leaving the Mammoth Hotel. The passengers were most likely park visitors arriving or departing to the Northern Pacific Railroad Depot, either in Cinnabar prior to 1903 or to the depot at Gardiner in or after 1903. The Yellowstone Park Transportation Company used these observation coaches to carry up to thirty-five people and their luggage. There was enough room for one guest to sit next to the driver, four forward-facing seats in the interior, one seat on the back, and seats on top. This was during the era with a heavy presence of soldiers at Fort Yellowstone, as illustrated by the two soldiers standing along the pathway. Built five years after the initial military installation of Camp Sheridan in 1886, Fort Yellowstone housed additional troops to protect the park's resources. These young men typically earned $13 a month. Some stayed after their duty ended or returned as park rangers when the U.S. Army left the park in 1918.

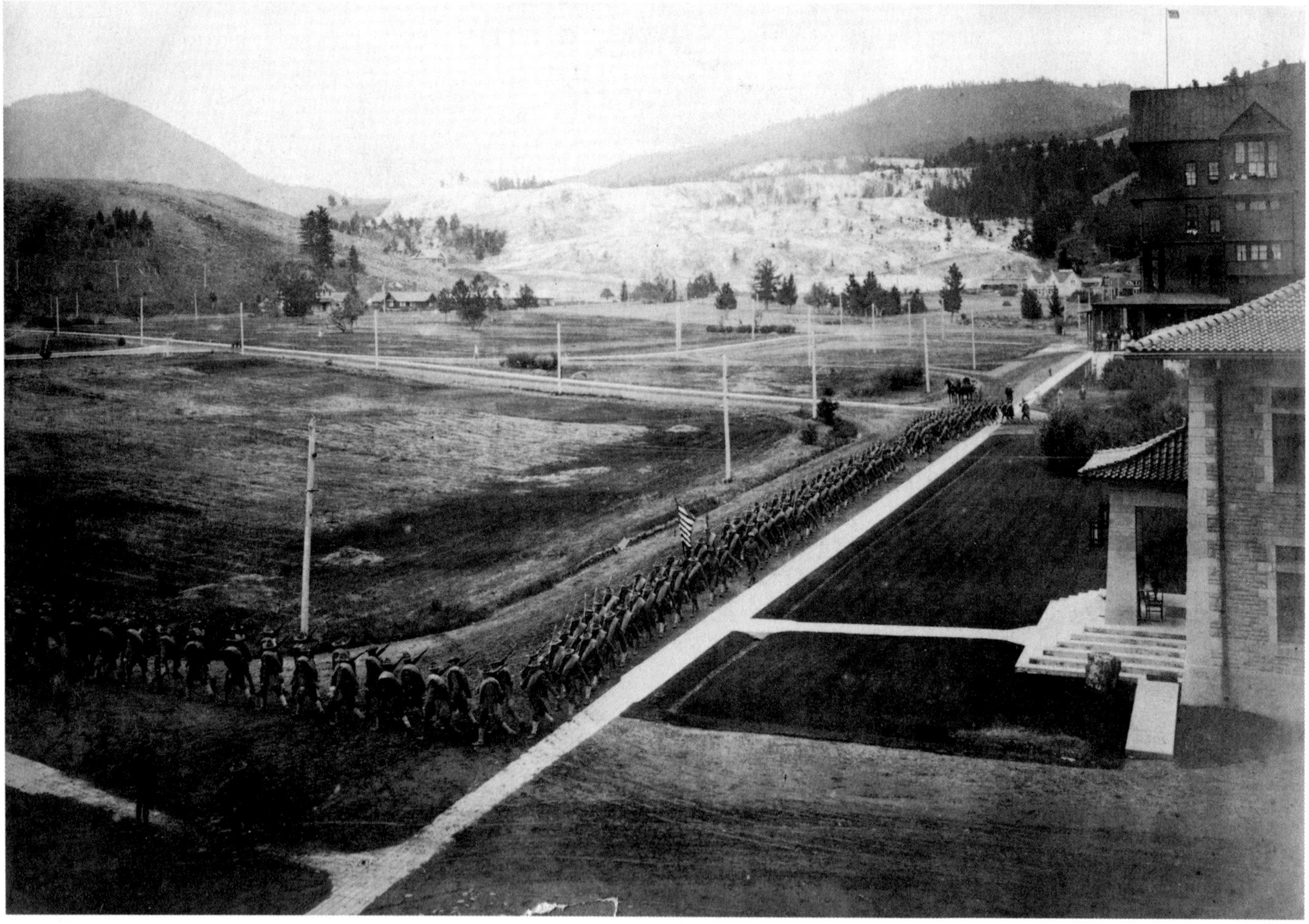

The Parade Ground was center stage for the troops, as in this photo of soldiers marching in formation on the road in front of the Mammoth Hot Springs Hotel at Fort Yellowstone. Every morning began to the sound of "Reveille" played by the post's bugler, followed by horse-mounted soldiers raising the flag. The post's bugler sounded once again in the evening, calling the troops to the grounds to lower the flag. At dusk, the cannon fired from Capitol Hill, and "Taps" played as the sun set to conclude the day. After outgrowing Camp Sheridan and needing winterized buildings, the military began construction of Fort Yellowstone in 1891. This photo was taken in or after 1903, because the stone office of the U.S. Army Corps of Engineers, called "The Pagoda" due to its hip-roof design, was built that year and is visible in the foreground.

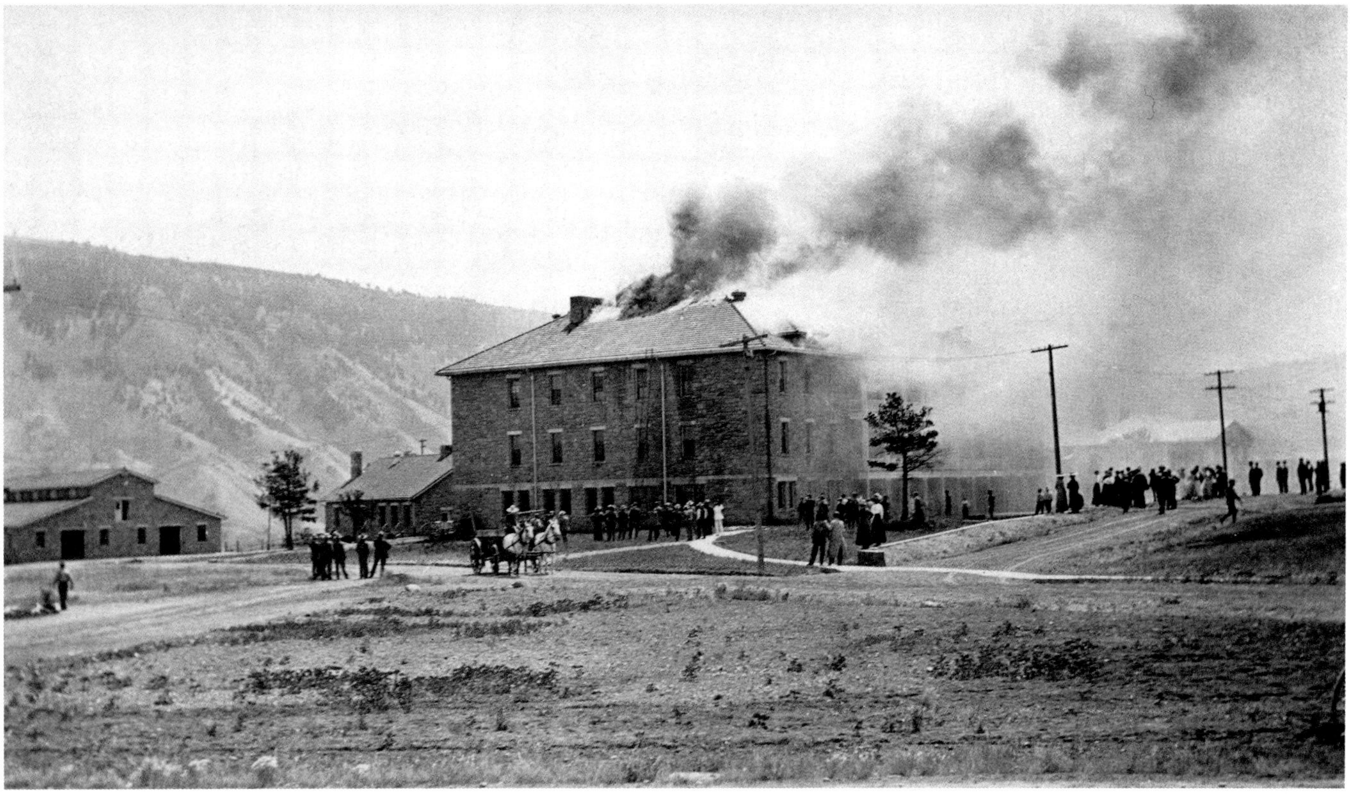

A photo by Rupert (probably the last name of the photographer) shows soldiers fighting the fire in the double barracks, which housed Troops F and G of the 1st Cavalry, on July 18, 1911, at Fort Yellowstone. The only reported injury was when a soldier fell three stories to the basement during the effort to extinguish the fire. It appears he survived. The fire, sparked by unknown causes, did not destroy the building, yet a 1972 structure report mentioned noticeable charring still evident in the rafters. The building stands today as the park's Administration Building.

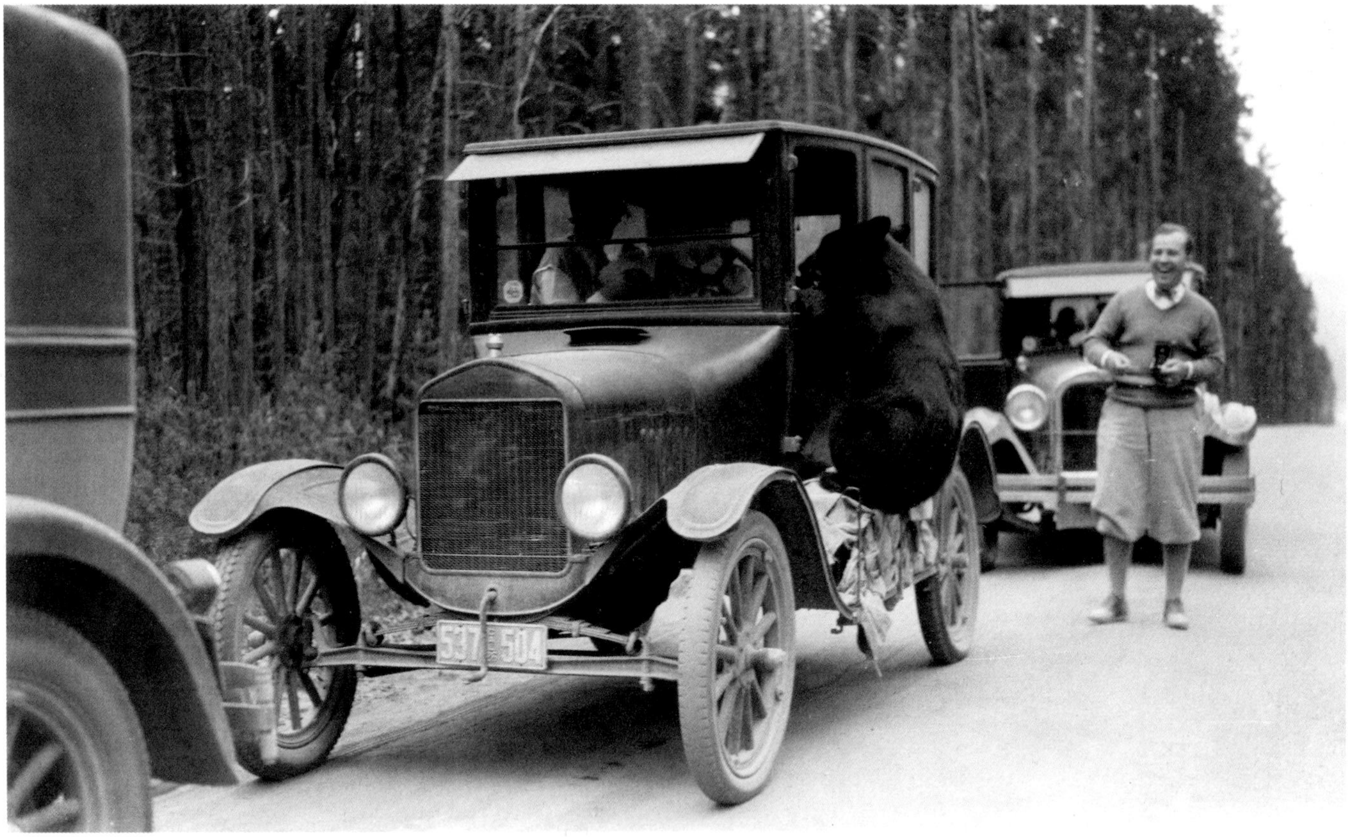

This 1926 photo is a comical shot of a black bear climbing onto a 1923-1925 Ford, Model-T Fordor Sedan, for a treat. The bear's boldness gives the standing gentleman, who holds a camera and might be the driver, a good reason to laugh. The bear is perched on what was most likely the family's tent, bundled and bound to the side of the car. At times, beggar bears damaged vehicles and gear in their attempts to secure a treat. The Fordor was the first four-door, touring automobile created by the Ford Motor Company. Selling for $725, it was also the most expensive. The license plate on the vehicle is from California. Notice the park entrance sticker on the passenger's side of the windshield. The car behind it is a 1925 or 1926 Dodge. *Photo courtesy of the Jay C. Lyndes Family Collection.*

CHAPTER 11

Wildlife Attractions

Wildlife has been a Yellowstone attraction as much as the park's thermal features and scenery. Enormous herds of elk roamed the high elevation meadows, and the park was the final bastion of wild bison.

Of course, bears have always been a key draw for visitors and employees alike.

From the early days, bears associated people with food, and many bears became regular guests to camps and hotels. They also took advantage of garbage dumps, and for a time there were so-called "lunch counters" where visitors could watch numerous bears feed while park rangers gave interpretive talks. "Holdup bears" that begged for food along roads was a recognized Yellowstone phenomenon. Today, the negative impacts of bears eating human food are well known, and feeding bears—or any park wildlife—is illegal.

Through the years, officials have adapted and abandoned various methods to "manage" the park's wildlife, changing as societal attitudes evolved and biological sciences reached new conclusions. One constant has been the park visitors and employees; they have always been enthralled with the park's wild creatures. Then and now, wildlife is the beating heart of Yellowstone.

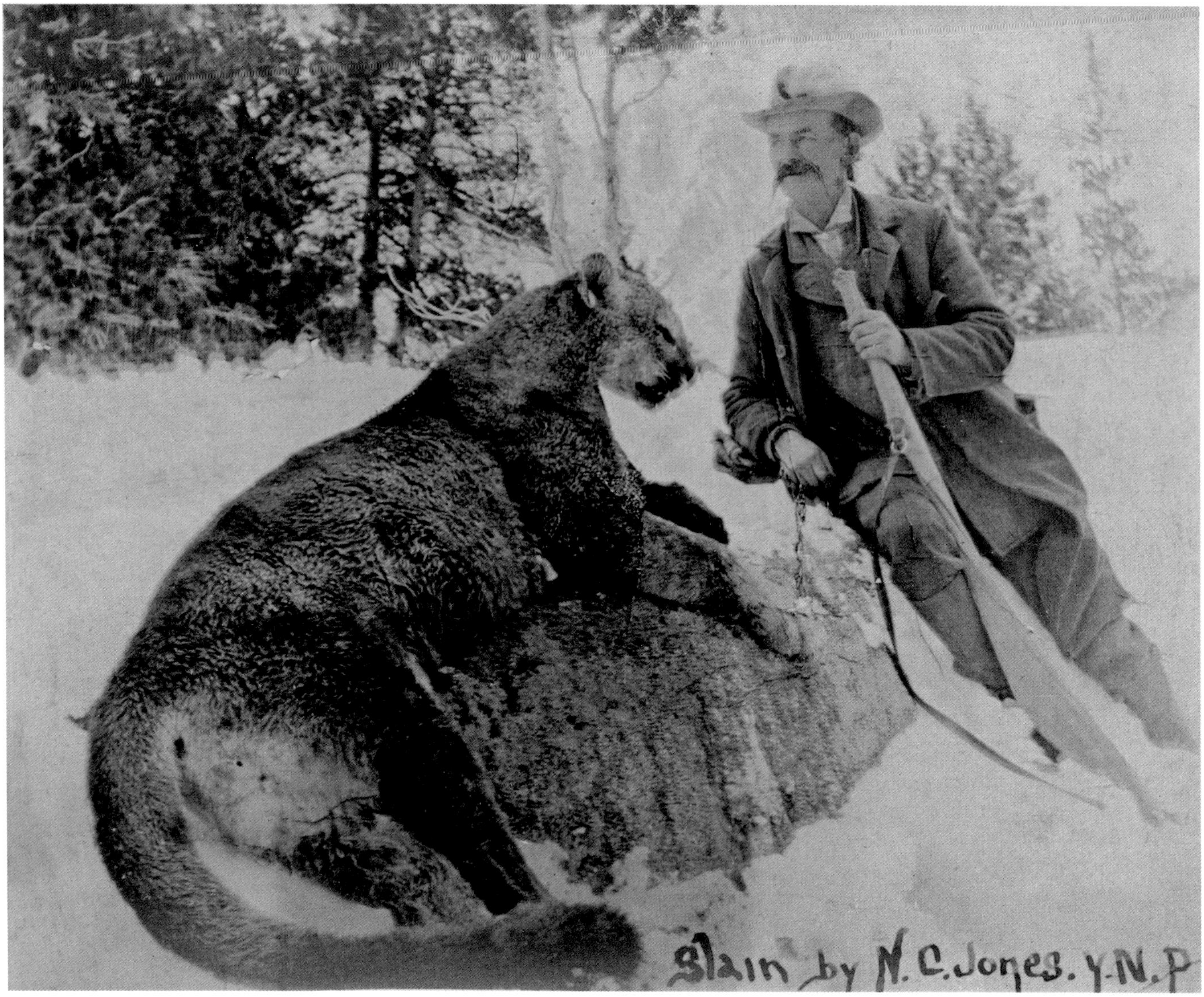

This circa-1900 image depicts the war on predators that was waged for decades in Yellowstone. Leaning against a large rock with his sheathed rifle in hand, N. C. Jones poses with a cougar he killed in the park. Shooting, trapping, and poisoning predators were common occurrences in the early days of the park, as well as throughout much of the West. These "beasts of waste and desolation," as Theodore Roosevelt referred to wolves, bears, coyotes, and mountain lions in 1885 during his time ranching in North Dakota, were viewed as a detriment to elk and "more desirable" species. Park officials shared a similar mindset, resulting in a thorough effort to trap, shoot, or poison everything from these apex predators to weasels and foxes. Within a couple of decades, Roosevelt had realized the importance of predators for the health of the herds, but it was not until 1931 that National Park Service Director Horace Albright curtailed the practice of actively killing them. By the 1920s mountain lions had been extirpated from Yellowstone. It was not until the early 1980s that a small but viable population reestablished itself within the park, followed by the government reintroduction of wolves in 1995.

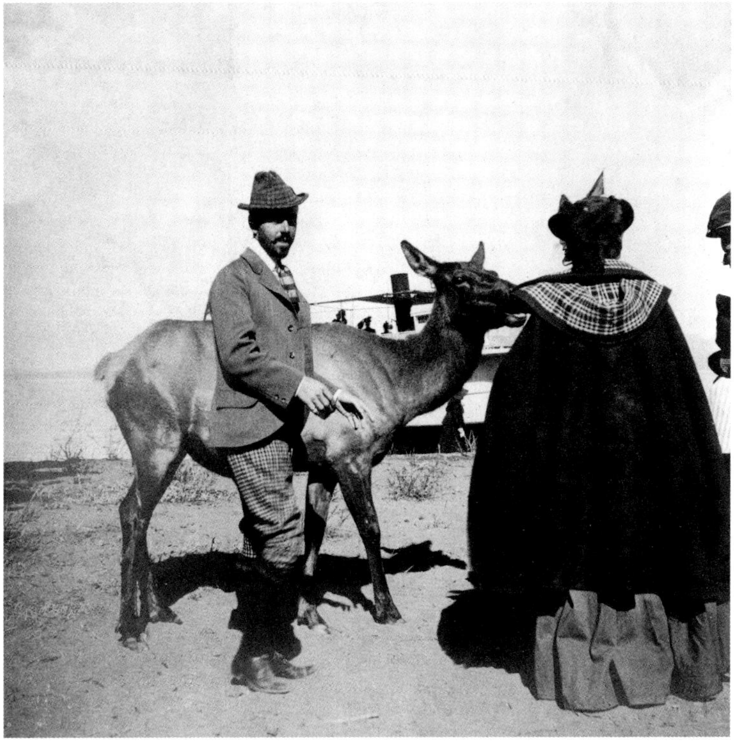

This image shows park visitors standing very close to a cow elk on Dot Island during their tour of Yellowstone Lake on the steamboat *Zillah*, which is partially visible in the background. E.C. Waters' Yellowstone Lake Boat Company transported visitors from Thumb Bay to Lake Hotel for a $2.50 fee above the cost of the stagecoach. He created his private zoo in 1896 precisely to encourage visitors to book a seat on the *Zillah*. The visitors are fashionably attired for the early 1900s, with the gentleman's plaid trousers and Homburg style of hat and the woman's long cloak and upswept hair style.

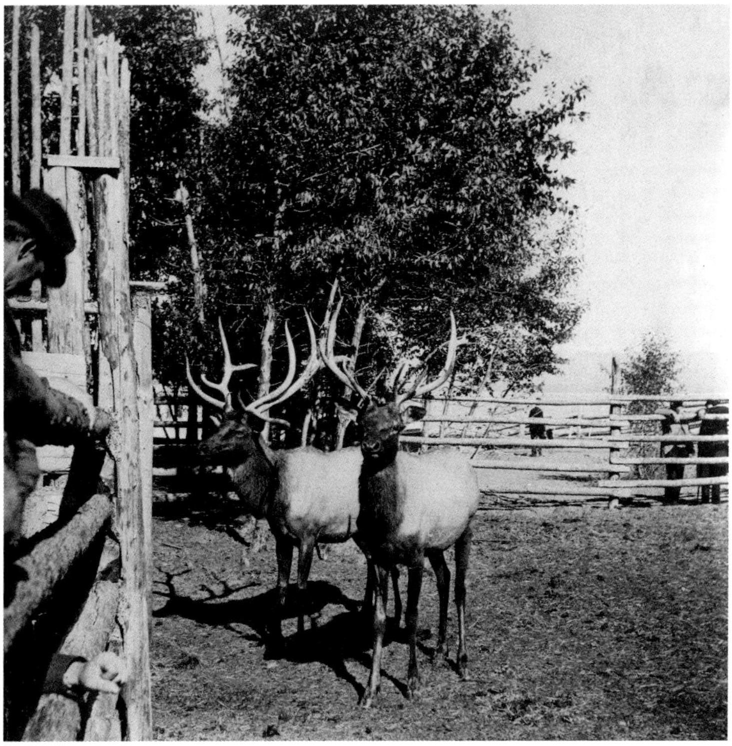

In 1896, Ela Collins (E.C.) Waters, the ambitious and unprincipled entrepreneur of the Yellowstone Lake Boat Company, established a small zoo on Dot Island, a seemingly inconsequential speck of land in Yellowstone Lake near the West Thumb. While it appears out of place for a national park to host a zoo of the park's wildlife, Waters felt it was a benefit to visitors, allowing them to be close to animals they often viewed at a distance, if at all. Of course, Waters also made money by taking visitors to his zoo. In this photo, park visitors watch a couple of bull elk that are fenced inside a log corral. The animals spent the summers on the island and were boated to a facility near Lake Hotel to spend the winter. Waters' wildlife show continued until 1907, when the park forced him to cease operation due to poor care of the animals and facility.

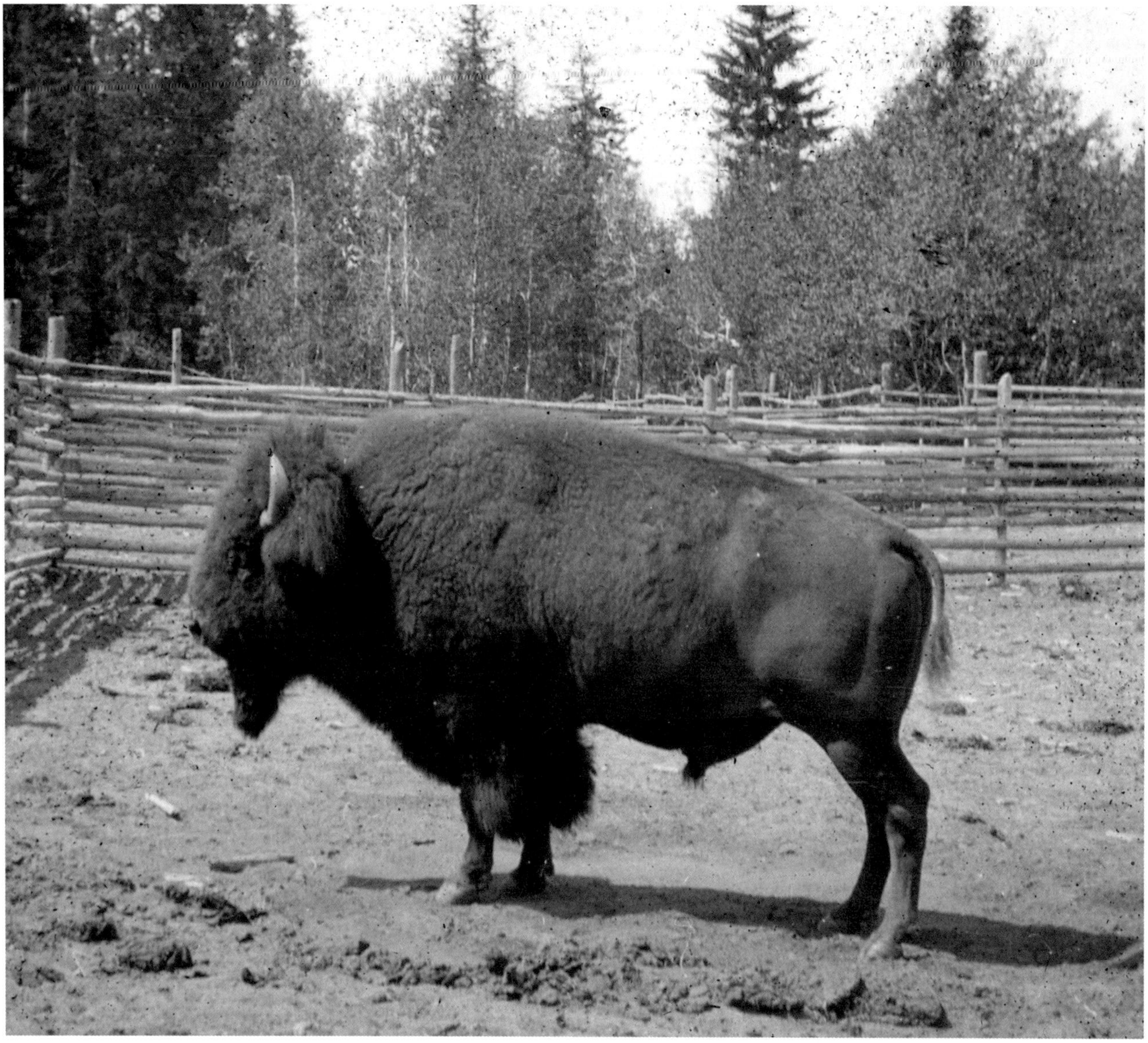

After receiving oral permission from Captain George Smith Anderson, the acting superintendent, to start his private zoo on Dot Island in 1896, E.C. Waters, proprietor of the Yellowstone Lake Boat Company, purchased two bull and two cow bison from a ranch in Goodnight, Texas. The animals traveled two weeks in a railcar to Fond de Lac, Wisconsin, where the handler, a cowboy named William Timmons, exchanged one of the bulls for a third cow before transporting them via rail to Cinnabar, Montana, where the line ended. From the station, Timmons brought them into the park in separate wagons, finally loading them onto on a barge towed by the *Zillah* to their summer residence on Dot Island. This photo taken by Franklin D. Edmunds is of the bull in a corral on Dot Island on July 29, 1905. When the zoo closed in 1907, the bison were released into the park, but there have been no reports of these animals assimilating within the population of the other park bison.

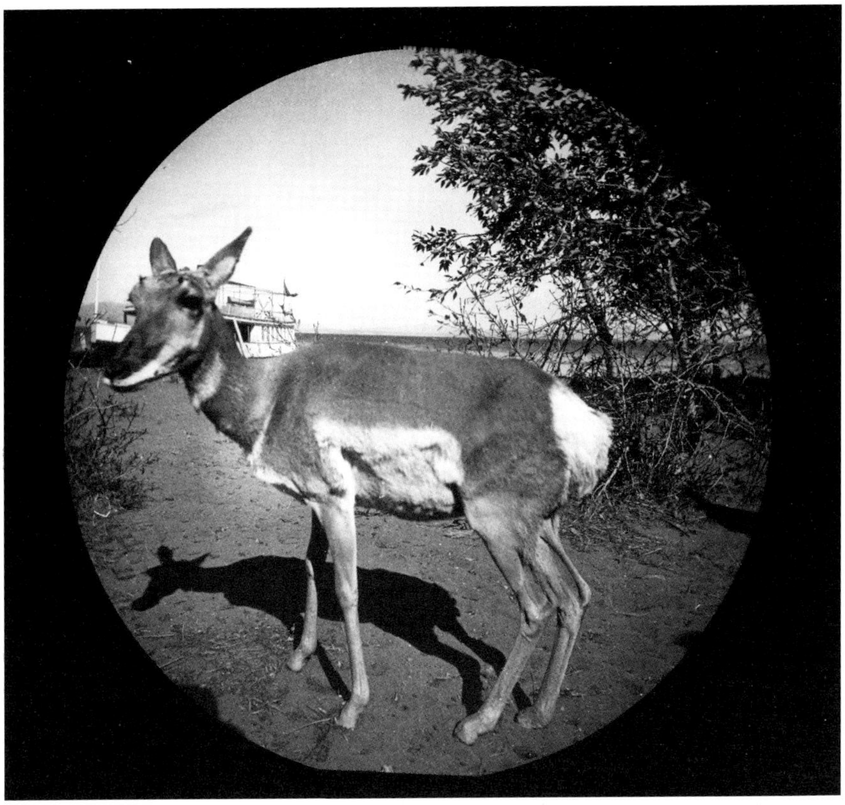

This is a round portrait matted from a Magic Lantern glass slide of a pronghorn on Dot Island with the steamship *Zillah* moored in the background, 1900 to 1907. When Acting Superintendent Captain George Smith Anderson gave E.C. Waters permission to start his private zoo on Dot Island, he was required to obtain all the animals from outside the park. The animals lived a miserable existence, corralled in small areas and fed scraps from Lake Hotel. The small zoo was part of Waters' relentless scheming to make money in the park in any way he could. In 1907, park officials finally banned him from the park for his obnoxious behavior and gross misdeeds, yet it was two more years before they were rid of him because he filed numerous lawsuits and had powerful friends.

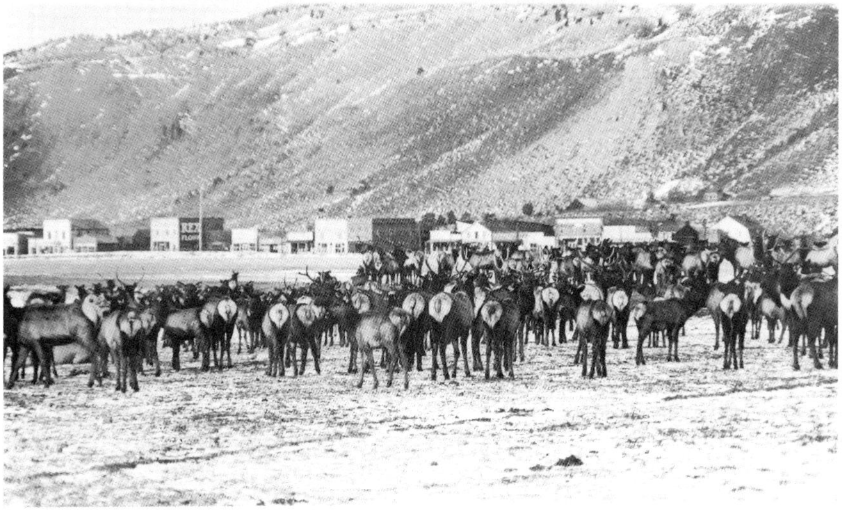

A large elk herd is seen at the north entrance of the park in this circa-1906 photo. The town of Gardiner, Montana, is in the background. As early as 1904, the U.S. Army fed elk and other ungulates during the winters to support the ever-growing population that park officials believed was beneficial. In 1919, Superintendent Horace Albright increased the program with managers feeding 1,500 tons of hay each winter to encourage the elk to remain within the park boundaries and out of the reach of hunters' rifles, as well as to mitigate harsh winters.

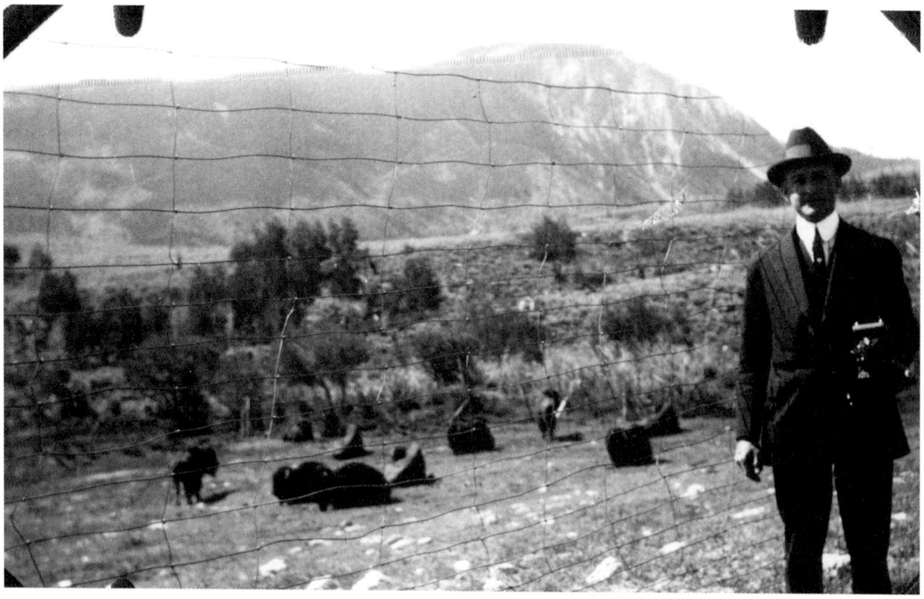

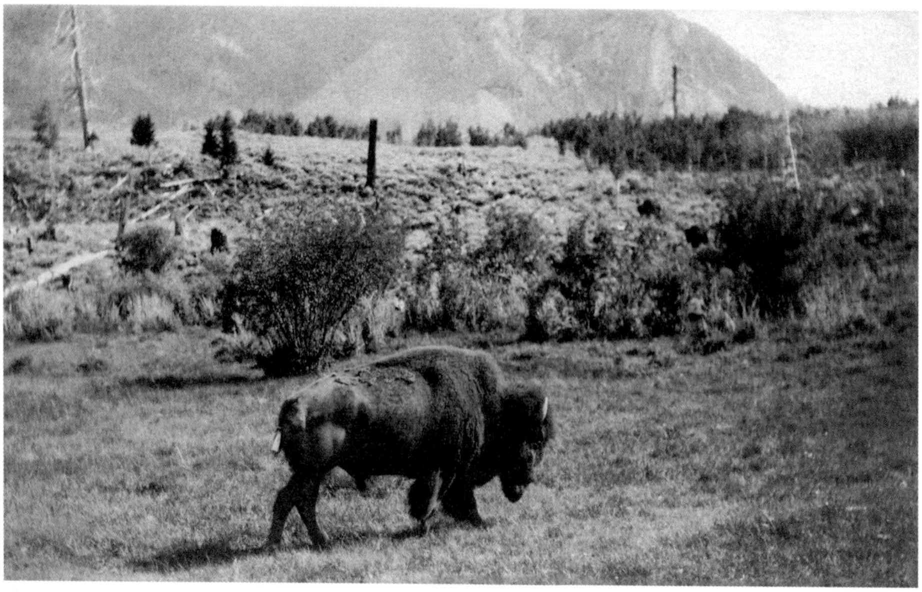

(Top) A park visitor stands in front of the "show herd," a tourist attraction at Mammoth Hot Springs. Bunsen Peak is in the background. (Bottom) A lone bison bull wanders past the camera within the enclosure, no date. Charles Jesse Jones, a Yellowstone National Park game warden also known as "Buffalo Jones," constructed the bison enclosure a mile south of Fort Yellowstone in 1902 as part of the park's effort to preserve these iconic symbols of the West. By the turn of the century, only 25 to 30 individuals of the once massive herds remained in Yellowstone after decades of over-hunting and outright poaching. To begin a breeding program, Jones purchased 15 cows and three bulls, keeping them at the Mammoth Hot Springs corral until 1907, when the herd was large enough to provide some animals for the Lamar Buffalo Ranch.

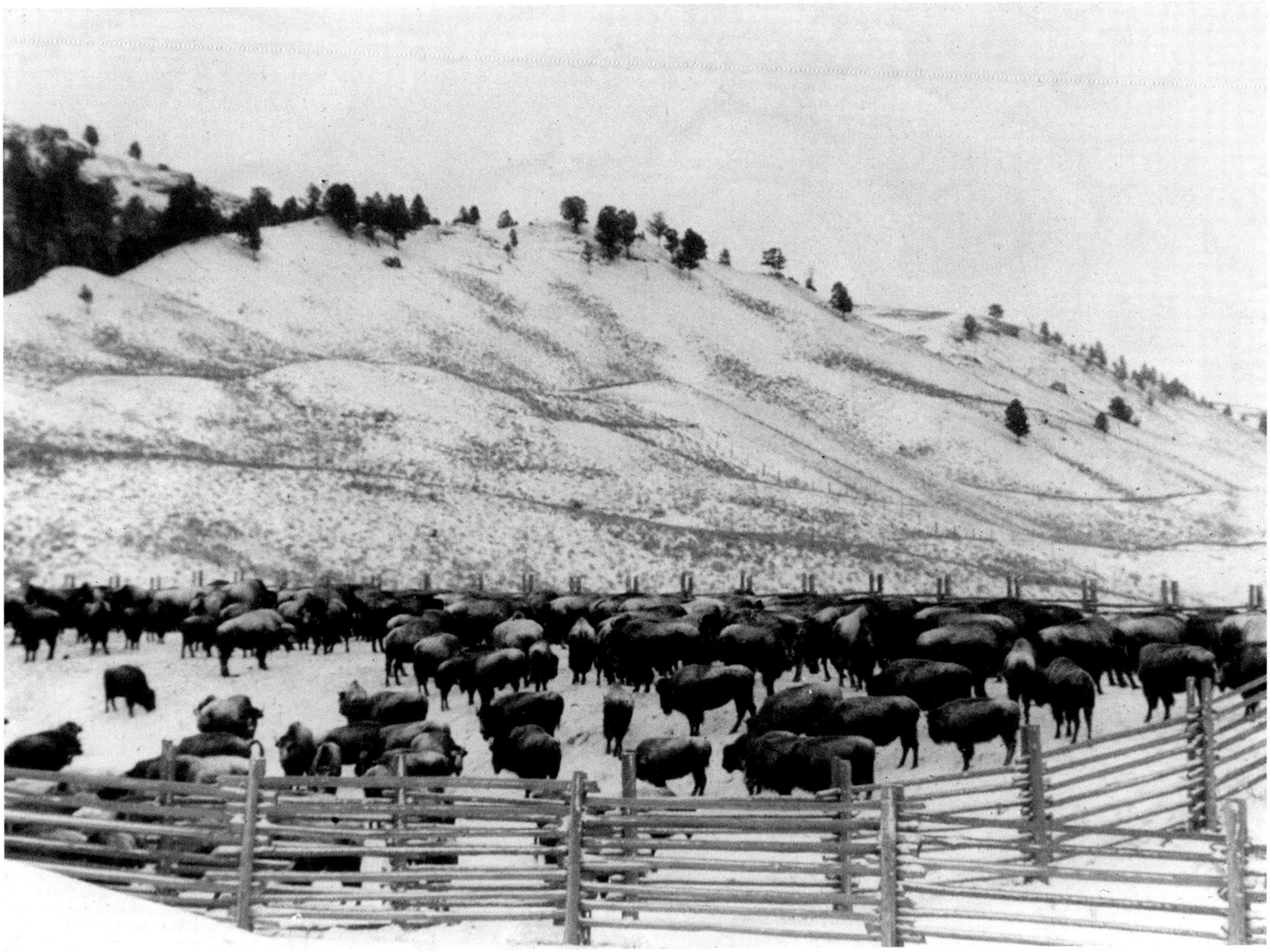

This photo was taken by biologist George Melendez Wright, who surveyed the park's wildlife for several years to gain a better understanding of the populations. It was taken in December 1932 of the growing herd at the Lamar Buffalo Ranch. Located east of Rose Creek in the Lamar Valley, the Buffalo Ranch was established in 1907, when 28 semi-domesticated bison were brought over from the original corral at Fort Yellowstone at Mammoth Hot Springs. After successfully increasing the bison population through decades of management, in the 1930s park officials relocated several groups throughout the park to establish self-sustaining herds. Today the buildings at the Buffalo Ranch are used by the Yellowstone Institute for public interpretive programs.

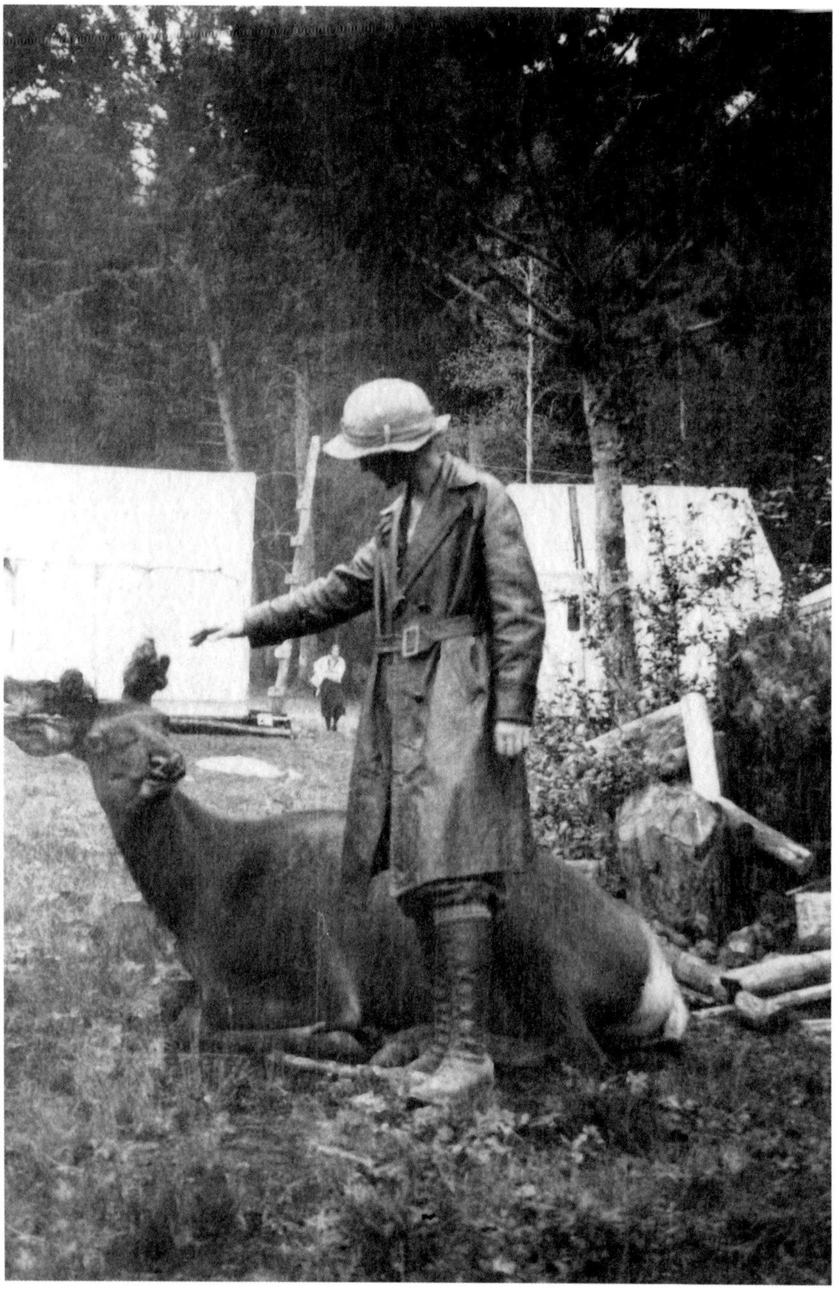

In the 1920s or 1930s, a female park visitor in a tent camp reaches out to pet a bull elk. The elk has deformed antlers, which sometimes occurs after an injury to the growing antlers or as the result of a hormone abnormality. The docile animal appears well habituated to people; perhaps it is a camp pet. The woman's knee-high, laced, leather hiking-boots, along with her knickers and cloche hat, was a typical hiking outfit for outdoor-minded ladies in the 1920s and 1930s.

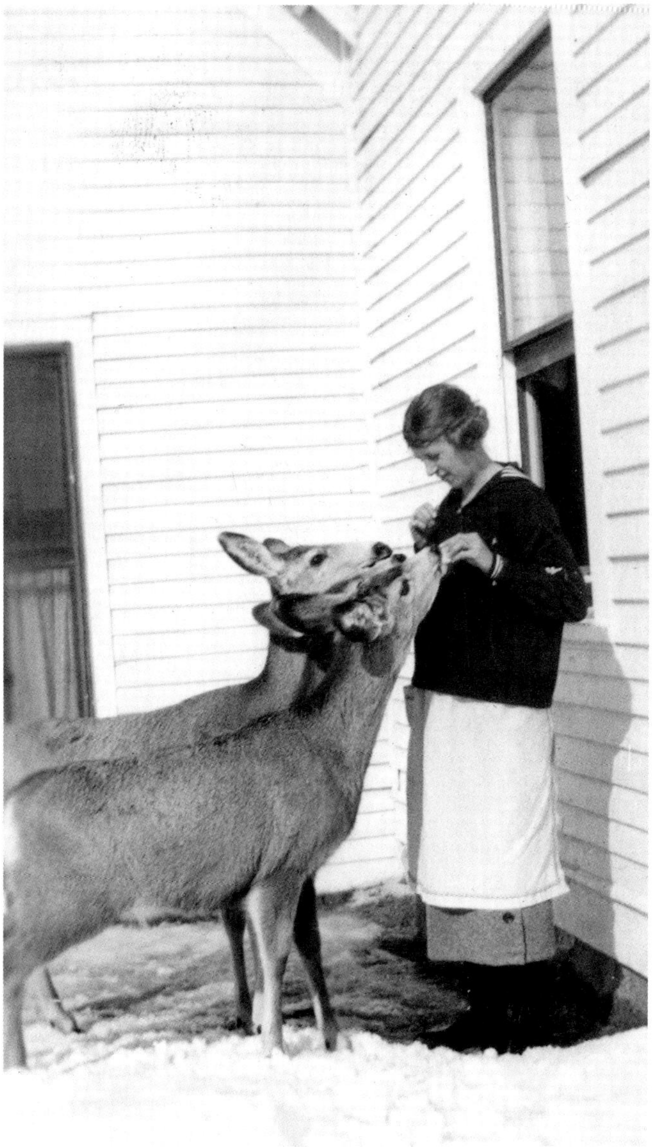

A female park employee wearing her work apron hand feeds mule deer fawns. Mule deer frequently occupied residential areas and readily accepted treats from well-meaning people. This practice is today illegal. This photo is from employee Matte Kincaid's 1922 Mammoth Hot Springs album.

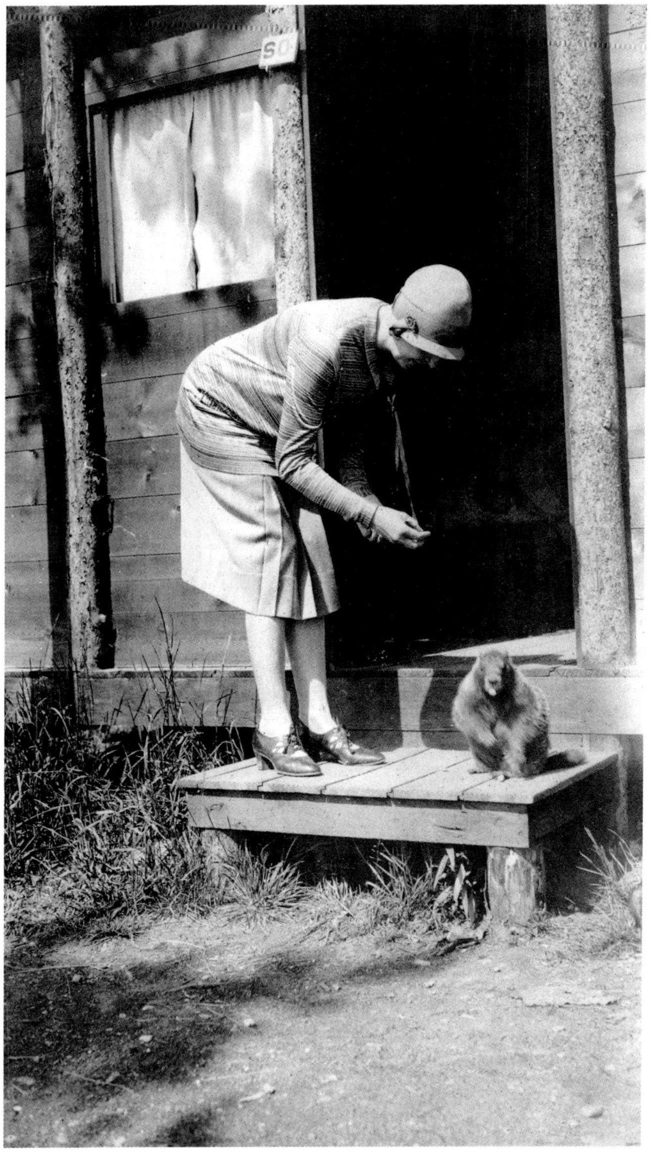

A female park visitor offers a treat to a yellow-bellied marmot on the porch of a Lake Camp guest cabin in July 1928. The burrowing rodents, which are much larger than ground squirrels, were notoriously bold beggars, taking up residence under guest cabins and in populated areas where they could easily beg for a snack and forage for food scraps.

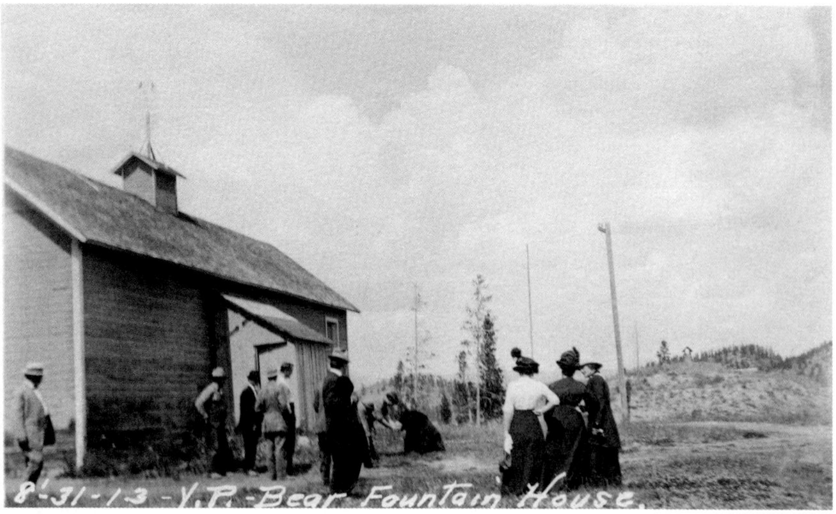

This unique photo shows park visitors feeding a large black bear behind Fountain Hotel on August 31, 1913. This is a rare view of outbuildings at this hotel, including what is thought to be the only known shot of the icehouse. Ice was a precious resource in the early 1900s. A laborious and dangerous job, it required workers to cut large blocks of ice from frozen lakes during the winter, sled the blocks to icehouses like this one, and pack the ice in sawdust insulation. Done properly, the ice kept well into the summer season. The Fountain Hotel was one of the first hotels, if not the first, to have a nearby garbage dump where visitors watched bears from a close distance. It is believed that in 1899, John Westlake, the son of Ellis Westlake, the manager of the Fountain Hotel from 1896-1900, took the famous photo of a black bear standing majestically in the dump with discarded food cans at its feet that was ultimately used as the Yellowstone Park Association's logo from the early 1900s.

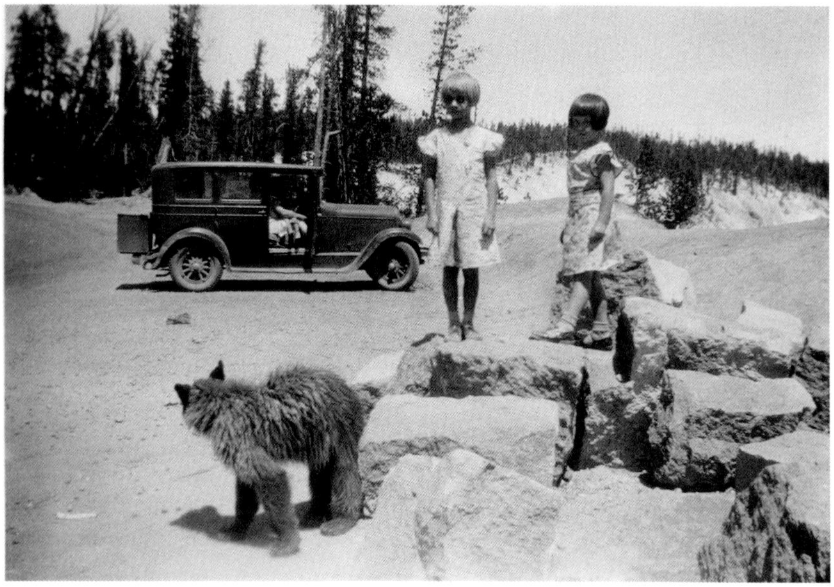

This photo shows a bear cub with two bobbed-haired young girls in the parking area along the north side of the Grand Canyon of the Yellowstone in 1934. Visitors often did not realize the potential hazards of having bears and people, especially children, in proximity with each other.

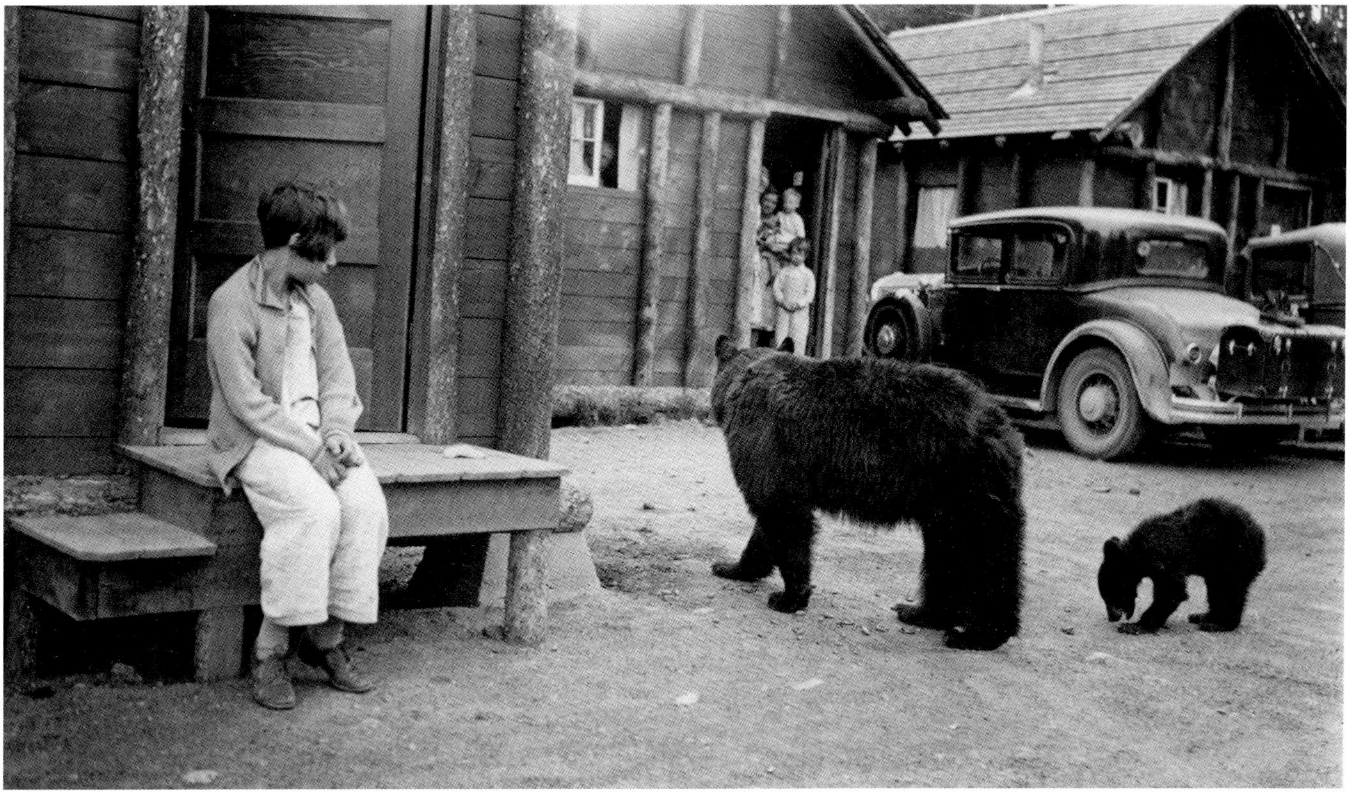

Black bears frequented guest cabins throughout the park because food was easily obtained from park visitors, who either fed the bears directly or stored food outside and the bears found it. In this 1931 photo, a young girl sits on the porch of, most likely, her family's cabin with a mother black bear and her cub merely feet away. In the background, a family watches from their cabin doorway.

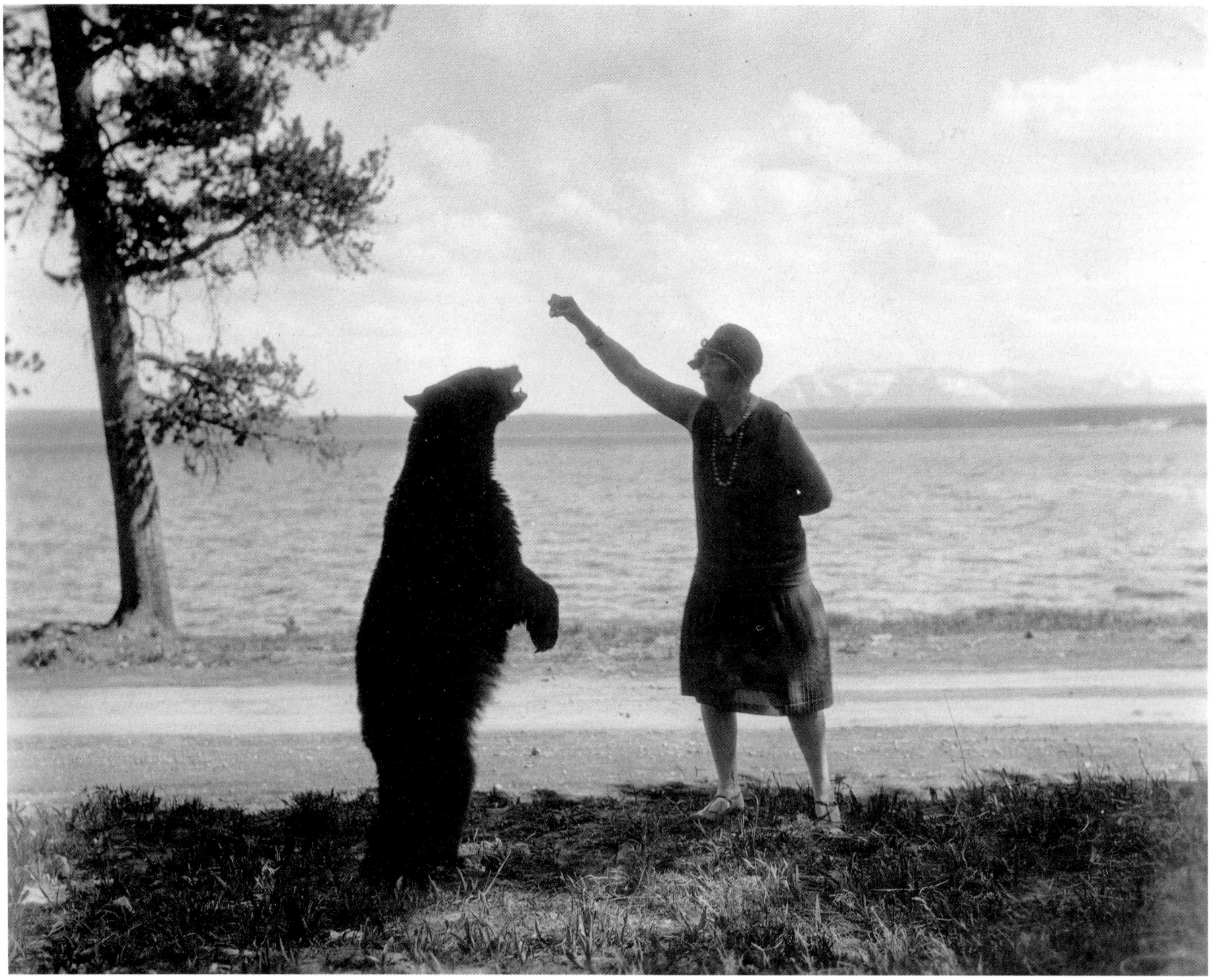

A begging black bear stands nearly as tall as the woman tourist offering him a treat at Yellowstone Lake in this 1929 photo. Although feeding bears in this manner was technically illegal at this time, Superintendent Horace Albright, who served from 1919 to 1929, believed that a positive visitor experience engaging with bears outweighed the negative risks. The woman is wearing a cloche hat, of the type that were popular in this era, particularly with ladies who wore a bobbed hairstyle.

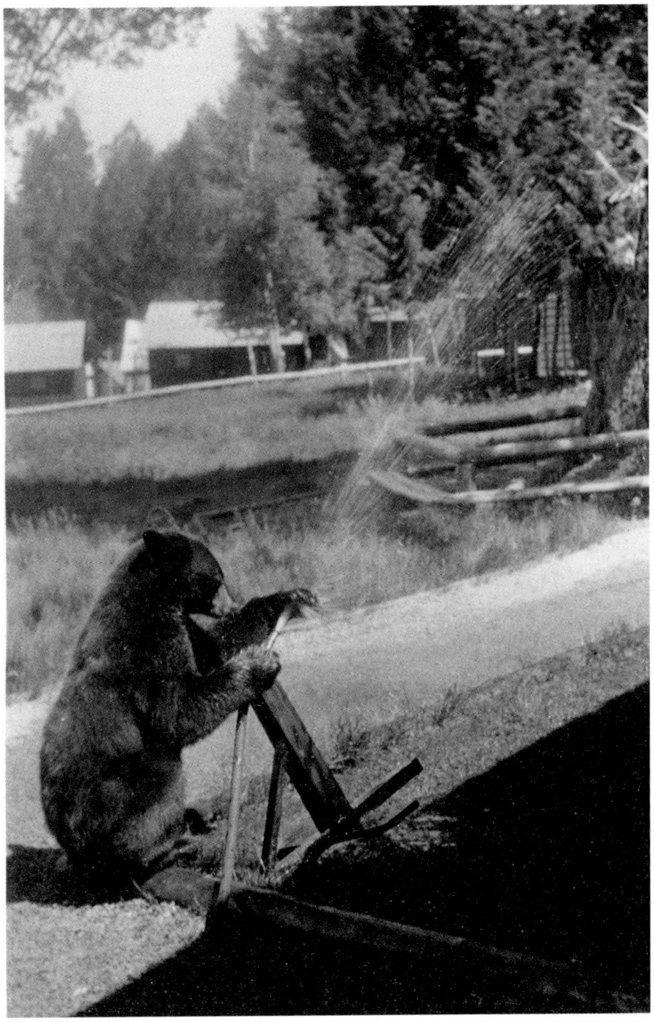

Black bears were well-known visitors to hotels, camps, and lodges because these places offered easy food. Other perks included playing with water sprinklers, as this black bear is doing at Roosevelt Lodge in 1927.

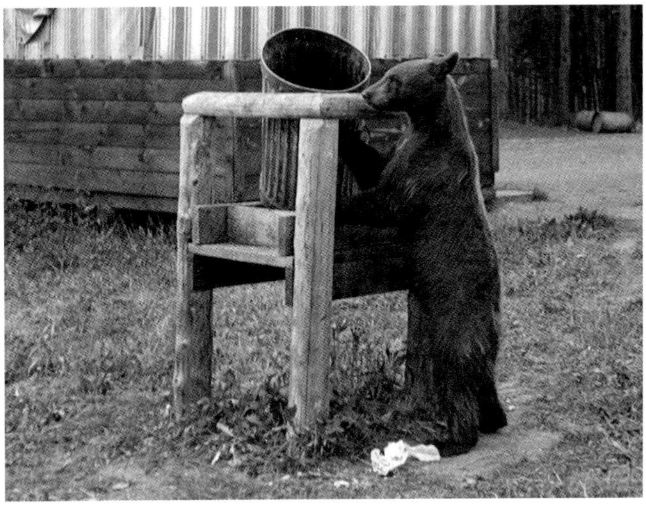

A young black bear digs into a trash can at Wylie Permanent Camping Company's Canyon Camp, which is indicated by the company's signature striped tent-tops over wooden cabin floors and walls. Before the days of bear-proof garbage cans, black bears frequently ate any debris left in garbage cans or near camps, including food-smelling glass and metal, to the detriment of the bears. The garbage cans were sometimes placed on raised wooden platforms to deter bears, as in this photo, but such attempts were futile.

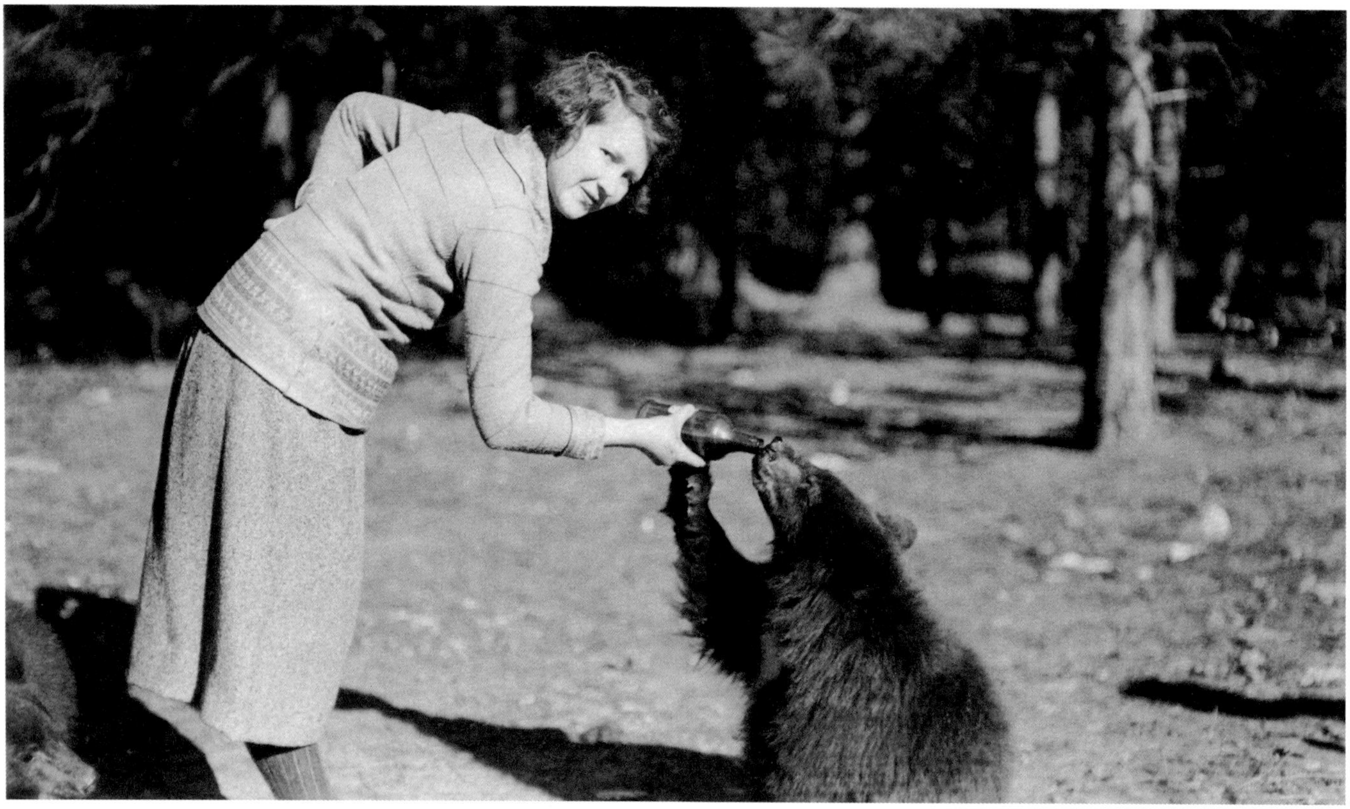

Treats took all forms for habituated Yellowstone bears. Here a black bear cub takes a swig from a bottle offered by a female park visitor, with the bear using its paw to steady her hand. The type of beverage is not known. This behavior demonstrates the tenuous relationship between wild animals and people when it comes to food. Hundreds of people in Yellowstone were hurt through the years, including a handful of fatalities from grizzlies in camps. Many people did not show much sympathy to those who illegally fed the bears; nonetheless, many bruins were euthanized after scratching or biting a guest, even when it was not a serious injury.

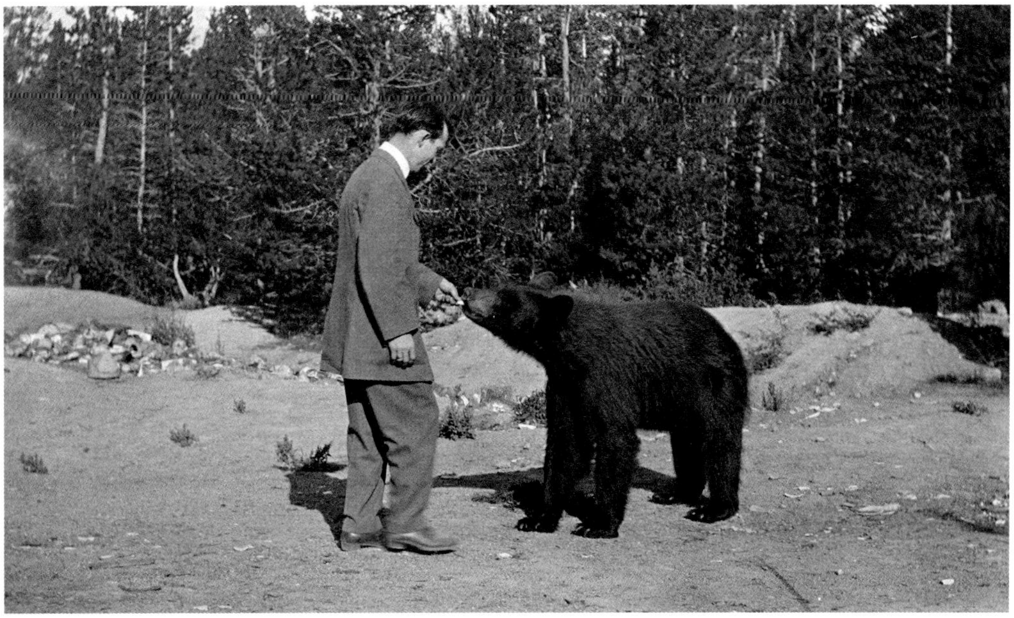

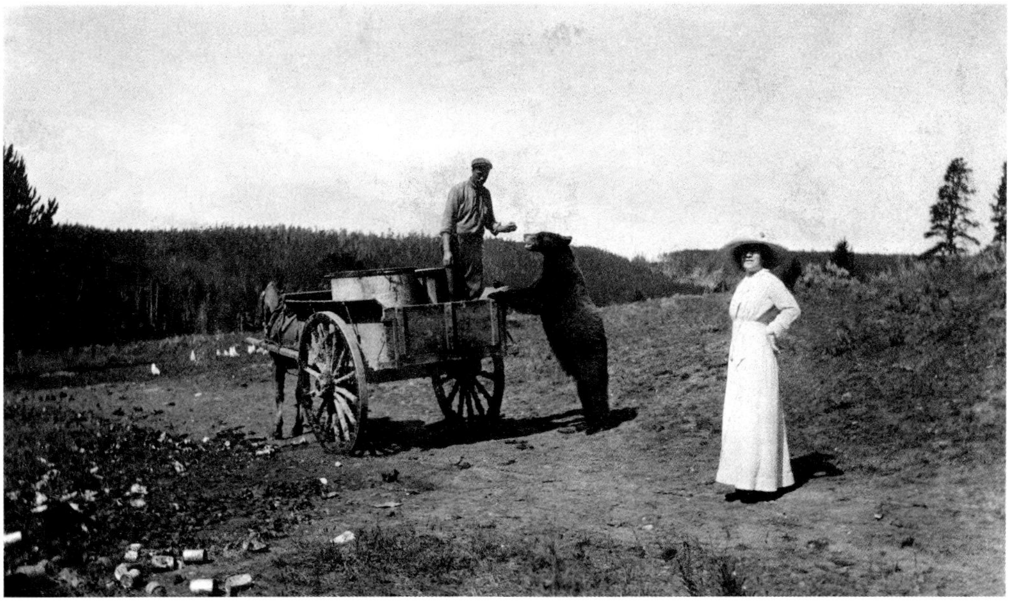

In the early days of Yellowstone, feeding wildlife was hugely popular, even though it was technically outlawed in 1902 by Acting Superintendent John Pitcher, and feeding a bear was the highlight of the practice. Some of the bears around the camps, lodges, and hotels had names because they were regular characters in those locations. A park visitor (top) feeds a black bear named "Jocko" at an unnamed garbage dump site. In the circa-1900 photo (bottom), a black bear stands at the end of a horse-drawn dump cart and receives a treat from the employee. A female park visitor went along for the feeding and poses in a full-length dress and wide-brimmed hat.

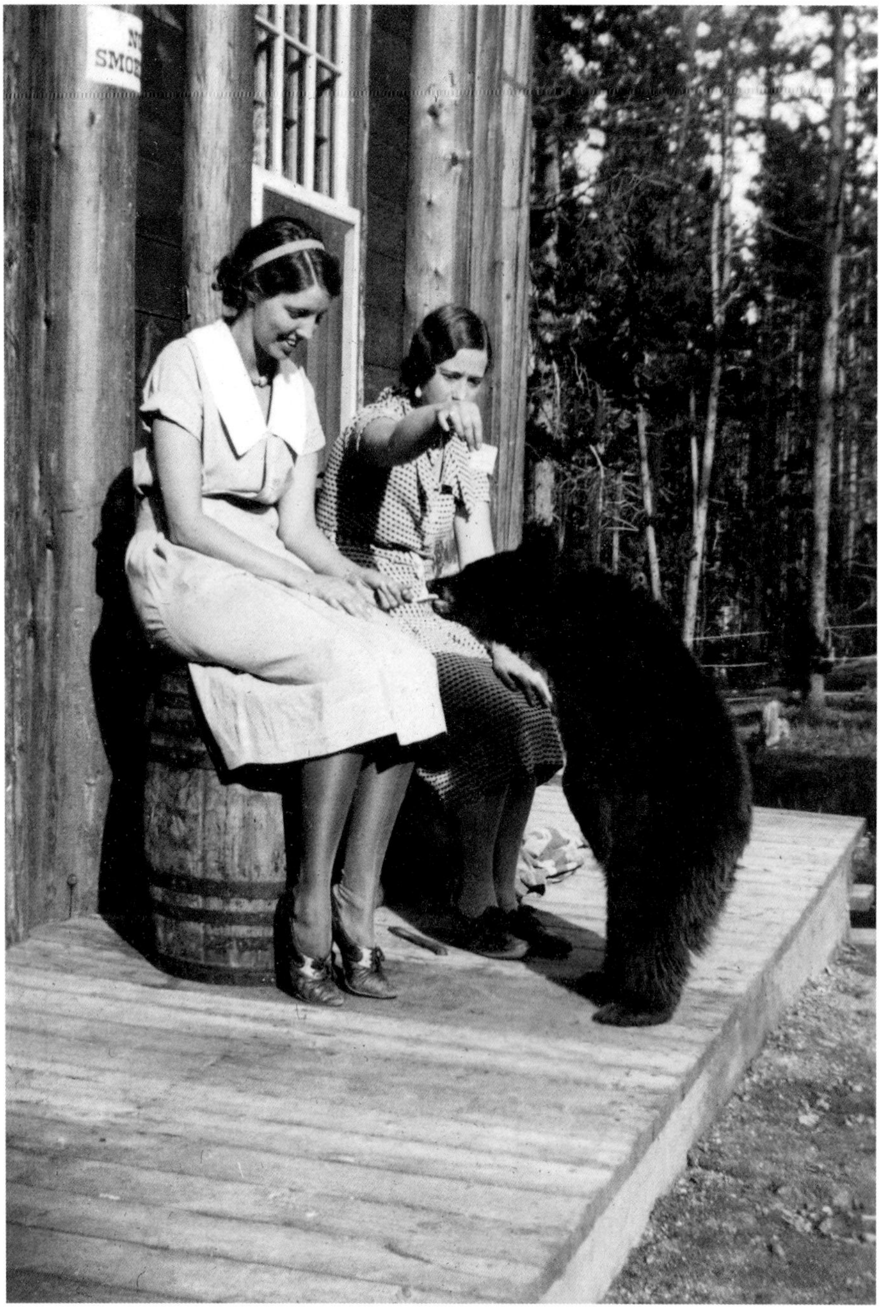

In this 1932 photo, a standing, black bear cub leans forward to gently take a cracker from the hand of a female park employee at Canyon Lodge. The woman on the left wears her work uniform and sleek stockings, while the young lady on the right wears a dotted dress and is most likely on her time off. This photo is from the Lois Davis park employee Canyon Lodge album.

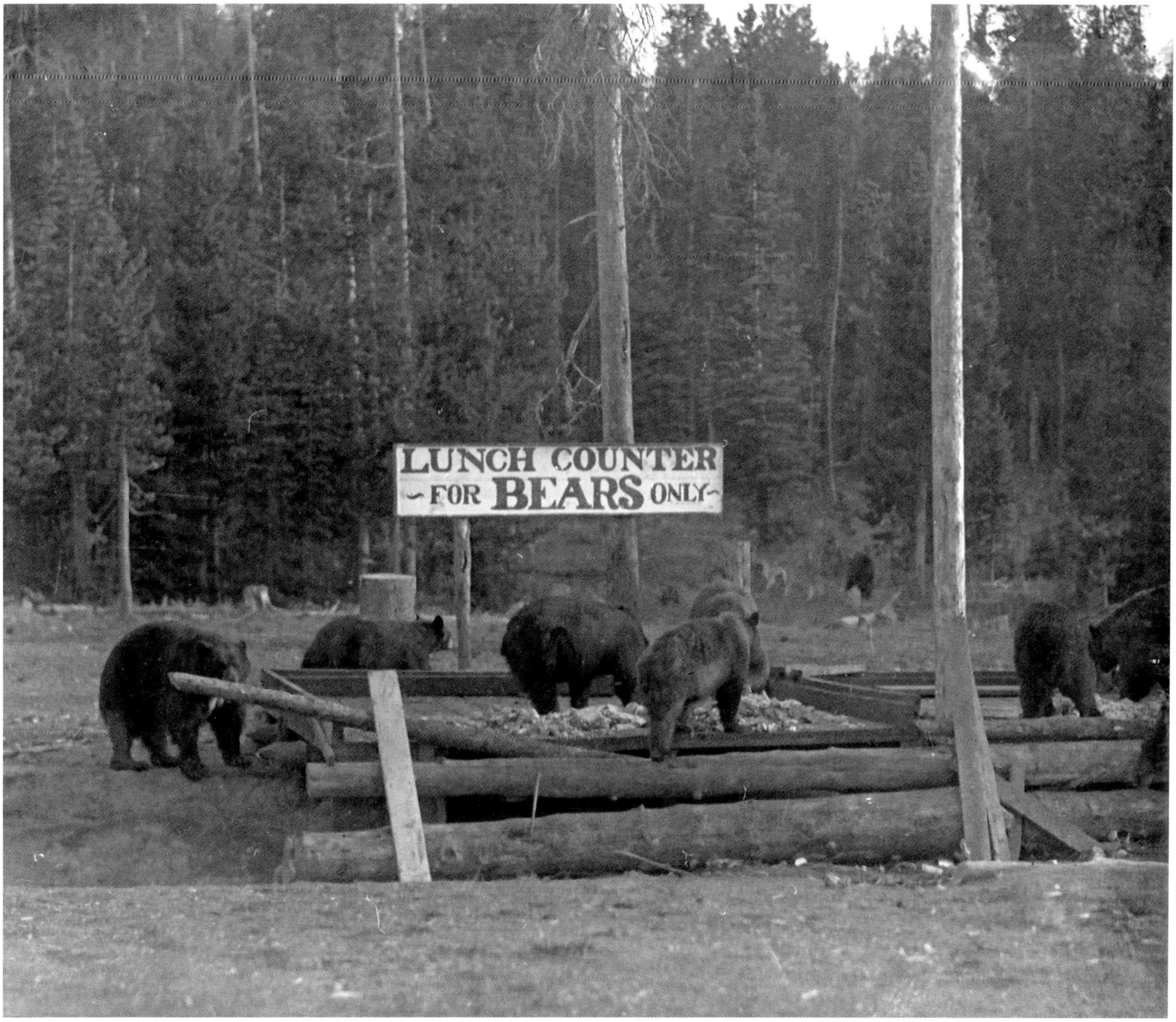

A group of apparently well-fed black bears dine at the "Lunch Counter for Bears Only" feeding grounds in the Old Faithful area. Official bear feeding for the delight of the guests started as early as 1889 and ended by 1935. In 1921, Superintendent Horace M. Albright built viewing stands around some of the dumps close to the hotels, including at Old Faithful and Canyon, where enormous crowds watched grizzly and black bears clean up the day's garbage. During these nightly shows, mounted, armed rangers gave wildlife talks to the enthralled crowds. The most well-known ranger at the Old Faithful area was Ranger Walter P. Martindale, who spoke to the crowd while seated on his horse a mere 50 feet from the bears.

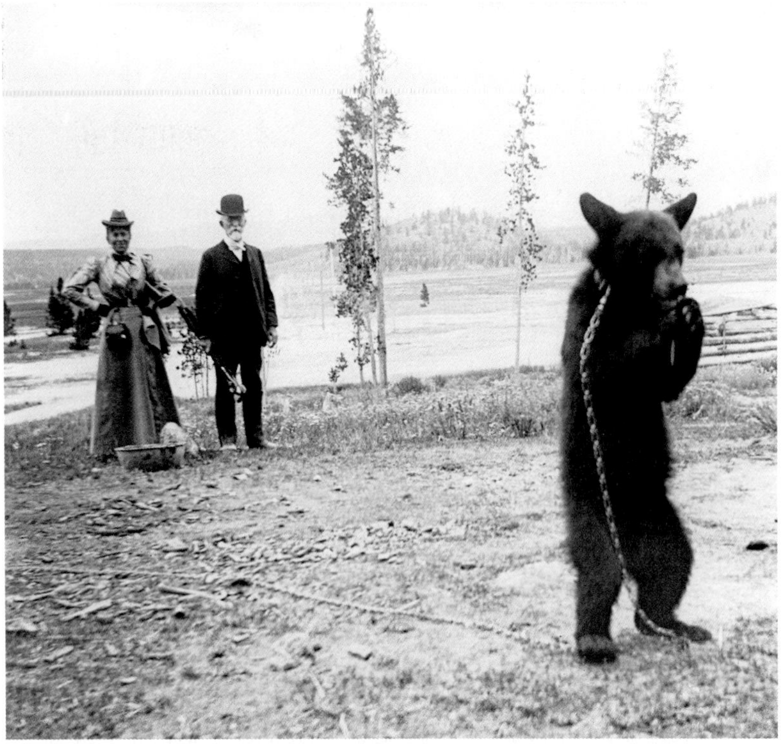

This 1905 photo is of a chained, black bear "display" cub with park visitors behind the Fountain Hotel. Captive bears were common at many hotels and camps, so visitors could watch a bear almost anytime they wanted. The woman wears a simple, full-length skirt that significantly drew in the waist, a holdover design from the dramatic silhouettes of the Victorian Era, but she also sports a small hat that was more functional for outdoor activities than the large, often ornate, bonnets popular in this era. The white-bearded gentleman in the bowler hat appears to be holding golf clubs in his right hand, although it is difficult to tell for sure. These well-dressed early visitors may have given the cub a treat, which it is eating while facing the camera.

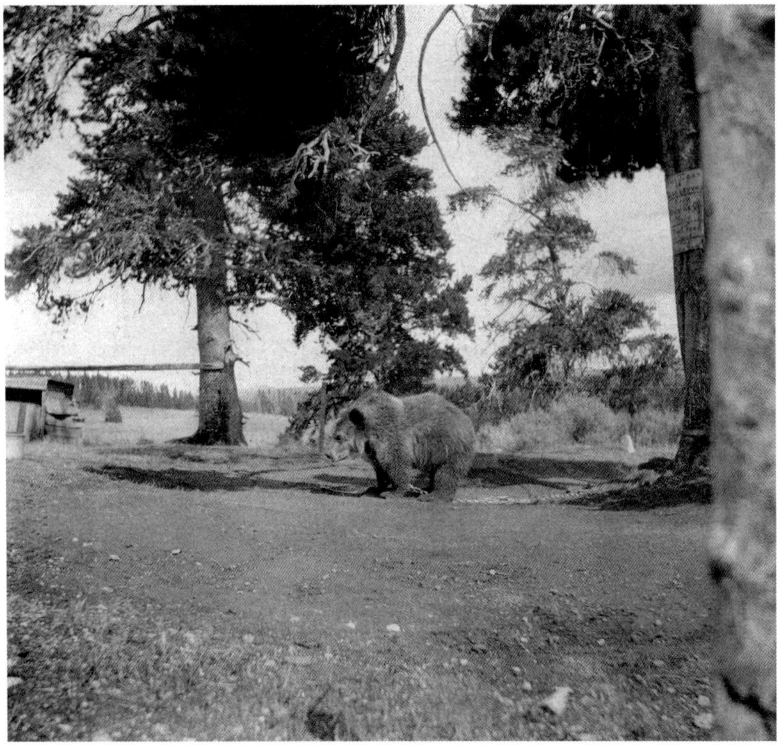

A young grizzly bear is chained to a nearby tree. This site is unknown. While it was fairly common to see captive black bears, not many grizzlies were on display. That's why this bear could possibly be the famous, captive grizzly named Mr. Dooley, even though the presumed "he" was a "she." Reportedly, around 1905-1907, Mr. Walker of the Canyon Hotel captured a grizzly cub and tethered the animal nearby to enthrall visitors. During her leashed confinement, the young grizzly rushed and snapped at guests. At the end of the season, Mr. Walker allowed the grizzly to "escape." Finally living on her own, the bear became well-behaved during subsequent seasons, calmly visiting camps to the delight of guests. Unfortunately, her trusting nature led her to be captured, once again, and she was shipped to the Washington Zoo where she spent the rest of her life.

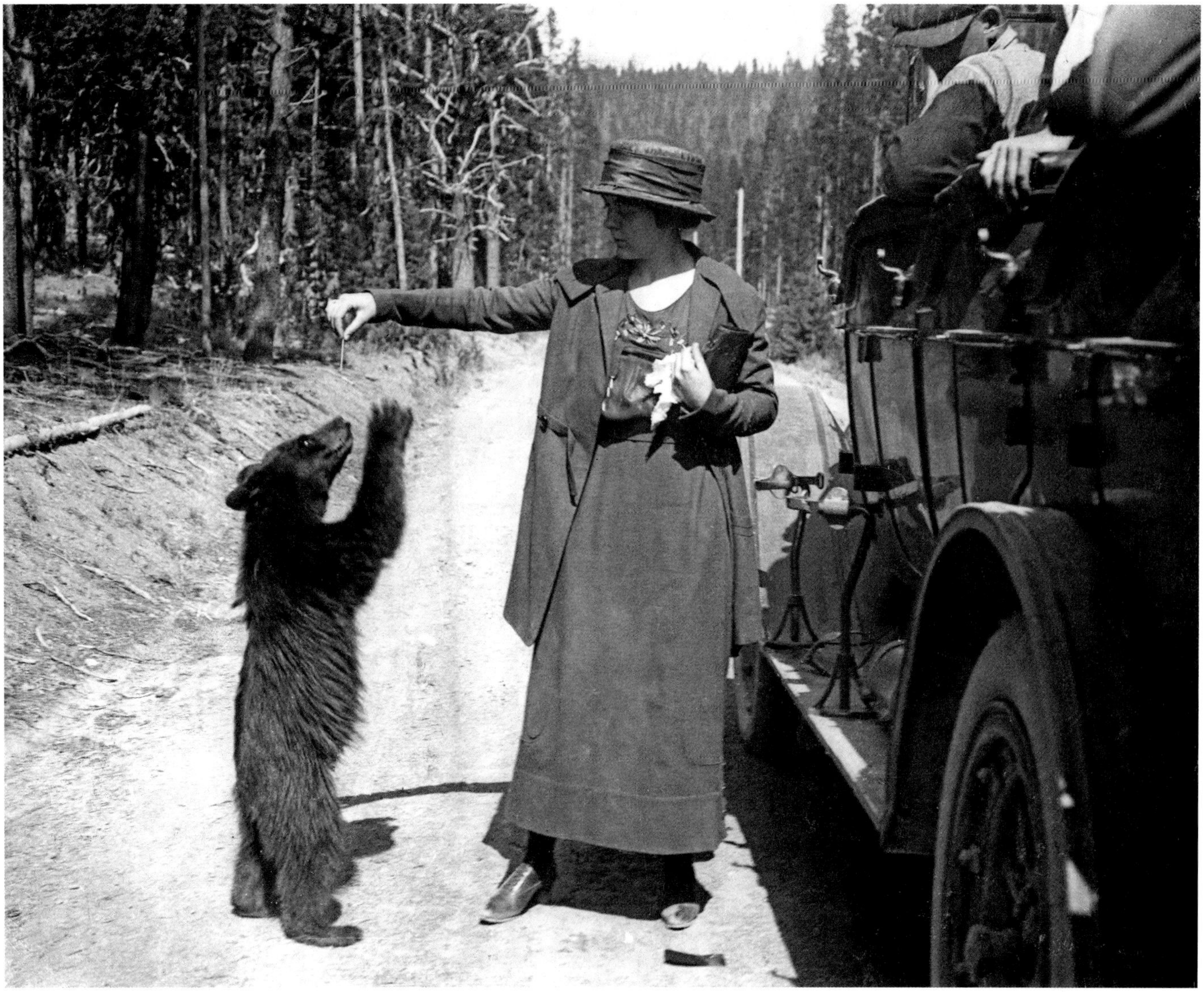

A female tourist holds a treat above the nose of a roadside black bear cub while passengers watch from the open-air park bus. After 1900, feeding black bears along roads increased as bears received food rewards from visitors traveling by stagecoach and from soldiers stationed in the park. By the mid-1920s, beggar bears were an attraction that rivaled geyser viewing in popularity. Once again, feeding and approaching bears are activities that are strictly prohibited today.

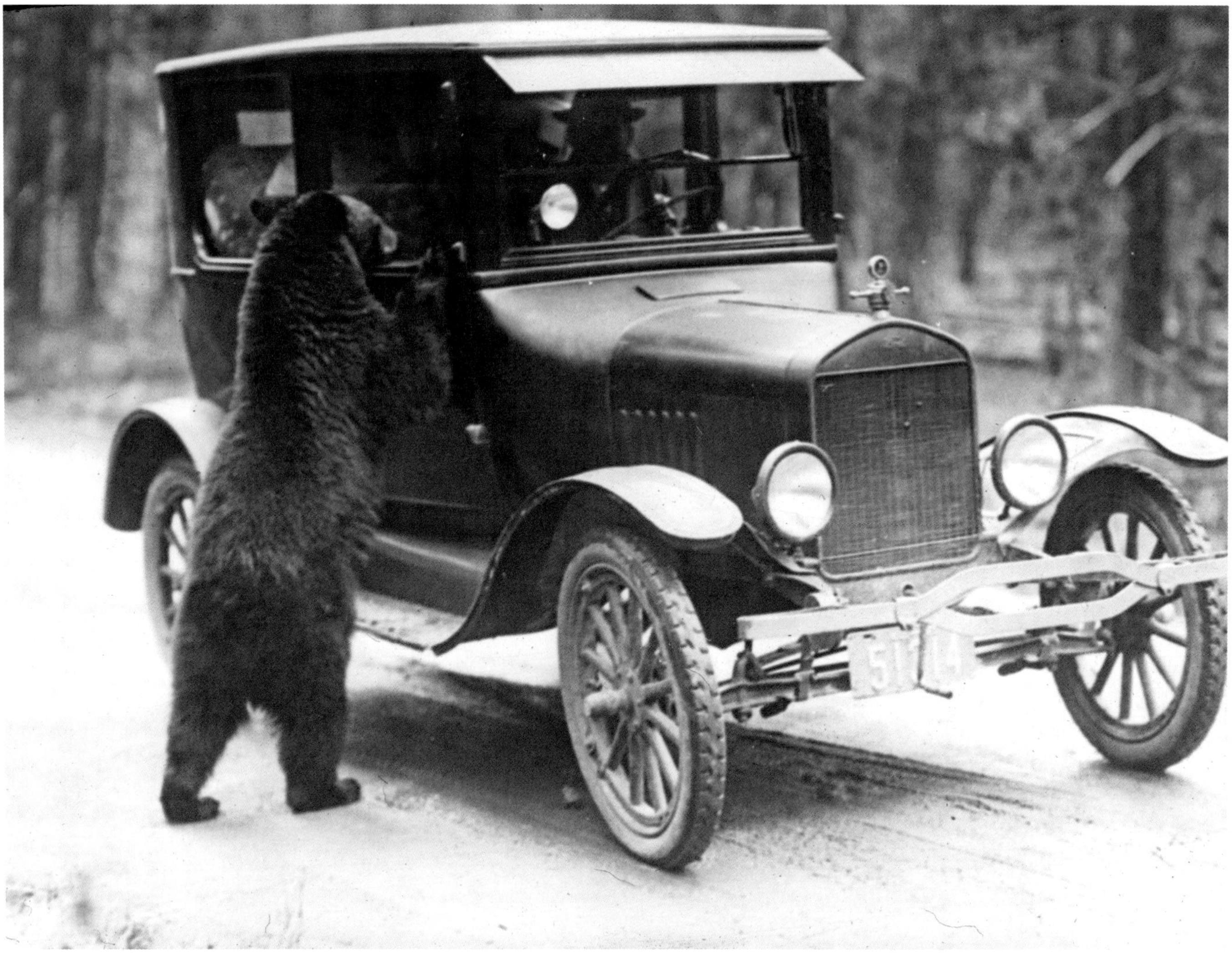

A Yellowstone "hold-up" bear looks for a treat through the passenger side window of a 1923-1925 Ford, Model-T, Tudor Sedan. An early "hold-up" or "beggar bear" reportedly occurred between 1917-1919 in the West Thumb area. The culprit was a young bear nicknamed "Jesse James" that stood up next to automobiles, looking for a treat. Bears are quick learners, and it did not take long for them to figure out that standing along the road, or leaning into cars, resulted in food rewards.

Michael H. Francis / Francis Historical Collections

Michael H. Francis is a recently retired wildlife photographer based out of Billings, Montana. He has thirty-five single-photographer books to his credit including, *Yellowstone Memories: 30 Years of Photographs & Stories, Watching Yellowstone & Grand Teton Wildlife*, and *Yellowstone Bears In The Wild,* all published by Riverbend Publishing. Mike worked in Yellowstone National Park for 15 seasons and during that time became interested in park history and collectibles, such as the many souvenirs found in the general stores and gift shops. Since 1974 he has collected thousands of historic images of the park, most of which have never been seen by the public. He is anxious to share these rare images with the world. Michael can be contacted at michael@michaelfrancisphoto.com

Amy Grisak

Freelance writer Amy Grisak began her media career carrying gear—and serving as sound recordist and associate producer—for nearly ten years while working on programs for National Geographic Television. Her introduction to Yellowstone National Park was during the filming of "Yellowstone: Realm of the Coyote," where she reveled in the unparalleled wildlife opportunities and fascinating geology.

Grisak eventually transitioned from television to freelance writing, pairing her nature photography with her stories and essays for the *Great Falls* (Montana) *Tribune* and other regional and national publications. She is the author of *Nature Guide to Glacier and Waterton National Parks* and an active member in the Outdoor Writers Association of America.

When she's not writing, Grisak co-hosts *Front Range Outdoors*, a Great Falls radio program where she discusses the wide range of outdoor recreation throughout Montana.

As soon as the snow recedes in the spring, Amy is on the trails with her two sons or fishing with her husband near their Great Falls' home. She loves exploring the stunning landscape she is blessed to call home.

Follow her work at amygrisak.com.

Lee H. Whittlesey

Lee Whittlesey's forty-five-year studies in the history of the Yellowstone region have made him an expert on Yellowstone's vast literature and have resulted in numerous publications. He is the author, co-author, or editor of sixteen books and more than fifty journal articles, including the forthcoming *"This Modern Saratoga of the Wilderness": A History of Mammoth Hot Springs* (2021); and *Stagecoaching Through Yellowstone* (2021). He recently published a new edition of his popular best-seller *Death in Yellowstone* (2014).

Whittlesey served as Park Historian for the National Park Service at Yellowstone National Park for 25 years, and previously served in that park as Archivist, Ranger Naturalist/Interpreter, Law Enforcement Ranger, and in numerous other positions. He has a master's degree in history from Montana State University and a law degree (Juris Doctor) from the University of Oklahoma. Idaho State University conferred upon him an Honorary Doctorate of Science and Humane Letters, and Montana State University awarded him an honorary Ph.D. in history.

Whittlesey has been featured on numerous television news broadcasts and documentaries about Yellowstone, including Ken Burns's PBS special, *The National Parks: America's Best Idea.* He is often interviewed on regional and local television.

Whittlesey retired as Park Historian for the National Park Service at Yellowstone National Park in 2018. He now lives in the Livingston, Montana, area, where he continues to write about Yellowstone.